MW00534425

THE FORMATION OF LATIN AMERICAN NATIONS

THE FORMATION OF LATIN AMERICAN NATIONS

FROM LATE ANTIQUITY TO EARLY MODERNITY

THOMAS WARD

UNIVERSITY OF OKLAHOMA PRESS : NORMAN

Publication of this book is made possible through the generosity of Edith Kinney Gaylord.

Portions of chapter 2 were previously published, in a form since revised, in "From the 'People' to the Nation: An Emerging Notion in Sahagún, Ixtlilxóchitl and Muñoz Camargo," *Estudios de Cultura Náhuatl* 32 (2001): 223–34. Reproduced by permission of Universidad Nacional Autónoma de Mexico.

Portions of chapter 4 were previously published, in a form since revised, in "Expanding Ethnicity in Sixteenth-Century Anahuac: Ideologies of Ethnicity and Gender in the Nation-Building Process," *MLN* 116.2 (March 2001): 419–52. Reproduced by permission of The Johns Hopkins University Press.

Library of Congress Cataloging-in-Publication Data

Name: Ward, Thomas, 1953–
Title: The formation of Latin American nations : from late antiquity to early modernity / Thomas Ward.
Description: Norman : University of Oklahoma Press, 2018. | Includes bibliographical references and index.
Identifiers: LCCN 2018016620 | ISBN 978-0-8061-6150-1 (hardcover : alk. paper)
Subjects: LCSH: Latin America—History—To 1600. | Latin America—Historiography. | Latin America—Discovery and exploration—Spanish. | Mexico—History—Conquest, 1519–1540. | Aztecs—First contact with Europeans. | Indians of Mexico—First contact with Europeans.
Classification: LCC F1411 .W37 2018 | DDC 980/.01—dc23
LC record available at https://lccn.loc.gov/2018016620

The paper in this book meets the guidelines for permanence and durability of the Committee on Production Guidelines for Book Longevity of the Council on Library Resources, Inc. ∞

1 2 3 4 5 6 7 8 9 10

To Úrsula, of course

. . . porque en recontar cosas modernas hay peligro de hazer graues ofensas.

Agustín de Zárate, "Epístola dedicatoria," *Historia del descubrimiento y conqvista del Perv*, p. iiii (overleaf)

Modern people living in state-level societies usually think that hierarchy is normal and that superordination and subordination are natural or universal.

Bruhns and Stothert, *Women in Ancient America*, 214

All the territorial possessions of all the political establishments in the earth—including America, of course—consist of pilferings from other people's wash. No tribe howsoever insignificant and no nation howsoever mighty, occupies a foot of land not stolen. When the English, the French, and the Spaniards reached America, the Indian tribes had been raiding each other's territorial clotheslines for ages and every acre of ground in the continent had been stolen and restolen five hundred times.

Mark Twain, *Following the Equator*, 1:298–99

CONTENTS

ILLUSTRATIONS

MAPS

FIGURES

PREFACE

This book is about the formation of nations in Latin America before the arrival of the Spanish and how those entities changed after contact with them. What I have tried to do is start the story from the perspective of Amerindian cultures, not from the Spanish perspective, the usual point of departure. As is well known, victors in wars are given the power to rewrite history. Beyond that, victors can write about the people they have defeated and subjugated in a way that suits their own purposes. It took me a long time to find the way to invert this paradigm, but the seeds were sown during my years as a graduate student at the University of Connecticut.

After arriving in Mexico City in the mid-1980s to bury myself in the reading list for my PhD comprehensive exams (it seemed a good place), I discovered Miguel León Portilla's *Visión de los vencidos* (*Broken Spears*). This anthology was not something I had ever read for class. So I plunged into it, and from it, I began to develop an awareness of non-European chroniclers who had a story to tell different from the one proffered in the canonical writings. Later, in the midst of Quincentenary celebrations and protestations,

I began teaching courses at what was then Loyola College. These offerings included both European and indigenous or mestizo chroniclers. The first course, "Mexican Civilization," suggested by my then department chair, Gisèle Child-Olmsted, surveyed thirty centuries of cultural achievement. Another, "Mexican Chronicles," explored historical episodes such as the massacre in Cholula's Atrium of God from a variety of perspectives, including those offered by Hernán Cortés, Bernal Díaz del Castillo, Bartolomé de las Casas, Fernando de Alva Ixtlilxóchitl and Diego Muñoz Camargo. Those early courses made me aware that whereas the impact of the Renaissance on the first hundred years of the colonial era was substantial, it did not eclipse Amerindian knowledge, despite trying to do so. I am grateful to Miguel León Portilla not only for publishing his eye-opening anthology but also for publishing an early segment of my research on Alva Ixtlilxóchitl, Muñoz Camargo and Sahagún in *Estudios de Cultura Náhuatl* in 2001. Another, appearing in the journal *MLN*, eventually won the Mid-Atlantic Council for Latin American Studies' Harold Eugene Davis Prize for the "best article" in the year 2002. Those articles mark the early origins of this book and are built upon in varying degrees in several of the Mexican segments of this book.

From this teaching and research, I stumbled across an important truth: that there were contrasting viewpoints regarding what is generally called the Conquest. I came to realize that the events themselves, with their inevitable military analysis, might be important for history but were not as interesting as the cultural configurations they glossed over. Because of the biases inherent in the chronicle, I turned to other kinds of sources: readings in ethnohistory, archeology, and anthropology helped me gain a fuller picture of several precontact cultures. A yearlong series of visits to the Library of Congress in 2006 allowed me to spend considerable time with the documents of the Jay I. Kislak Collection as well as rare correspondence in the Special Collections reading room. The collection director and curator, Arthur Dunkelman, was most helpful in making Nahua maps, letters handwritten by Las Casas, and a wealth of other manuscripts and rare books available to me. The librarians in the Hispanic Reading room opened up their microfilm library to me. The next summer, a Title VI Summer Research Fellowship sponsored by the UNC-Duke Consortium on Latin American Studies revealed new kinds of sources to me. At the University of North Carolina-Chapel Hill, the Bernard J. Flatow Collection of sixteenth and seventeenth-century first editions (see Ilgen) allowed me hands-on access. I am grateful to the knowledgeable Teresa Chapa for orienting me to materials at the UNC library. The Odriozola Peruvian Collection at Duke University contained correspondence between individuals as well as contemporary legislation that added to my understanding of how colonialism operated. Duke's Special Collections librarians were of great support.

Numerous people have helped me along the way with this project. I would like to mention Luis B. Eyzaguirre, may he rest in peace, who taught an interesting graduate seminar that placed the chronicles in the same context of some of the great Humanist masters and piqued my curiosity about the sixteenth century. My gratitude goes to Joseph Wieczorek, Virginia Marino, Howard Giskin, Jesús Díaz Caballero, Wilfredo Kapsoli Escudero, and Colleen Ebacher for helpful early commentary. Later discussions I had with Raquel Chang Rodríguez, Sara Castro-Klarén, Christian Fernández, and others helped me hone the idea of the nation I was working with and also alerted me to works that might have remained off my radar. Sara, in particular, helped me to understand the importance of theory in understanding colonial realities. I am in debt to colleagues in the Department of Modern Languages at Loyola. Already mentioned is Gisèle Child-Olmsted. Leslie Zarker Morgan read several sections and Randall Donaldson and Sharon Diane Nell proofread a proposal that eventually led to the Title VI Summer Fellowship, as well as two summer grants and two sabbaticals. The grants were awarded by the Research and Sabbatical Committee and the Grants Office at Loyola University in 2005 and 2007. The sabbatical in 2006 facilitated my completing the bulk of the research for this project, and another in 2013 allowed me to complete Chapters 4 and 5, embark on a massive endeavor of organization, and polish the final version of the manuscript. I would especially like to thank Nancy Dufau and Stacy Bass from Loyola's Grants Office for their professional help in the process. Loyola's Center for the Humanities aided me with funding for a research assistant various semesters and a summer. The grantees, Hannah O'Neill (spring 2006), Brianna Kosteca (spring 2007), and Renata Titus-Aguilera (summer and fall 2008) were without par in finding and scanning documents, photocopying, transcribing, and editing. The Center for the Humanities also most graciously helped with funds to cover mapmaking and indexing costs. Thanks also go to Mary Beverungen, Cindy McCabe, Peggy Field, Ginny Harper, Nicholas Triggs, and Christy Dentler of Interlibrary Loan Services at the Loyola/Notre Dame Library in the great city of Baltimore for their conscientious help in locating historical materials and secondary sources.

I am grateful to Joseph Tulchin, who brought me into the project to publish a second edition of the *Encyclopedia of Latin American History and Culture* (2008), and to Erick Langer and Jay Kinsbrunner, may he rest in peace, who both kept me busy with my editing responsibilities. My work for the *Encyclopedia* made me think about periods and places in Latin America I might not normally have considered. Mapmaker Erin Greb in New York City made five of the most wonderful maps for me. Finally, the anonymous readers for the University of Oklahoma Press have provided a wealth of feedback to keep me from my foibles and to get me to make certain points with greater clarity. I am grateful to them for the detailed work they did. I am in awe of the editors and proofreaders at the University of Oklahoma Press, Alessandra Tamulevich, Steven Baker, and Maura McAndrew, who all had patience with me and faith in my manuscript. It goes without saying, however, that any errors I have made are my own.

ABBREVIATIONS FOR SOURCES FREQUENTLY CITED IN THE TEXT

For full bibliographic information for published works, see the bibliography.

AZ	*The Aztecs under Spanish Rule,* by Gibson
CP-1^{era}	*Crónica del Perú: primera parte,* by Cieza de León
CP-3^{era}	*Crónica del Perú: tercera parte,* by Cieza de León
CDR	*Cartas de relación,* by Cortés, 1983 edition by Alcalá
CR	*Comentarios Reales,* by Inca Garcilaso de la Vega, 1943 edition by Rosenblat
GH/FC	*General History,* by Sahagún (The Florentine Codex)
HG	*Historia general,* by Sahagún
HI	*Historia de los indios de la Nueva España,* by Motolinía
HV	*Historia verdadera de la conquista de la nueva España,* by Díaz del Castillo, 1982 edition by Sáenz de Santa María
HT	*Historia de Tlaxcala,* by Muñoz Camargo, 1986 edition by Vázquez
HDC	*Historia del descvbrimiento y conquista del Peru,* by Zárate, first edition

NAC *The Nahuas after the Conquest,* by Lockhart
NS *Nahuas and Spaniards,* by Lockhart
NU *Nacimiento de una utopía,* by Burga
OC *Obras completas,* by Sor Juana Inés de la Cruz
OH *Obras históricas,* by Fernando de Alva Ixtlilxóchitl, 1997 edition by O'Gorman
PNC *Primer nueva crónica y buen gobierno,* by Guamán Poma de Ayala
PV *Popol Vuh,* part and chapter numbers refer to divisions in the Recinos and the Goetz/Morley editions
TD *Textos y documentos,* by Colón
TR *Tratados,* by Las Casas
TSC *Tlaxcala in the Sixteenth Century,* by Gibson
YE Yale Edition of the *Complete Works* of More

THE FORMATION OF LATIN AMERICAN NATIONS

INTRODUCTION

This book on the formation of Latin American nations is the second volume of what is becoming a trilogy that seeks to decolonize our research methodologies with respect to Amerindian cultures in the Americas. While the first book, *Decolonizing Indigeneity*, establishes four possible approaches to decolonial interpretation, the second, *The Formation of Latin American Nations*, puts in practice those approaches as it traces the contours of cultural components of several indigenous nations of late antiquity and their dispersal into early modernity, when transatlantic colonialism was instituted up and down the Atlantic coast and parts of the Pacific coast.[1] Before getting to that, it must be stated that these two terms, "late antiquity" and "early modernity," are from our time and are not the ones used by the people who lived in those two periods and those diverse places. Given the diversity of cultural trajectories and the multiplicity of perspectives that bring them into focus, no perfect terminology exists, nor is there a consistent system of periodization applicable uniformly to all areas. The cultures of late antiquity flowed in their own ways, sometimes in isolation, often not, and not always in the same direction.

Generally, though, in archaeological terms, Mesoamerican cultures flowed from Paleolithic through the Preclassic or Formative, through the Classic, and into the Late Classic, this last being the Mexica (Aztec) period and the interval in which the K'iche' nation coalesced from its Mayan roots. Andean cultures flowed from the pre-ceramic stage through the Early, Middle, and Late horizons, this last being the Inka age. Without distorting these cultures, the general and nonculturally specific rubric of "antiquity" encompasses all these periods and places in the Americas. This was the general sense applied to the term in Hewett's 1936 *Ancient Life in Mexico and Central America* and in Lumbreras's *The Peoples and Cultures of Ancient Peru* (1974; originally published in 1969 as *De los pueblos, las culturas y las artes del antiguo Perú*). North, Central, and South America were all brought under this rubric in Kubler's 1962 *The Art and Architecture of Ancient America: The Mexican, Maya, and Andean Peoples.* We say "antiquity" as it encapsulates all these pre-contact cultures over eons in these diverse regions, but when we say "late antiquity," we focus on the last centuries (Late Classic Mesoamerica and Late Horizon Peru) before the seismic shift that occurred after 1492.

The same can be said about the expression "early modern." It is a somewhat imprecise expression referring to Europe and thus creating an oxymoron, as suggested by Euan Cameron, referring to the period beginning after the waning of the Middle Ages (marked as ending at different times in the various European countries) and expiring as the nineteenth century began.[2] It can be as imprecise and variegated as expressed in different languages and referring to different countries as are the equally imprecise terms Renaissance (it begins in Italy and ends elsewhere) and Siglo de Oro (actually two centuries in Spain). Referring to Spain, James Casey explains, "The early modern period lacks, almost by definition, the clear features of its predecessor and successor, the medieval and modern worlds."[3] In other words, it was a time of change. Despite the imprecision of the designation, the period has certain distinguishing features, one of which is indispensable to deciphering its mysteries. Casey clarifies: "One of the characteristics of the early modern world was the acceleration of that process conveniently if loosely described as the transition from feudalism to capitalism."[4] But this was not necessarily the case with Latin America, where feudal or feudal-like institutions such as chattel slavery survived into the nineteenth century and debt peonage still exists today. Nevertheless, as discussed in chapter 5, *obrajes* (wool mills), natural resource mining, agricultural production, and mercantilist trade were all in play during the sixteenth century. While "early modern" can have an economic meaning (Prak, *Early Modern Capitalism*), it can also have religious meaning (Miola, *Early Modern Catholicism*), historical meaning (Herzog, *Defining Nations Immigrants and Citizens in Early Modern Spain and Spanish America*), and cultural meaning, with which I employ it here.[5] For Latin America, the term "early modern" can be roughly synonymous with the colonial era, but looks at other aspects of society not always conjured in the word "colonial." In some cases, it may be more precise to talk about early modern enclaves, as the Conquest was uneven and still continuing against the Ranqueles, for example, during the nineteenth century, and against the K'iche' during the twentieth.

It may surprise the reader to see the term "nation" so widely applied to fifteenth- and sixteenth-century politico-cultural organization. It is used here in the fifteenth- and sixteenth-century Spanish language sense, which as will be discussed, is quite different from the modern and postmodern usage. The nation during its passage from late antiquity to early modern, as defined by a variety of sources, consists of a septet of defining determinants including ethnicity and ethnic diffusion, lineage as it pertains to class, memory/history, religion, language, gender, and the human migration and/or long-distance trade resulting in cultural interaction. Each of these factors, to varying degrees, informs the pre- and early modern container we call "the nation." The nation, understood here as a group of peoples with a real or ideal common origin with a shared belief system, was not a static arrangement, and frequently entered into a process we can describe as ethnic blending, or forming new hybrid configurations. When referring to Amerindian societies the word "nation" has been used interchangeably with the words "tribe," "pueblo," or people. In sixteenth-century Spanish, *tribu* (tribe) was not generally used. In the 1739 *Diccionario de la lengua castellana,* the term refers to Israeli and Arab divisions of peoples but not to Amerindians.[6] The words "nations," "pueblos," and others were common signifiers in sixteenth-century Spanish prose, and the semiotic differences between them constitutes one line of inquiry in this book.[7] In essence, we will look at several Amerindian peoples and the elements that gave form to their nations so that we can then map out how Spaniards appropriated or rejected them after the post-1492 invasions. Chapter 1 sets the stage for the book and paints some broad strokes about sixteenth century conceptualizations of the nation based on ethnicity, culture, migrations, borders, and trade, and how some twentieth- or twenty-first-century conceptualizations reject those elements as constituting nationness, in some cases denying their importance in the configuration of the nation.

For both late-antiquity and early modern peoples, ethnicity was perhaps an obvious means for delimiting nations, although that is not a category and term peoples from either period would have used in describing themselves. Chapters 2 and 3 make manifest the pre-Hispanic origins of the ethnic nation, simply called *nación* in the Spanish of the time, by taking into account language, religion, lineage, and cultural diffusion and then how the facets of ethnicity were modified, reoriented, and projected during the first century of transatlantic colonialism. Specifically, chapter 2 focuses on the Mesoamerican chronicles, understanding this term broadly, with special emphasis on those by Hernán Cortés, Bernal Díaz del Castillo, Bernardino de Sahagún, Diego Muñoz Camargo, Fernando de Alva Ixtlilxóchitl, and the *Popol Wuj* to extrapolate the time before contact with Spaniards and then document the changes after that juncture. Maps and recent anthropological and archeological investigation fill in significant gaps. Special attention will be given to lineage, the Nahua social-organization structure known as *altepetl* (pl. *altepeme*), and the triple ideals of Toltecayotl, or Toltecness; Hispanidad, or Hispanicness; and something we might call Chichimecayotl, or Chichimecness, a contested category in a multilayered cultural borderlands.

Chapter 3 deals with colonial writings on the Andes, including primarily Agustín de Zárate, Pedro Cieza de León, Inca Garcilaso de la Vega, Blas Valera, and Felipe Guaman Poma de Ayala.[8] After setting out the issues regarding the nations of late-antiquity Colombia, this chapter will turn to the central Andes to discuss the millenarian social structures known as *ayllu* and *panaka* as root organizations even when contested or ignored in the face of colonial bias. Special attention will then be dedicated to a particular language, Qheswa, and a people who called themselves "Qheswa" but who, paradoxically, were not Inkakuna (sing. Inka), the supreme rulers who diffused the Qheswa language through the mountains as a cultural and linguistic ideal similar to Toltecayotl.[9] Unlike the Mesoamerican case of Toltecayotl, however, the Andean ideal did not have a recognizable name, although it was associated with Qheswa, known as the "General Language."

The subordination of women has persisted throughout the ages, and asymmetrical relationships between women and men can play a role when distinct groups come together. Chapter 4 searches for pre-Hispanic patterns of gender relations, both intra- and interethnic, and determines how those patterns then affected the inchoate transatlantic society that formed as Amerindian women were "encountered" by Spanish men. Postcontact women took on various roles ranging from elite actors to agents of their own destinies to intercultural conduits of power to be exchanged, as well as victims of rape and of slavery. On a basic level, the child-bearing relationship between a man and a woman formed the kernel of the nation-unit no matter what the particular group called it, and when said man and woman were from different nation-units, the nature of their respective nations was modified. Many of the sources employed in chapters 2 and 3 also furnish evidence for this chapter.

The sixteenth and seventeenth centuries are pivotal for these processes and configurations as they integrated into what Immanuel Wallerstein and his successors call the World-System. As this system coalesced, it brought into the European economic and cultural fold smaller networks that were thriving in the Western Hemisphere before 1492. Interaction with the master system allowed diverse peoples to come together directly or indirectly under new, more sophisticated, and more profound hierarchical modes of organization. Besides human migration, chapter 5 looks at cross-cultural trade's impact on the nation. This trade could take form from the exchange of icons for religious reasons, or the commoditization of those same artifacts in an expanding long-distance circuit. Whereas much inquiry on these matters has focused on the expansion of the European circuit, we will look at a variety of sources that reveal expansive trading networks in the Americas predating the so-called Conquest before looking at their incorporation into the transatlantic circuit.[10]

Why should we care about the moment when early modernity begins to flow into and reorganize late antiquity? The answer to this question has to do with a past that can be instructive to the present. As Papadopoulos and Urton write in the introduction to their edited volume on value in the ancient world, "The study of the past is more than just the study of ancient people, artifacts, events, and processes. At a broader, behavioral level, it is more about the relationship between people, material objects, processes, and space or place."[11] It is this relationship between people and their communities, the relationships communities have with each other, and the objects and trade routes that bind them together that help to forge culture. Those relationships suffered an unexpected turning point when Europeans came to the Indies with their products and products from the Indies flowed back to Europe, forever changing both hemispheres. Yet there were constants between late antiquity and early modernity, as there are between those eras and our current one. There was urban planning in late antiquity as there was in early modernity, and of course, there still is in our time. Likewise, there were wars in late antiquity—the arrival of the Europeans was defined by war—and we continue to have wars. There was trade then as now, and there were nations then as now, even if the nuances of this term's meaning have changed over the centuries. Because aspects of the human condition are eternal, we can learn more about ourselves from those cultures and communities from so long ago.

The early modern juncture is pivotal in the reorganization of the world because it incubates the origins of a capitalist world economic order and the establishment of an Ecumenical Christian Republic, both of which glossed over millenary ethnonational identities palpitating just below the surface. Besides the reach of Western Civilization, generally considered a positive phase in history, there is a "darker side of the Renaissance," to use Walter Mignolo's phrase, which subordinated peoples while integrating them into the Atlantic system. The silhouette of nations obscured on the "darker side" are illuminated and revealed with interdisciplinary readings of Nahuatl, K'iche', Qheswa, and Spanish-language documentation enriching our understanding of the event that Spaniards called (and school textbooks still call), the Conquest.

Such awareness deepens our appreciation of the Americas in three ways. First, it sheds light on society and its institutions during the first century of the colonial interval. This is because previous investigation was based first on the chronicles, then on Qheswa-language texts translated during the 1960s, and then on Nahuatl texts that surfaced in the 1970s, together with those that resulted from the cracking of the Mayan code in the latter half of the twentieth century. We will attempt to collapse these erstwhile trends into one heterophilological quilt of comprehension, defining Hispanic and diverse indigenous worldviews during the colonial interval. Second, as we dig deeper into colonial-era reality to unveil the latent condition of coloniality that would later limit the nation's relationship to "Independence," we expand our grasp of how colonialism lurks behind the advances of what is commonly described as Western Civilization. One of the ingredients of coloniality, a condition studied by Aníbal Quijano, is hegemony: when people who are subordinated accept, even to a degree, their subordination. Inasmuch as nations must interact with other nations, both within one state apparatus and between states as part of the evolving World-System, hegemony is formed and they cannot be considered totally free. Third, five centuries of suppressing national attributes limits our ability to unearth in unfettered fashion the raw data necessary for defining the identities of peoples organized as recognized and unrecognized nations. Indigenous and mestizo authors' works were given form by enduring altepetl cultures in Mexico and persevering panaka (pl. *panakakuna*) or ayllu (pl. *ayllukuna*) relationships in Peru, realities only recently coming to light. An example from each exemplifies these continuities.

Regarding the former, Jongsoo Lee notes differences of perspective regarding the fifteenth-century Acolhua (pl. Acolhuaque) leader Nezahualcoyotl that exist between Acolhuan and Mexicatl sources.[12] This divergence causes Lee to look with suspicion at Acolhuan sources that favor Nezahualcoyotl's own standpoint. Regarding the latter, José Antonio Mazzotti stresses that Inca Garcilaso de la Vega was from the Qhapaq Ayllu panaka, one branch of the royal family. This panaka-centric optic caused several prominent social scientists and historians (think González de la Rosa and Rostworowski) to look at Garcilaso as a suspicious historiographical source for Inkan history.[13] The persistent loyalty to the altepetl, ayllu, or other configuration giving form to the stories recorded by mestizo and Amerindian authors must be taken into account, even when writing in Spanish. Besides community standards, as Stephanie Merrim thoughtfully observes, a chronicle's author injected his own worldview into it, "endowing it with an autobiographical dimension."[14] Moreover, Rolena Adorno discovers political and financial dimensions, for example, in Díaz del Castillo's *Historia verdadera de la conquista de la Nueva España* resulting from his engagement with Bartolomé de las Casas.[15] Certainly all chroniclers had some type of bias, ranging from the kind of memory that results from personal experience to attentiveness to ethnic nation, justifying encomienda holdings, and rationalizing the "Conquest" itself. However, if one identifies the bias, one can read between the lines.

Bias and numerous other factors resulting from reading pre-Hispanic communities through the filter of colonialism create, Rocío Cortés reminds us, a real challenge in interpreting the meaning of the norms of those communities.[16] She recognizes, for example, that texts authored during the colonial era (she mentions the *Crónica mexicana* by Hernando de Alvarado Tezozomoc and the *Historia de las Indias de Nueva España* by Diego Durán) can simultaneously "reveal" and "conceal" as they narrate events from long ago.[17] Beyond individual authors and informants, auspiciously, a plethora of other kinds of sources help us to read between the lines, so to speak. Legal records exist, which, because the law was set up to favor those who have political and economic influence, tend to present things from the perspective of power. Even from that vantage point, if we acknowledge power's biases, it is possible to detect the precontact structures of nationness. Archaeology and all of its illuminating discoveries add another dimension to our knowledge, a slice of the pie unavailable to the colonial chroniclers.[18] With the twentieth century comes natural science and social science groundwork, which by studying the present, projects light back onto the past. A great body of research is being produced on how to read nonalphabetic sources, such as the Andean *khipu,* the Mayan epigraph, or the Nahua pictorial manuscript. Different pieces of the puzzle come together to create a more complete picture of those communities of people who came before.

This interdisciplinary approach draws on theories of transculturation, hybridity, coloniality and gender, and postulates two varieties of cultural appropriation, the vertical and the horizontal. These can be defined, respectively, as digging into one's own past (a journey through time), and appropriating another's culture after political and religious conquest, interethnic marriage, commodification of women or cultural objects (a journey through space). In a Newtonian sense, time is vertical, as one can only descend backwards on the genealogical tree, whereas space is horizontal and omnidirectional, because movement tends to advance from one territory to another in any two-dimensional direction possible. Cultures can also subsume each other simultaneously. Movement on a bidimensional plane causes new hybrid vertices of perspectives on the past to form.

A number of themes and paradigms emerge from my readings of this particular set of chronicles. By reading these in the context of anthropological and archeological discovery, as well as genetic research, we become acquainted with Amerindian-friendly and gender-friendly concepts of the nation. By allowing for other interdisciplinarily derived information to fill in the blanks, we read between the proverbial lines. The schema of interweaving horizontal and vertical appropriation allows us to recognize the primordial role of women in the latter case, and in the former, the primordial role of myth, history, and lineage in the process of nation forming. Conspicuous in this latter case is the role of "literature" (logogrammatic, fine-line drawing, *qelqa,* khipu, oral) in precontact nations.

The realization that certain continuities between late antiquity and the early modern exist goes against the popular misconception that there was a lightning-bolt conquest and peoples became Hispanic immediately

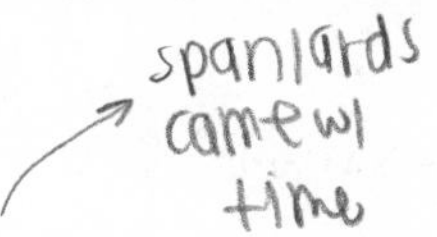

(magically?) after their encounter with the Spanish. However, following in the footsteps of Burga, Flores Galindo, León Portilla, Lockhart, Restall, Mignolo and others, the research presented in this book shows that the transition from late antiquity to early modernity is complex and nuanced. This is because various cultural modules arrived in the latter period as an unbroken chain, even if modified, while others were suppressed or forced underground. Thus the transition is uneven, and perhaps even incomplete. Furthermore, because abundant primary sources were unknown and even ignored, and because Spanish historiography reigned supreme, then and now, our interpretations of those events and societies of long ago can become distorted. Overcoming our bias based on Spanish bias requires reading not only between the lines, but also against the grain of both the chronicles and a sizable amount of the subsequent commentary, much of which has yet to go through a thorough process of decolonization. What is revealed is that Amerindian actors of the precontact and early postcontact periods are not solely the recipients of action; they are national actors (in late antiquity and early modern ways) in their own right, even when their own procedures of governance are modified or outright taken away from them. Spaniards clearly used elements of native governance when it served their purposes.

An appraisal of the terrible acts of violence committed by Spaniards against indigenous men, and especially women, should not imply that the English, the Dutch, and the French in their good time and spheres of influence did not commit acts equally horrendous to expand their nations. Discussing the violent acts Spaniards committed against Amerindians has nothing to do with the rhetorical ploy in politics known as *leyenda negra,* or "Black Legend" fostered by the English and other enemies of Spain during the early modern period and later. The term was coined by the renowned late-nineteenth-century author Emilia Pardo Bazán to label the discourse of Spain's critics, who described the country's culture as *déchéance,* or decadence.[19] Pardo Bazán underscored that it was *légende,* not *histoire.*[20] The "legend" and the mythologies associated with it came to refer to the actions of the Spanish in the New World and, as Stephanie Kirk notes, "circulate[d] among the various European imperial territories."[21] It was propagated especially in the Anglosphere to suggest Spaniards were "bad" colonists, as opposed to the English, the "good" ones.

That legend was nothing more than a political contrivance by the English to justify their own plundering in the New World and other regions.[22] The emphasis on the thoughts and deeds of the Spanish as described in the early modern period has to do with this book's focus on the Spanish-speaking areas of the Americas. An equally opportune approach would be one comparing English, Spanish, French, and Dutch colonialisms.[23] There can be no privileging of one colonialism over the other. The discussion of Spanish actions here has to do with the activity not in and of itself, but as an activity that redirected the trajectories of formation of Latin American nations during the sixteenth century.

Finally, despite my emphasis on indigenous and mixed-heritage writers, I cannot pretend to represent heterogeneous cultures from a non-Western vantage point. I can only try to, in the words of Hans-Georg Gadamer, "make conscious the prejudices governing [my] own understanding, so that the text, as another's meaning, can be isolated and valued on its own."[24] It is necessary to resolve the paradox of ethnographic inquiry that Jacques Derrida spells out: "it is primarily a European science employing traditional concepts, however much it may struggle against them. Consequently, whether he wants to or not—and this does not depend on a decision on his part—the ethnologist accepts into his discourse the premises of ethnocentrism at the very moment when he is employed in denouncing them."[25] Fabian takes this a step further and recognizes that social science itself "came to be linked to colonialism and imperialism."[26] While Fabian is referring to the nineteenth century, this relationship is also manifest during the sixteenth, when Franciscans and Jesuits became the first ethnographers as part of their mission to spread Catholicism. It is also manifest in the twenty-first, when cultural histories such as this must work against the grain in order to assimilate prior knowledge and then to decolonize it.

Many studies of the nation begin at the nineteenth century, when Germany and Italy as we know them today took shape and when many Latin American nations declared their independence. Thus we have Ernest Renan's seminal essay, "Qu'est-ce qu'une nation?" from the late nineteenth century, and Federico Chabod's 1961 *L'idea di nazione*. Scholarship on the nation began to flower in the twentieth century with works such as Benedict Anderson's 1983 *Imagined Communities* and Eric Hobsbawm's 1990 *Nations and Nationalism since 1780*. Other scholars, such as Anthony Smith in his *The Ethnic Origins of Nations* (1986) and *The Antiquity of Nations* (2004), broadened the scope and glimpsed pre-Enlightenment configurations of nations. Smith was mainly concerned with Europe, for example, the connections between the ancient

Greeks and modern-day Greeks. Much less interest has been generated on pre-Enlightenment nations in the Americas, which is our focus here.

With this awareness and new focus on sixteenth-century nations, we can approach indigenous viewpoints. We must admit though, we can never render those viewpoints as insiders. What is important is not arriving, but trying to arrive, moving across a cultural bridge. As curious readers in the Anglosphere, we cannot truly sympathize with Qheswa, K'iche', or Nahuatl-speaking peoples from their own perspectives. Much the way Las Casas offered a critique of the Empire from within the Empire or the way Walter Mignolo condemns alphabetical writing from within the standards of alphabetical writing, the present study reads between colonialism's lines from within the neocolonialist grid.

CHAPTER ONE

THE "BIRTH" OF LATIN AMERICAN NATIONS

> The nation appears today as a contested category, diversely construed from different perspectives and positionalities, a signifier always in tension with what it is supposed to represent or signify. In Latin America, even as imagined communities, nations are still fragmented entities (in terms of territory, regional diversity, social inclusiveness, and racial and ethnic make-up), striving for some unity of purpose.
>
> Salvatore, *Murder and Violence in Latin America*

Since the idea of the nation and the word to describe the idea came into being during the Middle Ages, its meaning has modulated with events such as the so-called Conquest, the Enlightenment, and nineteenth-century state formation in Europe and the Americas. The progression from "people" to ethnic group, then to nation, and from there to a postethnic concept of nation reigning among certain academics and politicians today makes the semiotic meaning of the term "nation" unstable during our time. Indeed, this term, as well as the adjective "ethnic," mean many things to many people. Sociologists Floya Anthias and Nira Yuval-Davis remind us in their book *Women-Nation-State,* "The very conceptualization of 'ethnic' and 'national' groupings and the concepts of ethnic culture, ethnicity and racism have led to much difficulty."[1] This is because, as Alarcón, Kaplan, and Moallem call to our attention in *Between Woman and Nation,* "it is a commonplace of our time to note that nation-state formations are influenced, underpinned, and even founded by ideas rooted in the Enlightenment and liberalism of the West."[2] Those liberal ideas, devoid of ethnic formulations, however, are still unachieved in our time. Think Kurds, Palestinians, the Rohingya people, and modern-day Amerindians who, while different from the cultures of late antiquity, are still excluded from nation-state formulations.

In the world of late antiquity, the Kuna people of Panama had a notion they called Abya Yala that referred to the land and thus the American continents. Their distant relatives, the Nasa Community, living today under the gun in Cauca Valley in Colombia, have a term, Kwe'sx Kiwe Wala, meaning Our Big Land. Inkakuna conceptualized their empire as Tawantinsuyo, which referred to the four cardinal directions. The Mexica (imprecisely called Aztecs) and their Triple Alliance could have described their country as Anahuac, a noun taken from the name of the valley where they founded their capital city and eventually subordinated many groups of people.[3] The cultures of late antiquity are revealing because they show a pre-Enlightenment concept of nation. In addition, if the reader believes racial, ethnic, and gender differences still inform our view of the nation, then the cultures of late antiquity and early modernity may have something to say to us.[4] These ingredients of nation were submerged during the colonial era because they were deemed unnecessary, even as that era evolved, ended, and was folded into Enlightenment and subsequent postcolonial, postracial, and postethnic conceptualizations.

Another issue comes up in a discussion of geographic categories. This book is entitled *The Formation of Latin American Nations*, but before the nineteenth century the expression "Latin America" had not yet been coined. A brief orientation on the idea of Latin America will be helpful before returning to the pre-Hispanic and early modern eras.[5] The region consists of various countries with variegated histories. Panama, for instance, did not become an independent country until it was detached from Colombia, which itself had split off from Gran Colombia, the latter a metamorphosis of New Granada. When Spaniards arrived in Tawantinsuyo they called it "Peru," and it officially became the Viceroyalty of Peru. It did not become the "Republic of Peru," more or less as we know it, until the nineteenth century. The Anahuac region and beyond immediately became the Viceroyalty of New Spain and did not emerge as the United Mexican States until after independence. The Central American confederation broke off from Mexico and eventually split into five distinct republics. The region as a whole became known as Spanish America, but as the nineteenth century came under French influence, it became recognized as Latin America, the preferred but not exclusive term today. "Hispanic America" is another possible designation, and Great Britain and Spain still seem to prefer the appellation "Spanish America," both of which exclude Portuguese-speaking Brazil, Francophone islands, and parts of Canada. The complexities and vagaries of the long arc of these politically configuring processes are outside the scope of this book. What I do throughout this study is focus on the origins of nations with special attention to the regions known as Mesoamerica and the Andes. In this chapter, I try to clear up some of the denotative and connotative issues regarding the term "nation" before shifting focus to late ancient and early modern notions of the nation in Latin America.

COMPETING PERSPECTIVES ON THE NATION

People might think of the nation as a modern enterprise, developed since the late eighteenth and nineteenth centuries. A number of world-shaping events come to mind: the spectacular birth of the United States on July 4, 1776, the explosive reconfiguration of the French nation after July 14, 1789, the long Mexican war for independence between 1810 and 1821, San Martín's emotional proclamation of Peruvian independence on July 28, 1821, the final thrust for Italian unification between 1861 and 1871, and the proclamation of the German Empire on July 18, 1871. In the context of these great paradigm-shifting events in the transatlantic world, the nineteenth-century French philologist Ernest Renan held that nations are born and that they die. He states unequivocally in his famous essay "What Is a Nation?" that "nations possess not even one iota of the eternal" (Les nations ne sont pas quelque chose d'éternel).[6] In the Americas, these modern constructions supposed unencumbering nations from European origins, adopting what Thomas Holt describes as "a new consciousness of we-ness," where "people must now picture themselves as part of a physical and conceptual abstraction."[7] This view, unhinged from ethnicity, is much like Renan's conception of "a spiritual family" (une famille spirituelle).[8] The nation is a place, according to one *New York Times* article, "where loyalty is less about particular places or tribes than particular ideas." It is a place where people "are not constrained by accidents of birth."[9] This conceptualization of the nation as a mindset tends to coincide with the idea of postethnic nations.

Today the idea of the nation in the West is generally held to be a unitary grouping of peoples regardless of race, ethnicity, or gender. Hobsbawm's view in his oft-cited *Nations and Nationalism since 1780* is typical and prescriptive: "The basic characteristic of the modern nation and everything connected with it is its modernity."[10] Anderson, who published his wildly popular *Imagined Communities* in 1983, just before Hobsbawm began to prepare the 1985 lectures that eventually would become his masterpiece *Nations and Nationalism*,[11] seems to suggest that "national consciousness" becomes possible only with the advent of print cultures.[12] Taking his intellectual cues from Anderson, Hobsbawm studied the various editions of the *Diccionario* of the Spanish Royal Academy and concluded that in Spain, the notion of state was not linked to that of nation until the 1884 edition of the *Diccionario*. He quotes directly from the *Diccionario de la lengua castellana* from 1734. The word *nación* only meant "'the aggregate of the inhabitants of a province, a country or a kingdom.'"[13] It was not until 150 years later, in the 1884 dictionary, when the idea of nation became linked with that of state.

Here we are concerned with culture, ethnicity, and nation, and it is important to consider the possibility that *in the past* the contours of the nation were not necessarily viewed as contiguous to those of the state. This was the case in the European view and especially in the larger empires in this hemisphere, such as the Triple Alliance and Tawantinsuyo, although not inexorably so in the smaller polities where nation and governance (frequently controlled by a hereditary ruler) may have coincided. Moreover, *in the present* some scholars view the nation as noncontiguous to the "ethnic group." Consider the thought of Adrian Hastings, who, using Hobsbawm as a point of departure, concludes, "An ethnicity is a group of people with a shared cultural identity and spoken language. It constitutes the major distinguishing element in all pre-national societies, but may survive as a strong subdivision with a loyalty of its own within established nations."[14] Anthony Smith also distinguishes between ethnic group and nation, but from another perspective: with ethnicity, "the link with a territory may be only historical and symbolic," while nations "possess territories."[15] Thus, we can conclude that while an ethnic group may or may not dwell on the land associated with it, nations must reside on the land with which they are associated. Hastings, because he did not read texts from the time Europeans encountered Amerindian communities, separates ethnicity from nation and supposes nation can exist separate from ethnicity. Smith's distinction is conditional because it is based on political control of territory, whereas Hastings's seems essentialist in that it is based on language and identity. This post-Enlightenment conceptualization that extracts ethnicity from nation seems to be what Hastings is envisioning when he alludes to the ethnicities existing within nations, not constituting them. There are too many ethnicities and nations on the planet to prove or disprove this hypothesis with absolute certainty, but, as we will see below, it would be an error to argue that ethnicity must necessarily be dislodged from nation. In late antiquity the nation was based on what we call ethnicity, and so it remained in early modernity, but universal Christianity and King Charles's Holy Roman Empire began to work against ethnic forces at play within the nation.

Taking the Europeanist theory of the nation as postulated by Anderson, Hobsbawm, Hastings, and others to be universal, as many scholars do, leads to the misconception that the Nahua *altepetl,* the Mixtec *ñuu,* the Yucatec *cah,* the K'iche' *amaq',* and the Qheswaphone *ayllu* were only stateless "aggregates of inhabitants," which was not the case.[16] We know many of the polities of Colombia, Guatemala, and Yucatán, as well as the imperialist Mexica and Inkakuna, were governed by states and state-like structures before 1492. The idea of stateless communities is one convenient way to argue for European superiority over those communities.

Furthermore, if there is a state, there is generally a nation. Indeed, a notable percentage of early modern authors writing in Spanish (both Hispanic and Amerindian identified) found entities such as altepetl, ñuu, cah, amaq', ayllu, and others could be represented with the term "nación." Those authors who avoided the term "nación" were saying something about their conceptualizations of Amerindian political status. This inquiry into the formation of Latin American nations discusses previous incarnations of this concept, referred to by many names, including "nación," in the Americas that were linked to lineage, ethnicity, gender, and territory. As the period of late antiquity transitioned into the early modern one, indigenous terminology on social organization was generally rejected and replaced with various terms such as "nación," "province," and even "kingdom."

If race (still) matters, as the public intellectual Cornel West blazoned across the cover of one of his books, the possibility of a color-blind nation free from hierarchical thinking and based on citizenship for all is thrown into doubt. It might be overly pessimistic to think the modern nation in race-free form put forth by free-market theorists and globalization advocates is not possible in the future. However, we have come a lot less distance than we imagine. Ethnic cleansing occurred recently in Rwanda and the former Yugoslavia; Russia has reclaimed parts of Ukraine based on ethnic principle; people from one Latin American country are not easily accepted as nationals in another Latin American country; and people from those countries are not freely accepted in the United States. Our overlapping neocolonizing and decolonizing national models still have much to learn from colonizing and colonized nations of the sixteenth century. To get there, we must understand as national constructions the organizational patterns and practices of pre- and postcontact peoples during the frames immediately before the advent of the Spanish and in the decades after their arrival in the region.

We cannot consider these matters adequately if we do not mention the realities in Spain that informed the minds of conquistadors, encomenderos, priests, administrators, and even colonists. What was happening there was a consolidating of socio-ethnic forces—Basques, Andalusians, and Castilians—all under the banner of "Spanish." This was an eternal process going back to before the Roman Empire and, as we will see, an eternal process in Mesoamerica and the Andes. The reader will realize that traditional notions had been coalescing (not unlike in Spain) and they continued to so with new elements as "early modern" began to take root. However, even in Spain, the ethnic factor is a rudimentary one, and even today, the forces of ethnicity are so strong that Catalonia and the Basque Country still toy with the idea of forging ethnic nations separate from Castile-dominated Spain. Thus, there are always alternative concepts of modernity.

There is an additional point of comparison to Spain, New Spain, and Peru. Not even the power of the postethnic vein of Western discourse can camouflage the fact that Great Britain is likewise not "one" nation. A brief discussion of the United Kingdom is helpful because most readers of this book in English are familiar with it. Its example highlights both the Enlightenment ideal tending toward postethnicity and the ethnocultural reality of the nation it tries to leave behind. Frank Welsh takes note of this in his history of the United Kingdom: "Inhabitants of other countries can define themselves as 'French,' 'German' or even 'Italian' without great difficulty, but those of the British Isles may wish to be known as English, Scottish, Welsh, Irish, or British, to say nothing of Jersymen, Guernseymen or Manx."[17] While author Welsh may have been unaware of local sentiments in Germany, France, or Italy, his observations on the United Kingdom are relevant to our understanding of Spain and the New World. Tellingly, he titled his book *The Four Nations: A History of the United Kingdom*. The "four" refers to the English, Scottish, Welsh, and Irish. There was already backtracking from the unitary ideal of the United Kingdom when Ireland, except for the northern province, left in 1922. Recent voting in the case of Scotland is illuminating. Indeed, much has been made of the "national" differences in the Brexit vote between the English and the Scottish.[18] To say it right out, the ideal is the United Kingdom, but the reality is the four nations still coming to grips with that ideal installed on May 1, 1707, when Great Britain was born.[19] What makes the idea of nation presented in this book on the sixteenth century and earlier seem somewhat outré is that it responds to previously deemphasized peoples as nations and that it is not blinded by the postethnic ideal, which is so compelling. We want this ideal, but it is difficult to obtain.

Two other points need to be made. First, besides modern notions of the nation, earlier conceptions persist to counterbalance modern ones, or to inform them, causing or creating a kind of heterogeneous modernity. These may be notions such as the previously mentioned Scotland, Catalonia, and Kwe'sx Kiwe Wala. As ethnographer Katinka Weber cautions, even in our time, people in Bolivia still identify with the *nación aymara,* the *nación guaraní,* or with the *nación chiquitana.*[20] For McKim Marriot, these terms and the process that occurs as they float to the surface refer to what philosopher F. S. C. Northrup has described as the "resurgence of submerged civilizations."[21] These notions endure despite "Bolivia" being the shared ideal. Tellingly, this ideal itself has changed to take into account the ethnic nation. Since 2009, this country is officially calling itself the Plurinational State of Bolivia, with many official languages, including Aymara, Qheswa, Guarani, Spanish, and dozens of others. Each "nation" included in the Plurinational State is an *etnia,* a term that, as established by Smith, means "ethnic community."[22]

Second, despite the Spanish American countries being differentiated ethnically, culturally, and politically, shared within and between each country is a kind of pan-Hispanic mantle centered on the massive etnia described as Las Españas, which is based on a common tongue, Roman law, and other considerations. For this reason, Madrid takes an interest in restoring colonial buildings in cities like Lima, includes representative Latin American "academies" in the Spanish Royal Academy of the Language, and continues to link economically to the Caribbean, Mexico, Central America, and the southern continent with business enterprises such as Telefónica, Repsol, Mapfre, and Sol Meliá. Contrast this with places like the United States, where Spanish economic investment is more limited.

This is not a uniquely Hispanic tendency. In the United States, with its "one nation under god" motto, there is pressure for all to speak English and the legal system is based on Anglo Saxon common law norms. Within US borders the melting pot ideal implies that all people, regardless of their origins, fold into the Anglo ideal. In addition, in international affairs, a kind of Anglo-Saxon alliance exists that stands out among the heterogeneity of world political configurations. The United States and Great Britain have a "special relationship" not shared with any other country (although Prime Minister Merkel has proposed such a relationship for Germany). Such macro ethnic determinants still carry weight despite their sometimes-coercive interaction with microethnic constituencies.

First and foremost, "to invent" is not a useful verb for envisaging nations as they coalesce. It comes too close to Benedict Anderson's neoliberal theory of the nation. His theory implies that Creole pioneers (the descendants of Spaniards) pass over the national substances with a print culture that favors an elitist and/or decultured state. An "imagined" state such as this one is primed for an increasing linkage with global economics. Conversely, nature, or *naturaleza* in archaic Spanish, as the *Diccionario* of the Royal Academy reveals, could have the same meaning as "nationality," especially in the sense of "origins that someone has according to the city or country where they were born" (Origen que alguien tiene según la ciudad o país en que ha nacido).[23] This definition approximates both Inca Garcilaso de la Vega and Fernando de Alva Ixtlilxóchitl's notions of the nation, which incorporate the idea of belonging to a place. After all, "nación" derives from *nacer*: to be born, to be born in a particular place, in a particular family.

To conclude this line of thinking, an awareness of what we might call etnia, nación, or ethnic nation, because it came from nature and tradition, was not problematic in the period of late antiquity. These kinds of communities with identities were taken as a given; they simply existed. Heraclio Bonilla notes that the problematizing of these communities that came with the rise of a concern for what has been called the "ethnic" or "Indian" problem "was a direct consequence of the Conquest and colonization that Spain imposed in this region from the beginning of the Sixteenth Century" (fue una consecuencia directa de la Conquista y la colonización que España impuso en esta región desde los inicios del siglo XVI).[24] The problematizing of ethnic groups by both conservative and liberal intellectuals and politicians because they did not fit into European models began with the Conquest and continues to the present moment.

ESSENTIAL ELEMENTS OF THE NATION

To offer a working definition of the nation liberated from the enduring colonialities of our time and place, a series of attributes can serve, not as an iron-plated mold, but as a type of barometer by which to measure an earlier time and place when the noun "nación" came into postcontact discourse. For the sake of illustration, we can review some specific traits codified in the *Popol Vuh,* now spelled as *Popol Wuj,* to give form to the idea of nationness and serve as a template for further discussion. Many elements in this compilation, put together in the middle of the sixteenth century, have ancient origins among the Maya that then achieved cohesiveness among the Postclassic K'iche' of Guatemala (see map 1). The text constitutes a primary example of a K'iche'-centric discourse elaborated with less Spanish influence than other contemporary documents. It is not that the *Popol Wuj* is more up to this task than other contemporary writing, such as that of Diego Muñoz Camargo, Fernando de Alva Ixtlilxóchitl, or Inca Garcilaso de la Vega, which holds value and is thoroughly discussed in the chapters that follow. It is simply logical to begin this discussion with a text less filtered and accommodated than Muñoz, Alva Ixtlilxóchitl, or Garcilaso, and especially because it is one of the best-known piece of *indigenous* literature in the Americas.[25] Moreover, it is a representative work that for Arturo Arias "constitutes the heart of the Mesoamerican cultural matrix."[26]

While the *Popol Wuj* is one of the best-known pieces of indigenous literature, López emphasizes, "its existence and survival have been linked with the fate of the community and culture to which it pertains and continues to pertain."[27] That community, again, is the K'iche' nation. The idea of nación in the early postcontact era is one way to represent the idea of amaq', which the *Popol Wuj*'s first translator, Father Francisco Ximénez, rendered as "pueblo," meaning people or nation.[28] Here the *wuj,* or book or document, serves us well because from it we can extrapolate the representative traits of the late-antiquity, Postclassic (AD 900–1524) amaq'. These are kinship and ethnic, class, and gender hierarchies, along with territory, religion, army formation, culture, and language.[29] Of course, these traits can be found earlier. What matters here is that they survived from those earlier periods on a long arc to remain in force during late antiquity, the period that came up against early modernity.

(1) One basic ingredient of the amaq', or premodern nation, is simply a *kinship group.* The idea of the family associated with biological reproduction

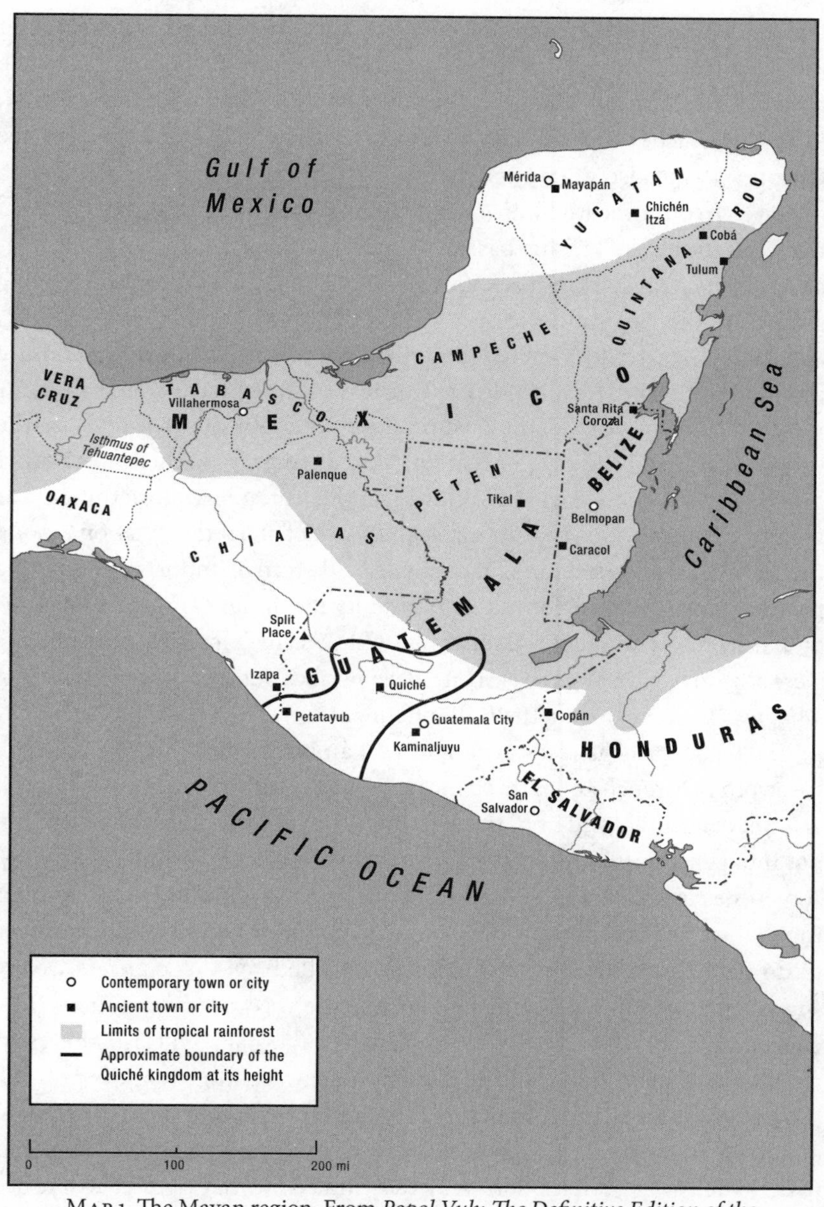

MAP 1. The Mayan region. From *Popol Vuh: The Definitive Edition of the Mayan Book of the Dawn of Life and the Glories of Kings and Gods.* 2nd ed. (New York: Simon and Schuster, 1996), 20.
Map by Erin Greb Cartography.

is, as Holt emphasizes, "perceived to be essential to the reproduction of the nation."[30] We detect this in the *Popol Wuj*, where three lineages are established that lead from Balam Acab to house of Nihaib, from Balam Quitze to the house of Cavec, from Mahucutah to the house of Ahau (Qoahau) (*PV*, IV, v). In this, K'iche' were similar to Mexica (see Chapter 2) and Inkakuna (see Chapter 3), who also valued and manipulated lineage as an ethic conception of power. In our time well-known and dominant families still play important roles, but the idea of kinship has been (unevenly!) replaced by political ideology, conservatism harking back toward the beginning and liberalism moving away from that beginning.

(2) The hierarchies organized by means of *race*, *class*, and *gender* are essential to this process. While the K'iche' would not have understood our modern concept of race, they would have taken for granted lineage (the three houses) and the kind of markers that distinguished them from other groups such as the Kaqchikels.[31] Lineage, the initial basis for ethnicity, as seen in Chapter 2, was also an integral feature of altepetl formation among the Mexica, and as seen in Chapter 3, it held similar importance for Inka panaka. Lineage has to do with late antiquity meanings of the term "nation" and, it seems, with medieval meanings of the term "race." These meanings were still strong during the early modern period, but there are indicators of what was to come during the Enlightenment.

The term "race" is just as fraught with ambiguities as "nation," but the two words say much about this concept. While the idea of race as we know it was not conceptualized until the end of the seventeenth century and was not put into general use until made common by nineteenth-century sociology, sometimes in sixteenth-century usage the word "nación" was synonymous to what we would call race. Indeed, both *raza*, or race, and *nación* have to do with lineage and what the Romans called *gens*, or clan. As we are suggesting, common descent is integral to the way race (and nation) were conceptualized. We can link the idea of nation to what Ivan Hannaford says about race: "It was not until the late seventeenth century that the pre-idea began to have a specific connotation different from that of *gens* (Latin, clan) and to be used in conjunction with a new term 'ethnic group.'"[32] "Clan" has to do with lineage, but "nation" is already linked to what would become our twenty-first-century notion of race, as depicted in the colonial chronicles. This usage can be delineated with Inca Garcilaso de la Vega, who wrote not in an indigenous language like the *Popol Wuj*, but in beautiful Renaissance

Spanish. Garcilaso provides colonial contextualizing for the *Popol Wuj*, because unlike the case of the K'iche' text, he wrote it for a Spanish readership. In an interesting chapter of the *Comentarios reales* (1609; *Royal Commentaries*, 1685) called "New Names to Name Different Generations" (Nombres nuevos para nombrar diversas generaciones), he discusses Spaniards and blacks, who he describes as *naciones*. He adds that when these naciones mix, then "others" (otras) emerge. When he affirms that "they call us mestizos" (nos llaman mestizos), he explains that this means "we are mixed from both nations" (somos mezclados de ambas naciones), implying the "Indians" were also nations (*CR*, IX, xxxi). Why would "nación" be a more common designation than "raza" during that period? Corominas tells us that in sixteenth-century Spanish, the utterance "raza" usually had unfavorable nuances.[33] Thus in this period, before the descriptor "race" had become common linguistic currency, "nation" denoted the idea. English speakers may be somewhat jolted by the early modern usage of "nación." To soften the blow, Harold Livermore, for example, translates "nación" in this chapter of Garcilaso as "race," and *generaciones* as "racial groups."[34] But if "nación" with its sixteenth century connotations can possibly throw off a twenty-first-century reader, "race" with its twenty-first-century connotations veils sixteenth-century realities. In an effort to move closer to late antiquity and early modern realities, we use the word "nation" as it was used five centuries ago, which is the manner intended in the book's title.

Class, the presence of a ranked society, has been presumed and embraced at least from the Olmec period in Central Mexico (1800–250 BC) and from the time of the Caral-Aspero complex of settlements in Peru (2500–2000 BC).[35] We see a ruling class in the *Popol Wuj* that is derived from lineage. The nation, in that text and in the thousand years it took to compose, was viewed as the lineage of the ruling elite, not necessarily of the clans of the everyday workers. Class was not something limited to antiquity, it was also integral to the early moderns' thirst for titles and wealth, and it survives to the present day in the form of tax codes favoring oligarchy formation, airline and train passenger ticket tiers, some amusement park ticket categories, distinctions between public and private schools, kinds of bank accounts and trusts, and exclusive clubs. Lineage leads to aristocratic notions of class, and lineage is formed when men and women are joined connubially.

In addition to hierarchies constructed with a class and race system, as Elizabeth Dore underscores, "*gender* is [also] a fundamental category of social organization and a major means by which social relations and inequality are structured."[36] Among the Postclassic Maya, as seen in Chapter 4, wives were bought and sisters sold as a way of forging nations. The K'iche', as depicted in the *Popol Wuj*, assigned value to women. Within the amaq', dissentions grew because of jealousy, wife and sister prices, and their inability to drink *chicha*, a kind of corn beer, together (*PV*, IV, viii). The value assigned to women is further discussed in Chapter 4, which details how the early dynasty Mexica married into other ethnic groups to improve their class standing, and how the Inkakuna offered women as interethnic gifts as a way to broker power. In all three cases, the social role of women was integral to nation formation and expansion. Without question, gender and class were inexorably linked, at least among the upper echelons of society. Such racial, class, and gendered rankings must be taken into account when deducing the features of the nation. Even today, liberal notions of the raceless and classless nation are Utopian. As Holt cautions, "Actual nations must be fashioned from existing identities that are gendered, racialized, and classified."[37] That is to say that gender, race (or ethnicity), and class must be acknowledged as the stuff of which nations were and are made. That which comes before informs what comes after. Today, the idealists and positive thinkers among us struggle to get beyond race, class, and gender subordination. We have come up with "isms" to describe the persistence of these forms of subordination: racism, classism, and sexism. These words were coined to represent aspects of the persistence of structures and tendencies that come from the past.

(3) An association with a *territory*, real or claimed, is integral to the idea of the nation. Maps are indicative of territorial associations. Buildings and other infrastructure that develop the territory are also symbolic of the nation. Both the territory and the monuments constructed on it hold value.[38] When the K'iche' abandoned their capital at Izmachi, they came to the town of Q'umarkaj, commonly known by its Nahuatl name, Utatlan. There, the *Popol Wuj* tells us, they built houses and a temple to God (*PV*, IV, viii). They "constructed the city of the gullies with lime and boulders" (construyeron de cal y canto la ciudad de los barrancos) (*PV*, IV, ix). Ruud Van Akkeren summarizes the kinds of edifices found in the central plaza of K'iche' Postclassic urban centers. He refers to "five classes of buildings that are commonly found in a plaza. Four of them have a more or less defined function: the elongated house, the pyramid temple, the altar and the ball court. A fifth type of building has been called 'Council House.'"[39] In this, the K'iche' coincided with their

late antiquity contemporaries, the Mexica and the Inkakuna, who also built great monuments and edifices in their capitals, Tenochtitlan and Qosqo. These practices in late antiquity are no different from modern nations whose capitals—think Buenos Aires, Lima, or Mexico City—try to represent their nations with magnificent presidential palaces, national senate buildings, cathedrals, and other symbolic structures.

(4) *Religious beliefs* shape identity. For the K'iche' of the *Popol Wuj,* Tohil, a deity associated with Ecatl and Quetzalcoatl, was unifying. His name represented the aforementioned dynastic houses, the Nihaib, the Cavec, and the Ahau. He makes the K'iche' great when he gives them fire. In a more general sense, a theological appreciation of maize, from which humanity sprang, is the locus of organization for Mayan peoples. Religion formed nations in the time of the Classic Maya and of Teotihuacan and, in various ways, still does today. In some Latin American nations, such as Paraguay, the constitution requires the president to be Catholic. However, religion—even if linked to the nation as it appears to be in the *Popol Wuj,* does not need to be correlative to one particular nation. *Popol Wuj* scholar Quiroa, referring to this primary text, notes that "its contents have been generalized to apply to virtually all of the ancient Maya religions."[40]

(5) The *formation of armies* is integral to shaping modern nations and, as Malcolm Deas suggests, most certainly was for pre-Columbian ranked-society nations.[41] Whether or not we like to admit it, war is a primary force in the project of nation-building or nation-weakening, depending upon a conflict's outcome. The *Popol Wuj* recounts that when the rulers Gag-Quibab and Cavizimah fought wars with various nations on their borders, their towns and fields were divided. These nations were the Rabinal, the Kaqchikel, and Zaculeu, and besides having their land partitioned or destroyed, many of their people ended up as slaves (*PV,* IV, x). Warfare can be a mode of forging rankings among nations just as hierarchies of people can be formed within nations. War was so integral to the Mexica that they had a war deity, Huitzilopochtli, who was primordial to their identity. Just as with the K'iche', the post-Independence history of Latin America is replete with examples of wars between nations, internal conflicts erupting between actors within one nation, and between "modern" states and ethnic and/or revolutionary insurgencies within those states.

(6) Construction of a *national culture* can include banners, textiles, maps, or other forms of codification of words or concepts (such as the *khipu* or *amatl*

bark paper). The *Popol Wuj* itself serves as a repository for the hallmarks of K'iche'-ness—deities, mythological heroes, tricksters, rulers, wars, territories, and women as mediums to foster kinship influence.[42] Lords "knew there was a place where [all this] could be seen, that there was a book that they called the *Popol Wuj*" (Sabrían bien que había donde podían verlo, que existía un libro por ellos llamado *Popol Vuh*) (*PV*, IV, xi). Again, "nation" in this sense can be hyper-local or it can be expansive. It can represent one altepetl, a group of four altepeme, or it can embrace the ideal of Toltecayotl. The *Popol Wuj* favors certain lineages over others. In our time, allegorical images on money, flags, and even corporate logos can codify and promote national cultures.

(7) Legends, history, and language, commonly studied in the humanities, are often *patriotic constructions* that give cohesiveness to the nation. The *Popol Wuj* highlights that the Kaqchikels' tongue is different from the tongue of the K'iche', because their gods were different (*PV*, III, ix). Legends and history can come together in one unified and coherent intellectual system. The sacred text opens by declaring itself "the old stories, the beginning and the origin of all that was done in the town of K'iche'" (las antiguas historias, el principio y el origen de todo lo que se hizo en la ciudad de Quiché) (*PV*, I, "Preámbulo"). As translators Morley and Goetz explain in a footnote, these are stories derived from oral tradition and "picture writings" (*PV*, I, Preamble, n. 2). After the process of *Breaking the Maya Code* during the twentieth century (see Coe), we know it was codified in script. Sections of the *Popol Wuj* reach back to those ninth-century stories and codify them in the decades after the Spaniards' arrival. In the pessimism of that event, the document's authors lament in their closing that the life of kings among the K'iche' can "no longer be seen," and that it "came to an end" (*PV*, IV, xii).[43] Indeed, those stories remained underground for centuries. While the moment of the Conquest's gloominess was not unwarranted, the *Popol Wuj*'s publication during the nineteenth century by Karl von Scherzer and Charles Étienne Brasseur de Bourbourg allowed the legends it contains to re-enter tradition and inform later works. These included the Nobel Laureate Miguel Angel Asturias's *Hombres de maíz* (*Men of Maize*) and the testimony of another Guatemalan who also won a Nobel Prize, this one for peace. Rigoberta Menchú's testimony, offered to anthropologist Elizabeth Burgos, links certain perspectives on the modern K'iche' nation to its roots. Often the legends, history, and language introduced by these kinds of texts are suppressed or kidnapped and redirected by the discourse of modern nation states.

We may want to agree with Renan's view that the nation should be based not on race, language, religion, economic interests, or geography but on "a spiritual principle" (un principe spiritual), on "a plebiscite held each and every day" (un plébiscite de tous les jours).[44] As the French intellectual asserts, doing so increases liberty for all. Yet politics, economics, and people themselves cling to their ethnicities, territories, religions, and economic interests, and nations generally have deep roots in the past. Once this has been recognized, the phenomenon can be studied, and once understood more fully, more light can be shed on the present day. The nation can pass through stages, successive governments, and evolving ethnic compositions. The issue is that varying strategies engage with the past. Some countries like Iran, Turkey, China, Japan, and even Scotland derive pleasure from their deep-seated, uninterrupted, roots. Others like France have had enough "republics" that they can number them, and since the Middle Ages, France and Spain have tended to reject the notion of subethnicities in favor of an inclusive homogenizing ideal of the nation-state, monarchic at first, imperialistic or democratic later. On the surface, this model seems to work for Latin America, the colonial regime brushed heterogeneous elements under the proverbial rug, a tendency that remains a feature of Criolla history and identity. Those rudimentary elements are often perceived as nonessential, or inferior, to the nation-state's identity. Here, we are concerned by and large with regions such as Mesoamerica and the Andes evolving between ethnic, meta-ethnic, and anti-ethnic conceptualizations and configurations.

Defining historical horizons in Mexico have comprised the Olmec horizon, the Teotihuacan complex, the Tolteca (sing. Toltecatl) surge, the Mexica-led triple alliance, the New Spain viceroyalty, and the United Mexican States. Peru has had just as long and varied a trajectory. R. Alan Covey has shown in his book, *How the Incas Built Their Heartland*, that a good number of the traits that gave form to the Inka nation were from earlier formations: the Huari, or Wari, horizon and the Killke people. These were built on even earlier formations known as Tiwanaku and Chavin.[45] We know a substantial slice of Tawantinsuyo has survived the colonial era, because over five million people still speak Qheswa in Bolivia and Peru alone.

Memories are an integral feature of the nation and were passed on during the apogee and decline of the Wari State. They survived as myth or as ayllu structures (as argued by Silverblatt)[46] during the Inka period. They endured throughout the colonial era (Thupaq Amaru II). The belief in *Incarrí* was still held to be true in the 1950s and perhaps survives until the present day.[47] Some academics working on this recognize the imperative to count on such stabilizing continuities because, as Sara Castro-Klarén reminds us, "the memory of the past is disputed, contradictory, multiple, and contestatory."[48] Struggling to liberate our worldview from colonial camouflages, it follows that nations are not invented, but instead are constantly "reinventing" themselves as they "reconfigure" their spiritual *and* material substance, in solitary conditions as a kind of monologue, in contact with other nations as a kind of dialogue. The past is always forcing its way into the present, while the nation simultaneously intersects with other nations contemporary to it at each successive moment in time.

Two essential problems reside in the way the nation is viewed in our time. One is that some specialists are calling for the end of the nation-state, or simply claim that it is extinct, in "full retreat," in the throes of extreme transformation, on the verge of extinction, or that it is limiting to world economies. William Robinson, a sociologist, maintains that the nation has simply not been that important in "diverse economic, political, social, and cultural processes."[49] The other is that nations of the industrial revolution tend to reject the existence of earlier national structures. To deny past constructions, even if those ethnicities were not the dominant ones, is to take away some of the substance of the present. Typical, in this regard, is a rhetorical strategy that presents new nations suddenly bursting on the scene in the nineteenth century.[50] This is a misconception. In short, as we shall see, the word "nation" was quite common in late Renaissance Spanish, a central point in the arguments contained in this book. This is not merely an Iberian phenomenon; the word is listed in the *Oxford English Dictionary* citing a medieval usage (from around 1350) where the phase can be found, "God's work of all kinds and tongues and folks and *nations*" (goddes werk of alle kyndes & tunges & folkes & *nacions*).[51] Despite the religious intent of this passage that refers to the Apocalypse, the association of people, language, and nation was clear during the Middle Ages. During the Spanish Renaissance, in the midst of multiple transatlantic conquests, Bishop Antonio de Guevara recognizes the existence of countless distinct historical nations, as he proclaims in his 1529 *Relox de príncipes:*

> Great and diverse was the multitude of *past nations,* including the Syrians, Assyrians, Persians, Medians, Macedonians, Greeks, Scythians, Argives, Corinthians, Caledonians, Indians, Athenians,

> Lacedaemonians, Africans, Vandals, Swabians, Alanis, Huns, Germans, Britons, Hebrews, Palestinians, Gauls, Iberians, Lidonians, Moors, Lusitanians, Goths and Hispanics.

> Grande y muy diversa fue la muchedumbre de las *naciones passadas,* conviene a saber: sirios, assirios, persas, medos, macedonios, griegos, scithas, argivos, corinthos, caldeos, indos, athenienses, lacedemonios, afros, vándalos, suevos, alanos, hunnos, germanos, britanos, hebreos, palestinos, gallos, yberos, lidos, mauros, lusitanos, godos y hispanos.[52]

It is not that all cognoscenti favored or perceived the nation in these terms. Guevara's awareness of cultural diversity across the Old World generated the animosity of humanists such as Pedro de Rhúa. Sara Beckjord goes further and explains that even Erasmists considered Guevara's works to be "prototypes" of lying or pseudo-history.[53] Humanists were concerned with a European unity based on Latin. Focusing on national heterogeneities would not help with that goal. Yet it is undeniable that the idea of a nation filtered into that time's worldview and, as will be seen, it influenced trajectories of the transmuting political structures of the New World.

Much like the failures inherent in our contemporary perceptions of the nation, the sixteenth-century conceptualization excluded vast swaths of populations to create a singular and elite notion. By cutting multitudinous peoples out of the story and fabric of the official nation, ejecting them from the land (typical English practice), or forcing them to work the land (typical Spanish practice), the late Renaissance construct becomes/remains unjust.[54] Happily, the idea of correcting a historiographical trajectory in our time is not an irresolvable quandary. It must first be admitted, as Walter Mignolo does, that "lurking beneath the European story of discovery are the histories, experiences, and silenced conceptual narratives of those who were disqualified as human beings, as historical actors, and as capable of thinking and understanding."[55] We depart from two premises on this issue. One: the nation can serve as a tool to resist economic expansion when it is unfair, concomitantly serving to insert its people into what could be called an alternative mode, from the roots up, what Edgar Montiel calls "humanist worldization." Two: the modern nation has its origins at least as early as the Renaissance, and the study of the nations of that time, both in their Amerindian and European formalizations, can illuminate aspects of both the disqualified human beings and the *gente decente*, the "decent people" who came to be in control.

Finally, a remark about the infinite depths of the nation in time is necessary. It may be impossible to say what the very first nation was, or what the first nations were, except from perhaps a theological perspective. This is true because memory of the first nations has been lost. Moreover, the further we go back in time, the more difficult it is to pinpoint exactly what the nations of anterior domains were. Even though this book posits that the "birth" of Latin American nations comes during the moment when their constituent elements came together in the early modern period, it is still possible to name precursors to those configurations. We must wait for new scientific, social-scientific, and humanistic methodologies to continue to flesh out nations that existed before those embodied by Mexica, Maya, and Inkakuna (that is, Teotihuacan, the Olmeca, the Wari). The current stage of archeological, historical, and cultural groundwork, however, represents a more than adequate starting point to wrap our minds around the sixteenth-century nation with a sufficient degree of sources even if some day science allows us to go back further than is presently possible.

Because dominant Europe saw itself as bringing "civilization" to the Indies, it attempted to suffocate knowledge that was contrary to its mission, and therefore indigenous responses to transoceanic expansion may be less than apparent. Rarely did Andeans win legal battles. Nevertheless, the legal documents produced can still serve to nuance national histories in later centuries. If the colonizer's version of events is well disseminated, the autochthonous one has only recently begun to come into focus, both through those documents and through what has been called ethnohistory. In addition to the prejudices inherent in the Spanish-language paperwork, an additional problem resides in the documentation, as revealed by the ethnolinguist Alfredo Torero:

> The utilization in Hispanic documents of a single term to designate indistinctly social phenomena as different as a language, a culture, a "nation," or even a socioeconomic category in order to impose tribute collection. Such was the case with the words *Aymara, Uro, Puquina, Uruquilla.*
>
> La utilización en los documentos hispánicos de un mismo término para designar indistintamente a fenómenos sociales tan diversos como una lengua, una cultura, una "nación," o incluso, una categoría socioeconómica para fines de imposición tributaria; y tal fue el caso de los vocablos *aymará, uro, puquina, uruqilla.*[56]

The damaging word, *indio*, or "Indian," reveals little linguistic, cultural, or ethnographic information about its supposed referent. As I have discussed in *Decolonizing Indigeneity*, the first book in a trilogy of which *The Formation of Latin American Nations* is the second, word choices can work toward defining nations or toward negating that which makes nations nations.[57] L. Antonio Curet discusses this situation and concludes, "The uncritical adoption and perpetuation of vague, colonial classification systems as 'natural' units . . . has created considerable confusion among scholars."[58] Sometimes a diminutive was used to connote superiority, as when the well-known twentieth-century historian Raúl Porras Barrenechea calls the historical figure Tumaco a "little Indian" (indiecillo).[59] Certainly Porras acquired this word form from the chronicles he was reading, but the fact that he could not find a more balanced form of expression renders his objectivity suspicious. Hence, between limited or biased views and an imprecision in denoting distinctive groups, cultures, and languages, all sources are suspect to a degree. Here I proceed with linguistic- and prejudice-aware caution as I seek to unearth the foundation of the nations of late antiquity and the colonial system imposed on them by comparing Old and New World sources in the bright light of archeological, anthropological, linguistic, literary, historiographical, and biological (DNA) research, all taking into account the new indigenous language-philology born during the 1960s and '70s. By sifting through dense layers of biases, a more objective field of vision than has previously been possible emerges.

THE ENDURING NATURE OF THE NATION

Latin American nations were not born with Thupaq Amaru II, Father Hidalgo, or Bernardo de Monteagudo, nor did the people who lived under colonial rule become "Spanish" after Columbus, Cortés, and Pizarro—they never did, at least not completely. What the first Americans did was resist or fuse, accommodate, and renegotiate with the Spaniards and the Africans who accompanied them, forging a new hybrid society. Whereas today a Guatemalan, a Mexican, a Peruvian, or even an Argentinean share with each other a common language, some literary affinities, some types of Hispanic political structures including Roman Law, the Napoleonic Code, and even a familiarity with *caudillismo*, a present-day citizen from any of those four countries is poles apart from a contemporary Spaniard—despite the Peruvian historian José de la Riva-Agüero's youthful protestations to the contrary. This is because the social, economic, racial, cultural, and yes, literary heritage of these countries' citizens, despite some shared elite literary movements during the nineteenth century, is an ocean apart from that of the Spanish, with millenarian beginnings and five centuries of divergent, complex, and nuanced influences.

The gap between Spanish and Latin American cultural alignments is a topic for another day, another scholar. Rather my intention is to state in unequivocal terms that pre-Hispanic peoples organized themselves as nations in the sixteenth-century Spaniards' understanding of that term, even when the Spaniards did not accept people unlike themselves as nations. Why is this important? When Spaniards denied the attribute we are calling nationness here, they instituted one of the attributes of what Aníbal Quijano describes as coloniality. Denying to others what they claim for themselves works toward instituting a hierarchy of nations based on a false presumption. The acknowledgement of nationness during the sixteenth century and before is important because the origins of Latin American nations are not found in the nineteenth (or eighteenth!) century, as commonly held by theorists such as Anderson, but instead, in part, in the remote origins of these American continents and in the successive moments when those configurations sustained contact with other configurations contemporary to them. To go back thousands of years to the Olmeca, the Wari, or the Moche would be the ideal approach, for therein lie important formative materials of Latin American nations. Archeologists have made exciting discoveries that bring to light organized states, in the case of the Moche (see Chimú area, map 6), and even some type of cultural unit, in the case of the Olmeca (southeast of Veracruz, map 2).[60]

Admittedly, one can only learn so much when going back across millennia to find and verify ethnic origins. The Maya case is indicative. Archaeology documents a generalized proto-Maya or Olmec culture during the Preclassic period (1800–250 BC). Yet for Robert Sharer, "The ethnic identity of the Preclassic populations in the southern [highland] Maya Area is not clear, given the near impossibility of correlating linguistic groups with archaeological remains." Even so, it can be generalized that a non-ethnic-specific pan-Maya early horizon is discernible during the Preclassic period, one that Sharer recognizes as including similar characteristics in "architecture, sculpture, writing, and calendrics," all serving ruling elites who used them "to reinforce authority within these initial state systems."[61] The subsequent splendor of the Classic cah underscores the development of these same traits. The wars and conquests described in the historical writing connote interethnic conflict between distinguishable national entities, some of which can be extrapolated back in time, as might be the case at Chichen Itza. Yet it is not until the Postclassic era when boundaries become

Map 2. Mexico and Northern Central America. From Charles Gibson, *The Aztecs Under Spanish Rule: A History of the Indians of the Valley of Mexico, 1519–1810* (Stanford: Stanford University Press, 1964), xi.

increasingly co-relatable to etnia, as evidenced in texts like the *Annals of the Cakchiquels,* the *Título de Totonicapán,* and the *Popol Wuj.*

Despite the difficulties of establishing language and ethnicity in earlier epochs, a number of New World nations were thriving two millennia ago. Because there has been a total revaluation of the Moche (see Chimú linguistic area in map 6), the result of recent archeological finds including the tomb of the Lord of Sipan, they can serve as a fascinating example in this regard. The Moche are a culture that captured the popular imagination with the discovery of the Lord of Sipan during the 1980s and '90s, carbon dated to around AD 290, which revealed a thriving culture in the period of Moche III (AD 200–450). If we proceed through the dark depths of anthropological time, we can affirm there was some kind of nation unified enough to achieve collective public works projects. Tom Dillehay, working with the Moche IV (AD 450–550) and V (AD 550–800) stages, offers insight on these achievements in varying contexts. These include farmlands, canals, aqueducts, furrows, protective fortifications on hilltops and around towns, ceremonial complexes, and an artisan class, as established by the fine and detailed pottery left behind.[62] However, the nature of that nation has been disputed. It is safe to say there was a Moche culture spread out in the Lambayeque region of what is today Peru, which, depending on which of the six phases comes under discussion, differed in political organization and cultural expression.

As Dillehay convincingly argues, Moche culture had both urban and rural components. Large ceremonial centers, intermediate settlements, and small rural outposts are apparent. There was an elite sector, most likely associated with the centers, that organized a hierarchical style of life. Dillehay explains that three data sets confirm this hierarchy: the "type of grave goods in burials; the representation of presumed social stratification in art; and settlement patterns." Yet this would be only one aspect of what a Moche nation might look like because, and Dillehay makes this clear, the rural areas may have enjoyed more political independence than has been traditionally thought. It would be unwise to attribute the loose linkage to ethnic differences, since that has not been confirmed. We can simply contemplate with Dillehay the possibility of "factional competition both within and among local Moche communities" as well as "relations with other non-urban communities and distant lands independent of an urban center."[63] Yet neither competitiveness nor suburbanity cancels nationness. One need look no further than the Unites States to verify competition between towns, states, and regions and urban and suburban communities, the latter developing a lifestyle given form by a somewhat successful attempt to avoid cities. In addition, we can suppose there may have been a common Moche culture; one unified enough to undertake a large public works project, a seventy-five-kilometer intervalley canal whose construction would have required a developed bureaucracy capable of organizing the project over a one-hundred-year span.[64] We can speculate that only peoples of one etnia, who may or may not have had slaves, would have the mutual sympathy required for such an undertaking. It is a shame the canal was not finished. We can only wonder why it was not, to what degree the late Moche were an integrated nation, and if a limited level of integration was a factor in the project's noncompletion.

Until we adequately decipher the narrative of the Moche fine-line drawings or those early Olmec glyphs, no truly readable documentary record exists until we come to the Maya of the first millennium.[65] Later there would be Nahua, K'iche', and Qheswa records, though these have been largely scorned or even destroyed (as with the Nahua amatl, the K'iche' wuj, and the Andean khipu). The khipu (pl. *khipukuna*) is an interesting case because it does not exclusively represent the State, or even the nation for that matter. As Porras Barrenechea explains, on the one hand, the khipukuna represented different subject matter, the reigns of individual Inkakuna, of specific battles, the law, the calendar, demographics, or other statistics. On the other, the noted historian continues, at least in terms of history, the *khipukamayoqkuna* (sing. *khipukamayoq*) were associated with a panaka, a sort of royal ayllu formed with the members of a particular Inka's family. It was they, in fact, who deliberated "if there should remain any fame of him [the Inka who had just died] for having won some battle, for his valor, or good government" (si debía quedar fama de aquel por haber vencido en alguna batalla, por su valentía o buen gobierno). Because the khipukamayoqkuna (the keepers of the khipukuna) were associated with different panakakuna, a khipukamayoq from one panaka would not necessarily be able to read a device from another panaka.[66] We must conclude, therefore, there may have been an Inkan nation, but—as Guaman Poma de Ayala's letter blatantly flaunts—there was not one master narrative, nor was it homogeneous. It was more like a panaka-organized quilt into which Inka strands of influence flowed.

While we understand that nation configurations reach back millennia, it is the sixteenth-century stage of development that documents the time right before the Spaniards' arrival in this hemisphere. This is the point of departure, not only because records written with the alphabet begin to exist, but because that moment was the flash point of civilizations crashing together. Restall, Souza, and Terraciano remind us that even after the advent of the Spanish, each Nahua, Mixtec, and Mayan ethnic state (altepetl, ñuu, and cah, respectively) "maintained a distinct native and local identity."[67] The same was true in the Andes. In his analysis of the Archivo Histórico of the Ministry of Finance in Peru, Tom Zuidema reaches a startling conclusion. He finds in these 1821–54 tax records that as late as "three-hundred years after the Spanish conquest, many of the precontact ayllu appeared to have survived."[68] Zuidema arrived at this conclusion after spending some ten years reading the Spanish-language chronicles, as well as consulting documents in the Archivo Nacional del Perú searching for clues on the pre-European *ayllukuna* (sing. ayllu) and their structures. Although they may not have survived in the Republican era in the purest of form, many of them did coincide in name or geographic area, even though diverse processes of cultural synthesis have taken place and continue to do so.

Ayllukuna and comparable organizations in other regions were not impenetrable fortresses. Drawing on Dennis Tedlock's explorations, Rolena Adorno concludes that principles of cultural organization have been "more toward integration, rather than separation, accumulation rather than substitution, and interpenetration rather than exclusivity."[69] Oral traditions and hieroglyphics were still apparent during the nineteenth century, though they were insufficiently examined at that time.[70] They were joined by an outpouring of indigenous, mestizo, and Spanish chronicles that found their way into print during that time. Juan Ginés de Sepúlveda, Bartolomé de las Casas, Alva Ixtlilxóchitl, Pedro Cieza de León, the *Popol Wuj*, and others began to find audiences that deemed them worthy of study, and foundational cultural studies essays on them have been written by José Martí and Riva-Agüero. Prescott drew on them when he published two works, *History of the Conquest of Mexico* in 1843 and *Conquest of Peru* in 1847, which fired the imagination and became bestselling volumes of Latin Americianist historiography. Early in the twentieth century Guaman Poma's masterpiece came to light, and this process of revealing the deeper and nuanced nation continues as he is taught extensively in schools and universities in Peru. These literary, oral, and social science trajectories blended with other sources throughout Republican age and are detectible in prominent novelists from diverse nineteenth- and twentieth-century contexts such as Juana Manuela Gorriti, Clorinda Matto de Turner, Miguel Angel Asturias, Juan Rulfo, Gioconda Belli, William Ospina, José María Arguedas, and others.

This is no mere case for dusting off an earlier version of the nation forgotten in archives, although that is part of it. This is also a case of recognizing a lack of clear boundaries between one period and another. There is no exact point when Chichimeca (sing. Chichimecatl) became Tlaxcalteca (sing. Tlaxcaltecatl), or when Warikuna (sing. Wari) became Inkakuna, or even if these transitions were complete because these processes are more like osmosis than the cut of a knife. Chichimecatl culture lived on in the Tlaxcalteca; the Wari heritage persisted in the Inka and colonial intervals.[71] As Mignolo reminds us, the *letrados*' suppression of indigenous modes of expression "does not necessarily result in the suppression of cognitive patterns rooted in the collective memory."[72] Group consciousness lives on in the people and in the archives. As Mazzotti theorizes in his *Coros mestizos del Inca Garcilaso* (*Incan Insights: el Inca Garcilaso's Hints to Andean Readers*), there may have been an Andean audience that found a reflection of themselves in the *Royal Commentaries*. Christian Fernández adds that various seventeenth-century chronicles, such as in Salinas y Córdova, Calancha, Cobo, and Anello Oliva, cited the Inca Garcilaso, and thus one chronicler is folded into another.[73] Prescott himself had Inka Garcilaso's history read to him.

Deeper in the in the national fabric lies an autochthonous *Incaísmo*. Jean-Philippe Husson has published an anonymous tragedy that dates from around

1555, the same time Cieza de León and Agustín de Zárate were issuing their chronicles. *Ataw Wallpa q p'uchuka ku y ni n pa wanka n,* titled by Husson in French as *La mort D'Ataw Wallpa ou La fin de l'Empire des Incas,* shows the dream of the Inka's return was palpable.[74] Jesús Díaz Caballero comments on the return of the Inka motif that survived during the colonial era, giving form to Thupaq Amaru's rebellion. He calls it a "accumulated tradition of popular Inkanism, parallel to and earlier than learned Inkanism incarnate with the enlightened reception of the *Royal Commentaries*" (tradición acumulada de incaísmo popular . . . paralela y anterior al incaísmo letrado representado por la recepción iluminista de los *Comentarios reales*).[75] Wilfredo Kapsoli has reached similar conclusions in his *Retorno del Inca* (The Inka's return). This ever-intensifying tradition continued to reformulate itself during the twentieth century, as Manuel Burga has brought to light in his *Nacimiento de una utopia* (Birth of a utopia).[76]

A similar process occurs in Mexico that seemingly culminates in Francisco Javier Clavijero, who had to write his magnum opus *Historia Antigua de México* (1780–81; *Ancient History of Mexico*, 1787) while in exile in Italy because he was expelled with the Jesuits from the colonies in 1787 by King Charles III. As noted by Joselyn Almeida, the Nahuatl-fluent Clavijero presented a "southern" perspective on the Americas that challenged the dominant view enshrined in William Robertson's *History of America* (1777).[77] Even though written in exile, the information Clavijero extracted from the underside of history eventually wove itself into back into the fabric of Mexican cultural and political history. This is interesting, as Adorno infers, because seventeenth-century writings "played a role in the development of a narrative tradition that carried with it and transformed its own carefully chosen antecedents."[78] As suggested, the indigenous nation also survives in the patterns of the family, of song, of dance, and even in political organization. Testimonial documents such as Gregorio Condori's or Menchú's show an appreciation and respect (even if confusing timelines) for the indigenous nations of their forbears, which they do not distinguish from their own nations. Just as representatives of Inkakuna and Spanish warriors go at it in the theatre, popular pageants, and even as opposing chessboard armies, Menchú reconstitutes Tecun Uman, who resisted Pedro de Alvarado's invasion of El Quiché for as long as he could, and whose memory still holds meaning for the K'iche' people.

Besides the collective memory, the cultural architecture, and the linguistic forms that survive, the pre-Hispanic nation endures in other ways, still resisting the legacy of colonialism. Occasionally these memories, architectures, and languages would burst out of the colonialist box, as in the case of the Juan Santos Atawallpa and Thupaq Amaru II rebellions in 1742 and 1780, respectively.[79] These uprisings were not isolated, local, or purely Qheswa phenomena. The Thupaq Katari revolt occurred in Upper Peru, where the Bolivian Plurinational State now resides.[80] After 1810, 1824, and 1826, they have continued to the present. Florencia Mallon writes about the nineteenth century and states, "The rebellions were widespread and threatened to become social revolutions."[81] Noteworthy was the rebellion spearheaded by Coronel Juan Bustamante in Huancané (1867–68), just some forty years after independence.[82] Even after that century had transpired, other cases, including the 1915 Rumi Maqui rebellion in Puno, captured the public spirit. Rumi Maqui influenced the noted essayist José Carlos Mariátegui's writing.[83] The sociological study of pre-Hispanic memory and the colonial and the post-independence reworking of it merit more attention than is possible in a book on late antiquity's passage of reaccommodation into the early modern period. Suffice to say, the rich bed of sources on these matters still needs to be funneled to the surface.

This survival of the indigenous nation cries out for another look at the moments right before and after first contact. It is precisely the sixteenth century when a solid series of sources call out through time as a beachhead on which later interdisciplinary explorers can land and gain footing in order to better understand the temporal depth of national structures and ideologies and to push our understanding of the nation beyond what appears to be apparent in our own time. This beachhead is constructed with numerous types of media and sources. Because my particular background is literary, and to a lesser degree, historical and philosophical, that is the primary path I take in this interdisciplinary study. Additionally, to fill in the backstory, I draw from archaeology, anthropology, linguistics, legal documents, and biology. First, I must present the issues pertaining to the role and nature of the nation and the nation-state and of the interactions between nations.

THE NATION AND THE STATE

As we are discussing, nations have ethnic components, while states do not generally or necessarily have them. This is because nations are composed of people, and states, at least ideally, are composed of institutions and laws. If a nation is composed of one sole etnia and the state represents the nation, it logically follows that the state also represents that etnia. But if two or more ethnic groups constitute a "nation"—or in our terminology, if two nations reside in one geographical division—the state would have a more difficult time in representing both of them (think Canada, Belgium, and Paraguay). Sometimes a state openly favors one of the nations it represents over another (think Israel or Turkey). Other times states purport to govern in the name of all citizens they supposedly represent, whatever their background (think Costa Rica). Thus we have citizens who can be called Guatemalans, Peruvians, or Mexicans, but not all Guatemalans, Peruvians, or Mexicans might feel equally represented. This is because hierarchies exist, both within one nation (or etnia) and between the nations (or ethnic groups) under the aegis of the state.

Taking these possibilities in our stride, we can state that nations can be organized hierarchically or not. A non-hierarchal nation would suppose a common purpose among the people who constitute it, where a hierarchical one supposes competing agendas organized from above by a government or governments. Covey offers a number of characteristics inherent to states around the world. These include a four-tier settlement hierarchy, increasing centralization, the existence of palaces and administrative buildings (suggesting state institutions), the existence of exotic materials (suggesting long-distance trade), and "lasting territorial control beyond a day's walk of the principal settlement."[84] This definition could certainly refer to the empires of the Mexica and the Inkakuna, but it could also refer to entities such as the cah in the Yucatec regions. Covey describes it as "a centralized government that has a distinct ideology and shared ethnicity or citizenship."[85] Here we have the essential models: if the state derives its power from a common ethnic root, then the nation-state would reflect realities in late antiquity; if the state derives its power from citizenship, then it would reflect the system the early modern Spaniards held for themselves, but not for their African slaves and not for Amerindian peoples.

Once hierarchies are ingrained, it would be silly to think of a nation without a state apparatus. The scholarly Jesuit Juan de Mariana (1536–1624), in his well-known *De rege et regis institutione* (1599), points to three oppositional pairs of ways to organize a state: monarchy or tyranny, aristocracy or oligarchy, and republic or democracy. Organized in this fashion, a monarchy holds power in the hands of a king but becomes a tyranny when the king abuses that power, treating his subjects with cruelty. An aristocracy's power is organized at the level of nobility but is virtuous, whereas an oligarchy's, also organized at the level of nobility, holds the accumulation of wealth above other interests. A republic is a state in which all people share in governance according to their rank, while in a democracy all people share in it irrespective of merit or class.[86] These contrasting options were open to discussion during the late sixteenth century, but as would have been usual given royal patronage, Mariana selects a monarchy as the best choice with a stern warning against tyranny (however, he may have been the first during the Renaissance to allow for tyrannicide when necessary).

The application of European statecraft history when trying to map out the trajectory of the nation in the Western Hemisphere can present problems. Referring to the present time, W. M. Spellman writes, "Ours is without question a national state-dominated society." For him, the unifying state had not taken hold during the Middle Ages because "systems of authority were plural in nature and local in setting." He goes on to mention monasteries, villages, manors, and kinship groups that were heterogeneous foci of authority.[87] This fragmentation, perhaps he is insinuating, began with the collapse of the Roman Empire, and reaches a critical stage when "by 1500 there were literally hundreds of more or less independent political units in Europe." Spellman is referring to "The Continent" and extrapolates a universal from it. However, state development also occurred in the Americas. By no other means did Spaniards figure out mechanisms so quickly for tribute and labor extraction. They simply eliminated the Inka and Mexicatl rulers and inserted themselves at the summit of power they immediately began manipulating. They could not have done that if there had not been a state apparatus over which they could exercise control. Yet Spellman can serve as an opening to discuss early modern political thought as we bring Erasmus into the discussion.

How did these European entities unite? Spellman explains they were amalgamated by "state-building programs" that agglomerated and absorbed.[88] Erasmus comments on the state frequently in his 1516 *Education of a Christian Prince*, dedicated to the prince who was to become Charles I of Spain. Drawing on Aristotle, he teaches that a Christian monarch should do what is good for his public, not what is good for him personally.[89] In it, he anticipates Mariana's *De rege et regis* by concluding the following: "Although there are many kinds of states, it is pretty well agreed among the philosophers that the most healthy form is monarchy"[90] Yet Jardine, in her translation, renders different kinds of words and expressions as state, including "republica," "respublica," and "rerum publicaum."[91] What these terms hold in common is the idea of "public." Although some local chiefdoms, or polities, in the Indies were not in essence states, it would be difficult to reject the existence of a *res publica*. Such nomenclature becomes even more useful for larger political structures, such as those that existed in places described as Tawantinsuyo or Anahuac. This is why European models and theory often distort New World realities. For if, as Spellman theorizes, the modern state could not be born until politics were separated from theology,[92] one would have to argue against the existence of Inka or Mexicatl statecraft, which would be a gross error.

To offer an example of pre-Hispanic state development, we turn to Tawantinsuyo. Covey distinguishes between the state and the people: "Even if many local groups were not directly governed by the Wari state, there is evidence that they participated in religious rituals and perhaps public feasts that were sponsored by Wari officials." That reality would carry on into the Inka time. Covey offers some examples where Wari structures evolved into Inka ones, despite a difference in their respective cultures of governance. These include "an urban capital, standardized state architecture, and the development of roads and intensive maize agriculture to facilitate state functions." He concludes, "The Inca state was based on Andean principles of social organization and inspired by power relationships introduced hundreds of years earlier by Wari settlers." He completes the thought: "State formation must be viewed as a long-term local development rather than a direct borrowing."[93] Regardless of when on the timeline the state came into being in the diverse regions of the globe, and regardless of the actual details in defining it, the state is integral to our conceptualization of the nation-state, and thus also has the potential to influence the nation, "both coercively and consensually," as Dore puts it. The ways the state can channel its power are, she writes, "through law, social welfare, and economic and social policy, as well as through attempts to regulate the norms of public culture."[94] Because these channels are given form through the culture or cultures that inform the state—the difference between Roman law based on codes and Anglo-Saxon law based on precedent—they also can be considered integral to the nation.

However, we must caution that not all actors in the nation and state were supporting the interests of *res publica*. This was a primary characteristic of Spanish rule in the Americas. Here is a central problem of colonialism and its legacy. Sociologist Portocarrero has written at length on how many of the state actors during the colonial age were transatlantic transgressors, working to take advantage of Amerindians and behaving in a way later described as *viveza criolla*. These transgressors looked for ways to get what they could out of the Royal Treasury, or even divert funds and wealth before it could get to the national coffers in Madrid. He writes:

> It is symptomatic that the practice of transgressing began with the authorities themselves whose function it was to force compliance with the law. The colonial administration, comprised of Spaniards, tended to see Peru as a kind of booty that could be plundered by means of abuse and extortion, to make illicit earnings exploiting the Indians and the Royal Treasury. With time, the bad example spread to all social classes so that in a way abuse and bribery were "democratized." The "dirty trick" became so popularized that it was even appropriated by the Andean migrant [to the city] who, in the new urban medium, becomes like a *Criollo,* or wises up, now prepared to take advantage of those that are now like what he was before.

> Es sintomático que la práctica de la trasgresión haya comenzado por las mismas autoridades cuya función era hacer cumplir las leyes. La administración colonial, compuesta de españoles, tendió a ver en el Perú una suerte de botín que podía ser saqueado mediante el abuso y la extorsión, realizar ganancias ilícitas explotando a los indios y al Tesoro Real. Con los años, el mal ejemplo cundió hacia todos los sectores sociales de manera que el abuso y la coima se "democratizaron." La "pendejada" se popularizó llegando incluso al migrante andino que, en el nuevo medio urbano, se acriolla o se aviva y entonces, ya es capaz de aprovecharse de los que ahora son lo que él fue.

Thus in the colonial state, a get-ahead-at-all-costs attitude metastasizes down through the social strata to plebeian levels. Portocarrero's analysis shows how "coloniality," while initially racialized as studied by Aníbal Quijano, moves into mindsets that cause people to mimic behaviors. But it all begins at the pinnacle of power.

Even at the highest strata in the viceregal system, there was a level of unpredictability and even instability. Portocarrero elaborates, "The viceroys accepted, but at the same time, failed to comply with royal edicts emanating from Spain" (los virreyes aceptaban, pero al mismo tiempo, incumplían las reales cédulas desde España). There could be certain "hypocrisy" in the behavior of colonial actors of power, or, as Portocarrero puts it, "the hypocrisy could not have been greater" (la hipocresía no puede ser mayor).[95] *Viveza criolla* was an element that arrived in the Indies, and it came to have—albeit as an unnamed behavioral trait—a definitive altering impact on the people of the nations here as they came in contact with the new ruling class. Fundamental to this transgressive and transformative process are deceit and selfishness, two hallmarks of capitalist behavior when individuals strive to improve their own material wealth, not the common good of the nation. Thus at the onset of the Conquest, certain tendencies suggest an incipient capitalist modernity linked to an inchoate state bureaucracy, even when formed by an emerging coloniality.

MIGRATIONS, TRADE, AND OTHER FORMS OF HUMAN INTERACTION

Neither the nation nor the nation-state has existed in a vacuum. Each and every nation lives and breathes in a larger context defined by other nations and the relationships between them. Nations have everyday contact with their neighbors and from time to time have contact with peoples from far afield. Columbus is a readily recognizable example of Europe's expansion. Mercantilism was a primary aspect of his dealings in spices and in precious metals. Of course, there was Amerindian and Arab-Muslim resistance to European expansion, and European fear of Arab-Muslim expansion. This uneasiness was codified in Garcilaso de la Vega (1501?–36), the estimable poet of the Renaissance (not to be confused with his homonymous relative, El Inca), who speaks in his second elegy of a "sandy Libya, the source of all things poisonous and fierce" (la arenosa Libia, engendradora/de toda cosa ponzoñosa y fiera).[96] Peoples in contact are evident even earlier. Courcelles quotes from St. Augustine's *City of God,* which "calls citizens out of all nations, and gathers together a society of pilgrims of all languages."[97] She then postulates that from this theological perspective, "a new planetary order might be established, thanks to the mosaic of the celestial city exiled on the earth."[98] Even Erasmus, who tended to stay away from the theme of the "Conquest," corresponds with the teenage Prince Charles and recommends good Christian education for someone who will rule "not over a mere cottage but over so many peoples, so many countries, and even over the world."[99]

Conversely, Latin-speaking Europe was still fragmenting into nations associated with particular vernacular tongues and with emerging and divergent notions of Christianity at the time it embarked upon its conquests across the seas. After the Council of Trent, Catholics struggled against the Protestants for the hearts and minds of Europeans, battling against Islam as Spain went to war against the Ottoman Empire, and combating perceived paganism in the New World. Such concerns and beliefs fueled Catholic imperialism. Part of the religious thrust was to bring heterogeneous peoples into the fold. Guaman Poma, who never left Peru, was aware of world ethnicities. Writing at the dawn of the seventeenth century, overcoming the limitations of a purely Yarovilcan heritage, he recognizes "Indians, blacks, Christian Spaniards, Turks, Jews, and Moors" (yndios, negros y españoles cristianos, turcos, judíos, moros) (*PNC*, 949 [963]). Some of these categories would have been apparent in Peru and others not so much, including "heretics" such as the Moors and Turks, who were troubling the minds of Europeans but not Amerindians.

What was the effect of the European sixteenth century on indigenous peoples? The Yucatec Maya, in the *Book of Chilam Balam of Chumayel*, described its effects in the following manner:

> The priests of ours were to come to an end when misery was introduced, when Christianity was introduced by the real Christians. Then with the true God, the true Dios, came the beginning of our misery. It was the beginning of tribute, the beginning of church dues, the beginning of strife with purse snatching, the beginning of strife with blow-guns, the beginning of strife by trampling on people, the beginning of robbery with violence, the beginning of forced debts, the beginning of debts enforced by false testimony, the beginning of individual strife, a beginning of vexation, a beginning of robbery with violence.[100]

Cultural, political, and economic intercourse during that time could have been a good thing if people shared what was theirs within a structure of truly unencumbered trade. Yet all kinds of hierarchies offered possibilities for unequal trade and even forced labor, human trafficking, and other forms of severe exploitation. Such realities must be acknowledged as elements of what we call colonialism. Even Thomas More's *Utopia,* a progressive text for its time, could accept a colonialism that shears other peoples of their nationness. More, one of Erasmus's contemporaries, allowed for general colonization practices in those cases where other peoples had let their land lie fallow. In those cases, the Utopians "consider it a most just cause for war when a people . . . do . . . not use its soil but keeps it idle" (*YE* 4:136–37). In this view whereby fertile land goes to those who will use it, he anticipates the debates that were soon to rage on the Spanish peninsula regarding so-called "just war" against Inkakuna, Mexica, K'iche', and other peoples.

More's England was suffering from a lack of land due to an enclosure movement that fenced in farming land so sheep could be raised. From that perspective, he conceives of a just war in terms of a people's right to satisfy their hunger, a view later used to justify English expansion in North America starting with the Jamestown and Plymouth colonies in the second decade of the sixteenth century. Similar arguments would be enunciated by John Locke, who held that the civil state had not yet taken hold in North America, a continent still organized as a natural state. It was the civil state's duty to elicit a transformation of the natural one. According to Locke, appropriation of land is one way a natural society could be transformed into a civil one.[101] The Spanish debate will be different. It will be framed in terms of "civilization" and "barbarism." Chapters 4 and 5 will begin by examining the very early migrations over the Beringia land mass that connected Asia and the Americas, and then discuss more fully both pre- and post-Colombian movement of peoples and objects.

ETHNICITIES, NATIONS, AND THE BORDERS BETWEEN THEM

Despite the narrow-mindedness of the Spanish chronicles, they do establish that ethnicity plays an overarching role in defining nations. This was unquestionably true when Spain and Portugal were expanding their empires and creating subclasses of people who were of non-European origin. Unfortunately, because the terms "ethnicity" and "nation" both evoke multiple meanings, differentiating the relationship between them could be akin to splitting hairs. Happily, our time has fostered momentous research on the nation and the impact of ethnicity upon it.[102] Ethnicity can be different things to different people in different places. Smith distinguishes three common perspectives on ethnicity. For some, "it has a primordial quality," for others, it "is situational," and for still others, it is "a type of cultural collectivity."[103] This brings us back to the conditionalist-essentialist dichotomy discussed previously. Primordial conceptualizations lean toward essentialism when they are based on language and culture. Conceptualizations fall under the rubric of conditionalism when they are situational. Both of these are types of collectivities. From these ways of looking at things, we can conclude that ethnicity is fluid in time and space, related to the perspective from which it is contemplated. The same is true with our complex understanding of the nation. As discussed, the gist of the term has been hotly debated since the publication of Anderson's *Imagined Communities* in 1983. Yet, again, it is Smith who proffers an excellent working definition: "A named human population sharing a historic territory, common myths and historical memories, a mass, popular culture, a common economy and common legal rights and duties for all members."[104] Although the ethnic groups who inhabited Anahuac at the time of the Spanish invasion might not completely satisfy Smith's requirements for nationhood, their members did share common territory, myths, history, and legal codes. They could also be described as being a "named human population," understood as nations in a sixteenth-century sense, or proto-nations from the perspective of modernity. Although it may seem strange to the twenty-first-century reader, some, although not all, sixteenth-century chroniclers, both Spanish and mestizo, viewed them as "nations." As discussed, these nations did not live in vacuums.

Recent theory on transculturation, heterogeneity, hybridization, and diversity awareness have provided a vocabulary to describe a process that occurs when men and women of distinctive ethnicities must face each other across some kind of border.[105] Prior to the Europeans' arrival, indigenous groups were constantly coming together and redefining their relationships. After the Spaniards' onslaught, such tendencies only became more pronounced and more generalized. Matthew Restall encapsulates this idea as follows: "Whether as squads of Huejotzincan warriors helping to topple the Mexica empire, a Nahua from Azcapotzalco leading his men into a Maya village, or an enslaved native Nicaraguan woman serving a conquistador in Peru, native peoples are everywhere in the Conquest alongside the Spaniards."[106] Mexica princes also participated in Pánfilo Narváez's ill-fated mission to Florida, and Tlaxcalan tutors taught the Floridian natives who returned to Mexico with Álvar Núñez Cabeza de Vaca.[107] We can only imagine what Floridians thought when they encountered Nahua and Spanish people, and how amazed they must have been when they found themselves in New Spain (Mexico) among even larger numbers of them. When ideologies of dissimilar ethnic groups come together, the possibility exists for what Mignolo has termed "border thinking."[108] Mignolo gets this idea from Gloria Anzaldúa who, as a Chicana separated from Mexico by a fence, described the barrier as "an open wound" (una herida abierta).[109] It is the pain that comes from cultural contact at the border that allows for new forms of thinking. According to Mignolo, this kind of thinking is not possible from the perspective of modernity.[110] Consequently, the study of interethnicity must begin as early in recorded history as possible. In the case of the Americas, that early point in time would originate with the early classical Mayan glyphs. Beyond that, if no key is found to decipher the fine-line drawing, the khipu, *and* the *tocapos,* the bulk of recorded history stems from the introduction of alphabetic writing in the sixteenth century.[111] An appropriate place to evaluate the contours of early nationalities could be the place Mignolo describes as "the exterior borders of the modern/colonial world system."[112] These borders, the same ones holding indigenous and mestizo voices largely submerged, are useful places because it is there that ethnicity-crushing modernity has least taken hold. What better place to begin exists than colonial Latin America? This inquiry can aide in interpreting more objectively the complex "shock" eventuated when Spaniards and Nahua, Spaniards and K'iche', and Spaniards and Andeans were violently thrown together to build new societies.

The idea of forging nations by means of ethnicity has been a European tendency (for example, medieval Spain and France, post-Soviet Eastern Europe, post-US invasion of Iraq) and is fundamental to other cultures. Such is the case of the Nahua, the Spanish, and their composite progeny. The heterogeneous character of New Spain was apparent at the end of the sixteenth century. As Irving Leonard summarizes, "The progressive mixing of diverse elements had created a veritable kaleidoscope of shades, complexions, and social castes."[113] Every two that came together represented an opportunity for border thinking. It is not my intent to describe those processes from a sociological or anthropological perspective. Here we will be concerned with ideology, the history of ideas as they relate notions of nations in contact with other nations as they evolved.

In the pages that follow, we will make ourselves aware of the origins of an ideology that not only allowed for ethnic blending, but also encouraged it. These customs existed in spite of the hegemonic doctrines of *pureza de sangre,* or blood purity, and in spite of popular expressions such as *salta atrás* ("throw back"), *No te entiendo* ("I don't understand you," meaning a skin tone that suggests an unknown race), and *Ahí te estás* ("There you are"), this last actually a precise expression that signifies 43.14 percent white, 51.35 percent indigenous, and 5.5 percent black, which implied a negative bias toward interethnic fraternizing.[114] The origins of the ideologies favoring and disfavoring the melding of cultures can be found in the colonial chronicles,[115] the Nahuatl philological materials recently come to light, and in the songs and dances of Qheswa- and Aymara-speaking peoples.

CHAPTER TWO

FROM PEOPLE TO NATION

MESOAMERICA

This chapter concentrates on the Nahua of Central Mexico to learn about the ideals to which they aspired as they formed distinct nations.[1] Their journey toward these ideals advances via two tendencies we can describe as horizontal and vertical cultural appropriation. The horizontal occurs when two or more groups in contact influence one another. One weighty aspect of what occurred has to do with disparate non-Nahua groups that appropriate elements of Toltec culture. These acquirings are horizontal because they occurred on a two-dimensional geographical plane where social borrowings had to come from neighboring communities. The vertical distinguishes itself from the horizontal because it is a process whereby groups take elements of their own past and institutionalize them, such as when the Mexica take the story of Tenoch and Aztlan and glorify it. The vertical, then, is a reaching back in time. It is an internal process within the nation, while the horizontal allows a nation to interact with another external to it. It is precisely when cultural self-fortification (a vertical process reaching back to the past) blends with cross-cultural appropriation (a horizontal process traceable geographically) that the perfect conditions for nation formation coalesce, because although nations know how they hold themselves to be, it is when they enter into contact with other nations that they must evaluate themselves, often making changes in the process. To understand the nature of both kinds of cultural appropriation before and after contact with Europeans, I will consider various chronicles, both Spanish and Nahua-Spanish mestizo, while simultaneously drawing on a contextualizing interdisciplinary field of inquiry Matthew Restall describes as the "New Philology."

The first aim here is to understand the nomadic or semisedentary concept of people, and how, through vertical and horizontal appropriation, it matured into the Nahua sedentary and imperial models of altepetl, as well as the cultural ideals known as Toltecayotl and the less-studied Chichimecayotl. To get to that point it is necessary to briefly consider the conquistador-chroniclers Bernal Díaz del Castillo (1492?–1584) and Hernán Cortés (1485–1547) and their resistance to the term "nation" when describing new world polities. We will then review the findings produced by the "New Philology" and consider that knowledge set with respect to the chronicle in order to understand what went on in the central basin of Mexico during late antiquity. From this vantage point, relatively free from the colonizing bias of the conquistadors, we can turn toward exploring the processes of horizontal and vertical cultural appropriation, including the foundation mythology of the cultural heroes Topiltzin and Huemac, from which the Toltec ideal springs. Integral to this discussion is the concept of the altepetl, including its quadrangular structure as well as an array of conceptualizations of the term "nación," a word that appears frequently in some chronicles but not in others. On this basis, we will concentrate on these features in the thought of the informants of Bernardino de Sahagún (1499–1590), in the writing of Diego Muñoz Camargo (1528–1600), and in Fernando de Alva Ixtlilxóchitl (1579–1650).

The second aim is to understand how, with new pulling and pushing in the realm of culture—what Fernando Ortiz describes as transculturation—these precontact cultural and political constructions of the altepetl in turn melded with the early modern concept of nation the Spanish were importing. Indeed, one prong of this investigation is to uncover the altepetl concept concealed by the term "nación" in the best of cases, or negated completely in the worst of cases. That said, surprising similarities between the Nahua and Spanish ways of life can be seen. Central to what happened in the lands that became known as New Spain were the inverse processes of *populating* and *depopulating*, which caused chaos and allowed for further cover-up of altepetl structures and the insertion of notions of the nation centered on Spaniards, not on the Nahua. A close reading of Muñoz Camargo and Alva Ixtlilxóchitl shows how they interfaced in different ways with the Spanish concept of nation, after which Sor Juana Inés de la Cruz (1651–95) has her own take, which provides even greater depth and breadth to the discussion. The chapter concludes with a discussion of how Hobsbawm's proto-nationalism paradigm applies as religion and language become integral ingredients of the nation.

Among the authors who denied the condition of nationness to the Nahua, we include primary actors in the Conquest, such as Díaz del Castillo and Cortés. A more nuanced take on Amerindian nationness can be found in the authors of the next generation, which was intercultural and resulted from Spanish-Nahua liaisons, as in the case of Muñoz Camargo. Notable in Díaz del Castillo's canonically authoritative chronicle is his avoidance of the term "nación."[2] Díaz was not interested in representing indigenous people, nor was he curious enough about them to describe them except as part of the monumental story he narrates. But it is not just a great story he tells. As Rolena Adorno convincingly argues, Bernal Díaz's primary purpose for drafting his *Historia verdadera de la conquista de la Nueva España* (*The True History of the Conquest of New Spain*) was to defend the concept of just war and justify his encomienda holdings.[3] In order to argue for just war, one cannot classify as nations the people "deserving" of such military aggression. Since they cannot be conceptualized as being on the same level as the conquering people, they must be viewed as less, so that they can logically be subordinated in the minds of the invaders. Such a bias throws into doubt the chronicler's broader quest for the "true history."[4] It also impedes his ability to regard the altepeme of the Chololteca (sing. Chololtecatl), Tenocha (sing. Tenochcatl), and Tlaxcalteca as nations obfuscating this possibility for subsequent historiography.

When Díaz recounts his experience, he refers to the political/social structures of the Tlaxcalteca or Chololteca as towns (*HV*, 112a, 116a), cities (*HV*, 152a, 156a), provinces (*HV*, 113a), or regions (comarcas) (*HV*, 138a), and the region's proper names as Cempoal, Tlaxcallan, or Chalollan (the last two referred to by their more common spellings, Tlaxcala and Cholula).[5] The people from these municipalities are referred to as "los de Cempoal" (*HV*, 126a), "los de Tlaxcala" (*HV*, 119a), or "los de Cholula" (*HV*, 155a) (for the last two, see map 5), meaning the ones from Cempoal, the ones from Tlaxcala, and so on. Despite his staying away from calling these configurations nations, countries, monarchies, or republics—all terms in use at that time—and despite the passing over of civil structures when he describes the Nahua, Díaz does perceive cultural variation among the diverse entities.[6] He notices religious differences, and comments that each province had its own deity (*HV,* 196a). Districts were ruled over by "little kings" (reyezuelos) (*HV,* 286a), who were probably altepetl leaders known as *tlatoque* (sing. *tlatoani).* In the earlier Guatemala manuscript Díaz writes that "kings" ruled over provinces (*HV,* 285b), not nations as a Western observer might anticipate. Not unexpectedly, Díaz eschews the terms "altepetl" and "tlatoani."

A review of Hernán Cortés's letters reveals a lexicon paralleling Díaz's word choices. He comments on towns, cities, and provinces, but not nations or altepeme.[7] In the battle for Tenochtitlan, he simply calls the city's residents "indios," or Indians (*CDR,* 82a). He is not able to go any further in recognizing their qualifications with respect to nationness. Even the mixed-heritage writers who were born immediately after the Spanish onslaught hesitated about designation of nationality. Diego Muñoz Camargo, born in 1528—the first decade, that is, after the first Iberian forays into Mesoamerica—denies the label "nation" to groups such as the Chichimeca, although he does call Cholula a nation and Tlaxcala, whence he came, a republic (*HT,* 212–13). His complex attitude toward indigenous nations is perhaps unsurprising, as his homonymous father was a conquistador who, as noted by Charles Gibson, had arrived in Mexico in 1524,[8] and his mother was a Nahua (I discuss this fact and its result later in the chapter).

While the term "altepetl" was generally excluded from the early chroniclers' lexicon, the term "nation" became more common as the sixteenth century matured. Authors who arrived or were born a generation or two after the initial Spanish advances frequently allow the appellation into their vocabularies. Father Diego Durán (1537?–88) accepts Mexica and other groups as naciones, as does another churchman, Toribio de Motolinía.[9] For their part, the chroniclers associated with the group Rocío Cortés labels the Intellectual Circle on Indigenous Matters proudly utilize the word "nación" when they refer to their maternal heritage.[10] Alva Ixtlilxóchitl refers to the "nación tulteca" and to the "nación chichimeca," and both he and Muñoz Camargo consider themselves members of the Spanish nation (*OH,* 2:34, 236; *HT,* 250).

Adorno, in her discussion of chroniclers like these, explains they developed this multifaceted way of seeing themselves because they "could not go back to any pristine, pre-Columbian state of mind."[11] We take advantage of the clues this hybrid mentality offers as we try to extrapolate back before 1521 or even 1492. To read between the lines, so to speak, we need to draw on other sources to help interpret the long arc of these processes of nation. Even with differences in terminology, all authors, indigenous,[12] mestizo, Spanish, or Criollo seem, nonetheless, to be aware of ethnic diversity and relate it to city, republic, or nation, despite the fact that 1492 marked the first attempts to suppress both New World social organization and awareness of it. Their works can verify an early interface between ethnicity and the Spanish nation, and for the Peninsular and Criollo world, the beginning of modernity dispersed as part of the first World-System that became truly global in nature.

THE NAHUA AND THE "NEW PHILOLOGY"

> Una sociedad se define no sólo por su actitud ante el futuro sino frente al pasado.
>
> Octavio Paz, *Las trampas de la fe*

The early chronicles document the process that ultimately allowed the Spanish and the Nahua to come together. Our limited perception of the multicultural societies who produced these annals deepened with the twentieth-century discovery of a gargantuan corpus of Nahuatl-language documentation. Gordon Whittaker notes that a sizeable amount of these materials represents the work of the Franciscan friars who had come to New Spain to evangelize.[13] Other genres come from court proceedings, town council meeting minutes, and other governmental activities. The study of this corpus, a new discipline that Restall has termed the "New Philology," has provided new insight into what Ileana Rodríguez, Walter D. Mignolo, José Rabasa, and others would call a subaltern society. These copious materials (wills, legal documents, titles, meeting minutes) have led James Lockhart and other ethnohistorians seemingly to shun the Spanish-language chronicles of the sixteenth century (*NS*, 161; *NAC*, 2–5). Lockhart's attitude departs from the belief that the Nahua must be assessed from the vantage point of the Nahua themselves. There is no reason not to concur with him on this matter up to a certain point. That said, it is somewhat of an overreaction to the prior tendency of focusing solely on the Spanish-authored documents. Both kinds of sources must be considered in unison, because each renders a unique perspective on the larger picture.

Despite Lockhart's well-placed misgivings, the early colonial chronicles remain significant for another reason: they document the birth of a new hybrid society and a new literature written in Spanish and sometimes Amerindian languages.[14] While Lockhart may appear to take matters to an extreme in dismissing the chronicles, he is reacting to views such as those expressed by José Joaquín Blanco, who claims that without the chronicles, "Mexican history would lack basic information that dispels the misty and fabulous legends that cover this remote period that preceded the arrival of the Spaniards."[15] While these punctilious pronouncements are accurate to a degree, there are fertile avenues to understanding the indigenous view of things: the mestizo chroniclers, the archeological record, the Nahuatl philological materials, and reading between the lines of the Spanish-authored documents. Cornejo Polar puts this in perspective. He explains,

> For too long, a "literature of the conquest" or a "literature of the Colony" were talked about as if they were exclusively written in Spanish. Later, a "literature of the vanquished" was added as a separate system. But in reality, we are dealing with a unique object whose identity is relative.

> Durante demasiado tiempo se habló de la "literatura de la conquista" o de la "literatura de la colonia" como si fueran exclusivamente las escritas en español, se añadió luego la "literatura de los vencidos" como un sistema aparte, pero en realidad se trata de un objeto único cuya identidad es estrictamente relacional.[16]

Without a doubt, we must accept the colonial chronicles as one "horizon of understanding" among several that constitute the pre-Hispanic knowledge set.[17] The chronicles contain ideologies that helped to define state ideology and a cultural history for a society that would become increasingly mestiza. As Adorno points out, the chroniclers were not trying to solve problems of historiography, but of culture.[18] The chronicle, now inserted into in a scholarly context redefined by an emerging Nahuatl philology, can open a broad window into New Spain. As Restall makes clear, "While native-language sources offer unique insights, the long-term goal is to use complementary sources in all available languages in order to gain as full an understanding as possible."[19] We must not forget that mestizo authors writing in Spanish would have been aware of the Spanish-language press. By 1600, before other regions of Latin America had a single print shop, Mexico City had six—some with multiple presses.[20] While writers were directing their works toward a European audience, the incipient local publishing industry would have shown them the importance of the printed word. That reality must not be overlooked any more than the new philological sources should be. What I am attempting here is a rereading of Spanish-language chroniclers, both of Old and New Worlds, along with Bernardino de Sahagún's informants, in a context with New Philological discoveries. Sahagún's informants add the precious perspective of Tenochtitlan-Tlatelolco learned men, the *huehuetlatolli,* which was almost lost, but fortunately survived.[21] The altepeme of Tenochtitlan and Tlatelolco were the primary targets of the Spanish war of conquest against the people who are sometimes imprecisely called Aztecs. The present treatment takes all these sources into account in order to outline and then extrapolate constructions and ideologies of protonationness in late antiquity, as well as to address their continuation, appropriation, and adoption during the burgeoning Novo-Hispanic tidal wave of culture.

When studying precontact historical events, the reader should be aware the Nahua did not hold the same aspirations of strict accuracy claimed by, although certainly not achieved by, Western historians. There are historical events detailed in the chronicles for which we cannot always determine the dates. Reflecting on this pursuit of "accuracy," historian Restall emphasizes, "Western thought has viewed history and myth as standing in opposition to each other."[22] This was not the case in Anahuac. Furthermore, as noted in the Introduction, Nahua history sometimes was linked more to the local altepetl than it was to the larger Nahuatl linguistic area, or even New Spain. Here we are concerned with Mexica, Chichimeca, and Tlaxcalteca, who did not differentiate history, myth, and legend to the degree the Spanish purported to or even to the lesser degree the Spanish actually achieved. As it happens, Nigel Davies explains, "the Mexicas were given to fairly constant revision of their own history, and in effect the process of creating myths and legends was continuous."[23] Another difficulty in grasping the Nahua epos resides in their cyclical concept of time.[24] For instance, the chronicles claim that the Toltec Empire both begins and ends with a leader named Topiltzin. These pitfalls, however, do not render pre-Hispanic history any less valuable than its "objective" Western variety. The Nahua past is paramount because it signifies a system of deeply held values that did not necessarily dissipate after 1521. Before examining those beliefs and practices, a few more words on history are necessary.

The Invasion itself presents an impediment to decoding the Mesoamerican past, because in the better part of the narratives, as explained by Susan Gillespie, "'history' was necessarily modified as an adjustment to the new conditions of [colonial] society."[25] Indigenous and mestizo writers had to show beyond a hair of doubt both their allegiances to the Crown and their Christian faith, and therefore had to organize their native material in terms of appropriate doctrine. This is true for the early Nahua informant, for the later Nahua scribe, and for the mestizo chronicler who wrote his material directly in Spanish. Consider the case of the informant who, as Jorge Klor de Alva cautions, "is in a subordinate position to the ethnographer." Such a condition would require strategies for survival, including hiding material or pleasing the ethnographer. On the other side of the coin, the ethnographer controls "the general plan" of documentation, circumscribing "the range of data to be gathered," limiting "the lexical items employed to those that attest a European/ Christian judgment," and using informants who are already partly assimilated into Hispanic and Catholic culture.[26] Even the Nahuatl-literate scribes had to be careful when they expressed native concepts in the legal documentation they drafted. Mestizo authors may have felt vulnerable because they wrote their histories in a Spanish-language format that would or could then be distributed in Spain. These late-Renaissance, baroque, or neoclassical works, crafted by the Nahua, Spaniards, Criollos, or mestizos, as Martin Lienhard cautions, should not be considered a pre-Hispanic prose.[27] They represent the birth of a subjective Indo-Hispanic literature whose interpretation requires special caution. Prudence is crucial because this colonial literature, although dependent on the metropole, was in many ways at odds with the works produced on that side of the Atlantic.[28] Moreover, the limitations placed on cultivating these texts are further complicated by their restricted circulation and the possibility of censorship. Lienhard recounts how Sahagún participated in the "kidnaping" of his own manuscripts to preserve them![29]

Notwithstanding the relative darkness of pre-1520 history and the interpretive obstacles sketched out above, we have come to appreciate that indigenous notions of nation, state, people, and land persisted among Nahua men and women well beyond the sixteenth century.[30] This realization has been achieved through recent philological investigation on extraliterary Nahuatl-language-source documents such as wills, testaments, and meeting minutes. This new research shows, as Lockhart concludes, "that in nearly every dimension there was far more continuity from the preconquest era than one thought" (*NS*, 185; *NAC*, 163).[31] When new philological research completed by Lockhart, Restall, and others is interfaced with the chronicles, a more nuanced appreciation of the "things of the Indies" is possible. In addition, one essential element we can glean from both the Nahuatl sources and the Spanish-language chronicles is an appreciation of border ontology between ethnic nations and how it worked in the nation-building process.[32]

HORIZONTAL AND VERTICAL CULTURES MEET IN THE CENTER

As mentioned, culture can move across both geographic and temporal borders. Ethnicity is a dynamic process responding to horizontal and vertical stimuli. It can be constructed as the ken of a cultural horizon that emerges when comparing one's peers to other contemporary etnias.[33] One's ethnicity ends where another's begins, but it is that place of intersection where border ontology emerges. Such comparisons can create a self-awareness based on difference. An example of this process transpired when the Mexica observed the northern Chichimeca: they saw them as inferior, thereby aggrandizing their own achievements. This type of construction is also possible when one culture subsumes elements of another's. Hence, when some Chichimeca first adapted features of the Toltec mother culture, they were horizontally absorbing an ideal, Toltecayotl, or Toltecness. Later, when they absorbed the Spanish language and the Catholic religion, they were absorbing early modern cultural ideals, Hispanicness and Christianity, horizontally.

Such horizontality constantly being reconfigured with the passage of time is not the only manner of cultural fortification. Ethnicity can also develop as a descending vertical or diachronic process whereby a group looks back to its own historical, mythological, or legendary past. This is less of a passive condition than an active way of life. Mining one's own folklore or preserving it through oral or written traditions is one example of this type of practice. As Alberto Moreiras puts it, this means to "dwell within that culture's hermeneutic circle."[34] Such atavistic practices tend to buttress a population's ethnological identity. Smith proposes that the recovery of a bygone ethnic era is an important ingredient in the creation of a national identity.[35] Such singularity was fundamental to the cultures of Anahuac. Gibson finds ethnic fixation on the past to be a common feature among the diverse Nahua groups, all of whom, as he spells out, "understood their own early history through a series of tribal narratives. Their original divisions into groups and the movements of these groups along recorded routes were subjects of keen historical interest to them" (*AZ*, 9). In the case of the Mexica, their ethnic antecedents stem from Aztlan and their leader from that time, Tenoch, both of which constituted a source of vertical pride. There was also a horizontal linking that occurred, less biological, more mythological and cultural, and related to their reverence for the culture emanating from Tollan, or Tula (see maps 3 and 5). Such reverence brings us to the ideal of Toltecayotl, which, according to León-Portilla and Mignolo, implies the appropriation of the heritage of Tollan with its artisans and wise men.[36] After the Mexica completed an early period of ethnic blending with the Tolteca, they could from there on out stake a vertical claim to Toltecayotl. When they absorb Toltecayotl, a complex cultural operation occurs. They do not reject the verticality of their origins in Aztlan, but they pierce xenophobic elements of border ontology by laying claim to the Tolteca horizontally, allowing them then to drink from a second stream of verticality and form a new and nuanced reference point of interpretation.

But if Mexica and Chichimeca had to appropriate Toltecayotl horizontally, the Tolteca themselves, obviously, could fortify their bonds directly to their own past. This mythic-cultural root-defining tendency is commonplace in universal history. The relationship between the modern and ancient Greeks will illustrate this point: in history, the connection between these two groups appears to be direct. Smith demonstrates, however, there is little direct biological connection between them. But one needs only to *feel* a connection to experience its power. The modern Greeks feel a tie to the ancient Greeks, and that is what is meaningful. The same was true for the Mexica: they felt a link with the Tolteca, and that is what was significant.

Their bond with the Tolteca of yore held meaning for the Mexica, because—as with the Greeks—it bestowed upon them a feeling of chosenness. Smith concludes that "a myth of ethnic election" was integral to the Visigoths, Saxons, Franks, and Normans. Just as it was in these central medieval groups, so too was ethnic pride exhibited in Anahuac. The Mexica "felt" (Smith's word) themselves to be the torchbearers of the ancient civilization of the Tolteca, cultivating an identity that Smith calls "ethnic chosenness."[37] From their perspective, they *were* the descendants of the Tolteca. Ethnicity, then, while having an initial basis in biology, geography, and culture, can, upon further cultural absorption, evolve into an unbridled subjectivity.

THE (NOT SO) HIDDEN NATION-STATE: ALTEPEME IN COLLISION

Every bit as meaningful, especially after Spanish and Nahua worldviews crashed into each other, were the repercussions for the idea of nation. To master these issues, we must return to pre-Cortesian thought, where the idea of the nation does not seem to exist exactly as we "know" it, yet where we can detect its presence. Lockhart gets to the crux of the matter when he isolates a political and social structure denoting a type of "ethnic state" called altepetl (*NAC*, 14). In his Nahuatl dictionary, Siméon lists the meanings of "altepetl" as population, city, state, king, or sovereign.[38] The term implies "an organization of people holding sway over a given territory" (*NAC*, 14). Two central components here are land and people. In the case of the former, as Rebecca Horn observes, the term is a compound word combining *atl*, "water," with *tepetl*, "mountain." As such, it "immediately evokes a sense of territory."[39] The extension of this configuration could be considerable. Lockhart finds that during the sixteenth century, the entire Tlaxcalan kingdom, or even "countries" outside of New Spain such as Japan or Peru, could be understood as altepetl. However, he determines that the best translation for this noun might be "town" or "city," "comparable in size to the early Mediterranean city-states." The separateness of and divisions between altepeme imply a notion of distinctive ethnicity. Lockhart underscores how "each altepetl imagined itself a radically separate people" (*NAC*, 15). Restall, Souza, and Terraciano remind us that even "peoples of the ethnic states conquered by the Triple Alliance continued to rule themselves and retained their own local identity."[40] This irrespective of the not so small detail that the Nahua believed in a unified "humanity" composed of *maceualtin* (sing. *maceualli*), who were descended from the divine principle Ometecuhtli-Omecihuatl.[41]

Map 3 gives a general idea of where the ethnic nations were located. The Tepaneca of Azcapotzalco, the Acolhuaque (Chichimeca) of Tetzcoco, and the Culhua-Mexica of Tenochtitlan and Tlatelolco represented important centers of power. Gibson distinguishes nine "basic ethnic divisions at the time of the Spanish conquest" (*AZ*, 9). We list them with their singular forms as Otomi (sing. Otomitl), Culhuaque or Colhuaque (sing. Culhua, or Colhua), Cuitlahuaca (sing. Cuitlahuacatl), Mixquica (sing. Mixquicatl), Xochimilca (sing. Xochimilcatl), Chalca (sing. Chalcatl), Tepaneca (sing. Tepanecatl), Acolhuaque (sing. Acolhua), and Mexica (sing. Mexicatl). Still, it is not entirely clear that altepetl and ethnic specificity coincided perfectly. And again, as recognized by Horn, it had a geographic aspect.

Repeatedly throughout human development, urban planners have divided cities in half (such as in the Inkan capital of Qosqo) and then divided the halves again. Because of its obvious economic benefits, for example, Thomas

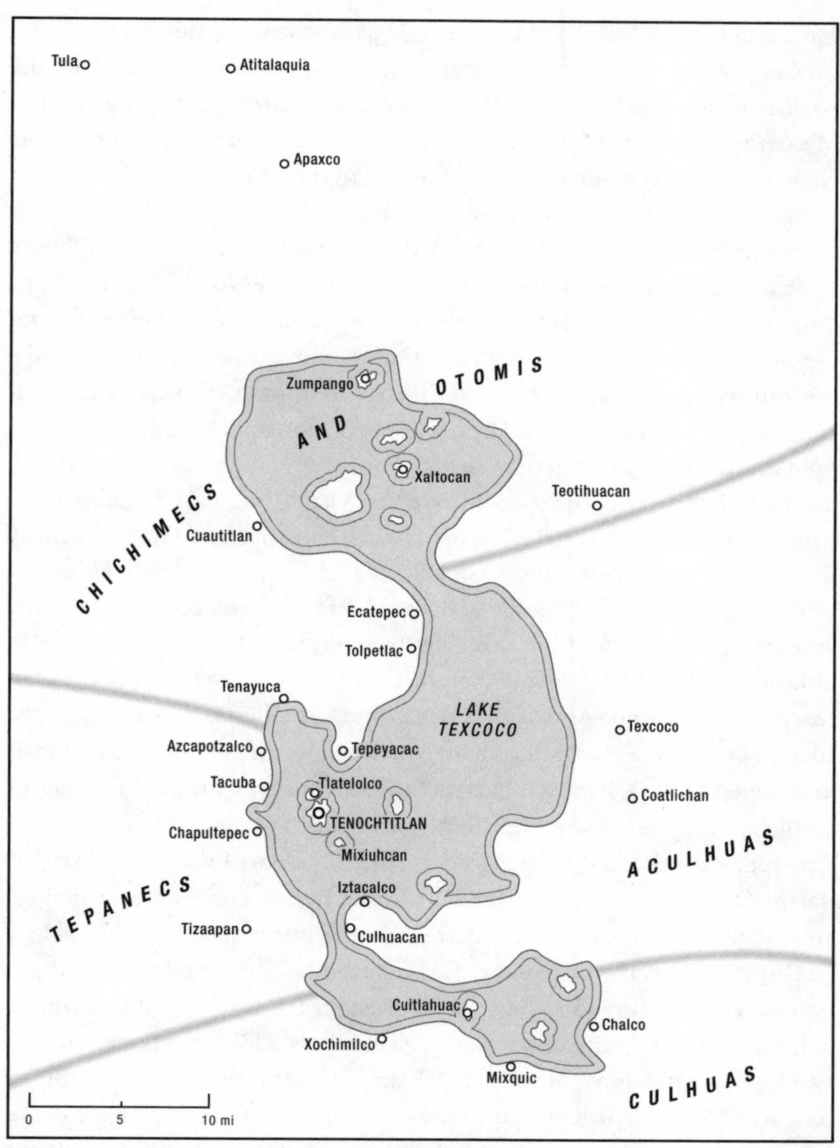

Map 3. Primary ethnic nations in Anahuac. From Nigel Davies, *The Aztecs* (Norman: University of Oklahoma Press, 1980), 19. *Map by Erin Greb Cartography.*

More divided his ideal city of Utopia into quadrants (*YE*, 4:136). Such a design further suggests a universality to the practice of quadripartition. As with the Andean people, the K'iche' saw the cosmos as divided into quadrants. Within Mesoamerican culture, the K'iche' provide context for understanding the Nahua. We observe this form of organizing in the *Popol Wuj*, a text that, for Restall, "seamlessly blends mythic and historical components into one epic narrative."[42] According to the *Popol Wuj*'s "Preamble," the world was thought to be divided into four angles, four corners. In order to get to Xibalba, or underworld, one has to pass four roads: one red, one black, one white, and one yellow, with green substituted for the yellow at one juncture. Just like the four roads, there are four gourds filled with flowers, each also a different color (*PV*, II, ii; II, viii; II, ix). The Lords of Xibalba send four messengers to kill Ixquic, who is protected by an equal number of owl messengers (*PV*, II, iii). These figures echo the stick-men deities, Vacub-Caquiz, Chimalmat (his wife), Zipacna, and Cabracan. The hero twins, Hunahpu and Ixbalanque, slay the first and last of these figures, constituting again a group of four. Hunahpu also kills Zipacna in the middle of the narrative segment, but not before the latter slaughters the four hundred boys, a multiple of four (*PV*, I, vi, ix, vii). This quartet formed by Vacub-Caquiz, Chimalmat, Zipacna, and Cabracan represents the four columns of the world, the four pillars of the cosmos. The colored crossroads coincide with an equal number of periods of creation as understood by the K'iche'. It is the fourth age when Ixquic invents the *milpa*, or cornfield, which allows for the fifth period, the age of humanity. This number also applies to the first K'iche' leaders, the founders of the four dynasties: Balam-Quitze, Balam-Acab, Mahucutah, and Iqui-Balam. These formations are no mere literary construction; they were cultural, social, and durable.

During the twentieth century, the K'iche's intellectual and activist, Rigoberta Menchú, seemed to have weak grasp of the traditional cosmology of her people, probably because of the colonialist cleansing of her culture and her training as a Catholic catechist.[43] Nevertheless, she is capable of serving as an eyewitness to practices during the ceremony of the dead, where the number four continues to hold meaning, as when "they put out four candles in the four cardinal points" (se ponen candelas en los cuatro puntos cardinales).[44] Barbara Tedlock also confirms the Nahua *calpulli*, an endogamous quadripartite way of organizing communities, was imported into the K'iche' area and called *calpules*, or *parcialidades*, in Spanish. She writes, in Momostenango "the four quarters were renamed after the conquest for the patron saints assigned to them—Santiago, Santa Ana, Santa Isabel, and Santa Catarina—and were continued as administrative divisions, just as were similar quarters in Mexico."[45] It becomes clear that some pre-Hispanic parceling found ways to survive in the Hispanic Christian world.

In a central Mexican context, these four subdivisions respected the standard Mesoamerican quadrilateral layout of the world. *Nahui,* the number four, can be converted to other forms such as *nauhcan,* in four places, to the four directions, or from the four directions.[46] Siméon lists *naulotl,* which actually means four ears of corn, of cocoa beans, of bananas, or of pillars—all important elements of Nahua civilization.[47] Alva Ixtlilxóchitl explains in the *Sumaria relación* how Xolotl, the legendary founder of the Chichimecatl nation, climbed to the top of Xocotl mountain and from there shot four arrows of fire partitioning the territory (the world) into quadrants (*OH,* 1:295). Such a notion infuses Toltecatl urban norms. During the great Tolteca migrations, when one contingent arrived at Culhuacan, a city was founded and the elites stayed there, while "the [other] four other groups spread out toward the four points of the world, north and south, west and east" (las cuatro se fueron hacia las cuatro partes del mundo, norte y sur, occidente y oriente). When the Tolteca from four neighborhoods came to live with the Chichimeca, they again occupied each of the quadrants (*OH,* 1:284, 2:34). Even without using the term "altepetl," about which we now know from the new philology, the mestizo chronicler unintentionally confirms its importance in the numerous references to quadrangular organization.

The Nahua were especially concerned with marking out space in an altepetl and then in larger districts. The previously mentioned first Chichimecatl leader, Xolotl, shot four arrows of fire, delimiting the quadratic scheme of his territory (the world). The altepetl can also be detected in Cartographic histories. When Dana Leibsohn studies the *Mapa pintado en papel europeo e aforrado en el indiano* (Painted Map on European Paper and Lined with Indian Paper) (1535), she notes that on both the left and right sides of the document "four culture heroes meet to discuss the boundaries of the *altepetl.*"[48] She suggests an ethnic link between each hero and its constituent altepetl, underscoring the ethnic anatomy of the political organization. As evident from map 4, the postcontact Nahua of Tolcoyuca were also interested in mapping out a locality, in this case an altepetl and parts of other altepeme. Quite clear on the map are the footprints that surround the area, creating a boundary. We can also recognize four sections, although unevenly distributed in terms of square feet.

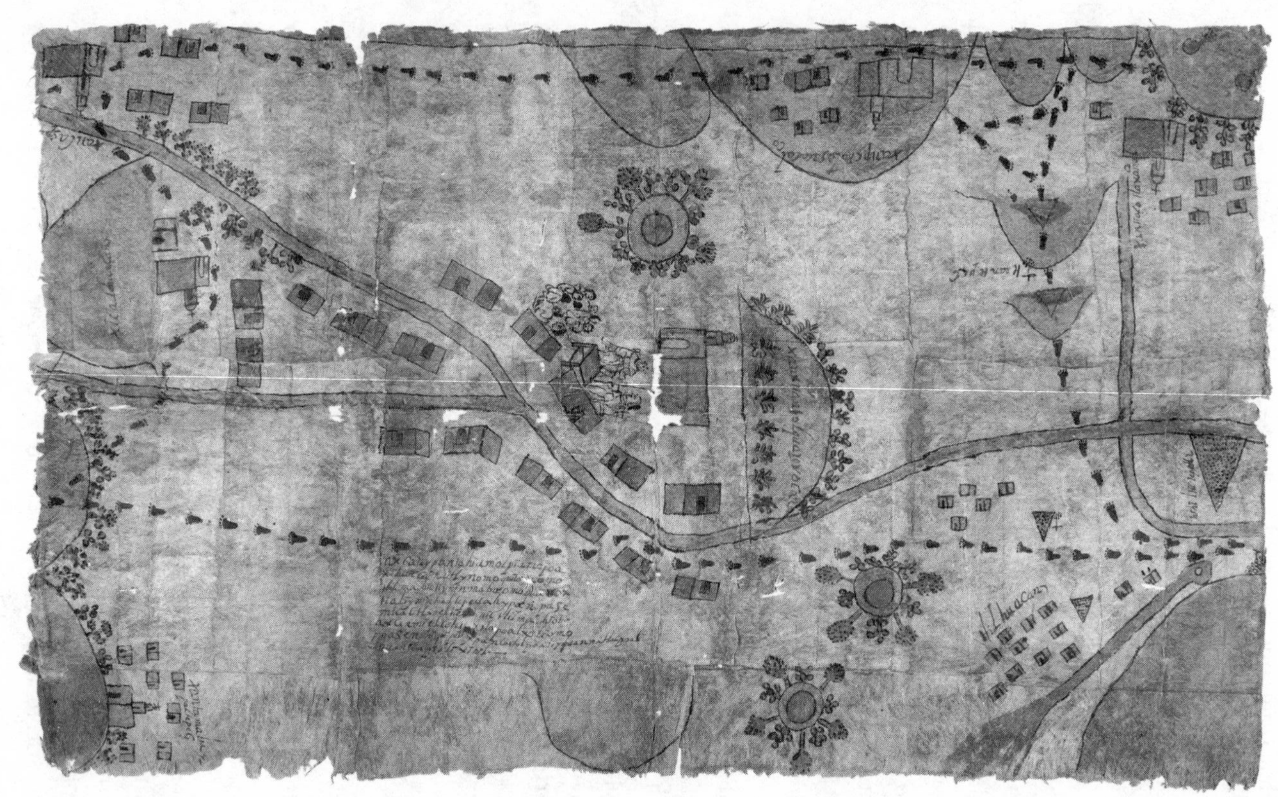

MAP 4. San Juan de Tolcayuca. Manuscript map on amate (fig tree bark) paper. Jay I. Kislak Collection, Rare Book and Special Collections Division, Library of Congress (7.1).

This way of organizing communities, however, was much more complex and goes beyond a mere correlation between territory and ethnicity. Lockhart finds in the Nahuatl records that "even the smallest and apparently most homogeneous altepetl was in a sense a confederation of distinct and competing ethnic groups" (*NAC*, 27). This multilevel ethnic awareness defined political and social relations between neighboring groups of Nahua (and with the Otomi) and organized ethnic diversity within each altepetl. To be sure, these altepeme could be made up of smaller altepeme. Leibsohn, after studying six maps or other cartographic documents from Cuauhtinchan, concludes the altepetl was composed of *calpulli, tlaxilacalli,* meaning big house and neighborhood, respectively, or even getting right down to the smallest unit, *teccalli,* a house.[49] These terms are intriguing, as they can even represent graduations on the social scale, because calpulli, according to Siméon's dictionary, can mean big house, a neighborhood, or even a small town.[50]

As suggested by the association of quatrilinear space and the four periods of creation, spatial awareness intertwined with temporal depth. Also studying a chart from Cuauhtinchan, Taylor makes a startling conclusion: "This map, unlike the familiar projection genre, is not about locating oneself physically but about performing a history; footprints indicate the movement of the Aztecs as they walked, carrying their gods with them, from Aztlan (what is now the southwestern United States) to Tenochtitlan in the valley of Mexico."[51] Thus, whereas spaces had a horizon quality to them, they also held temporal gravity where the past was ever working to define the present.

Besides water and land, space and time, another conspicuous conceptual component of the altepetl is "the people." While the notion of "the people" appears in Nahuatl texts such as Sahagún's, when it appeared in Spanish it became "city," "nation," or "republic," depending on the context. Sahagún rendered "the people" of his Nahua sources as *república.* In other cases, he used the word *ciudad* to represent "life." Anderson and Dibble's English-language translation appears to better approximate the original Nahuatl. Consider the table that follows this paragraph. There are various examples of this type, where a European filter creates the notion of a "republic" where none had heretofore existed. Such a filter, however, had a noble intent of inserting the Nahua into a framework where they could at least compete with the Spanish on the "civilized" ground they conceptualized.

Florentine Codex	**Sahagún's Translation**	**Anderson & Dibble's Translation**	**Siméon**
tlacanemjliztli (*GH/FC*, 10:176)	"tenían su república" (*HG*, 601)	"they were city dwellers" (*GH/FC*, 10:175)	"vida modesta, generosa, vida humana"
tlacanemjliztli (*GH/FC*, 10:176)	[Los otomíes] "vivían en poblado y tenían su república" (*HG*, 602)	"The Otomí had a civilized way of life" (*GH/FC*, 10:176)	"vida modesta, generosa, vida humana"
nauatlaca (*GH/FC*, 10:176)	"su república" (*HG*, 602)	"Nahua People" (*GH/FC*, 10:176)	"las tribus mexicanas" (Siméon, *Diccionario*, 599a, 306a)

Regarding the dynamic contact between groups in the Valley, it should come as no surprise that the borderline of who "the people" included was constantly moving and undergoing revision. As "the people" encountered other "people" and transcultured with them, the concept was transformed. What could be called a negative or inverse border ontology could also exist. When Sahagún's informants discuss the Tamine, for example, they set them apart from the Nahua or the Otomi (*GH/FC*, 10:171). Nahua identity could be seen as in opposition to some groups. To use Moreiras's expression, the hermeneutic circle does not close, expanding instead. This would still be a horizontal ethnic construction. However, it is even more complex: it can appropriate, resist, and become entrenched by digging deeper into its own past, what could be called the time factor. As mentioned, the Mexica revered their pilgrimage from Aztlan. They also looked up to their deity, Huitzilopochtli. When they spurned the Tamine, they had no choice but to do so from a vertical position that looked inward toward their own significant past. This ethnic pride would include a vertical awareness of that which came before. When they adapted Toltecayotl to amplify and to aggrandize their complex identity, both horizontal and vertical vectors gave form to this three-dimensional process, even if the horizontal appropriation of Toltecayotl also comprised a counterpoint to the Tamine rejection. Once this horizontal-vertical synthesis forged new borders that were sometimes porous and other times impermeable, there could be a cultural push and pull, resulting in new and unexpected alignments. This would persist after the "Conquest" as the Nahua struggled to adapt to a new reality.

After the Spanish annexed the Nahua, the "imperial conglomeration" broke down immediately "into its constituent ethnic altepetl" (*NAC*, 27). In the Nahuatl-language annals a good example of its prominent use can be found in the *Codex Chimalpahin*. The term's persistence in postcontact Nahuatl records confirms the hardiness of this political and cultural structure, even if not so apparent in the Spanish-language chronicles. While the Nahua word "altepetl" does not appear in Spanish, the Castilian word "nación" does, but not uniformly so.

"Nación" is absent in the lexicon used by the chroniclers who participated in the invasion. It does, however, surface in that of the later narrators, both Spanish and mestizo. The term's use by those later informants and authors indicates a shift in attitude toward native peoples and reorients colonial discourse to coincide with language usage in the "mother country." There, as the philologist Maravall finds, the term "nación" was common in prose of the sixteenth century, which is to say during the Mexican and Peruvian campaigns.[52] Thus its omission by certain authors is of interest.

The early chronicler's avoidance of the word connotes an ideology of Hispanic superiority and chosenness and may betray an agenda to justify obtaining riches from a people who were not from his nación, or any nation, and hence considered inferior. As mentioned, Díaz del Castillo stands out in this regard. Different are the clerical authors who, writing a little later, had an eye on evangelization. They embraced the designation to describe the object of their observations, all with the intent of spreading Christianity. Toribio de Motolinía (1490?–1568?) is one example of this trend. These chroniclers' use of the word suggests a greater familiarity with native peoples that came with prolonged contact. The Spanish concept of nation is also gradually claimed by the acculturated mestizo who, decades after the initial assaults by Cortés, blended it with the Nahua idea of "the people," the altepetl. This belief in distinctive ethnicities, then, was not lost with the so-called Conquest. The individual mestizo author, whose education was a product of the late Renaissance, the Reformation, and the Counterreformation, found the Nahua worldview not so far from the European construct he had learned in school. This multilayered idea of the nation became an early modern sieve, filtering elements of ethnicity in their vertical and horizontal sifting.

TOLLAN-TENOCHTITLAN AND SAHAGÚN

Before exploring the origins of Tenochtitlan and its even earlier cultural origins in the altepetl of Tollan, a look at the relationship between text, time, and ethnicity is necessary. Sahagún's *Florentine Codex,* an early compilation of Nahua knowledge from between 1545 and 1590, reveals an acute ethnic awareness. José Rabasa describes Sahagún's material as an anthropological referent that corresponds to a state of society anterior to the Western one, which was actually the Franciscan's intent.[53] However, the codex dates from after the destruction of the Mexicatl capital, and we must take it and extrapolate to a point earlier in time. It is possible to consider this ethnographic knowledge carefully, mindful of the bias in the interviewer's questions, and to draw on this rare corpus of knowledge surviving from the time that came before contact, as long as we recognize the limitations that result from the wholesale destruction of manuscripts and artifacts. Our interest is not in Tollan from an historical or artistic perspective, but as it existed in the minds of the Nahua during the sixteenth century.

In the hundred years before the arrival of the first Spaniards, Tenochtitlan was the perceived linchpin of the cosmos. All ethnicity that mattered stemmed from the metropolis, from the Templo Mayor, to be exact. Mignolo explains that different deities could be found in the four quadrants emanating from the Templo Mayor: the rain god (Tlaloc), the wind god (Ecatl or Quetzalcoatl), the earth god (Huitzilopochtli), and the fire god (Xiuhtecutli). These deities were not of equal importance during various periods and could take precedence over each other as the different ethnicities unfolded in time. Thus where Tlaloc dominated in the Teotihuacan horizon, Quetzalcoatl was dominant in Tollan (or Tula), culminating with Huitzilopochtli's preeminence in Tenochtitlan with the Mexica themselves (see map 3). Besides the displacement of the three cultural centers in space, as can be seen on map 3, each center had its apogee at different moments in time. Following Coe, Davies, and what is generally known, Teotihuacan thrived from AD 200 to 700, Tollan AD 800 to 1100, and Tenochtitlan AD 1300 to 1521.[54]

Here we are talking about primary deities relative to others in a polytheistic environment. Certainly Quetzalcoatl was apparent in Teotihuacan prior to the Toltec apogee in Tollan when he was supreme, and he persisted among the top deities in the very late Postclassic Tenochtitlan. Likewise, Tlaloc held more importance than Quetzalcoatl in Teotihuacan, just as Huitzilopochtli seems to have in Tenochtitlan. And in Tollan, Quetzalcoatl was primary despite the existence of myriad other deities. The focus here is on the emblematic deities of particular cultures at particular points in time, even though there were competing deities in all three places and times.[55] The deities and their interpretation constitute an important element of what we call culture.

So even in the face of a growing geometricity, the ethnic element was there without fail through time. There was, in effect, as Mignolo allows, complicity between the "ethnic center of cultures in expansion" and a "geometric rationalization of space."[56] The perhaps inchoate concept of a monotheistic deity known as *In Tloque Nahuaque* may have been affecting the *pipiltin* (sing. *pilli*), or nobility, initiating new structures that begin to privilege class over ethnicity.[57] These types of chrono-cultural speculations are thought-provoking and merit further study. What is of concern here, however, were the ethnic mechanisms driving the Nahua way of life and how the teeth of those mechanisms interlocked with the inverse gears of the Spanish machine of conquest.

In addition to their nomadic beginnings outside the trajectory being outlined here, any interpretation of Mexicatl ethnicity must include the group's adherence to the cultural ideal known as Toltecayotl. Tenochtitlan reflected Tollan, the royal city of the Tolteca, which according to Davies means "place of rushes."[58] Tenochtitlan's eventual fall from power finds meaning within the cyclical pattern established by Tollan's fall. Sahagún's informants delved into this topic in detail. The *Florentine Codex* suggests Topiltzin lost his legendary battle for Tollan because he had drunk an old man's white pulque (*GH/FC*, 3:17–18). His opponent, Huemac, took advantage of Topiltzin's inebriated state and ergo, he prevailed in the battle. Other interpretations, probably influenced by Christianity, place this great conflict in terms of good and evil. For his part, Davies puts forward another explanation that takes ethnicity into account.[59] For him, Tollan fell because of internecine tensions between two dominant groups, headed respectively by Topiltzin and Huemac. The Nonoalca under Huemac defeated Topiltzin's Nahua. To the physical world of ethnicity, a metaphysical dimension was added: Topiltzin's Nahua followers associated themselves with Quetzalcoatl, and Huemac's Nonoalca revered Tezcatlipoca as their principal deity. Ethnic conflict, thus, could take on theological dimensions.

The waning of Toltec supremacy would hold considerable significance for the Mexica. We must then ask if the revered mother culture waned because of a theological or ethnic war, or some combination of the two? Did the semidivine Topiltzin Quetzalcoatl really disappear to the east, promising to return someday as a member of another etnia? Within a Mesoamerican belief system that included destruction, creation, cyclical time, and ethnic awareness, this is conceivable. First, it must be stated with Nicholson that the different Nahua ethnic groups each held to be true a variant of the Quetzalcoatl cycle or cycles. Even Muñoz Camargo, the author covered in the next section, offers two versions.[60] At this juncture we are primarily interested in the Mexicatl strand codified with Sahagún's informants, who were from Tlatelolco. A deeper look at ethnicity becomes indispensable for an appreciation of Nahua culture at the time of first contact with the Iberians.

By going back even further than Teotihuacan, we can roughly divide cultural horizons in the central basin into four supreme epochs: the Olmeca, Teotihuacan, Tollan, and Tenochtitlan.[61] The number of cultural apogees coincides with the corresponding temporal vertices that made up the Mexicatl worldview and with the four cardinal directions. Each of the cultural culminating moments was defined by cultural diversity. Richard Lesure, in his study of figurine styles, suggests the Olmeca comingled with the non-Olmeca.[62] Meyer finds documentable evidence of ethnic neighborhoods at least as far back in the archeological record as Teotihuacan.[63] Richard Diehl concludes that the Tolteca of Tollan were also a multiethnic society.[64] This pluricultural trend continued after their decline, still detectable during the interval in which Tenochtitlan came to dominate. Gibson finds evidence of ethnic neighborhoods in Tetzcoco, Chimalhuacan, Tezayuca, and Azcapotzalco (*AZ*, 23, 189). Sahagún's work substantiates such divisions. Aside from the Tamine's separateness from the Otomi and the Nahua, which was also geographical (see map 3), there are countless other examples. Clendinnen concludes that "mixed populations were not rare, but the outsider group usually resided in a distinct section or ward of the town, with their separateness acknowledged."[65]

Gibson characterizes life in Anahuac as "numerous internal migrations," "refugee movements and some systematic administrative insertion of peoples of one tribe in the area of another." He concludes these ethnic movements eventuated "the formation of enclaves, not mixtures, of populations" (*AZ*, 22–23). However, history shows that enclaves are never totally impermeable. As is evident in the legendary histories, an intense ethnic mixing was taking place, and this was certainly the case with the Nahua. The Mexica, from the lowly maceualli, or peasant, to the sophisticated pilli, lived in a world of multiple ethnicities with experiences ranging from internecine warfare to coexistence, interethnic mingling, and to what we could call cultural journeys. The Mexica's genealogical saga has a nomadic origin, from what is today northwest Mexico or as far away as Upper California, New Mexico, or Texas. They may have been Chichimeca or a Chichimeca-like people. They did not disavow their humble origins in the place they called Aztlan, yet as they strove for something greater, their cultural history pointed toward the more developed Tolteca, whom they emulated. For this cultural reorientation, the Mexica had to appropriate a culture originally alien to them. Smith theorizes that when one culture borrows from another, it increases its chances of ethnic survival.[66] Mexicatl history supports this proposition. As they looked to the Tolteca, they refined their culture while becoming more powerful politically. Their history repeated the Tolteca's, a necessary component in a cyclical notion of time.

In the *Florentine Codex,* Sahagún's informants reveal the Tolteca were also called "Chichimeca," which typically refers to nomadic people from the north. This nomenclature suggests the Tolteca similarly may have had nomadic origins. Also known as the Nahuachichimeca, they were bilingual (*GH/FC,* 10:165, 10:175), meaning they were probably biethnic. The informants distinguish between the Toltec-Chichimeca, who spoke sophisticated Nahua o Nonoalca, and other groups—Chichimeca, Otomi, Tamine, and Teochichimeca—each of whom spoke a more "barbarous tongue." Despite these multiethnic surroundings, the bicultural Tolteca were able to develop generalized, identifiable characteristics. These included being learned, righteous, devout, rich, and tall (*GH/FC,* 10:167–71). Such positive traits created a model for other groups, who could elevate themselves through assimilation, a process documented in Sahagún's text. Consider the case of the Teochichimeca, the Other, the "Extreme," who lived on the plains or in the forests. Even though their mother tongue was said to be barbarous, the Chichimeca eventually acquired a second language, Nahuatl (*GH/FC,* 10:171, 175), the language of the learned Tolteca. This same process repeats later when the Tamine began to learn Nahuatl or the Otomi languages. During the course of history in the Valley, Tolteca, Acolhuaque, and Mexica could all claim Chichimecatl or nomadic origins (*GH,* 10:171, 196–97). Each gradually took on a higher level of cultural sophistication. These populations may have appropriated this more sophisticated culture in response to pressure from Toltecatl elites in neighboring cities.[67] The process may also have arisen from the human penchant to improve and move up on the social ladder. More likely, the different etnias may have been reacting to both forces, external and internal. Whatever the motivating factors, people who came together in the *omphalos* (Anahuac) ended up becoming cultured in the sense of Toltecayotl.

Tenochtitlan was the main city of the Mexica, a conglomeration of peoples. It claimed a diversity of origins, ranging from Mexica, Culhuaque, Chichimeca, and even Tepaneca and Acolhuaque. In spite of its diversity, the city constituted a more or less unified entity. For Clendinnen, at the time of the Spanish invasion, this unity was not necessarily historical: "By the sixteenth century shared land and the notion of a shared past had become more a matter of sentiment than a historically based actuality, but the sentiment remained potent."[68] Clendinnen's "sentiment" is analogous to Smith's "to feel." But it seems the sentiment and feeling must have originated with events, which brings us back to our theory of horizontal and vertical appropriation.

There was a felt cohesiveness on two levels. The first occurred between the various contemporary cultures and resulted horizontally from mutual sharing of culture. When this transculturation was not bilateral, it was not purely horizontal. Cross-cultural mating practices, as discussed in chapter 3, were part and parcel of the horizontal annexation that increased political power. After the horizontal journey, people gained access to new cultures that they could then mine vertically. Whether through peer pressure, individual volition, accident, or gendered relationships, groups directly assimilated Toltecayotl thriving in Culhuacan. Again, this prompted a cultural shift that allowed for a subsequent vertical resurrection of that which came before, the Toltecayotl ideal. Vertical appropriation and fortification brought with it a greater spiritual awareness and cultural authority. Nahua culture did not necessarily differentiate between spiritual and temporal elements and probably would have seen them as one integrated concept. Nevertheless, we can artificially separate temporal and spiritual power as an apparatus to distinguish between the two kinds of cultural journeying, horizontal (political) and vertical (spiritual). Neither mode of assimilation was wholly independent of the other, nor was the political viewed as distinct from the spiritual, yet differing social conditions in relation to the quest for power responded more to one or the other. Both modes of appropriation had their impact on the idea of "the people."

MUÑOZ CAMARGO, TLAXCALAN, BETWEEN TENOCHTITLAN AND CASTILE

Investigation carried out by Gloria Anzaldúa and Walter Mignolo on borderlands, borderlands theory, and cultural hybridity has looked at multiethnic realities in our time and in the past.[69] Proceeding in this manner, what Mignolo calls "border thinking," allows us to shed new light on the condition of nationness in the colonial chronicles. This and the following section look at two trailblazing colonial historians, Diego Muñoz Camargo and Fernando de Alva Ixtlilxóchitl, both border thinkers with roots in the group described by Rocío Cortés as the Intellectual Circle on Indigenous Matters, which was founded in the Colegio Imperial de Santa Cruz de Tlatelolco.[70] These two authors are similar, yet approach their ethnic nations from divergent stances, creating in the process a tapestry of tension and comprehension that elucidates the interlocking intricacies of ethnicity and colonialism. We start with Muñoz Camargo and his city Tlaxcala (see map 5).

In the period prior to the advent of the Spanish, a siege mentality had molded Tlaxcala's identity, developed in the shadow of the economic and military might of the Mexica. That defiance and resistance help to fuel a regional pride, formed in part from Tlaxcala's opposition to Tenochtitlan, but it caused great suffering among the Tlaxcalan people. Gibson remarks that due to its constant warfare with Tenochtitlan, Tlaxcala was cut down "from a position of opulence and flourishing trade to a state of comparative poverty" (*TSC*, 15). The clearest indicator of socio-economic disparity between the two altepeme resides in the kinds of fabric that each typically wore for clothing.

Clothing, as Mignolo discerns, is an element of *civitas* that functions as a sign "whose reading allowed the construction of social identities by the perception of social differences."[71] Díaz del Castillo sheds light on garment textiles when he refers to Cholula, or Cholollan, another altepetl linked to Mexicatl power. His previously mentioned proconquest bias is unlikely to distort his recounting of textile variation, because these details would not support one side or the other in the great encomienda debates that caused him to commit his chronicle to paper. He remembers the hallmark of the Tenocha and the Chololteca was the cotton finery they wore (*HV*, 149a–157a). This material is important, Muñoz Camargo tells us, because it is associated with Tehuitznahuatl, Quetzalcoatl's birthplace (*HT*, 95). The Tlaxcalteca, however, could not afford it and Díaz reports they were reduced to wearing clothing sewn from burlap (*HV*, 146a). This divergence

Map 5. Valley of Mexico. From Charles Gibson, *The Aztecs Under Spanish Rule: A History of the Indians of the Valley of Mexico, 1519–1810* (Stanford: Stanford University Press, 1964), xi.

in fabric types epitomized both ethnic differences and economic power in Mesoamerica. Upon the Spaniards' arrival, each category of fabric represented a symbol of nationality, as Díaz del Castillo verifies on numerous occasions. Therefore, the lowly henequen garments the besieged Tlaxcalan wore exemplified his or her rank in the pre-Hispanic geopolitical power grid.

Even though the Tlaxcalteca had forged a common identity, like the Mexica and the Acolhuaque, they resided in a kind of borderlands where multiple ethnicities interacted on a daily basis. It was the constant measuring of one's own cultures against neighboring cultures that allowed for cultural pride to develop. Chronicler Muñoz Camargo is aware of this diversity of cultures. He explains the earliest groups to inhabit the region were the Olmeca, the Xicalanca, and the Zacateca. Later, the Teochichimeca immigrated to the valley and melded with its inhabitants (*HT,* 83–84). Gibson corroborates these basic elements and this scheme of things, except he inserts the Otomi in the process somewhere between the three foundational ethnicities and the Teochichimeca. Even in the face of this cultural diversity, the Tlaxcalteca were able to meld the collective patriotism upon which Gibson remarks (*TSC*, 2–3, 5–6, 145). Such ethnic pride was necessary for Muñoz Camargo to be inspired to put to paper his detailed *Historia de Tlaxcala* (History of Tlaxcala), even when he himself had plural roots.[72]

While the honor of being the first Tlaxcaltecatl historian goes to Tadeo de Niza, Muñoz Camargo is also significant because much of what can be gleaned from later chronicles "is traceable" to his writings (*TSC*, 3, 13).[73] These were, for example, the central source for Fray Juan de Torquemada's 1615 *Monarquía Indiana* (Indian Monarchy).[74] He is a pivotal figure, moreover, because as the first Mesoamerican mixed-heritage author, his ideas institute an early defensive response to a complex colonial societal fabric. His work anticipates the next generation, which Alva Ixtlilxóchitl would come to embody.

Besides the distinct cultures at play in the Tlaxcala of late antiquity, there was also the dualist paradigm of early modernity. Marilyn Miller understands Muñoz Camargo as having brought two worldviews together in one text.[75] Each constituted a complex system of attitudes informed by class, ethnicity, and gender. We must consider the possibility the chronicler was aware of two distinct sets of discriminatory biases directed toward him, early modern Spanish and late ancient Mexica. From the Iberian perspective, while wealthy, Muñoz Camargo was not a nobleman. We know his mother held such low social rank that, according to Gibson, "no record remains" of her.[76] For conquistadors and *pobladores* from Spain, he was simply a middle-class merchant. Muñoz Camargo would have felt this contempt. Most likely he was not of the "Hispanic oligarchy" (oligarquía hispana) as one of his chronicle's editors, Germán Vázquez, maintains (*HT*, 44). Doors were closed to him in favor, first of peninsular Spaniards, and then of the newly forming Novo-Hispanic class.

From the Mexican perspective, the autochthonous side of Muñoz's family originated in Tlaxcala, an impoverished, henequen-clad nation surrounded by Tenochtitlan's sphere of cotton-confected fashion. He must have felt some condescension having grown up in Mexico City, the erstwhile seat of imperial culture. Central to our discussion is the chronicler's capacity to relate to one culture or the other, and his ability to repress intermittently one or the other, improving his chances for personal gain in the colonial milieu.

His family story is revealing. As a mestizo, Muñoz Camargo represented the intricate confluence of two vertical heritages. His father, also Diego Muñoz

Camargo, hailed from Extremadura and his mother, Tlaxcala. He identified with his father, who raised him in the viceregal capital.[77] Despite marrying Leonor Vázquez, a Tlaxcalan noblewoman,[78] he demonstrated an outward inclination toward Spanish, not Tlaxcalan culture. This is apparent by his excluding the honorific "don" from his name, distinguishing himself from the autochthonous elites, who by 1580 had adopted the "don."[79] Muñoz Camargo was able to walk between both cultures, becoming a leading businessman. After 1586, Gibson reports, he also became *procurador* to the indigenous government of Tlaxcala.[80]

Furthermore, these two vertical heritages were not interacting in a sterile laboratory environment. As noted, Muñoz Camargo came into adulthood while residing in colonial Mexico City, where multiple etnias were also neatly ensconced. All of them were potential horizontal psychological determinants. The most salient of these were the Mexica's descendants. They preserved the memory of their ancestors, who held the Tlaxcalteca in low esteem. Their collective *Weltanschauung* would influence Muñoz's view of the Tlaxcalteca and of himself. Even with these two indigenous influences, the vertical via his mother and the horizontal via his social contact with the Tenocha, the colonial chronicler identified with the forming Criollo elite. If he felt lacking with respect to the Tenocha, he could feel good about the Spanish.

So integrated into the Hispanic world was Muñoz Camargo that his commercial transactions involved, in the words of Mörner and Gibson, "land, houses, cattle, salt, slaves, cacao and other goods."[81] He owned black slaves, employed autochthonous laborers and, according to Gibson, became "one of the five or six largest entrepreneurs of sixteenth-century Tlaxcala."[82] As a consequence of the abuses he or members of his family committed, Muñoz Camargo eventually found himself expelled from Tlaxcala by royal decree in 1589.[83] This event is not unusual given that mestizos were prohibited from living in *pueblos de indios,* Indian towns. They were restricted to the *pueblos de españoles.* Tlaxcala had been awarded a special status, protected as a pueblo de indios because it had aided Cortés in his destruction of Tenochtitlan. Muñoz Camargo and his relatives were of mixed heritage and would not have been accepted as *indios.* Yet this royal *cédula,* as with countless before, was not respected and, as Mörner and Gibson discover, in 1593 we still "find him purchasing goods, dealing in land, engaging in legal actions, and still identified as a *vecino* of Tlaxcala."[84] In the sixteenth-century colonial world, Inca Garcilaso de la Vega reminds us, the term *vecino* referred to people who owned other people.[85]

Even though he would have been absorbed by his intense legal and commercial activity, Muñoz Camargo still had time to compose the work generally known as the *Historia de Tlaxcala*.[86] In it, his self-awareness as a Spanish subject is complete. He ponders the importance of converting "nations" (naciones) such as China and Japan to Christianity (*HT*, 263). When turning his sights on the Chichimeca cultures, the *a posteriori* attitude he developed after his 1591 trip north to relocate four hundred Tlaxcalan families to the Chichimecatl frontier was typically novo-Hispanic, dividing peoples into civilized and noncivilized categories. Assuming he most likely penned the lengthy chronicle between 1580 and 1595, he may have been working on it during his trip. Decoding his perception of the Chichimeca is requisite activity in approaching his notion of ethnicity.

Essential to appreciating Muñoz Camargo's thought is the idea that there were two classes of Chichimeca. The first are the Teochichimeca, whom we met in our discussion of Sahagún and who populated Tlaxcala on the heels of the Olmeca, the Xicalanca, and the Zacateca. He distinguishes those "sincere and ancient Chichimeca" (sinceros y antiguos chichimecas) from a second variety, the nomadic and warlike tribes who populated the northern frontier of Nahua lands during his own lifetime. While both could be "barbarians" (bárbaros), the former were exalted to the point they constituted "their own homeland" (su propia patria) (*HT*, 89, 250, 104, 105).[87] In neither case does Muñoz Camargo afford the Chichimeca the condition of nationness, even though in the case of the former, they lived among "these peoples, provinces and nations for a long time" (estas gentes, provincias y naciones muchos tiempos) (*HT*, 114). Who were the nations of "those times" (aquellos tiempos) (*HT*, 113)? Muñoz Camargo does not explain this in straightforward terms. But they were probably Tolteca, people like them, or other Quetzalcoatl-worshiping groups such as the Chololteca, whom he mentions on various occasions (*HT*, 114, for example). Given the earlier Chichimecatl group's prolonged contact with those "provinces and nations," they would have constituted a nation better than the nomadic warrior group of his time. Yet that is not how Muñoz Camargo viewed them.

Clearly, Muñoz Camargo did not consider himself to be of Chichimecatl stock. This is obvious in his diagnostic of the Chichimeca, yet he must have been aware that as a composite being whose Nahua origins were from Tlaxcala, he had at least partially descended from them. He skips over this point. In both cases the Tlaxcalan writer uses the term "Chichimeca" as synonymous with "barbarous." There is more: when he describes La Florida, he sees it as unpopulated and "of Chichimeca," a suggestion implying that whoever La Florida's inhabitants are, they are not capable of constituting "population" (*HT,* 260). This is not mere *a priori* posturing. Gibson has found evidence that "he appears to have been entrusted with the teaching of Indians brought back from Florida."[88] As mentioned earlier, these would have been the same individuals who came to Mexico City with the very famous Álvar Núñez Cabeza de Vaca.[89] By calling the Floridians "Chichimeca," the historian descends into the same narrow mind-set as did the Europeans. He fails to define them on their own terms (Mocoso, Timucua, early Seminole?), lumping all non-Europeans into a single group, seeing them as the inferior "Other." Muñoz Camargo's insinuation that Floridians were less than people denies them humanity. Was this cultural chauvinism impeding him from regarding those he called Chichimeca as "population" or "nation"? Was this the same insensitivity that inheres to the Spanish view repudiating indigenous heterogeneity? It is true that the geography and the distance between first, the Nahua center and the Chichimecatl lands, and second, between those lands and La Florida, may have been nebulous to Muñoz Camargo because of the limits of knowledge during the time he lived, the extreme distances, and the newness of it all. What we have here is a literate subaltern attributing characteristics to an even more subaltern group that constitutes "the Other" of "the Other." This *mise en abîme* can be described as metasubalterity. It is an alterity of an alterity, so profound that understanding its details requires an almost quixotic undertaking.

Muñoz Camargo's need to be "Spanish" impaired his ability to see the people he viewed as "barbarians" as nations. As a colonial subject, and even more so as a bilingual one, he had to prove his allegiance to the imperial homeland and work hard to prove his loyalty to the Crown. Given his dubious origins, he may have "passed" as a Spaniard at a time, as Miller reminds us, "when the collective identity of the European-American mestizo remains unformed and unregulated."[90] To fit in, to survive, and to flourish, therefore, he regarded himself, above all, as a member of the larger Hispanic nation, now mestiza, superior to the provinces of Chichimeca in the north (*HT,* 250). Consequently, to imagine this as a binary experience forged between "Indians" and "Europeans" would be overly simplistic, and thus distortive.

Just as there are many European nationalities, there are many kinds of "Indians." Contrasted against Muñoz Camargo's pejorative view of the

Chichimeca is his acceptance of Tlaxcala as a republic and of Cholula as a nation. The terms "gentility" (gentilidad) and "republic" (república) inform his idea of nationness (*HT*, 197, 206). The latter term is familiar to the reader, but the former term, *gentilidad*, is connected with lineage in premodern thought. To the postcolonial mind, it relates to the *gentilicio* of a people, rendered in English as ethnonym. "Gentilicio" can now be expressed using the neologism "demonym," defined by the *Oxford English Dictionary* as a "proper name by which a native or resident of a specific place is known."[91] Although this neologism does not yet appear in *Webster's*, it is a useful substitute for "gentilicio" in Spanish or "ethnonym" in English. Lineage has to do with the premodern nation, when the nación was intimately linked to the people who ruled over it. But Muñoz Camargo pertains neither to the premodern nor to late antiquity, and his idea of the republic has to do with early modern sensibilities.

The chronicler's view of the altepetl of Cholula and its interaction with Tlaxcala sheds light on the qualities that for him constitute nationness. When he narrates the events that end in the assassination of the Tlaxcalan ambassador to Cholula, he mentions the "terrible fear and sorrow in the Republic" (terrible espanto y pena en la República), a suitable reaction for an emissary who died "in the service of his homeland and Republic" (en servicio de su patria y República) (*HT*, 212–13). This sentiment explains why the Tlaxcalteca assisted Cortés in the alleged (probably true) massacre at Cholula, a political entity Muñoz terms "that nation and province" (aquella nación y provincia) (*HT*, 213). Such nomenclature probably reveals a multiple precontact altepetl arrangement. Cholula constituted an altepetl in its own right, with its own tlatoani, or ruler, its own deity, and its own territory, the three primary prerequisites Horn lists to constitute this type of political organization.[92] It could thereby appear to be a nation. Even so, the idea of a province also makes sense if the altepetl of Cholula linked up to other, larger altepetl, either Tlaxcala or Tenochtitlan, depending on one's political bias, this in the context of various competing altepeme (see map 5).

Muñoz's categorization of Cholula as a "nation" in its own right supervenes on its cultural and commercial authority, and its perceived autonomy. This self-rule may have been a consequence of its altepetl not rotating in the traditional Nahua pattern with either Tenochtitlan or Tlaxcala. Cholula's religious prestige resulted vertically from its adoration of Quetzalcoatl. Such reverence for this primary deity of the Tolteca lends credence to the idea of

Cholula's connection to Toltecayotl. Cholula first rose to power as an ally of Teotihuacan, but fell into decadence during the period of Teotihuacan's waning. After its subsequent subordination to the Tolteca, perhaps in the twelfth century, and after its inhabitants' ethnic blending with them, it could claim a vertical relationship with Toltecayotl and its central deity, Quetzalcoatl. As we will see, this is different from the Mexica, because important migrations were part of the process.

Its temporal power stemmed from an additional source. The European idea of a "province" is more subjective. Cholula had ties in one form or another to both the Triple Alliance and to Tlaxcala. The reference could refer to its commercial links to Tenochtitlan because it was a renowned trading hub. As Davies reports, it was a highly developed commercial center.[93] Moctezuma II, for example, dined on fine Chololtecatl earthenware. Irrespective of Mexicatl losses to its army (approximately one hundred years before the advent of the Spanish), some Chololteca rulers broke bread with other tlatoque in Tenochtitlan.[94] Thus its power also stemmed from temporal activity. The substance of "province" is interesting from a vertical perspective. Both municipalities revered the great Ecatl Quetzalcoatl, a deity associated with Toltecayotl. As we have seen, their inhabitants both wore cotton attire, a fabric associated with Quetzalcoatl's birthplace. These common characteristics could point to a vertical identity shared at least in part by both altepeme.

Despite commercial and religious ties to Tenochtitlan, it may have been that, at the juncture of Cortés's arrival, Cholula was also perceived as a rebellious province by the Tlaxcalteca. Consequently, tensions were high between the two altepeme. From its broad commercial clout, Cholula had elevated its economic status to a level superior to its rival. Its residents' use of cotton finery painfully set them apart from the hemp-clad Tlaxcalteca. The former's goal to remain free from the latter was crushed by the latter's alliance with the Spaniards.

Muñoz Camargo does not devalue Cholula's prestige as a nation, notwithstanding its enemy status. Calling a political entity a "nation" denotes respect. This is not the case, as discussed, when he considers Floridians. Despite his ranked scale of "civilization," Muñoz does acknowledge the idea of pre-Hispanic national separateness. Like other chroniclers, he recognizes an ethnocentric hierarchy in which each distinct culture felt itself superior, immolating individuals from other ethnicities. The Chololteca, for example, sacrificed to Quetzalcoatl victims who were not from their city. They were broadly from "other nations" (otras naciones) (*HT,* 214). Some of those were from Tlaxcala. The Mexica also offered up a great number of Tlaxcalteca, in their case to Huitzilopochtli during the holiday of Toxcatl. This is confirmed by Tetzcoco's paramount chronicler, Alva Ixtlilxóchitl (*OH,* 2:228). Such practices could explain why Pedro de Alvarado instigated the battle/massacre of Toxcatl, to avenge—or to appear to avenge—his Tlaxcalan allies' "humiliation." Alvarado may not have understood that interethnic practices of sacrifice were mutual. Or as is commonly inferred, he used and distorted custom and history to his own tactical advantage.

A comparison of Muñoz Camargo's views on Cholula and Tlaxcala sheds more light on the notions of altepetl and nation as he understood them. Both urban *omphali* were altepetl. Muñoz envisages them equally as nations, although he prefers to call Tlaxcala a republic (*HT,* 206, 231). He utilizes such terminology when the larger altepetl could coincide with those Spanish notions that allowed Tlaxcala to be, for a time, a relatively independent pueblo de indios. Regarding the altepetl, he seems to be aware of Tlaxcala's pre-Hispanic political geography. He grasped that there were four "lords" (señores) and four of what were called "cabeceras" in the Spanish of the time, and that the province was divided into halves (*HT,* 231, 115, 116). This is incontrovertibly an altepetl layout. However, when looking at the four sub-altepeme (tlaxilacalli?) constituting the larger unit (see figure 1), he adopts the Spanish term "cabecera" to describe them (*HT,* 231). Such usage distorts our understanding of Nahua socio-political arrangement, because "cabecera" conveys the notion of a hierarchical cabecera-sujeto administrative framework, meaning towns under the control of cities, while "altepetl" denotes a rotating governmental pattern organized by means of a power-sharing model based on parity between the parts.

Because Muñoz Camargo was writing, after all, for people who could read Spanish (he delivered the manuscript in its *Descripción de la ciudad y provincia de Tlaxcala* format to Philip II's royal library or bookstore in 1585), he may have felt the need to deliberately force the Nahua political structure into Spanish's linguistic system of signs. The possibility also exists that Muñoz simply did not grasp the concept of *quadrialtepetl* within the larger unit, implying that the autochthonous pattern remained hidden from him. This scenario is less likely. Muñoz Camargo was familiar with local history and custom. First, he dedicates half of his *Historia* to the Nahua origins of Tlaxcala. Second, as Miller points out, Muñoz was integrated sufficiently into the indigenous world to openly praise the Nahuatl language as being soft, dignified, and lovely (*HT*, 85) and to supply a lengthy glossary to make the work more accessible.[95]

That Muñoz Camargo was aware of the persistence of precontact political structures does not diminish the certitude that the altepetl was slowly giving way to a cabecera-sujeto political framework. For Gibson, the ascendancy of this manner of administration was detectable by mid-sixteenth century (*AZ*, 188–89). Yet Lockhart finds conclusive evidence that the altepetl, in one form or another, was still an integral aspect of government in some locales as late as the eighteenth century (*NAC*, 52–53). During Muñoz's time, this transition would have been inchoate. It is therefore noteworthy that he refrains from using the term altepetl in his reconstruction of Tlaxcala's national identity, preferring instead a Novo-Hispanic linguistic frame. Even so, that frame has cultural margins aligned with other margins at a border, making cultural interaction an integral part of the chronicler's worldview.

ALVA IXTLILXÓCHITL, TETZCOCAN WITH THE BEST OF THREE WORLDS

As Rocío Cortés observes, Mexico-Tenochtitlan, Tetzcoco, and Tlaxcala were "major centers" in the central basin where the Nahuatl language dominated (see maps 3 and 5).[96] If pre-Hispanic Tlaxcala defined its identity by its resistance to Tenochtitlan, Tetzcoco derived its, at least partly, from its adherence to that axis of power. With Tlacopan (Tacuba) and Tenochtitlan, it formed the Triple Alliance, the dominant political force in the valley when Cortés arrived.[97] Tetzcoco boasted an illustrious history characterized by sophisticated rulers and deep links to the Mexica. In addition, Tetzcoco could trace its lineage to the Chichimecatl people, and thus Tetzcocans cultivated something that along with Toltecayotl we might call Chichimecayotl, or Chichimecness.

The baroque author Fernando de Alva Ixtlilxóchitl, a student at the Colegio Imperial de Tlatelolco just before its demise, is perhaps the premier chronicler of Tetzcoco's history, so a few words about his historiographical situation would be prudent before continuing.[98] While here we are more interested in the author's concept of the nation than in his intentions, it is helpful to know that Alva Ixtlilxóchitl may have written his *Historia de la nación chichimeca* (History of the Chichimecatl nation) and other histories as a way to defend his family's privileged status in the colonial situation in which it found itself. Pablo García Loaeza, for example, argues that "all of Alva's texts, from the *Relación sucinta en forma de memorial* to the extensive *Historia de la nación*

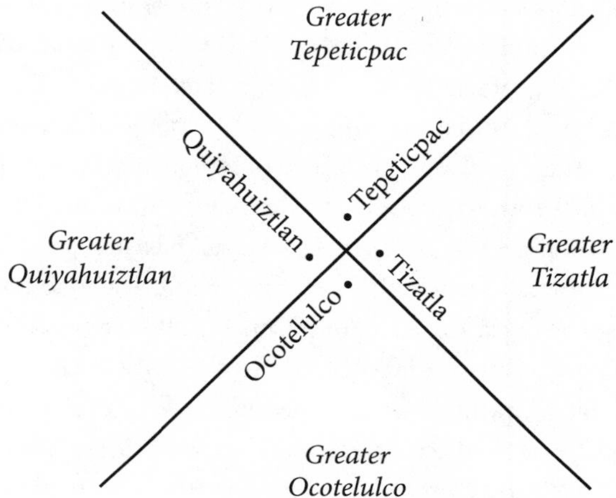

Figure 1. Tlaxcalan altepeme. From James Lockhart et al., *The Tlaxcalan Actas: A Compendium of the Records of the Cabildo of Tlaxcala (1545–1627)* (Salt Lake City: University of Utah Press, 1986), 4.

chichimeca, are extended *nobiliarios,* family histories intended to call attention to his lineage's nobility."[99] Certainly García Loaeza is on to something with respect to intentions, but from our perspective, so many centuries after the chronicler lived, it would be hard to say just how much of the chronicler's motivations were financial, how much they had to do with family pride, and how much they there were part of a creative impulse, or a combination of all three. Nor can we be sure if family prestige pressure was a primary factor because, as noted by Amber Brian, the chronicler's brother, Bartolomé de Alva, was also a writer. He was interested in translating Siglo de Oro plays into Nahuatl.[100] It is plausible the brothers talked about history and literature and may have been influencing each other. Indeed, the brothers may have transmitted this literary interest to Fernando's son, Juan, who would then safeguard these important manuscripts and ultimately give them to one of Mexico's two great baroque literary figures, Carlos de Sigüenza y Góngora.[101] Certainly it may have been the family's literary and historical interest that allowed these manuscripts to survive for posterity. All of these may have been factors, and whatever the hidden influences in his intentions, we are fortunate Alva Ixtlilxóchitl was concerned enough with the idea of Tetzcoco to write his histories, as without them, we could not study his ideas regarding the nation.

When he wrote what could be called an epos in prose, his best-known work the *Historia de la nación chichimeca,* Alva Ixtlilxóchitl consulted *amoxtli,* the Nahua semiotic receptacle of information created by a *tlacuilo,* or writer/painter, as well as oral sources and indigenous chronicles such as the one crafted by Alonso Axayacatl, an ethnic lord of Iztapalapa. At the same time, he turned to Spanish authors such as Torquemada, Motolinía, and López de Gómara. Alva Ixtlilxóchitl's chronicle can be read as such, a hybrid form, based on the chronicler-authored, orally informed, and tlacuilo-painted histories. Even so, as Leisa Kauffmann points out, it is "certainly modeled on European historical forms and ideas."[102] In this hybrid text, these three kinds of sources blend nicely together. The text-based and tlacuilo-painted histories are both preserved on a solid medium, be that paper or amoxtli. Moreover, these written sources are not so far from the oral ones, given that they, too, as Walter Ong reminds us, were "related somehow, directly or indirectly, to the world of sound, the natural habitat of language, to yield their meanings."[103] It should not be a surprise that Alva Ixtlilxóchitl could creatively weave his three sources into a seamless plane of expression. Given its final disposition as a book, though, one must recognize, as Mignolo does, that the work follows Western historiographical conventions.[104]

Alva Ixtlilxóchitl could trace his lineage directly back to a long line of distinguished Tetzcocan rulers, culminating with the poet-king Nezahualcoyotl (1402–72) and Ixtlilxochitl II (1521–31), two of the last three independent tlatoani of that altepetl. He could similarly claim bloodlines to Tenochtitlan's gentry, including Cuitlahuac (1520), the penultimate sovereign tlatoani. His old-line family, defined by unions between Acolhuaque (Tetzcocan) and Mexica, was well accustomed to interethnic links at the time of the Iberian invasion. As called to mind by Townsend and García Loaeza, some of the associations Tetzcoco had formed, such as its family ties with Azcapotzalco, were problematic and conflictive.[105] Here we are not so interested in those difficulties—human relations are often fraught with tension—but rather in the fact that precontact links were frequently forged willingly, perhaps energetically, with Culhuacan, Azcapotzalco, and Tenochtitlan, establishing a pattern. Tetzcoco's Chichimeca merely continued these culture-blending norms after Cortés seized power. His grandmother married Juan Grande, his mother Juan de Peraleda, both Spaniards. Alva Ixtlilxóchitl was, in the end, only one-quarter Nahua. From these three traditions—Tetzcoco, Tenochtitlan (with their links to Tollan), and Spain—he was able to draw strength vertically.

The compound name this historian eventually took symbolizes the coming together of two worlds, Alva Spanish and Ixtlilxochitl Nahua. Blanco finds it strange he took the Ixtlilxochitl surname at all, because patriarchal tradition would require he adapt the surnames of his father and grandfather, which would result in his being called Fernando Pérez Grande.[106] Another possibility might have been Fernando Peraleda Cortés (his father Juan de Peraleda, his mother Ana Cortés). It is hard to say, as naming practices during that time were more fluid than they are in ours. His contemporary from Peru, Inca Garcilaso de la Vega, also fashioned a name different from the one given at birth, Gómez Suárez de Figueroa. Alva Ixtlilxochitl's naming choice does reveal a desire to accentuate both sides of the Atlantic, this despite the strange penchant in his family to take the maternal surname "Cortés" to pass from generation to generation. Both names evidently come from Alva Ixtlilxóchitl's great-great-grandfather Ixtlilxochitl II, the brother of Cacama and the son of Nezahualpilli, who, during the Spanish onslaught, allied himself with Hernán Cortés. After he was baptized, he came to be known as Fernando Cortés Ixtlilxóchitl. This "Cortés" became part of the surname Alva Ixtlilxóchitl's children used: Juan, Ana, and Diego de Alva Cortés. The historian of Tetzcoco, then, although he departed from an amalgamated heritage and frequently needed to self-identify as "Spanish" to pursue privileges in the colonial setting, did not devalue his autochthonous side. His Nahua-themed *Historia* is truly a composite exposition, composed in a transatlantic language yet replete with an indigenous content that tries to complement and compete with European culture and religion.

His view was truly composite, as can be seen by at least two of his cultural practices, one originating in Europe, the other in Anahuac. First, similar to Muñoz Camargo, he wrote his *Historia de la nación chichimeca* in Castilian, cultivating the typical "chronicle" genre for Spanish readers. Second, unlike Muñoz Camargo, despite his legal travails in life, he self-identified as a Nahua in his writing, as illustrated by his use of the honorific "don." As alluded to earlier, this title came to imply status within the indigenous community (even while its use lapsed among Spaniards). This divergence in bearing between the two historians could also be ascribed to Alva Ixtlilxóchitl's noble lineage, of which he would have been proud. The Tlaxcalan chronicler, in comparison, could boast of no Nahua pedigree except his wife's.

Notwithstanding their differences, Muñoz Camargo and Alva Ixtlilxóchitl shared the tendency to integrate both Western and indigenous traits in their writing that served to translate and codify the autochthonous past.[107]

Comparable to his Tlaxcalan colleague in this regard, Alva Ixtlilxóchitl is noteworthy because he inserted Nahua tradition into the humanistic world of letters. As Adorno indicates, by "remembering" Anahuac's past in his writing, he erases "the spectacle of otherness" to which his culture was condemned. He thereby "reinstate[s] native history" into Hispanic literary and historical forms.[108] Though he was composite, Adorno cautions that he cannot be understood in a simple binary Spanish-Indian framework. He was a colonial subject caught in a balancing act: proud of his heritage, yet eager to be accepted by the colonial power's apparatus of Church and State.[109] Indeed, descriptors such as "binary" or "dual" do not take into account the complexities inherent in Alva Ixtlilxóchitl's family, which drew on lineages from at least four locations: Tetzcoco, Tenochtitlan, San Juan Teotihuacan, and Spain. Of course, Chichimecatl and Acolhua elements, understood as ethnonyms but not as demonyms, nonetheless represent additional consequential ingredients. Even though his hometown was San Juan de Teotihuacan, his writing represents a "redistribution of cultural space" achieved through his successful elevation of Tetzcocan heroes to the level of Cortés and his minions.[110] While it would be a tricky endeavor to verify all his cultural and historical details with precision, it is clear that Alva Ixtlilxóchitl's lexical choices say much about the mestizo concept of the nation during the early *Barroco de Indias* period.

Because we still have a great deal to learn about how the altepetl was viewed one hundred years after Cortés defeated Moctezuma, Cuitlahuac, and Cuauhtémoc, it is unclear just how much Alva Ixtlilxóchitl's preference for the term "nación" in his *Historia de la nación chichimeca* coincides with the precontact Nahua political system. Nevertheless, it is evident he applies the Spanish term to all ethnic groups. The Otomi, to cite an example, are thus classified (*OH,* 2:18). What is more, we know he did not apply this designation solely to those groups deemed "civilized." This sets him apart from Muñoz Camargo. When he records Cortés's deeds in Guaniganiga, he describes that locale's inhabitants as belonging to "those gentilic and barbarous nations" (aquellas naciones gentílicas y bárbaras) (*OH,* 2:195).[111] The use of the adjective "gentilic," meaning lineage, suggests the idea of a premodern nation. The use of the plural "aquellas" can also depict a confederation of peoples (*OH,* 2:203–4). This idea can likewise be found in the disparate people the Tetzcocans conquered, "the nations we have subjected" (las naciones que hemos sujetado) (*OH,* 2:135–36). Such a way of formulating things demonstrates that this chronicler conceived even weak ethnic-political entities in terms of nationness.

One sure method to delve into Alva Ixtlilxóchitl's perception of the nation is to examine the Chichimeca, that category of interest held by all central Mexican cultural groups. His idea of them differs from Muñoz Camargo's stance. For the chronicler of Tetzcoco, the Chichimeca constituted a nation even before they became a sedentary culture. In his attempts to fashion from ethnic memory a cultural ideal we might call Chichimecayotl, he projects nationhood on to the early Chichimeca, who initially did not make their homes in cities, but who ultimately founded Tetzcoco. Also included in this grouping were the late-arriving Acolhuaque, who would eventually fuse with the Chichimeca (*OH,* 2:17). Consequently, the "Chichimecatl Nation" is a cultural model, vertical with its remote origins embodied in Xolotl and the dynasty he engendered and horizontal by the Chichimeca and the Acolhuaque's mutual appropriation of each other's culture. Stated clearly, both vertical and horizontal forces sculpted the nation.

Chichimeca and Acolhuaque were each categorized as a nation. After fusing with each other, the new entity is still called "nation," adopting the designation of the former, probably as an accolade to the foundational Chichimecatl lord Xolotl, from whom Alva Ixtlilxóchitl claimed direct descendance.[112] This idea of lesser nations merging to become larger ones coincided with the pre-Cortesian altepetl that allowed for smaller altepeme to work in tandem to compose larger ones (see *NAC,* 14). There could also be a cabecera-influenced case: when Alva Ixtlilxóchitl refers to the tlatoani of Quihuztlan, whose pueblo presiding over others still constituted one nation (*OH,* 2:204). These distinct towns may well have been altepeme. Whether operating from the vantage point of the altepetl or from that of the Spanish cabecera-sujeto imperative, the cultural ingredient was manifest when describing each political entity. When two or more altepeme came together, obviously, the singular culture of each was integrated into the new composite entity.

The ideal of Chichimecayotl, however, was a contested category. Further discussion sheds additional light on Alva Ixtlilxóchitl's concept of the nation. The customary usage of Chichimeca can be found in Muñoz Camargo. For him, simply stated, this term renders the expression "savage men" (hombres salvajes) (*HT,* 87). This traditional interpretation signifies heritage of dogs, animals that run in packs and are nomadic, as the Chichimeca were. Siméon's dictionary substantiates this meaning.[113] It lists the root of the proper name to be *chichi,* having four denotations: dog, to nurse (as with milk), to sew or darn, and from *chichitl,* to salivate. Alva Ixtlilxóchitl takes exception to such definitions. For him phonic similarities have obscured the noun's true substance, which denotes eagles (*OH,* 2:15). By virtue of the obvious ornithological connection to the Tenochtitlan foundation myth, in which Huitzilopochtli's prediction of the eagle perched on a nopal and feeding on a serpent is fulfilled for the Mexica, this proper name invokes an advantageous linguistic position. This descendent of Tetzcocan rulers is able to configure a glorious narrative for the Chichimeca, a group associated with the celebrated Xolotl and his legacy. Alva Ixtlilxóchitl *feels* a historical connection with the Chichimeca, and that creates a sentiment of "ethnic chosenness" (as explained above). In addition, the notion of a "nación chichimeca" goes beyond the vertical link to origins, because Xolotl's descendants form a horizontal relationship with the Acolhuaque. Finally, besides these two ethnic elements, a third primary cultural ingredient is in play. That ingredient is Toltecayotl.

The Chichimeca came to occupy Tolteca lands after the fall of Topiltzin, somewhere after the year of *macuili tepatl.*[114] Because they lived with the Tolteca, they were able to horizontally appropriate their culture. Alva Ixtlilxóchitl lauds the culture of the Tolteca in cities such as Tollan, Cholula, and Tolantzinco (*OH,* 2:10, 13, 34). Across the board, as would the Mexica later, the Acolhuaque-Chichimeca proudly assimilated the learning of the Tolteca, whom they came to accept as a mother culture. Once they had accepted the Tolteca in this intimate way, they could then extract the ideal of Toltecayotl vertically to weave into the fabric of their culture. Ultimately, their learned culture flowered in the sublime Nezahualcoyotl and his son Nezahualpilli. Alva Ixtlilxóchitl describes the Chichimeca's eventual acceptance of the Tolteca: "[The King] Techotlalatzin had so much love for the Toltecatl nation that he not only consented to their living among Chichimeca, but also made it easy for them to make public sacrifices to their idols and to dedicate their temples, such as had not been permitted by his father Quinatzin." (Era tan grande el amor que [el rey] Techotlalatzin tenía a la nación tulteca, que no tan solamente les consintió vivir y poblar entre los chichimecas, sino que también les dio facultad para hacer sacrificios públicos a sus ídolos y dedicar los templos, lo que no había consentido ni admitido su padre Quinatzin) (*OH,* 2:35). The idea here is that the Chichimeca openly began to embrace the victims of the Toltecatl diaspora. After allowing them to practice their faith, the Tetzcocans started to adopt it. As they adopted it, which, as seen above, implies the adoration of Quetzalcoatl, they also merged the ideal of Chichimecayotl with the ideal of Toltecayotl. The horizontal appropriation of spiritual Toltecayotl indicated a desire to bond with a greatness that existed, but that had come before, and it endeavored to deepen spiritual connections with an earlier tradition, a kind of vertical cultural journeying only possible after crossing a horizontal bridge.

Again a word of caution: this is not a binary process. The process was multilayered and complex. Alva Ixtlilxóchitl's deeply layered concept of the Chichimecatl nationality achieves its influence from the sway the Tolteca held over Xolotl's descendants, realized by the vertical enhancement of their millenary cosmology, its rites, and its spirituality. By accepting Topiltzin's followers into their community and sharing physical space with them, the Chichimeca could then directly mine their sacred history, gaining the necessary spiritual authority to back up the new temporal power they acquired from melding horizontally with the Acolhua. Moreover, as a concomitant process, demonstrating the vigor of horizontal osmosis, the Chichimeca commandeered the appellation Acolhua, from which ultimately their kingdom derived its name, Acolhuacan.

The locale that branched out with increasing social contact defined identity. The previous vertical Chichimeca, the posterior vertical Tolteca, and the horizontal Acolhuaque links became defining features for the now influential Chichimecatl nation. Yet there were additional threads of culture. Along the same lines, Tetzcoco would derive its identity from its horizontal relationship to the Triple Alliance's supreme capital, Tenochtitlan. This fact can be demonstrated from Alva Ixtlilxóchitl himself. His complicated bloodlines are an example of how the tlatoque of the two altepeme had become kin related. Rulers of both were his ancestors.

The process by which Xolotl's Chichimeca merged first with the Acolhuaque, then with the Tolteca, and later with the Mexica is significant for postcontact history. These links established a pattern by which smaller etnias mushroomed by merging with adjacent ones. The verticality of Toltecness was different from the font originating with Xolotl and his descendants, because horizontality with the Tolteca needed to be established before Quetzalcoatl could be assimilated. This second vertical font, the one we call Toltecness, was able to blend with the first one, which we call Chichimecness, after it had horizontally blended into the framework of coeval cultural sharing between Chichimeca, Acolhuaque, and eventually, Mexica. To summarize: two vertical fonts of culture and three horizontal planes of culture all interacted with each other either as active forces or as the recuperation of echoes from the past.

The stage was set for the coming of a sixth vector, still another population, the Spanish.[115] In this context, the tlatoani Ixtlilxochitl II's initial greeting of Cortés before his arrival in Tenochtitlan, his acceptance of Christianity, and his alliance with the Spaniards initiates an even wider circle of horizontal appropriation. If weaker chiefdoms, or polities, could have been conquered by Chichimeca and maintain nation status, the Chichimeca themselves could come under transatlantic domination and still preserve their national status, at least for a while.

NOVO-HISPANOS AND POST-INDIOS IN THE NOVOALTEPETL KNOWN AS NEW SPAIN

Hispanidad, or Hispanicness, was a growing trend on the multicultural Iberian Peninsula populated by Romans, Celts, Goths, Almoravids, and Almohads and inhabited during the fifteenth and sixteenth centuries by Basques, Catalonians, Castilians, Galicians, Mudejars, Moriscos, and others. Hispanicness encapsulated the achievements of the Hispanic people in language, literature, and other cultural accoutrements such as city planning, religion, and especially the Reconquest of Spain from the Muslim caliphates and emirates. All of these ingredients—Catholicism, the Roman heritage, military achievement, the normalization of the vulgar tongue, and a growing body of literature—fortified a growing pride in Hispanic identity and what we are calling Hispanidad.

The standards of Hispanidad and Toltecayotl share important similarities. We have just finished with the latter, disseminated by wise men and artisans to immigrants such as the Mexica and the Chichimeca, and we now delve into the former, disseminated by humanists to Europeans and the people they were to conquer. The former found its most symbolic expression in Nebrija's *Gramática de la lengua castellana* (1492) and *Reglas de la ortografía castellana* (1517), which supposed the expansion of the territories increasingly known as "Spain." Along these lines falls Bernardo Aldrete's *Del origen y principio de la lengua castellana o romance que oi se usa en España* (1606). Mignolo dedicates a great deal of time to these early apologists of the Spanish language in the context of colonialism, so there is no need to go over them again here.[116] What is of concern at this juncture is the relationship between religion, legislation, language, and even clothing that constitutes the banner of Hispanidad compelled to unfurl itself across the globe. Assuredly, Spaniards saw themselves as the inheritors of the Romans. Hispanidad, then, paralleled Toltecayotl, whereas the Nahua saw themselves as the inheritors of the Tolteca. Where Spaniards imitated Romans, Chichimeca and Mexica imitated Tolteca. Mignolo, upon studying comparatively the idea of Toltequidad, immediately comes to the conclusion that "in the Latin West the equivalent concept would be *civilization*" implying Roman citizenship in particular and, in general, a community of citizens.[117] Just as *civitas* comes from Latin, the language of "civilization," Toltecayotl comes from Nahuatl, considered the most sophisticated language. Just as in Europe all learned men learned Latin, in the Nahua world, they learned Nahuatl. Because of the similarities between the templates for Hispanidad and Toltecayotl, from the 1520s on, indigenous peoples of the upper classes could easily "catch on" and learn oral and written Spanish to participate in Hispanicness.

Mexicatl and Spanish societies were both deeply religious and imperial. Both had rigidly hierarchical social constitutions. These similarities, however, were not apparent to Spaniards who saw Mexica as heathens and barbarians. Mignolo points out that the Catholic missionaries and the chroniclers never realized that Toltecayotl held an affinity with Hispanicness.[118] Gibson explains why. From his analysis on Nahua-Spanish relations in New Spain, he concludes the Spanish held indigenous modes of life to be exotic and not desirable, and they actually "exaggerated their own Spanish styles, as if to deny their provincial situation." They resisted adopting Nahua clothing or architecture styles. They filled in Tenochtitlan's canals to introduce "vehicular traffic and mule trains," leaving the "Indians to paddle the canoes." They even "ignored chinampa agricultural methods until the eighteenth century" (*AZ*, 8).[119] Lockhart adds to our understanding. He observes that Spaniards did not fathom the intricacies of the Nahua altepetl framework (*NAC*, 20). They saw instead a cabecera-sujeto relationship between cities and outlying areas. The dual-heritage authors coming on the heels of the Spanish authors adapted this same terminology, obscuring the pulsating reality of Nahua political life that continued to thrive under the Hispanic mantle.

Yet in a broad sense, Mexica and Spanish truly held a great deal in common with respect to the nation and the distinctiveness that informs it, so much so that Octavio Paz concludes in his *Laberinto de la soledad* (1950; *Labyrinth of Solitude*, 1961) that the Mexican fondness of ceremony, formulae, and order comes from its double heritage, Spanish and indigenous.[120] More concretely, Mexica and Castilians both came from a multiethnic, heterogeneous milieu and defined themselves as exceptional in opposition to that heterogeneous milieu. The former contrasted themselves with the Otomi, the Chichimeca, the Tlaxcalteca, and an assortment of other groups; the latter with Basques, Catalonians, Galicians, and Moors, among others. Díaz del Castillo became aware of this cultural heterogeneity common to both the Spanish and to the Nahua. He takes note that in the diverse kingdoms of the Spanish monarch, there exists "much diversity among peoples" (mucha diversidad de gentes) (*HV*, 244a). When Moctezuma inquired about the tension between Pánfilo de Narváez and Cortés, Spaniards told the Mexicatl sovereign that Narváez was from Vizcaya, a province whose people could be compared to the Otomi (see map 3). They explained that Basques were different from Castilians in the same way Otomi were different from Mexica. According to Díaz del Castillo, the Basques and the Otomi both spoke a "reserved language" (*HV*, 244a). Thus we have commonalities in hierarchical language relationships and in deep-seated religion, fondness for ceremony, order and formulae, the concept of exceptionality within heterogeneity, and a strong cultural and religious ideal (Hispanidad and Toltecayotl).

In the decades after Spanish annexation, indigenous groups were preoccupied with space and frequently petitioned the Crown for land rights and for cabecera status, which would allow for the collection of tribute (*AZ*, 32–57, 194–219). The accumulation of land had constituted a salient aspect of Mexicatl expansion at least since the heyday of Itzcoatl.[121] However, with the adoption of the notion of the cabecera-sujeto relationship, the structure of the altepetl weakened. Nevertheless, both had to do with land. As previously mentioned, the possession of territory is, for Smith, a principal distinguishing factor between being solely an etnia and constituting a nation.[122] To that national characteristic in a ranked society, among other attributes, we must add tribute extraction. Often, levy collection was the responsibility of the local tlatoque who, after taking their cut, would pass on the required percentage to the authorities. Accordingly, Nahua tribute extraction norms and Spanish tax collection requirements become fixed in one process. The combination of land parameters, etnia, and the remnants of the Triple Alliance state apparatus imply the survival of important elements of the altepetl framework into the sixteenth century and beyond, despite the petitions for cabecera status. The altepetl survived as it blended into what were called parcialidades, and became an aspect of Novo-Hispanic norms that we can playfully describe as a *novoaltepetl.*

What else can we say about the novoaltepetl? After the institution of the viceroyalty and the setting in motion of the colonial gears of absorption, the importance of the vertical Nahua past would slowly go underground while horizontal cultural contact flowed out further across altepetl frontiers. This was neither a thoughtful process nor a tranquil one. This post-invasion trend arose directly from the social cataclysm that came with the defeat of Mexicatl sovereignty. It is helpful to read the letters of Hernán Cortés back to back with the *Brevísima relación de la destrucción de las Indias* of Bartolomé de las Casas (1474–1566) to get to an idea of the back-and-forth nature of the cataclysm. Aside from the obvious divergence between their respective ideologies, one can feel two opposite forces emanating from their texts: *poblar* and *despoblar*, that is, populating and depopulating. Cortés begins this process and Las Casas responds to it. Cortés's invasion of Mexico is a classic case of colonialism given form by "white settlers." Richard Gott describes the attributes of this variety of colonialism:

> The characteristics of the white settler states of the European empires are generally familiar. The settlers sought to expropriate the land, and to evict or exterminate the existing population; they sought where possible to exploit the surviving indigenous labour force to work on the land; they sought to secure for themselves a European standard of living, to justify or make sense of their global migration; and they treated the indigenous peoples with extreme prejudice, drafting laws to ensure that those who survived the wars of extermination remained largely without rights, as second or third class citizens.[123]

The mechanics of the colonial processes Gott outlines here are described in the colonial chronicles with these two verbs, "poblar" and "despoblar." This idea of "poblar" utterly disregards the people who already resided in a particular space; they, accordingly, would need to be killed, displaced, or re-cultured. This colonial tactic was accepted hook, line, and sinker by scholars who subsequently studied European colonialism. Consider the attitude revealed by the famous Harvard historian Bernard Bailyn (b. 1922) in the title of one of his books, *The Peopling of British North America* (1986).[124] This title, written just over thirty years ago, suggests that there were no people in North America when the British reached these shores. Of course, the Spanish were already in North America, but before any of the Europeans arrived, Amerindians were there—and they were "people."[125] These kinds of biases need to be overcome to appreciate more accurately those earlier times. This brings us back to sixteenth-century issues.

In his "Fourth Letter," Cortés glorifies his strategy of "populating," that is, settling specific areas with Spaniards. Two examples of this practice are the encampments at Espíritu Santo and Segura de la Frontera. In the former's location, Cortés indicates, "a village was founded and populated" (se pobló y fundó una villa). In the case of the latter, Cortés specifically commands his men "to look for a convenient place in that province and populate it" (en aquella provincia buscase un sitio conveniente y poblase en él). Another is the site of Tenochtitlan. After its destruction, the conquistador's plan was to repopulate it with Spaniards. Doing so would make it "the most noble and populous city that exists in the populated world" (la más noble y populosa ciudad que hay en lo poblado del mundo) (*CDR*, 176a–177a, 197b). It is often overlooked that before its annexation to Spain, Tenochtitlan was bigger and grander than many European capital cities. Clendinnen puts this into perspective. When Spaniards arrived, Tenochtitlan boasted a population of some two hundred thousand people, dwarfing Seville, the largest city in Spain, which had a population of only sixty to seventy thousand people in 1500.[126]

There are ample examples of the obsession (for this is what it was) with populating. Why was "populating" such a burning issue? Cortés himself admits the alternative would have been to allow for the baser behaviors of the conquistadors, destroying these lands to get their riches and then simply leaving them (*CDR*, 205b). One of the main thrusts of the war of acquisition, then, was to populate the newly encountered lands with Europeans, distracting them from the gold-lust and concomitantly swelling the territorial perimeter of the national axis. Such a policy also demonstrates the innate link between nationality and land: simply by populating Anahuac with ethnic Spaniards, the territory became Spanish.

That is one side of the story. Las Casas offers an inverse and concomitant version of those events. In the wake of the advancing Spanish troops, countless indigenous towns were left depopulated. This is a principal theme in the trenchant *Brevísima relación,* even though its author employed the literary device of hyperbole in the representation of the exact numbers of population decline. Hyperbole or not, population decline was a verifiable phenomenon that befell many communities throughout the emerging Spanish Empire. Massimo Livi-Bacci, basing his conclusions on tribute roles and other sources, observes that the population of central Mexico plummeted "from 2.7 million people in 1568 to 1.4 million in 1595."[127] These later dates take into account neither the number of people who died in the Conquest wars themselves nor the people who died of diseases, such as small pox, that preceded the Spanish infiltration (described by Sahagún's informants). Referring to Pánuco, Ipilcingo, Tututepeque (or Cutupeque), and Colima, Las Casas informs the reader that there was "depopulating" of those areas (*TR*, I, 75–77). This process was not absolute, for there were invariably survivors left to fend for themselves. As could be expected, they were uprooted either by force or through their own will to survive. They then had to be resettled in other locations and would have to accommodate to those local variants of culture.

These two great trends, poblar and despoblar, eventuated an immediate condition of disorder and confusion that tended to break down the barriers between the different altepeme. Indeed, from the chaos, social order collapsed from both the European and Nahua perspectives. However, we should not conclude here that the poblar and despoblar trends resulted solely from the Conquest. As is well known, great migrations characterized the annals of the Nahua past. The pilgrimage of the Mexica from Aztlan to Tenochtitlan is, perhaps, the best known. Muñoz Camargo recovers an oral tradition that "remembers" the epic movements of the Chichimeca who went from place to place, populating: "Armies disappeared so that they could go and populate the lands that were found unoccupied" (se desaparecieron los ejércitos para ir a poblar las tierras que se hallasen desocupadas). Muñoz Camargo offers historical precision when he mentions Toquetzaltecuhtli, Iyohuallatomac, and Quetzalxiuhtli, who went off "to populate the province of Quauhquechollan and a big town in Cohuatepec" (a poblar la provincia de Quauhquechollan y asentaron un poblazón en Cohuatepec) (*HT*, 99–101). Munoz Camargo's narrative is interesting because it reveals these kinds of social movements that foreshadowed the advent of the Spanish.

In postcontact situations, any sort of interethnic intercourse was possible, regardless of policies to keep Nahua and Spaniards apart. Human migration was common before the coming of the Europeans and it continued after their arrival. Only now, the goal was the extraction of wealth, not the fostering of great civilizations. Migrations became more widespread, took on new traits, and deeply affected all people. In two examples, Mexica participated in de Soto's *entrada* into La Florida and Mayans were sent to Peru as slaves. Let us not forget that Spaniards were also involved with deep and often permanent migrations, leaving family behind on the Peninsula and forging new relationships in the Western Hemisphere, even if these were hegemonic. The chaos and social turmoil became so egregious, as Mignolo remarks, that the crown became aware of "pueblos de españoles that have become depopulated" (pueblos de españoles que han sido despoblado).[128] From this disarray, a new order would emerge that would affect all peoples: Nahua, Spaniards, and their slaves.

Besides colonial resettling of Nahua groups to allow for their physical separation as pueblos de indios, a rigid system of racial cleavage was established. Robert Jackson writes, "The Spanish government legislated a caste system . . . that established legal distinctions between people of predominately European ancestry and of indigenous or African ancestry."[129] While this legal yet theoretical racial zoning was imposed from "above," substantial contact occurred "below": between disparate indigenous ethnic groups, and between all these groups and the Spanish, along with their slaves of African origin. Such mixing was a fact of life. That Imperial legislation became necessary to create *castas* as a mixed-race pigeonhole demonstrates the existence of interethnic mingling.

The influx of Iberian settlers into indigenous areas such as Tlaxcala would only speed up the disintegration of local cultural and legal traditions. Muñoz Camargo's biography, as discussed, illustrates this point. Even though there was a royal cédula issued in 1589 that prohibited his entrance in Tlaxcala, he continued to thrive there economically after that date. For Gibson, incursions of whites into Nahua areas negatively affected their "prosperity and prestige," a process that would only accelerate. Land, an inherent element of nationness, was a critical feature of Iberian dominance over Nahua areas (*TSC*, 79–84, 87–88). As these processes flowed their courses, a new larger, but hybrid, altepetl called "New Spain" slowly began to emerge.

In Tlaxcala the four altepeme gradually gave way in the face of early modern Hispanization. While some of the altepetl's features may have continued to operate, government standards became increasingly Hispanicized (*TSC*, 122). First the tlatoani became a governor, then a generation later, an "elected" cabildo, consisting of ordinary alcaldes (judges) and regidores (councilmen), was put in place along with a governorship that sometimes rotated among members of the tlatoani's family.[130] In this context, numerous Nahua municipal leaders went to petition the viceroy in Mexico City, and some even went to Spain to present their grievances personally to the king. Generally, these had to do with governance or with property. Muñoz Camargo himself went on one of these delegations, accompanying a group of Tlaxcalan noblemen. The hybridization processes could only lead to a broader awareness of Tlaxcala as a cog in a larger system of human relations. This increasing Hispanization came with a decline of population, indigenous values, and patriotism. Gibson describes a process that evolved from "local chauvinism" and a "campaign for privilege" to an emotional state more like nostalgia than pride (*TSC*, 194). Despite those losses, enough local self-esteem survived to inflame the passion of chronicler Muñoz Camargo, who had grown up in Mexico City, and Alva Ixtlilxóchitl, who still took pride in his millenary Chichimecatl origins.

Relevant to this is the parallel tale of *mestizaje*. As Spaniards were committing generalized abuses against the people they came across, they also were taking multiple bed partners to satisfy their sexual urges. The polygynous reality of the early colony rapidly created a new composite social class. Eventually, as the Catalonian anthropologist Claudio Esteva-Fabregat reminds us, "mestizo interests came to outweigh demographically and socially even those of the European Criollos, until finally displacing them from the rule and sentiment of Ibero-America."[131] That dislodgment would take centuries, and still has not run its course. During the first one hundred years of the Spanish presence, Spanish relationships with the altepeme remained much starker.

Any discussion of early modern Hispanization and the inverse power of local chauvinism must begin in the context of a colonialism that exacerbated local cultural and political fissures. Such was the case with the Totonaca and Tlaxcalteca, who saw themselves as distinct from the Mexica and aligned themselves with Cortés's forces in the war. Ethnic divisions exacerbated by colonialist incursions are not solely a Mexican story. What happened there is no different from what happened in Peru only ten years later. In Peru, Huancas, or Wankakuna, sided with Pizarro against Inkakuna. Colonialism is a divide-and-conquer process that leaves residual wounds, as suggested by the Chicana author Gloria Anzaldúa in her highly regarded 1987 hybrid book, *Borderlands/La Frontera*. The realities Anzaldúa observed in the 1980s find their origins in previous centuries.

Writing several decades after the emergence of the Spanish Empire in Mesoamerica, Muñoz Camargo is covered in residue from which he cannot seem to escape. When he comments on Cortés's advance through Cholula, he conceptualizes a Tlaxcalan-Spanish national confederation from the moment of the initial Spanish advances. This was actually not the case, as the Tlaxcalteca initially resisted in three fierce battles. Unhinging his story line from history, he describes the advance of "*our* armies" (nuestros ejércitos) on Tenochtitlan (*HT*, 214; my emphasis).[132] Evoking the Tlaxcalan-Spanish alliance implies that pre-Cortesian national differences between Tlaxcalteca and Mexica still had not subsided during Muñoz's lifetime. As a result of historical hatred, it was easier for the Tlaxcalteca to fuse horizontally with Spaniards than with Mexica. Muñoz himself may have self-identified with the Spanish as a way of compensating for Tlaxcala's inferior status vis-à-vis the pre-Cortesian economic omnipotence of the Triple Alliance. Certainly, part of his self-identification with things Hispanic had to do with accommodation to power, the coloniality of power, in order to get ahead.[133]

Tlaxcala offers one perspective, Tetzcoco offers another, and Tenochtitlan, still another, yet all nonetheless eventually ended up as part of New Spain. If precontact Tetzcoco was an altepetl, and if the three altepeme that constituted the Triple Alliance could together be a larger altepetl (theoretically, there should be a fourth to allow for rotating tlatoque), there is no reason why this expanded altepetl could not also view itself as a sub-altepetl of a still larger altepetl. Alva Ixtlilxóchitl refers to this entity in the *Historia de la nación chichimeca* as "our Spanish nation" (nuestra nación española) (*OH*, 2:236). The people who make up "our Spanish nation" are none other than "our Spaniards" (nuestros españoles), people he refers to and identifies with, in the exact moment they find themselves in the process of "marrying into" (emparentar con) Tlaxcalan lineages, linking two peoples inexorably (*OH*, 2:214). He uses the expression "Nuestros españoles" twice more in the *Historia chichimeca*, further establishing his relationship to Spaniards in his narrative with the possessive "nuestros" (*OH*, 2:235, 250).[134] This novo-Hispanic situation is interesting because some scholars still feel compelled to racialize these chroniclers.

For example, some authorities feel the need to think of Alva Ixtlilxóchitl as a castizo or mestizo, colonial categories assigned to him. However, as the court documents published by Edmundo O'Gorman show, not only did he self-identify as a Spaniard, his neighbors also considered him and his family Spanish (*OH*, 2:361). Being Spanish would imply citizenship, where belonging to one of the colonial racial categories would tend to deny that privilege. It is not surprising that he would self-identify with the Spanish in his life while simultaneously concerning himself with his gentilidad, or lineage, that emanated from Tetzcoco. This would be something like a Spaniard who felt proud of his local roots, be they Basque, Catalonian, or Galician. The only difference here is that Alva Ixtlilxóchitl's roots were neither on the Iberian

Peninsula nor were they "colonized" in the distant past. Adorno describes him as defined by a "complex and compromised subject position."[135] We can build on Adorno, O'Gorman, and our research here and describe Alva Ixtlilxóchitl as a competent writer, a deep-thinking historiographer who was not afraid of being an agent for himself historiographically, legally, and culturally in a hybrid manner. His Tetzcoco-centric view of history does not disparage things Hispanic and is written in a Spanish-language prose that allures the reader.

Looking back, he inserts the destruction of Tollan into a universal framework, as is broadly explored by Salvador Velazco in a thought-provoking book, *Visiones de Anáhuac.* First, Alva Ixtlilxóchitl gives the Nahuatl date, *ce tecpatl,* then the Christian one, 956. He then assigns a European context for the Toltecatl catastrophe: the reigns of the Castilian king, don García, and of the Roman Pontiff, Johannes XII (*OH,* 2:13). He presents the histories of Anahuac and Europe in a framework of cohesion and symmetry. The idea of parity would be consistent with the precontact understanding of altepetl organized into equal (albeit rotating) power foci. The altepetl notion served as a mechanism to put colonized and colonizer on a footing where they were commensurate with each other. This achievement is not simply a case of superimposing Spanishness on indigenous standards or of Spaniards pilfering Nahua traditions, although there was plenty of both. On top of that, as mentioned, there existed an Iberian historical convention within which the term "nation" also allowed for diverse local ethnic agents.

Another interesting literary example from a little later in the colonial interval is instructive in these matters. Sor Juana Inés de la Cruz produced the bulk of her output while a cloistered nun in a Hieronymite convent. Despite her double alterity resulting from being a woman and a nun, Sor Juana had both literary and social links with the world that existed outside the convent walls. She participated in the customs of the day and was aware of differences in the human condition that separated groups of peoples from each other. As a case in point, as Leonard notes, numerous convents of her day enjoyed "the services of personal slaves."[136] Sor Juana herself had a slave, a person of color also named Juana, a gift from her mother.[137] She eventually sold the slave, who was just four years her junior, yet she may subsequently have had others.[138] In her *villancicos,* or carols, the nun composer demonstrates familiarity with blacks who sing in churches as she represents, through her spelling, their manner of pronunciation (*OC,* 211, 217, 223, 240, etc.). As Marie-Cecile

Benassy-Berling points out, the black motif in Sor Juana is nothing new in literary tradition, apparent also in Lope de Vega and Góngora.[139] For Mabel Moraña, these diverse villancicos are a testimony to her multiculturalism.[140] Sor Juana's awareness of African contributions to culture in New Spain was not limited to darker-skinned people singing in churches; she also introduces African themes, such as the serpent.[141] Given her use of irony and baroque ornament, however, it is hard to determine her exact perception of the black slaves. Her late-seventeenth-century awareness of diversity would be limited more to an awareness of people of color, perhaps even a sympathy for them, than it would approximate twenty-first-century conceptions that seek out cultural, social, and political agency with respect to people of color. The same can be said for her conception of the Nahua.

On the one hand, Sor Juana celebrates the imposition of Christianity in Mexico; on the other, she seems to doubt its superiority over Nahua religion. As Moraña puts it, she found the inequities forced on the Americas by the European invasion to be distasteful.[142] Benassy-Berling and Carmela Zanelli both claim Sor Juana was more progressive in her views than Francisco de Vitoria, although she did not achieve the radicalism of Las Casas.[143] As part of her understanding of what we might call "diversity," the Hieronymites embraced Spanish views, even in the face of what Moraña describes as a growing Criolla consciousness.[144] We see in the 1692 "Dedication" to the second edition of her works that she boasts being of the "Vizcaya branch" (rama de Vizcaya). Unambiguously, her vertical lineage hails from "our Basque nation" (nuestra nación vascongada) (*OC*, 811a). It is with this vertical authority she creates characters who sing in Euskara in some of her villancicos. Not unexpectedly, Sor Juana is capable of horizontally expanding her national concept of Basques to include "our Spaniards" (nuestros españoles). In her *Repuesta a sor Filotea*, Sor Juana comments on "our republic" (nuestra república) (*OC*, 254b, 810a, 841b), making manifest that she visualized New Spain as politically one with the mother country.

As Sor Juana's "our Basque nation" reveals, the origins of the Spanish nation, like Mesoamerican nations, are not held in common. They hark back to an array of etnias, people from Andalucía, the Basque Country, Castile, Catalonia, al Andalus, and Galicia.[145] This is not so unlike Alva Ixtlilxóchitl's embrace of Tetzcoco while identifying as a Spaniard. His Tetzcoco is Sor Juana's Basque Country. Viewed from still another angle, the Spanish nation also stems from Christian, Jewish, and Moorish roots, or more precisely, from the first's dogged determination to stomp out the other two. Since the Islamic and Jewish religions were expelled or repressed in the peninsula after 1492, the nation is derived in part from forging a unity based on the suppression of those non-Christian religions. While such Catholic cohesiveness was achieved by force, it did imply linking disparate etnias at least on the surface. In this sense, "Spain" prefigured "revolutionary" notions of the nation that burst onto the world scene in 1776 and 1789. Under the political, religious, and cultural authority of Castile, this Spanish trend toward interethnic amalgamation would mushroom after 1492. Homogenizing practices developed in the homeland could then be exported as part of the imperial enterprise. This was possible because Hispanidad was not unlike Toltecayotl as a unified ideal, which nevertheless did not suppress microideals such as the Chichimecatl and the Tlaxcaltecatl ones, in the case of Muñoz Camargo and Alva Ixtlilxóchitl, and the Basque one, in the case of Sor Juana. Whatever their ethnic origins, all three authors considered themselves Spanish despite their interest in diverse communities residing in New Spain. The folding of Nahua customs into Iberian conventions allowed for the creation of a transoceanic nation as empire.

Iberian norms of cultural homogenization could not have been implemented in the Indies to the degree they were if similar ideals had not preexisted there. Unfortunately, intercultural practices in pre-Cortesian Mexico are hard to document. This is true for three reasons. The Spanish made a concerted effort to destroy local records, the Nahua hid elements of their culture as a form of resistance, and there was a process of cultural hybridization, as Jongsoo Lee makes clear in *The Allure of Nezahualcoyotl*. The essential upshot of these three parallel restricting operations is that a wealth of Nahua culture was lost or recast. Among what did survive, however, were Hispanicized Nahuatl documents that revealed the persistence of the altepetl as well as Spanish-language chronicles that codified the memory of ethnic migration, mixing, and expansion. The idea of the nation, linked to horizontal and vertical cultural practices, may have likewise referred to the altepetl layout. We have corroborated from Alva Ixtlilxóchitl's perspective that this notion can be applied to any group, whether the not-so-barbarous Chichimeca, the highly regarded Tolteca, the "barbarous" people of Guaniganiga, or the larger multiethnic Spanish Empire. Muñoz Camargo holds a kindred view, with the exception that he rejects the "barbarians" as nations. Such gaps between the two chroniclers' ideologies may have been brought about by Muñoz's greater Hispanicness, possibly resulting from his being born on the heels of the Spanish invasion, making his principles and notions much closer to Cortés and Díaz del Castillo. They could also reveal his need to show allegiance to things Spanish, his very person, a mestizo, being suspect. As might be expected, however, both authors had to operate within the fettered parameters allowed to colonial subjects. The pride they exhibited for their respective "national" cultures, even in the face of their mutual differences, reveals that they pushed Hispanic norms of discourse to the limit.

The colonial concept of the nation cohered to the sharing of certain ideals—religious, linguistic, cultural, and political—and a common expanding or infiltrating ethnicity (depending on one's perspective), a process that was not necessarily biological permuting as allowed by horizontal determinants from other cultures. Different etnias could likewise associate, through their common vertical connections, with an earlier mother culture. With Muñoz Camargo's multiple roots in Tenochtitlan, Tlaxcala, and Spain, the conflictive identity marbling he must have felt from them, and his need not to offend Church and State, his brand of Hispanicness becomes a paradigm for grasping the complexity of the subaltern condition. The same is true for Alva Ixtlilxóchitl. Since Tetzcoco's culture had blended with the peninsular, he was free to look back vertically, not only to Xolotl, Nezahualcoyotl, and Cuitlahuac, but also to the Pope and to a long line of Castilian kings. His antecedents were fertile, with roots in Acolhuacan and Tenochtitlan as well as Rome and Castile. He was able to feel proud of three cultural ideals—Chichimecness, Toltecness, and Hispanicness—which he attempted to explain and synthesize. Such a textured heritage allowed him to operate in an increasingly multicultural colonial world. Yet the pluralities of the kind Muñoz and Ixtlilxóchitl epitomized were precisely, as Paz reports, what the colonial government denied and suppressed.[146] Their works remained unpublished and kept largely under wraps until after political Independence in the nineteenth century. We could say, therefore, that Muñoz Camargo and Alva Ixtlilxóchitl were not mere chroniclers of deeds and events. Each in his own way was a time- and culture-traveling novo-Hispanic *tlamatini,* a sage and historian of his people, neither Nahua nor Spanish, a suppressed and unlabeled micronational resident in a new macro-altepetl known as New Spain, able to articulate his thought and project it to the future where it could resurface for all to read again in the bright light of decolonial inquiry.

FURTHER THOUGHTS ON ETHNICITY, PROTONATIONS, AND TRANSATLANTIC DIFFUSION

The wider European experience, exemplified by Spain's successful seizure of the Canary Islands in 1402, provided a model for cultivating an expanding "proto-nationalism," employed vigorously after 1492.[147] The Spanish belief in their divine mission generally kept them from perceiving that the people they encountered might have their own nations, even though, as we have verified in this chapter, their successors intermittently used that term to describe them, especially in later years. Columbus was not able to discern the five kingdoms of Bohío, known to us as Hispaniola.[148] Amerigo Vespucci, in a letter drafted seventeen years before Cortés was to reach Anahuac, shockingly professed that the locals were "of few words, or none" (de poca habla o ninguna). Furthermore, he asserted, they did not have laws, faith, or private property. Finally, he stated, they do not have "borders between kingdoms and provinces: they do not have a king" (límites de reinos, y de provincias: no tienen rey).[149] When applied to the Caribbean, Vespucci's way of construing the absence of territorial demarcations may have had a grain of truth to it, but only a grain. Later when Cortés arrived in Anahuac, he quickly recognized kingdoms based on ethnicity—just like in Europe. Even though Cortés recognized these divisions that for him were political, he did not respect them. They would only become a tool in his mission of conquest.

In *Nations and Nationalism,* Hobsbawm makes a distinction between two varieties of "proto-nationalism." The first forges links that go beyond the "actual spaces" where people reside, such as Christian links to a "wider world." The second, government sponsored, imposes norms of "generalization, extension and popularization."[150] In a Mexico that was slowly becoming early modern, these "proto-nationalisms" can be understood as Christianization and Hispanization. Benedict Anderson, whom Hobsbawm had read, maintains the conquistadors did not attempt "'Hispanization,'" and that they limited their endeavors to the "conversion of heathens and savages."[151] Walter Mignolo comments on Cortés's written request to Charles V for "spiritual assistance to Christianize the indigenous people, not necessarily to Hispanize them." Mignolo reminds us that the Franciscans became fluent in Nahuatl for their work, not forcing the Nahua to learn Spanish.[152] Yet those trailblazing attempts at conversion, including the tactic of destroying of idols, for instance, were destabilizing. In effect, they were laying the groundwork so later measures directed toward Hispanization could take root, even if those processes are still underway today.[153]

Mignolo suggests that the initial lack of interest in teaching Spanish could have resulted from King Charles's upbringing in Flanders. Later monarchs would fall into unbridled Spanishness, and there would be an increasing trend, as Mignolo notes, toward suppressing what he calls "nonalphabetic writing systems," documented in legislation promulgated by the crown from the sixteenth through eighteenth centuries.[154] This despite the mendicant orders who wrote their Nahuatl dictionaries, and despite the resilience of the Nahuatl tongue.[155]

There is a certain irony in the Spanish resistance to nonalphabetic semiotic systems. Alphabetic texts were not a common thing even among Spaniards, because the majority was illiterate. Others, the *letrados*, had to work their way through a veritable labyrinth of controls. Even a cursory look at the perfunctory materials that set in motion Joseph de Acosta's *Historia natural y moral de las Indias* (1590; *Natural and Moral History of the Indies*, 1880) reveal a tightly knit power structure that included the crown, the Inquisition, and the Jesuit Order (Acosta was a Jesuit); it even included stroking the ego of the King's daughter. From those documents, we can ascertain that the King had to give "license," that such a license was valid only for ten years, and that the work had to be signed by a notary, submitted to the Jesuit order for review by "learned and serious people" (personas doctas y graves), and then submitted to the Inquisition, who referred it to the chair of scripture at the University of Salamanca, where none other than the noted poet and Augustinian Friar Luis de León certified its Catholicism.[156] This double authority of Church and State served to stamp out heresy and ensure that the King's 1577 edict banning discussion of native customs was respected. In summary, it limited what kinds of books could be available.

If the imposition of Spanish as regal policy was a slow process, the importation of Spaniards, their governmental structures, and their business enterprises (the *poblar* tendency) had the immediate effect of fostering Hispanicness. With *encomenderos* (with their "grants of Indians"), *mercaderes* (with their wares to vend), and *corregidores* (with governmental authority) came the Spanish language, utilized in official governmental discourse and practical business conversations. Eventually, it would win out over Nahuatl and other indigenous tongues and would be used to evangelize the old-line *pipiltin*, who would adopt it along with the commercial class. It became the lingua franca of the New World from La Florida to Las Filipinas, from New Spain to the Antarctic.

During the colonial age, despite varied rates of success, Christianization and Hispanization formed two poles of a triangular ideology of conquest (the third was the quest for economic gain, not commented on overtly but the basis for untold actions of plunder). At the exact moment of the invasion of the lands now known as Mexico, the Spanish began to consider Mesoamerica part of Spain. The act of establishing the first Spanish city on the Mexican coast was symbolic. Without hesitation, Cortés founded Vera Cruz, based on religion (the name means "True Cross") and ethnicity (some Spaniards were left behind). Through dual efforts to Christianize and to Hispanize, the Crown could launch a two-pronged endeavor geared toward building a larger ethos, fostering both tendencies Hobsbawm describes. In the wake of the transatlantic invasion, economic forces (the encomienda, the mines, tribute gathering, and eventually the hacienda) reinforced both Christianization and Hispanization.

Diverse textual evidence suggests Spaniards brought with them an attitude that supposed the superiority of Hispanic culture. Esteva-Fabregat explains, "The dominant political position of Spanish culture over that of Indians and Africans assumed that the Spanish had a greater capacity to transform the way of living of the other racial groups than the others had to transform the Spanish."[157] This attitude, for example, caused Spaniards not to respect Mexicatl (or K'iche' or Inka) architecture. It allowed them to destroy buildings and to knock the tops off structures to build Spanish-style edifices on their foundations—all of this without any ethical or aesthetical quandaries.

While the Crown and certain religious sectors such as the mendicants did not see eye to eye on what we might call the colonialist connivance between Christianization and Hispanization, both were processes that worked hand in hand toward cultural and social fusion.[158] Despite their temporal interest, there can be no doubt the sovereigns were authentically concerned with bringing the word of Christ to the newly found lands. Even so, it would not have been lost on them that Christianization could give people with dissimilar origins a common social denominator. From the temporal perspective, the Crown similarly imposed norms of "generalization" in language, colonial government, book regulation, and the like that would work to erase social and ethnic differences between people. Gibson describes Hispanization as "a secular counterpart" to Christianization (*AZ*, 192). In countless institutional efforts, Christianization and Hispanization merged. This is the case with endeavors to promote monogamy and with the religious and cultural aspects of the system of encomienda that allowed grants of "Indians" to Spaniards who had had a hand in the Conquest.

Mercantilist impulses can function as a third class of "proto-nationalism," one that Hobsbawm does not mention. They can also work outside the nation, or even against the nation, as I discuss in chapter 5. The arrival of a money economy to Mexico directs another societal shift. Money, it goes without saying, makes people behave differently than they would if they were merely bartering or getting involved with collective projects. Capitalization, then, along with Christianization and Hispanization, worked to spur a new hybrid culture. This third tendency, unlike with Christianization and Hispanization, was advanced at first not by the Crown or the Papacy, but by individuals with private acquisition ambition. These entrepreneurs set up a system that allowed for the Nahua nation's insertion into the transatlantic system (see chapter 5).

The encomienda fit into this category. Although the monarchs slowly tried to curb the encomenderos' supremacy, they allowed the encomenderos broad economic authority in the first decades after the military campaigns. A private enterprise, the encomienda represented a temporary decentralization of the State, constituting a localized form of remunerative power. In fact, as Kauffmann notes, "the *encomienda* in New Spain and Peru was organized on the basis of what the Spanish knew of preconquest customs and traditions, some of which had parallels in Spain itself." The overriding feature of this system was "tribute extraction." For maximum results, Kauffmann continues, Spaniards were aware of local custom and they based such extraction on local amounts and kinds.[159] Gibson explains that during the years after the arrival of Cortés, the tax system benefitted "a privileged Spanish class." This ephemeral perquisite gradually reverted to the "Spanish political state" (*AZ*, 194, 219). The economic pressures exerted by capitalization fragmented indigenous communities enough so that, in their weakened condition, they could later be subordinated to other mercantile projects sponsored by the Crown, and in due time, to the rise of the hacienda system, which was largely independent of the State.

Economic interests were a homogenizing form of protonationalism because they often provoked geographic upheaval. Mining is a representative case. Robert Haskett finds the following from his research: "The regular movement of laborers to and from the mines increased contact among Indians from many regions and between a variety of non-Indians."[160] Such social contact would induce transculturation among befallen peoples. Transculturation is a complex give and take described by the Cuban anthropologist Ortiz in *Contrapunteo cubano* (1940; *Cuban Counterpoint,* 1995) to help understand human relationships in the development of cultures. He explains:

> We understand that the word *transculturation* best expresses the different phases of the transitive process from one culture to another. This is because it does not consist only of acquiring a distinct culture, which, strictly speaking, is what the Anglo-American word *acculturation* means, but also implies the loss or uprooting of a preceding culture, suggesting a partial deculturation. This back and forth signifies the subsequent creation of new cultural phenomena that could be labeled as neoculturation.
>
> Entendemos que el vocablo *transculturación* expresa mejor las diferentes fases del proceso transitivo de una cultura a otra, porque éste no consiste solamente en adquirir una distinta cultura, que es lo que en rigor indica la voz angloamericana *acculturation,* sino que el proceso implica también necesariamente la pérdida o desarraigo de una cultura precedente, lo que pudiera decirse una parcial desculturación, y además significa la consiguiente creación de nuevos fenómenos culturales que pudieran denominarse de neoculturación.[161]

It should not be considered arbitrary to use a theory developed in the Caribbean by a Cuban anthropologist during the twentieth century to describe the processes that gave form to sixteenth-century Mexico, as intercultural mixing is almost a universal phenomenon. Transculturation transpired in the areas that Spaniards overran. As discussed, we are not talking about two cultural processes, but abundant pre-Columbian cultures, the intricate relationships between them, and three proto-nationalistic transatlantic forces at work. Christianization, Hispanization, and capitalization worked in unison toward establishing by force a new unified national sentiment, "nuestros ejércitos," as Muñoz Camargo writes, "nuestra nación española," as Alva Ixtlilxóchitl puts it, and "nuestros españoles," the category Sor Juana claims as her own.

The political, religious, and economic blender, however, was not instantaneous, nor was it absolute. Twenty years after the overthrow of Mexico, Father Toribio de Motolinía, interpreting Easter of 1540, could still recognize people from twelve "nations" with twelve "different languages" (*HI,* 92a).

Theologically speaking, the existence of distinctive languages is not outside what is possible, even despite the commonly held adherence to monogenesis as a theory of the origins of humanity during that time. One of Motolinía's intellectual adversaries, Father Bartolomé de las Casas, surmised this to be a consequence of some type of human diaspora, where human lineage—after the second age on the earth (Noah's deluge)—extended all over the globe, forming races and nations. For Las Casas, the very act of these "lineages and family relationships" (linajes y parentelas), spreading out over distant lands, "was the cause of many and diverse great nations" (fue causa de grandes y muchas y diversas naciones).[162] Motolinía called these diverse pre-Hispanic nations provinces, which frequently were at war with one another (*HI,* 110b). As a proponent of Christianization, he saw a wealth of good in their coming together under the Christian God, achieving peace and justice.

Nevertheless, Motolinía's view of the Hispanic State was not so unitary. He favored the two traditional types of pueblos, one for Spaniards and another for the indigenous. The creation of separate pueblos was ideally meant to keep the corrupt Peninsular Spaniards away from the "innocent," so-called *tabla rasa*, of the original inhabitants. The Nahua were to be accepted into the nation of God, but not necessarily into the nation of Spaniards. Still, theory inevitably differs from practice. The two kinds of pueblos could not be kept apart. The Nahua, Mörner and Gibson report, "complained to the king about the abuses they were suffering from their Spanish, mestizo, mulatto, Negro and 'ladinized' Indian neighbors."[163] Even though there were custom-made laws for each of these groups, total separation was impossible. When Hispanicness, Christianity, and economic might operated hand in glove, the by-product was the ever-expanding mosaic of Hispanized mestizos, zambos, and indigenous peoples. All retained some element of their ancestors' pre-Hispanic past.

CHAPTER THREE

FROM PEOPLE TO NATION

THE ANDES

Readers who turn to chronicles sometimes get caught up in the deeds of the conquistadors, which can seem heroic or dastardly. When the Colombian author William Ospina read the chronicles to cull material for his 2005 historical novel *Ursúa*, he came to the latter conclusion. He writes,

> Nothing else occurred to the adventurers except to rob and enslave, and when they were hungry, they never thought of planting a spike of wheat, nor of taking up a hoe, but instead burdening peaceful populations that cultivated cotton and corn, and pinning their salvation on the perdition of others.
>
> A los aventureros no se les ocurría otra cosa que robar y esclavizar, y cuando tenían hambre no pensaban jamás en sembrar una espiga ni en empuñar un arado, sino en cargar sobre las poblaciones pacíficas que cultivaron algodón y maíz, y cifrar su salvación en la perdición de los otros.[1]

Ospina's depiction of the conquistadors is probably verisimilar to those historical realities and thus of human interest, but their behavior is not the only kind of information that readers can cull from the chronicles. These documents also contain a kind of anthropology *avant la lettre* that is useful for getting at the roots or origins of the nation.

Before discussing structures of power that organize the nation, a measure of the "civilization" of pre-Hispanic people needs to be established. The word "civilization" is fraught with contradictions, diverse meanings, and even racism and cultural elitism. Since the sixteenth century it has been juxtaposed to barbarism, frequently to justify conquest of the so-called "barbarians." The measure of "civilization" employed in *The Formation of Latin American Nations* is not the polemical notion from the sixteenth century (or from the twenty-first century for that matter), applied unevenly between groups from the east and west sides of the Atlantic. No, this is a different notion that comes from a decolonial methodology that reverses asymmetrical relationships to restore historical subjects' humanity. If we take the sixteenth-century concept of civilization as understood by jurists in Spain and by the conquistadors on the ground and universalize their Eurocentric understanding of it, it can be used to assess New World peoples in a way that reveals multifold New World peoples had many of the same attributes the Spanish had held as exceptional to themselves. Spaniards could not see these attributes because they wore colonialist blinders that were Christian, Hispanic, Renaissance, and Roman-oriented. From the decolonial vantage point of the twentieth-first century, the blinders can be less opaque, especially when looking back at the sixteenth.[2] By filtering colonialism out of the lens, a more objective gauge of social organization as applicable to peoples of the sixteenth century becomes visible. How does this work? Based on Spaniards' own criteria, their biases and suppositions about themselves, we can invert the "civilization" barometer and apply those very same suppositions to Amerindians. When the chauvinism opens up to become inclusive, it ceases to be chauvinism and a step is taken toward decoloniality. Executed thusly, this methodology serves as a template to see how Amerindians measure up to the Spanish and thereby decolonize our thought about them.[3]

This is a tricky proposition if we are engaged in evaluating the great urban centers of late antiquity. As Gustavo Verdesio calls to our attention, researchers and perhaps readers worldwide appear to be obsessed with the three great peoples: the Maya, the Mexica, and the Inkakuna (again, plural for Inka). He suggests that the West is fascinated with this trio because they actually resembled the European nations that were conquering them (as suggested in the previous chapter). He explains: "They had, in some cases, a complex bureaucracy, a regular army, institutions of education, commerce, complex systems of belief, and other forms of social organization." Consequently, if we were to compile a detailed list of "civilization" indicators and compare European and Amerindian societies, the concomitance between them would be generally on a par, except of course with regard to the American lack of horses, steel, the wheel, gunpowder, and, in some cases, a writing script.[4] There are also differences with conceptions of nation, divinity, honesty, and economics. Yet the similarities, as we have seen, are intriguing. Verdesio is concerned that admiration of the three greats has to do with "a certain evolutionist prejudice that pervades contemporary standards and values." He reminds us that "it is an undeniable fact that those complex societies coexisted with others who chose to organize themselves in different ways." The societies he has in mind are those that "organized themselves in myriad ways that include the subsistence patterns of hunter-gatherers, foragers, and early agriculturalists" and who resided in "the Amazon basin, the plains of present-day Argentina, Uruguay, Venezuela, and Brazil, and the cold regions of Argentinean Patagonia and southern Chile."[5] While those cultures may appear to some scholars as "less developed," they had the positive side in that they were less hierarchical and probably more democratic than the big three. These are all good points worthy of discussion, and nomadic peoples can offer a point of comparison to urban peoples.

Perhaps to Verdesio's dismay (if he were to read this), this book is primarily about Qheswa and Nahuatl-speaking peoples, and to a lesser degree, the K'iche', a people with Mayan origins. It has sections on the Moche in Peru and the polities of Colombia. Regarding the big three, it was precisely in Mexicatl and Inka areas (the Mayan areas are problematic in this regard because there was no unified state apparatus) that accelerated top-to-bottom ethnic blending occurred. This chapter focuses specifically on the Andes. We begin with the regions that encompass modern Colombia and the people who lived there, which in a way address Verdesio's misgivings. The Colombian chiefdoms, or polities, will serve as a reference point for the upcoming discussion on the Inkakuna, but they are also interesting and hold value in and of themselves. I survey the Colombian polities not because they are more important than the Patagonia or other places of interest to Verdesio, but because they provide interesting cultural information about the Andean cultural complex.

One of the problems with drawing on early modern sources in South America is that the chroniclers who laid them out were not anthropologists (obviously) and were not disinterested in their material (also obviously). To begin with, they were educated in the humanist tradition or lived and worked with people who had been educated in that tradition, and they automatically saw events in the New World as subordinated to Rome and to what they saw as Charles V's successor state to Rome.[6] They became perhaps unwitting agents of empire interested in extending Spanish political power and, to a somewhat lesser degree, Roman Catholicism. In some cases, humanist traditions came into play and reconfigured subjective knowledge, as when the Imperial Treasurer Agustín de Zárate asserted that the first Peruvians (this category included most South Americans at that time) migrated from Plato's Atlantis ("Declaracion," *HDC* [1]). As Teodoro Hampe Martínez points out, Atlantis was not the only reference to the Greco-Roman World in Zárate's writing.[7] The Christian mentality, consciously or not, worked to wipe out indigenous knowledge, offering instead Judeo-Christian-centered paradigms for apprehending the new realities being encountered. This is no surprise because the chronicler—any chronicler—as Kathleen Ross cautions, suffers from "the characteristic disdain afforded to non-Christian rituals by Spanish observers."[8] Let us explore this a bit. Tellingly, the Spanish chronicler Pedro Cieza de León explains in his *Crónica del Perú* that he wants to deal with "the rites and customs that the natural Indians formerly had" (los ritos y costumbres que tenían antiguamente los indios naturales) (*CP-1^era^*, fol. 4, pp. 9–10). With the word "formerly," in one stroke, he sets up a human palimpsest. As the reader may already know, a palimpsest is an animal-skin parchment that was used before the introduction of paper in Europe, sometime after the capture of Toledo from the Moors in 1085. Medieval monks erased Greek or Roman texts on these parchments and then inscribed on them Christian theological tracts. The human palimpsest becomes a useful metaphor for apprehending Spanish attitudes and practices. It is more precise than the notion of the sometimes-used *tabla rasa* to explain what the Spanish were doing to Amerindians' minds, because indigenous peoples did not have blank minds. In the same mode as monks and their palimpsests, Spaniards intended to erase from indigenous minds their cultures, their narratives, and their customs, to then re-record in those biological storage spaces a Spanish culture, and primarily the Christian religion.

We should not admit defeat and say no information can be gleaned from the chronicles simply because they are tainted with palimpsest-like coloniality. To accept as much would imply that there remains only a colonial situation for which "there is no remedy," as the early-seventeenth-century roaming scholar-author Felipe Guaman Poma de Ayala lamented. To accede to that defeating attitude in our time is to accept the heritage of the colonial situation in scholarship as insurmountable. In order to overcome the colonialities of our time, we must go back to the colonial period and separate oil from water. We must get over what Lucy Maddox, commenting on peoples overrun by the English (but her commentary is equally applicable to peoples overrun by the Spanish), refers to as "the almost universally shared assumption that there were only two options for the Indians: to become civilized, or to become extinct."[9] This can be done by trying to dissect a series of complex relationships formed between the original Americans, who were there before the Spanish; Spaniards themselves; Africans, the descendants of these groups; and the new hybrid groups that formed, including their descendants. While absolute extinction never occurred, postcontact peoples were subject to the ebb and flow of the depopulating of their polities and the populating of those and other diverse areas with Spaniards. The result of these ebbs and flows is complex, but there are numerous clues to apprehending those realities.

CIEZA DE LEÓN AND EARLY ANTHROPOLOGICAL KNOWLEDGE OF THE POLITIES OF COLOMBIA

To begin, it is important to consider the geographic area under discussion. The chronicler Cieza de León viewed the inhabitants of the territories that comprise present-day Colombia as part of what he understood as "Peru," and there was no entity "Colombia" in the sense we know it today. As Peter Wade reminds us, this country did not exist in the beginning of colonial times or the end of indigenous times, the period of our analysis. He offers some historical depth when he explains, "What now roughly corresponds to Panama, Colombia and Ecuador were combined in 1718 into the Viceroyalty of Santa Fe de Bogotá, composed of the Audiencias of Quito and Santa Fe de Bogotá."[10] The viceroyalty transmuted into the Gran Colombia at independence, and then in 1830, into the Republic of New Granada, which includes present-day Venezuela and Ecuador. Eventually, the Republic became the Granadine Confederation and then the United Colombian States in 1863, which included only modern Colombia and Panama—this last country split off from the mother trunk by the United States in 1903 to build the cross-isthmian canal. Within the borders of post-1903 Colombia resided the polities upon which this section focuses.

Pedro Cieza de León is pivotal to this inquiry because he is an early Spanish chronicler who wrote about this region. His opus magnum is the five-part *Crónica del Perú*, but again, early modern Peru encompassed all of South America, including Colombia, on which he wrote engaging chapters. This makes sense, as he lived there and observed many things before he went to Peru proper (as we understand that configuration today) in 1546, in the middle of the Spanish civil wars between the Pizarro and Almagro factions.[11] Cieza de León's observations on the region known today as Colombia are useful, primary even, because the first indigenous documents do not come until decades later. In *Beyond the Lettered City*, Rappaport and Cummins discuss one Muisca hereditary chief from the town of Turmeque. Don Diego de Torres began producing "innumerable legal petitions in impeccable Castilian Spanish," but only after the year 1574. In a petition to the king in 1584, part of "a legal battle to regain the rights to his chiefdom," he included two anonymous European-style maps, one of which situated Turmeque in the Province of Tunja, and the other of Santa Fe de Bogotá. Rappaport and Cummins emphasize that these two maps "are the earliest cartographic documents we know for Colombia."[12] There is also an epic poem, the first part published in 1588, which offers a literary version of the Muisca of Tunja. Because that heroic work, the *Elegías de varones ilustres de Indias* by Juan de Castellanos, was published at the late date of 1588, and because, like Don Diego de Torres's petitions, it centers on Tunja, it falls outside the geographical space and time frame of what this book is able to consider. Cieza, therefore, represents an early view of things indigenous in the western region, however imperfect that Hispanic perspective was. His observations are the closest we have to the point when late antiquity is transformed into the early modern period. His writing provides a first look at indigenous people at the exact moment they were exposed to Spaniards.

Pedro Cieza de León's *Crónica del Perú* archived a kind of early anthropological knowledge as much as could be attainable during the 1550s.[13] Despite organizing reflections on this region with this chronicle written by a Spaniard, it is possible to shed some of the heritage of colonialism by first gaining insight into early Colombia through Colombia itself, not through Spain.

We begin with the polities, or *señoríos,* which were there before people from Spain knew they were there. This is clear from Cieza's writing, even though this genre of prose can be tarnished by the biases we know Spanish authors held as they came into contact with people who were from outside their realm of knowledge.[14] Reading texts such as Cieza's with our bias-detection radar turned on helps us filter out bias from the inchoate anthropological material. Archeology, comparative textual analysis, and even DNA testing are helpful tools for getting beyond those biases. If one consults these diverse genres of information fonts and filters in tandem, it is possible to see a more complete depiction of those precontact peoples at the very moment they become transatlantic colonial subjects than one can viewing solely through a narrowly focused Spanish lens.

When Cieza de León documented his long journey down the Andean mountain range, he compiled a large quantity of ethnographic material providing insight into peoples' power structures, gender relations, bellicose activities, territory, language, urbanism, place names, trade circuits, and other traits of nationality. However terrible Cieza's colleagues' forays though those lands were for the people encountered there, his chronicle provides material of considerable value. The nineteenth-century historian Sir Clements Markham notes a kind of paradox regarding Cieza de León and the *Crónica del Perú.* On the one hand, as a boy-soldier, "he was bred amidst scenes of cruelty, pillage, and wanton destruction" that was the reality of Spanish in South America.[15] On the other, "his sympathy with the conquered people, and generous appreciation of their many good qualities, give a special charm to his narrative."[16] This sympathy on his part, and reading between the lines on our part, represent two logical mechanisms to filter out long-term irradiating coloniality, while filling in the blank spaces with information derived from the other kinds of sources. In this fashion, we approach an understanding of these precontact peoples at the moment they were coming under Spanish domination.

Positioning this region before Peru in this chapter makes logical sense for two reasons. One has to do with Cieza de León, who began his *Chronicle of Peru* in the North Andes and worked his way down the cordilleras toward diverse Qheswa- and Aymara- speaking districts. The other has to do with notions of urbanity and of empire. Polities of the varieties found in Colombia were exactly the types of ethno-political-social structures the Inkakuna in the Central Andes were folding into a vast far-flung empire whose ideal was linguistic, political, and economic integration. The northern polities therefore make an interesting starting point to reveal several forms of Andean social organization. Cieza initiates his southern descent in present-day Panama and then continues into the cordilleras of Colombia.

In these lands a patchwork of polities predominated. Mary Helms comments on an "organization diversity of the numerous rank societies distributed through its three Andean Cordilleras and the Caribbean lowlands."[17] These societies, "densely settled" in Wade's opinion,[18] sometimes called *señoríos* by the chroniclers, are often rendered as chiefdoms in English, a word with damaging connotations. "Polity" is a more connotatively neutral expression. Cieza was capable of calling certain of these polities "nations." Because of our post-Enlightenment training, we might feel compelled to describe these entities as "ethnic nations." Nevertheless, nación, without the modifier, is the designation Cieza applied. When writing of those in Antioquia and beyond, Cieza de León refers to the existence of "these nations stretching all the way to the Pacific on the west coast road" (Estiéndose estas naciones hasta la mar del Sur la vía del poniente) (*CP-1^{era}*, fol. 24 [xiii] [*sic*] p. 54). Here we are interested primarily in Antioquia and Cauca, looking at those social structures that must have existed right before the Spaniards' arrival and how they combined with those transatlantic ones imposed as they arrived. What are the features of these polities that make them culturally germane to understanding the formation of Latin American nations?

These polities were ranked societies, suggesting they might have eventually been incorporated into Tawantinsuyo if the Inkakuna had resolved their civil war. The polities did, in fact, assimilate well with the Spanish (as discussed in the next chapter with regards to DNA testing). Additionally, studying the peoples of Popayán and other regions of Colombia, is indeed a response to Verdesio's above-cited call to look at people outside the realm of the two large empires. Societies have the right to organize themselves as they see fit, and it is precisely the heterogeneous varieties of statecraft that make for interesting research.

For the same reason, the range of urban nations in the Andes, from Urabá to Qosqo (also spelled Cusco and Cuzco), is interesting.[19] Here we can certainly see Cieza de León's way of organizing people, a system that perceived the nature of ranked societies, the essence of a particular form of nation, not apposite to all native peoples, but organic to the Andes. Cieza's travels purvey a wealth of information good for posterity's awareness. Curiously though, his anthropological data does not precisely coincide with the great archeological groups whose artwork can be found in museums and on the Internet. He makes no references to Muisca or Nariño in his work.[20] However, we do find other cultures of interest.

Polities: Houses, Farms, Temples, and Leaders

This section focuses on how diverse polities in Antioquia, Cauca, and the Valley of Cauca resided in urban settings where people lived in homes, cultivated agriculture, produced materials for trade, worshiped divinities, and were governed by paramount leaders. This segment will close with the depopulation of these kinds of hubs, uneven as it was, followed by the populating of them again with Spaniards. We begin at the extreme north of South America. The geographical name Urabá comes from a cacique, a Taino or Arawak word meaning "hereditary lord," who governed a town on the east coast of the gulf that still carries his name.[21] Despite his governing a sovereign entity, the Spanish tried to establish themselves in Urabá's dominions. As early as 1504, Juan de la Cosa had "plundered ninety-one hundred pesos worth of gold kettledrums, earrings, pendants, and small idols from tribes living on the eastern shore."[22] Around 1511, two competing companies under the direction of Alonso de Ojeda and Diego de Nicuesa respectively, in Duncan's words, "attempted to found rival settlements on opposites [*sic*] sides of the gulf of Urabá."[23] Accordingly, various social forces were at play in the lands of Urabá.

It is difficult to ascertain with certainty to which etnia Cieza de León refers in his discussion of this area. It is probably safe to say it was not Chibcha, and it may have been a branch of Carib. For this reason, it is not surprising that reports of cannibalism surfaced, as that group was notorious among the Spanish for that cultural trait.[24] We can also conjecture that the Spanish incursions of 1504, 1511, and others had some kind of demographic and perhaps cultural impact on Urabá's residents. Furthermore, disease epidemics almost always preceded the Spanish, causing terrible health issues and even death among the people residing there. This likely happened in Urabá, making it especially difficult to determine who the people were in that location. We do know that Cieza was referring to the site or sites of successive Spanish towns called San Sebastian, the first, probably just a fort, established by Ojeda.[25]

Cieza de León reports that the people in the 1540s lived in small "branch-made shelters" (ramadas) made from "posts" (estantes) in which they slept on hammocks (*CP-1^era^*, fol. 19 [ix], p. 43). He declares, "They have no house of worship." Yet he may have settled on such a position in order to build up to his logical conclusion, "They have no house of worship," because "they certainly talk to the devil" (no tienen casa ni templo de adoración alguna), (ciertamente hablan con el diablo) (*CP-1^{era}*, fol. 20v, p. 46). If they did indeed talk to the devil, they would need to be converted to Christianity. Conversion implied submission. Yet there was an even more consequential concern here for the Iberians. Cieza doubtlessly looked for such a temple as an indicator of empire, as was the case for the central Mexico and as would be for the central Andes. As MacCormack concludes from her reading of this chronicler, "Cieza grasped clearly the importance of Inca religion as a religion of empire."[26] An empire implied a larger, yet more efficient conquest because the emperor controlled more people, and with what the Spanish learned in Mexico about strategies of deceit, it was easy to knock off an imperial lord and take over his control network. The presence or absence of temples might have been one mode to distinguish polities from empires. From an archaeological vantage point, the absence of a temple, if indeed none existed, may imply a non-ranked society or perhaps a lesser-ranked one since there was certainly a leader, Urabá.

The charge of devil worship often became an excuse for conquest. However, this is quite likely a type of religious distortion, as evidently Cieza did not speak the local language to follow exactly what local people were discussing and/or venerating; it is impossible to understand the nuances of a culture if one cannot understand their language. An ideological slant of this type is expected, due to the Spanish impetus and (ultimately quite successful) penchant for bringing Catholicism to these lands and its judgment of them as measured against Catholic values. Nevertheless, it seems safe to conclude with some certainty from Cieza's observations that there was no temple structure. For why would this chronicler bear false witness about its absence? If he were predisposed to argue there was devil-worship, a temple building would certainly fortify his argument, as it certainly did for those Spaniards justifying conquest in Central Mexico and as it would later, in the case of an idol in the *Templo Pintado* of Pachakamaq outside the present-day city of Lima. Putting the religious debate aside here, as there may have been enough ranking for a cacique to emerge from a group with few class divisions, we can deduce there may have been a level of urban planning, but perhaps not enough for a sacerdotal hierarchy. Other than that, the details of the society that resided in Urabá remains clouded by the mists of time.

Moving south along the Sierra Abibe we come to the larger polity of Guaca, possibly a large multiethnic jurisdiction, which Jorge Orlando Melo suggests was perhaps in the throes of incipient statehood at the time of the Europeans' arrival.[27] We are referring to the current-day Antioquia Department in or near the contemporary capital city of Medellin. Melo is on the right track because Nutibara, sometimes called Atibara, ruled this Carib or Carib-like kingdom (initially limited to Guaca) that he was expanding. The Villamaríns note that Nutibara had "annexed the gold-rich Abibe area, appointed Quinuchú as its governor, and collected tribute from its people."[28] The ethnic composition of these peoples was again not likely Chibcha, more likely a subgroup of the Caribs, such as the Katio, the Embera Chamí, or related peoples.[29]

We know much more about this population than we do about the residents of Urabá. Cieza de León indicates that the peoples of Guaca eat from healthy stockpiles of fruit, fish, poultry, swine, and so on (muchos puercos, pescado, aues, y otras cosas que en aquellas tierras se crían) (*CP-1^era^*, fol. 23 [xiii], p. 52). Cieza shows himself to be the cultural comparatist when he notes that the agriculture of Guaca is more developed than on the coast: "Here, there are none of the weeds that can be found in Urabá" (Por aquí no hay de la mala hierba de Vraba). He hints at the cultivation of cotton and the commerce associated with it when he describes "a great quantity of cotton blankets, very painted" (gran cantidad de mantas de algodón muy pintadas) (*CP-1^era^*, fol. 22v, p. 50). Even a modicum of this kind of evidence suggests a ranked society involved in trade. There is good quality and diversity of agriculture. The stocks of fish and fruits also suggest sedentary living; the fish caught by migrant anglers are an indicator of trade with the coast, the fruit suggesting local groves or further indications of trade. Either way, both products suggest sedentary existence. Like the finely crafted gold jewelry (*CP-1^era^*, fol. 23 [xiii], p. 52), the *mantas,* or blankets, are a concrete sign of social standing and suggest women's participation in matrifocal civic activities beyond the home. We mentioned textiles in this regard with respect to Mexico, and this is also the case with these Andean societies.

Cieza de León's description of the blankets he encountered at Guaca as "painted" may have resulted from his associating them with the Nahua painted manuscripts; he also may have been referring to woven patterns in the fabric. Moreover, even if Cieza did not get so far as to understand these forms of expression, we know messages were imbedded in the designs, beginning with some kind of ethnic indicator much like flags, national animals, or birds in our time can be, except more intricate. It should not be so controversial to suggest the images and patterns woven into textiles are a form of text.

Ong underscores that alphabetic, interknitted, or oral texts all share a root meaning, which is to "weave," giving textile expression a special place in a discussion of texts.[30] These are the origins of semiotic expression in the Old World and in the New. In Qosqo, for example, we know that the textiles' semiotic planes of expression recorded the calendar. John Murra comments on these perishable calendars, so very unlike the Classic Mayan versions, etched into stone and thereby preserved for posterity.[31]

An obvious indicator of sedentary living among Nutibara's people is the presence of urban communities. In Guaca, Cieza de León finds "numerous large wooden thatched-roof dwellings" (muchas casas muy grandes de madera, la cobertura de vna paja larga) (*CP-1era*, fol. 22v, p. 51). The idea of "large" seems to set the Guacans apart from Urabás. Unlike on the coast, now there is some type of organized religion embodied in a "large temple or house" (vna grande casa o templo), even if, again, Cieza claims they it used to worship the devil (*CP-1era*, fol. 23 [xiii], 52). However, the historian admits that in this house or another, people get married (*CP-1era*, fol. 23v, 53), another usually religious enhancement to urban organization. This structured ritual system, along with a paramount leader, agricultural production, and trade, suggests sedentary living in an organized hierarchy with at least two tiers, perhaps three. Cieza does not consider Nutibaran religion on par with Catholicism; he could not in that time and place, with the cultural baggage he was carrying and the peer pressure he would have been up against. His ethnographic documentation does reveal, however, some type of organized religion embodied in the "large temple or house." That combined with cultural expression, agriculture, and trade suggests the qualities of nationness as understood during the sixteenth century.

Further south along the cordillera we come to the city of Cali, today the capital of the Valle del Cauca Department (not to be confused with the Cauca Department to the south), where some of the same kinds of traits can be observed. We return to fabrics, an important component of culture in the Americas. Cieza de León observes that the people of Cali "walk around naked generally, although, now in this time, they wear tee-shirts and ponchos made of cotton" (Andan desnudos generalmente, aunque ya en este tiempo los más traen camisetas y mantas de algodón) (*CP-1era*, fol. 44 [xxxiii], p. 97). The *camiseta,* a tee shirt or jersey, appears to have been a postconquest innovation, the manta, something like a poncho or serape, being the traditional garb worn by the inhabitants of these regions at the time of the Spanish invasion.

Whether manta or camiseta, the woven fabric indicates textile production. Helms explains that the elites were often "clad in exceptionally fine textiles."[32] Hence, the production of cloth suggests the possibility of ranked society.

The next area of interest is still further south. Scholar Henri Lehmann explains that upon the Spanish's arrival, the Popayán Valley, today in the Department of Cauca (not to be confused with the Department of the Valley of Cauca to the north) was densely populated with distinctive ethnic groups he calls "tribes."[33] The mid-sixteenth-century chronicler Zárate talks of "la prouincia de Popayan," (*HDC* [4]), a mere "province" from the Spanish perspective during Zárate and Cieza de León's time. Nevertheless, as Melo infers, there might have been a process of organizing various polities into some form of a state at the time the Spanish arrived.[34] Lehmann accepts this possibility and recounts the existence of some kind of limited confederation of the Moguex-Coconuco peoples, "who fought the advance of [the Conquistador] Balalcázar, and we may infer that there existed among them a relative subordination of tribal interests at that time."[35] Besides the Moguex and the Coconuco, Troyan lists the Piajo, the Nasa, the Guanaca, and the Payanense peoples as prominent groups in the region. This brings us to the inescapable conclusion that there were layers of ethnographic complexity. Troyan explains that these groups were configured with subgroups that also had their own names.[36] Beyond this, we cannot hypothesize what kind of ranking these peoples might have fostered if their trajectory had been left unchecked.

Cieza also talks of "esta prouincia de Popayán." Even though he associates it with "Perú," he notes that "the people and the disposition of the land is very different" (es muy diferente la gente, la disposición de la tierra) (*CP-1^{era}*, fol. 25 [xv], 57). It is worth mentioning that Cieza distinguishes the people who inhabit Tawantinsuyo from those that inhabit Popayán. Whereas the latter are "untamable and daring" (tan indómitos y porfiados), the former "serve well and are tamed because they have greater reasoning abilities" (siruen bien y son domables: porque tienen más razón) (*CP-1^{era}*, fol. 26 [xvi], 58). He arrives at this conclusion because of organizational differences between the two peoples and what those differences mean in terms of susceptibility for conquest. Subjects of an empire would generally be more reluctant to pursue a local strategy, the omnipresent fear of the emperor on the horizon. This might not be so within a polity where ranking is less stretched and folks might feel more openness to contribute ideas. Additionally, local-polity caciques would have greater flexibility to act then would a local lord subordinated to a state-level ruler. Cieza de León uses a word common in the Spanish lexicon of that time to connote the idea of localness (and other kinds of attributes that were condescending) in Popayán. The Payaneses, he writes, "have always been and still are *behetrías*" (han sido siempre y lo son behetrías) (*CP-1^{era}*, fol. 26 [xvi], 58). This word connotes much when talking about nationness. José Antonio Mazzotti explains that for Cieza de León, "behetría" implies "small populations without any political relationship between them, each state remaining under the control of a local boss" (pequeñas poblaciones sin vínculo político alguno entre sí, quedando cada población al mando de un jefe local).[37] Cieza suggests an ordering that was even less than a polity when he affirms, "They did not have lords among them that made them fear" (No vuo entre ellos señores que se hiziessen temer), which is to say, no cacique structure existed in Popayán (*CP,* fol. 25 [xv], p. 58). As Spaniards learned in Mexico, they could control empires by controlling the tlatoani. They confirmed this in the central Andes with the summary execution of Atawallpa in 1533. It is harder to control and manipulate a web of polities than a state with central vertical control. The Payaneses were people, as Villamarín and Villamarín point out, on which the Europeans could not depend for provisioning.[38] In other words, the inhabitants of Popayán organized themselves with a noncentralized dispersal of power—what the Spanish called "behetría"—that could not easily be manipulated. Even further to the south, Spaniards only had to murder the Inka ruler to throw Tawantinsuyo into chaos and "milk it dry," so to speak, through a kind of capillary action. However, even if the Payaneses did not have a cacique, they were sufficiently sedentary and organized that Covey proposes that if Inka state building had been left unchecked, Chibcha and Payanese peoples in the Cauca Valley would have eventually become incorporated.[39] This says something about the Payanese relationship to the qualities inherent to the nation as construed during the early, early modern period.

Also in the Department of Cauca lies the municipality of Coconuco, which even today has two indigenous groups, the municipality's namesake and the Puracé. Regarding the former, Cieza de León talks about two valleys descending from the Payanese mountain range. These valleys "in times past were densely populated, and now they still are with some Indians they call Coconucos, although not as much, and certainly not more than before" (en los tiempos passados fueron muy poblados y agora también lo son, aunque no tanto, ni con mucho, de vnos indios a quien llaman los Coconucos) (*CP-1^{era}*, fol. 47 [xxxvii], 104). Lehmann tells us the Coconuco language was spoken "along the Río Grande, between San Isidro and Paletará" with the Puracé volcano to the north, and "the upper Cauca River to the south."[40] In the eighteenth century, the Jesuit historian Juan de Velasco observed that both groups still spoke their "guttural" language.[41] Lehmann clarifies that the Coconuco language has been extinct since the nineteenth century, but does survive to name the flora and fauna as well as the geographical features of the land.[42] Perhaps some of the forces working to make the language extinct were human migrations. Joanne Rappaport explains: "During the seventeenth and eighteenth centuries, a substantial layer of *resguardo* residents spent time working on Spanish plantations surrounding Popayán, while in the nineteenth century, many were absent from their communities extracting quinine from the forests for the Colombian and international markets."[43] The study of such a complex trajectory through the centuries requires compiling and synthesizing the research of historians, sociologists, anthropologists, and literary theorists; here we are concerned primarily with the hairline fracture between precontact and postcontact nations. Another crucial question that perhaps cannot be answered completely also comes from Rappaport. She wonders about the kind of "historical interpretation" indigenous people "develop in their struggle to survive as an autonomous people."[44] This "historical interpretation," developed by the indigenous at the time of contact with Europeans and after, is difficult to ascertain with total certainty, and much remains to be accomplished. But some information established by the chroniclers sheds some light that can be brightened even more with social science, and in the next chapter with natural science (DNA testing).

Here, to the detriment of a truly authentic indigenous representation, it is logical to begin with the chroniclers, because they are the ones who set the standards for what has been discussed over the last five centuries. Again, we must read between the lines when we ask, what were the Coconucos like during the sixteenth century? Speaking generally about the towns subject to or surrounding Popayán, and perhaps referring to the Coconucos, Cieza clarifies:

> And the Indians of this land came upon a lot of gold that legally was seven karats and some more and some less. They also had fine gold, which served to make jewelry, but compared to [the quantity] of that [gold] of lower quality, it was rare. These people are very war-like and

such meat-eaters and Caribs, like those from the provinces of Arma, Pozo and Antioquia.

Y los indios desta tierra alcançauan mucho oro de baxa ley de a siete quilates: y alguno a más y otro menos. También posseyeron oro fino, de que hazían joyas: pero en comparación de lo baxo fue poco. Son muy guerreros y tan carniceros y caribes, como los de la prouincia de Arma, y Pozo, y Antiocha. (*CP-1^{era}*, fol. 48v, 106)

Cieza de León appreciates the metalworking qualities developed by the people whose descendants would become Colombians, a characteristic setting them apart from people in other regions of this hemisphere. Yet to the Spanish mind, being "war-like" and "meat-eaters" lowers them on the scale of what they viewed as civilization. Yet specifically referring to the Coconucos, he explains that they "do not incur in the abominable sin of eating human flesh" (no vsan el abominable peccado de comer la humana carne) (*CP-1^{era}*, fol. 49 [xxxix], 107). This would be a cultural differentiation between the Coconucos and the ethnic nations of the Caribs. Needless to say, we should consider this assertion only with trepidation. The Spanish called any polity they wanted to discredit Caribs, and because nothing was more abominable to them than cannibalism, the correction of cannibalism became a good excuse for imposing the encomienda system.

Depopulating and Populating: from Indigenous Nations to the Hispanic Nation

We know that some of these precontact features, structures, and practices survived into the early modern era. But some of them, such as the Coconuco language, did not. Others permuted after they were poured into the well of transculturation. From the beginning, Spaniards began forming their new society on the backs of the people who lived there. They were able to impose new subordinating structures of encomienda, slavery, and pueblos de indios or repurpose preexisting ones, such as the *coatequitl* and the *mita*. They were able to dominate the people they were conquering with relative ease because the people often came from ranked societies that enjoyed urban ways of living. Calero mentions Antioquia, Pasto, Popayán, Timaná, Cali, Cartago, Anserma, and Arma as early Spanish settlements.[45] Few trajectories of resistance and assimilation are easily traceable over the long haul; they tend to take on a zigzag pattern, with apparent fade-outs and surges. Old World diseases frequently preceded Spanish military deployments, which caused fade-outs. Spaniards repeatedly found depopulated towns in their paths, and the survivors often found it attractive to cohabitate with the Europeans. T. Lynn Smith explains, "The manner in which the Indians receded before the whites varied greatly from one part of what is now Colombia to another. Along the coastal plains in the north, in Antioquia, and in the Cauca Valley, the changes came about swiftly and violently, while along the heavily populated slopes of the eastern cordillera and far to the south in the upland portions of Nariño, the changes were slow and gradual."[46] Sánchez-Albornoz adds, "The native population shrank by more or less a quarter of its former size in the first three decades after the conquest," and worse yet, as Wade explains, "The Indian population suffered a particularly rapid and drastic decline: by 1778, they were less than 6 percent of the [Antioquia] province's inhabitants."[47] Wade underscores two of the many reasons for demographic collapse: "disease and conquest" and not adapting well to subservient labor.[48] It is important to add, however, that the indigenous population also waned because some of its descendants did not fall into the category "Indians" but instead were classified as "mestizos." Some perhaps simply switched cultural codes of their own volition and began to pass as mestizos.

Despite being Spanish and participating in the Spanish wars to "pacify" the southern hemisphere, Cieza de León, something like Las Casas, could see its negative population effects.[49] I discussed this depopulating phenomenon with respect to Cortés and Las Casas in chapter 2's section, "Alva Ixtlilxóchitl, Tetzcocan with the Best of Three Worlds." Referring to the Pearl Islands, Cieza de León explains: "They used to be populated by their natural inhabitants, but now there is not one. Those [Spanish] who are now its lords have blacks and Indians from Nicaragua and Cubagua who take care of their livestock" (Solían ser pobladas de naturales: mas en este tiempo ya no ay ninguno. Los que son señores de ellas, tienen negros y [*sic*] indios de Nicaragua, y Cubagua que les guardan los ganados) (*CP-1^{era}*, fol. 14 [iiii], p. 31).[50] There can be no doubt: the people who inhabited those Pearl Islands died either from Spanish treachery, from European diseases, or both, or they fled in the face of a Spanish incursion. But they left something behind—be it crops, textiles, or even a structure or two—which the Spanish were able to appropriate.

With respect to Antioquia, Cieza de León moves from the realm of early anthropology to architectural description upon suggesting a great urban population once existed there. He reaches this conclusion from his observations of the numerous structures, a testament to a now forgotten cultural horizon: "Formerly these valleys were greatly populated as we can see from their buildings and tombs, of which there are many to see." (Antiguamente auía gran poblado en estos valles, según nos lo dan a entender sus edificios y sepulturas que tiene muchas y muy de ver) (*CP-1*[era], fol. 24 [xiii] [*sic*], p. 54). What is lacking here is an awareness of when these urban sites may have been depopulated. Did that happen at the end of an earlier cultural horizon, or just before the march of the Spaniards? We cannot know solely from Cieza de León.

In a place called Corome, however, Cieza intimates an inverse relationship between the Spaniards' arrival and indigenous depopulation. An inverse relationship is formed between the indigenous and the Europeans: "The Spanish come in to conquer, and [the indigenous] have been greatly diminished" (y entrados los Españoles a conquistarlos, y, se han disminuydo [*sic*] en gran cantidad) (*CP-1*[era], fol. 26v, p. 59). Similarly, he observes the local inhabitants occasionally destroy their achievements rather than surrender them, such is the case with another city, probably Antioquia: "After the Spaniards entered this town, the Indians burnt it. They have never wanted to return and repopulate it again" (Entrados los Españoles en este pueblo, lo quemaron los Indios, y nunca han querido boluer más a poblarlo) (*CP-1*[era], fol. 26v, p. 60). This assertion conveys a reality in which indigenous people sometimes would commit cultural suicide rather than integrate into the new nation being formed right before their eyes. But the suicide is never completely achieved. In the same place, great migrations also occur. Every summer, the blacks the Spaniards imported and the remaining indigenous, who were already there, extract gold from the waters in ever increasing amounts (*CP-1*[era], fol. 27 [xvii], p. 60). Not all Spaniards were ethnocidal slayers, however. One, Luis Sánchez, a priest in Popayán, worked against these powerful antisocial trends by writing a *memorial* that was of pure Las Casian inspiration.[51] In summary, the Spanish advance was not only a push and pull with indigenous nations, but also with themselves, because there were always those who had their doubts.

Besides the human suffering it inflicted, the populating and depopulating of certain areas also impedes the task of looking back and describing these urbane societies anthropologically, because primary sources of information—people—have been extinguished. Even in twentieth-century scholarship, indigenous people are denied the humanity afforded to Spaniards.

Indeed in some rhetorical modes the indigenous, in the worst of cases, are extinguished almost exclusively, and in the best ones are downgraded to the status of "Indians," peoples without culture, urbanity, or polity. To offer one example, the distinguished historian Porras Barrenechea, upon discussing the Spanish incursions into the Urabá region, writes that San Sebastián was "the first city founded on the continent" (la primera ciudad que se fundó en el continente).[52] It would be accurate if he had said the "first Spanish city," but as discussed in this book, many cities were established in the American continents before the Spanish. It is as if modern-day historiography itself continues to erase those urban centers of late antiquity initially obscured by early modern annalists.

INKAKUNA, CHIMÚ, AND THEIR PRECURSORS AS DIVERSITY IN TIME AND SPACE

If we continue our descent along the mountain range, we come to the lands eventually known as Peru, the realm of the Inkakuna. However, since the first European contact with the Andes, knowledge of so many other peoples in the region besides Inkakuna has been generally ignored or suppressed. This was Verdesio's concern in the larger South American orbit, and it is certainly the case with the precursor Colombian people, just discussed, who have been eclipsed by the intense interest in the Inkakuna. The same is true of the Chimú, a master culture conquered by Inkakuna during the latter half of the fourteenth century (see map 6).

This is not only a geographical preference; it is also a preference unfolding along a complex succession of cultures on the South American continent. This suppression is a partial result of what Michael Moseley describes as "the Colonial legal policy of accepting the situation under Inca rule as the *terminus post quem*," an approach that "curtailed Spanish inquiry into pre-Inca conditions."[53] Contrary to this omnilinear and thus dubious construction of Andean identity that begins and ends with the Inkakuna, various verifiable cultural horizons preceded them. These were so frequently in flux it could be hard to say when one ceased to exist in time and when its successor took up the wand of authority. Such would be the problem if we wanted to discern at what point the Wari nation, or some remnant of the Wari nation, became the Inka nation, which is Covey's concern in his compelling *How the Incas Built Their Heartland.* He demonstrates how the Inkakuna rose from Wari ashes. We know this because the accoutrements of Inka culture,

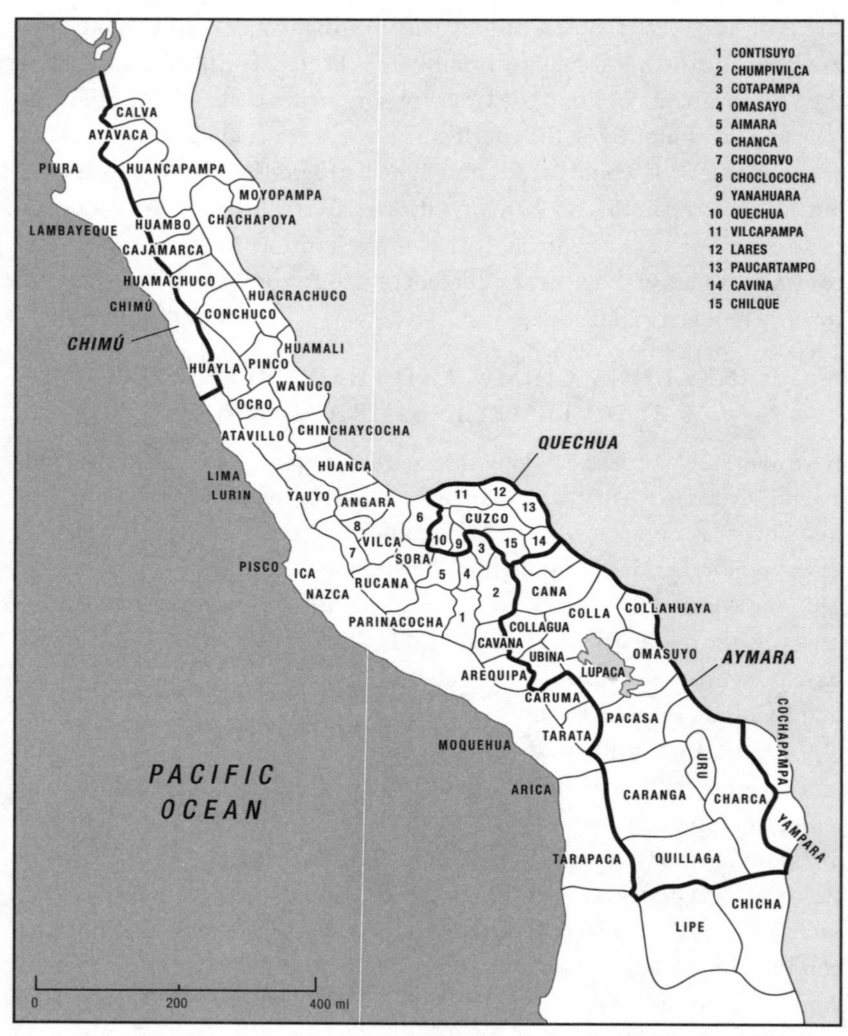

MAP 6. Member nations of Tawantinsuyo during Atahualpa's Government, corresponding to the present-day Peru and Bolivia. From Wikimedia Commons. *Map by Erin Greb Cartography.*

the khipu and elaborate textiles, can be found in Wari excavations. Karen Bruhns writes: "Quipus are known in a fully developed form from the first major conquest state that we know of, that of the Huari. They probably have a greater antiquity."[54] We now know the device goes as far back as Caral, as discovered by Shady, "invented" in the third millennium BC.[55] Oral narratives and archeology both point to the fact that long before Inkakuna, there were nations, and before those nations, there were others. As Tom Zuidema argues, even Wiracocha was an Inkan appropriation of Wari culture.[56] Brooke Larson sums up the fluidic ethnonational realities of pre-Hispanic peoples in the central sierra: "This was no pristine social landscape of permanent tribes or pure ethnicities. Long before the Europeans invaded the Andes in 1532, chiefdoms inhabited a world of constant flux, tension, and transformation during the dizzying expansion of Tawantinsuyo.[57] There was diversity on the Inkan time line, such as the Wari, and there was diversity in geography with other cultures contemporary to Inkakuna, such as Wankakuna and Chankakuna (called Huancas and Chancas in the chronicles), that were also located in the central sierra. Another culture to the north was the Chimú, who the Inkakuna eventually conquered during the 1460s or 1470s. There was no unified culture either in time or in space except in a generalized Andean sense (see map 6).

The Chimú offer an interesting example of a culture contemporary to the Inkakuna because they appear in the chronicles and we know a substantial amount of archaeological information about their antecedents. The precursors to late-antiquity Chimú culture included evolving stages of development known as Moche, or Mochica, culture, among others.[58] The Moche may not have been a state before the Moche V period, ranging from AD 550 to 800. Even though that configuration appeared to be a nation with a unified culture, the so-called fine-line style of narrative engraved on their pottery in that cultural and temporal moment, the Moche had not achieved ethnic unification. Izumi Shimada explains, "Much of the labor service is believed to have been provided by non-Mochica residents (inferred Gallinazo ethnicity) resettled to the Southern Pediment largely from agricultural marginal lands in the Lambayeque and adjacent valleys."[59] Thus, even within one nation there were people from other nations. We will examine the Moche more fully in chapter 4. Here our focus is on the Inkakuna.

On the ground in a real-life kind of way, society of late antiquity, irrespective of local cultural variants, was an urban one employing artisans, stone cutters, bricklayers, and road builders, all of whom worked within the style of their local culture. Variations may have resulted from cross-cultural contact. Inka ceramics, for example, hold similarities with earlier Wari artifacts, but each had a distinctive style. The same is true for Chimú art with respect to the different stages of Moche, some of which themselves reveal the influence of Wari and Tiwanaku. Divergent styles developed through contact between peoples from disparate lineages and traditions.

Upon their arrival, the Spanish might have constituted one additional tradition among many, but they insisted on policies to reorganize systematically that which came before. Iñigo García Bryce brings this into focus: "Despite a remarkable pre-Hispanic tradition of craftsmanship, Spanish rule broke earlier patterns and established new institutions intended to incorporate native populations into a Hispanized way of life."[60] The break, however, was not an absolute one, as elements survived in one way or another. One of the tactics employed to change the Andean way of life was to foster colonial mentalities through books, legal practices, and religion that took into account local conventions only when it suited those mentalities. While Andean diversity contemporary to the Spanish was recognized, it was not taken into account and all groups were simply called "Indians." Any thrust of local culture to burst to the colonial surface, such as the Taki Unquy—the worship of *huacas,* or *wakakuna*—was considered subversive. But in agriculture, cuisine, the evolution of Spanish, and the mixing of peoples themselves, there were certain fusing continuities, and the more rural the space, the more Andean the culture there remained. Inkan oral history itself entered into Renaissance historiography when the son of a conquistador and an Inka ñusta, or princess, lived and made friends in Spain, where he earned the distinction of being the first Peruvian-born historian.

Inca Garcilaso: Panaka Troubles in the Face of Provinces, Nations, and Republics

We turn now to one of the more famous and widely read of the chroniclers who wrote about Peru, the Inca Garcilaso de la Vega. His writing demonstrates how one bicultural author viewed the nation as he projected his notion of it back to late antiquity. Garcilaso is helpful because he shows the importance of the panaka, the family line, as he writes of provinces, nations, and republics. His writing recognizes the heterogeneous reality of Andean nations, but it also extols the Inkan thrust toward homogeneity. Both of these aspects come together to give form to divergent border ontologies, defining the nation as they glorify that which came before while simultaneously entering into new horizontal relationships. While some commentators have unfairly censored Garcilaso's *Royal Commentaries* as fiction,[61] it would be imprudent to swing too far in the other direction and accept the text as pure and objective history. As is the case with all chronicles, we must examine the *Royal Commentaries* in the political and social context of the time. Works of this type were authored by colonial subjects who tried to make an argument beneficial to themselves or their group while remaining rhetorically feasible and not creating political, social, or religious problems for themselves or their people. When we do not take this delicate situation of coloniality into account, extreme censure can result, as with this one offered by the Peruvian historian José Durand:

> Evasions, omissions, silence, and forgetfulness are features that frequently surface in Garcilaso's work. And perhaps it is not unnecessary to point out that these same features generally present themselves in the American Indian, famous for his or her reserve, fear, and suspicion.
>
> Rodeos, omisiones, silencio, olvido, son rasgos que se presentan de continuo en la obra de Garcilaso. Y quizá no fuera inútil apuntar que estos mismos rasgos también se presentan, por lo general, en el indio americano, bien conocido por su reserva, recelo y desconfianza.[62]

It seems incredible that Durand, a prominent twentieth-century historian who did not die until 1990 and who lived, researched, and taught in Peru, Mexico, France, and the United States, could ascribe these characteristics to Garcilaso and—even more outrageous—could then extrapolate them to the "Indians" throughout the Americas without taking into account unique cultures all transculturating, accommodating, and resisting colonialism and its attendant Hispanism, or English- or French-ness, in varied and sometimes jagged ways. Durand's essentialist jump from Garcilaso's historiography to a generalized disdain of Amerindians could result from his character, his education, his ideas, his world view, perhaps from the heritage of colonialism filtering into Criollo culture of which he was a part, or different combinations of these elements. Part of our task here is to overcome what Aníbal Quijano designates the coloniality of power, or more precisely the enduring coloniality of Criollo power, to move in the direction of representing indigeneity with verisimilitude as much as we can, however difficult that is given the present state of research.

Unlike Cieza de León, who was justifying the occupation by his compatriots and simultaneously evaluating it (the latter attitude acquired after the events, upon reflection, possibly upon reading Las Casas), the *Royal Commentaries* were more combative without obviously being so. As another twentieth-century Peruvian historian, Alberto Flores Galindo, points out, Garcilaso's primary work was "a polemical text destined to confront the Toledan chroniclers" (un texto polémico destinado a enfrentar a los cronistas toledanos). Flores Galindo is referring to the texts written at the behest of Viceroy Toledo that painted Inkakuna as tyrants, thereby justifying the continuing conquest of the Andes and depicting Spaniards as liberators.[63] Flores Galindo mentions Pedro Sarmiento de Gamboa's Toledan *Historia indica* in this regard. For no other reason did the Biblioteca de Autores Españoles include the *Historia indica* in the four-volume recompilation of Garcilaso's complete works. Flores Galindo best sums up the Toledan ideology encapsulated in Sarmiento de Gamboa's work: "The Inkakuna appear as latter-day governors, tyrants and usurpers who expand their Empire by force, to the detriment of other older and more traditional sovereigns" (los incas aparecen como gobernantes recientes, tiranos y usurpadores, que expanden el imperio por la fuerza, a costa de los derechos de otros monarcas más antiguos y tradicionales).[64] The Inkakuna had been certainly expanding their realm when the Spanish arrived, sometimes by force, sometimes by negotiation, but there is no reason to suppose this was worse than the newcomers who were also expanding their realm. Perhaps, we could argue, since the Inkakuna were closer in a cultural sense to the people they were absorbing, their "conquests" were less severe than the Spanish Conquest. To offer an example, both the Inka system and the Spanish system used the mita, but in the former case the model was one of reciprocal benefit between the empire and the local community, while in the latter case the model was one of tribute extraction. The Iberian model was, despite the outward trappings of Christianity, profoundly anti-Christian, a fact that could not be highlighted in any way that would show its hypocritical nature. Its mission was to obscure those colonial era realities that went against Christian doctrine. Imperial discourse of the time, especially the Toledan discourse in Peru, might fall into the category of language described by George Orwell in his novel *1984* as "newspeak," or as we might say in our time, doublespeak: the deliberate slanting of the meaning of words in order to create an inverse interpretation of events that may seem logical on the surface, but conceals the truth. Spaniards accused Inkakuna of the very thing they were doing, a diversionary rhetorical strategy to gaslight their own people into thinking their own actions were better than those of the Inkakuna. Toledo needed to further the imperial push, and to do that he needed to come up with a "newspeak," an alternative way of thinking and writing about the Inkakuna that justified the Spanish presence.[65]

The inconsistencies in the Toledan posture are blaring. Policies passed over cultural heterogeneity in favor of Hispanic homogeneity, but when such heterogeneity could serve to justify the overthrow of Inka homogeneity, it was employed duplicitously to meet Spanish ends. Garcilaso dismisses the Toledan viewpoint disseminated to justify the Forty-Years War (1532–72) and presents Inkakuna as a monumental civilizing and homogenizing force preparing the path to Christianity.[66] His view does not disavow cultural diversity, but emphasizes that the Inkakuna worked in favor of a unified cultural model which, if we think about it given the place and time he wrote, anticipated what the Spanish would do as they imposed their colonial system.

Garcilaso had to take on these conquest-justifying arguments subtly, given that he had to get his work by censors. One aspect of his technique consisted of simply feigning to gloss the previous chroniclers, thereby not appearing too harsh in his criticism of them; another involved formulating a rhetoric by which Inkakuna were civilizing "primitive" peoples to prepare them for the one God of Christianity. When we consider these biases that were countermanding other biases, it becomes clear that the text is caught in an ideological grid in which the nation is being mapped in terms of the pre-Inkan, Inkan, and post-Inkan. Garcilaso viewed, or rhetorically viewed, the pre-Inkan and the non-Inkan peoples contemporary to him as barbarous, and he viewed the post-Inkan world as a place where Spaniards and Inkakuna continued to act in tandem as civilizing forces. Garcilaso covers over a heterogeneous cultural landscape not only because his readers who reduced non-Spaniards to "Indians" would not understand it, but because he also wanted to defend Inkan achievements in the face of Toledan criticism.

But there can be no dispute; multifold heterogeneous ethnic nations thrived in the Andes. Covey notes, for example, "considerable cultural variation" in the diversity of burial practices. Some polities that Inkakuna incorporated into their regime were Qanas, Kanchis, Qollas, Lupaqas, Pacajes, Qarankas, Killaka-Asanaqui, and the Charka confederation.[67] The existence of ethnic nations is confirmed by the distinguished Peruvian ethnohistorian María Rostworowski. She concludes that Tawantinsuyo, in effect, comprised a conglomeration of local cultures only loosely integrated into the Inka State.[68] These cultures were in constant flux, whirling in and out of different kinds of arrangements with each other and with the Inkakuna. After the invasion, these provinces of Peru were reconfigured as a province of Spain, the imperial capital no longer Qosqo, but Madrid.

For the Renaissance-trained Inca Garcilaso de la Vega, the Inkakuna presided over a "Republic," and in some cases an "empire," as with the rulers Wiracocha and Pachakutiq (*CR,* III, xxv; VII, x).[69] The empire was composed of provinces such as Charca, Colla, Qosqo, Rimac, and Quito that had been folded into the larger organization (*CR,* I, vi). The idea of an Inka republic was not a revelation. As discussed in the section on Mexico, Muñoz Camargo conceived of a "Republic of Tlaxcala" large enough to pose a threat to the Triple Alliance. The appellation was also applicable in Peru, as can be seen from the chroniclers. In geographical terms, "republic" can coincide with "kingdom," and in this vein fifty years earlier, we find Cieza de León referring to the "great kingdom of Peru" (gran reyno del Perú), composed of "such a variety of provinces" (tanta variedad de prouincias) (*CP-1*[era], pp. 3, 6; fol. 3v, p. 7). Garcilaso also coincides with Cieza de León's contemporary, Agustín de Zárate, the Royal Treasurer, who speaks of the "provinces of Peru" (prouincias del Peru) (*HDC* [1]). Likewise, he correlates with the ideas of his own contemporary (even though he was probably not aware of him), the wandering scholar Felipe Guaman Poma de Ayala, who acknowledges this organizational and political reality during the colonial era by recognizing "towns" (corregimiento[s]), "cities" (ciudades), and "provinces" (provincia[s]), all subservient to the kingdom (rreyno) (*PNC* 510 [514]). We talk more about provinces in a postcontact reality when we broach the topic of demarcation in the penultimate section of this chapter. For now, suffice to say, the cultures that gave form to Garcilaso, Cieza de León, Zárate, and Guaman Poma's precontact "provinces" had their peculiarities. This brings us to the early modern idea of nation.

Many chronicles, Spanish, indigenous, and mestizo, boldly applied the European term "nations" to these ethnic groups, some of which were quite large. Sarmiento de Gamboa, by way of illustration, relates how Titu Atauchi, one of Waskar's generals, was involved in the campaigns "to conquer the nations of Pumacocha" (a conquistar a las naciones de Pomacocha).[70] Thus, even pro-Spanish chroniclers were capable of recognizing the qualities of what they understood as nationness inherent in Andean diversity. In a general sense, despite his Inkan panoptic, Inca Garcilaso is capable of differentiating between what he understood as distinct nations. Discussing the Jesuit historian Blas Valera, for example, he explains that his colleague was interested in distinguishing "the customs that each nation had" (las costumbres que cada nación tenía). Garcilaso is also capable of calling some nations "barbarian people" (gente bárbara) that needed to be brought into the Inkan fold (*CR*, I, xi; III, i). Two points should be made here. Regarding the first, he calls people conquered "barbarian people" as a way to show that Inkakuna were bringing the different groups up to the level needed to prepare them for the advent of Christianity, an argument made as a rhetorical choice to counter the Spanish view of Inkakuna as tyrants. Regarding "the customs that each nation had," we realize Garcilaso did patently recognize different nations in the Andes, each one associated with a particular variant of culture.

We can now offer a few specifics with respect to the nation. According to Garcilaso's view, the neighboring Chankakuna were "gran provinces" and collectively, a "nation" (*CR*, V, xxiv).[71] The commentator informs his readers the Chankakuna were a "nation" (nación) who "were proud of descending from a lion, and they worshiped the lion as god" (jáctanse descender de un león, y assí lo tenían y adoraban por dios). He also discloses that "under this proper name Chankakuna, come many other nations, the likes of Hancohuallu, Utunsulla, Uramarca, Uillca, and others" (Debaxo dese apellido Chanca se encierran otras muchas naciones, como son Hancohuallu, Utunsulla, Uramarca, Uillca, y otras). Each of these had its own deity. Thus, we can have nations inside of nations. Yet the diverse Chankakuna divided over submission to the Inkakuna; one faction decided to submit and the other, not (*CR*, IV, xv). Garcilaso also employs double terminology when he refers to the more distant Wankakuna. They were a "province" and a "nation." Province has to do more with territoriality, nation with lineage. The Wankakuna were not just a town. Even though idiosyncratic groups of Wankakuna disputed borders between their towns, "all of them were of one nation" (ser todos de una nación). These people based their nation on "their ancient lineage" (su antigua gentilidad). This old-line pedigree was one of the ingredients that helped define the nation. Another that added cultural form to this nation was, as Garcilaso explains, the national deity, the dog. Much like the Chichimeca of Central Mexico, the Wankakuna had to contend with negative epithets, theirs being *comeperro*, or dog eaters (*CR*, VI, x). Other groups, like those who lived in the province of Chucurpu, were nations (or provinces), even though they were fierce. Areas such as Tarma, Pumpu, and Huaillas, or Huaylas, were classified as provinces, while Huaylas could also fall into the category of nation. Yet peoples who lived to the east, in the area known as Antisuyo, meaning the Amazon jungle, were not called nations. They were people who had no government, no *kuraka*, and their provinces had no names (*CR*, VI, xi).

There were transcultural aspects of diffusion as local peoples came into contact with Inkakuna through reciprocal arrangements or through outright war. As the Inka state incorporated these groups into their realm, they allowed local traditions to remain in place. While Inkakuna forced Wankakuna to give up their dog deity, they allowed them to continue adoring their "man-idol." In similar fashion, the Chucurpu gave up worshiping the tiger deity. After absorption, all sectors gave up animal deities uniformly "because they did not permit the adoration of animal figures" (porque no consintieron adorar figuras de animales) (*CR*, VI, x). This suggests a standardized imperial policy directed toward all micronations being conquered, moving them culturally closer to the Inkakuna and their cultural umbrella.

There was also a process of educating. After reciprocal integration into the realm, or after a successful war of inclusion, the Inkakuna instituted the first phase of cultural, religious, and political control with military forts and garrisons. The case of the Chucurpu was typical. After some initial battles, they agreed to subordinate themselves to Qosqo's power. Inkan authorities left behind governors and clerics to oversee education. It appears these same authority figures administered the "the estate of the Sun and of the Inca" (hacienda del Sol y del Inca). A garrison of military personal was stationed there to protect recent conquests (*CR*, VI, xii). Those religious convictions that did not challenge Inka orthodoxy were allowed. Yet though the Inkakuna tolerated some local traditions, they instituted imperial worship of the sun without fail. This implied constructing sun temples, *acllahuasi*, or *akllawasi* (the house of virgins), and importing a clerical structure (*CR*, VI, xii). In a 1533 letter, Hernando Pizarro writes of the houses of chosen women in all the towns (*NU*, 113). The Akllawasi of Pachakamaq can be seen in figure 2.

Camayd-Freixas makes an interesting though perhaps incomplete observation on these matters. For him, Garcilaso, while making forays into European notions of boundaries such as those in Spain, Italy, or France, "reverts to the Indian concept of space based, not on boundaries, but on boundless directions radiating from a center."[72] Camayd-Freixas is referring to the *ceque* concept

Figure 2. Akllawasi at Pachakamaq.
Photograph by Håkan Svensson. Courtesy of Wikimedia Commons.

so brilliantly analyzed by Zuidema. While there was a concept of space emanating from a central point, there was likewise a quadrangular notion of space. Zárate indicates that Qosqo "is divided into four estates" (se divide en quatro estancias) (*HDC*, 17 overleaf). The word "estancia," suggesting a notion akin to "hacienda," distorts the urban landscape by imposing a commercial (and feudal) coating over noncommercial districts, and the number four unambiguously refers to quadrants. Zárate then goes on to name the four *suyos* he calls *quarteles*, spelling them as Collasuyo, Chinchasuyo, Condesuyo, and Andesuyo (*HDC*, 17 overleaf-18). The fact that he calls these suyos provinces implies delimiting borders between them. Such borders would have been porous, however.

Borders inside Tawantinsuyo were indeed porous. Murra explains that after the Inkakuna expanded the boundaries of their territory, they moved state *mitmaqkuna* (sing. *mitmaq*), Hispanized as *mitimaes*, into the new areas "to ensure Inca rule and revenues."[73] There was also a reverse movement, as when Inkakuna removed skilled Chimú artisans to Qosqo and other cities.[74] Murra clarifies and makes vivid what Inka expansion meant beyond human migrations, painting a picture of what it was like for the Lupaqa to come under

Inka domination. First, the people were moved, then the fortification walls were torn down, and then the Inka highway system was constructed.[75] In this manner, a boundary was removed and transportation across that point then became easier—normal, even. Murra does not say so, but if the Inkakuna used Lupaqa fortification materials to build their roads, the symbolism would be inescapable. The boundary moved to the backside of Lupaqa territory, and Tawantinsuyo extended its frontier. After annexation, the people of a given etnia were relocated all over The Four Directions.

The Wankakuna from the Jauja region may have used some type of land markers demarcating where one town ended and another began. However, Garcilaso writes, "They had factions and disputes about cultivatable land and about the boundaries of each town" (tenían vandos y pendencias sobre las tierras de labor and sobre los términos de cada pueblo) (*CR*, VI, x). Thus, if we accept Garcilaso's take on this, the Inkakuna were not the only ones to establish territory markers. The Four Directions were not boundless, however. Military garrisons were sometimes necessary at the expanding demarcating limit of Tawantinsuyo, suggesting a border zone between it and local unincorporated polities.[76]

Some might argue that there could be a European overlay on the colonial representation of these territorial constructs. After all, Garcilaso was living in Spain when he wrote his oeuvre. It also true that the quadrangular method of organizing territories, and even the world, is common to numerous cultures. We saw this in the chapter on the Nahua. For his *Darker Side of the Renaissance,* Walter Mignolo did extensive research and found this type of configuration in Mesoamerica, the Andes, the Navajo nation, and ancient China, as well as in Christian and Jewish cosmologies.[77] However, Mignolo reminds us that sixteenth-century colonialists writing early New World history—including the Spanish chroniclers, the missionaries, and even the Franciscans—"were silent about Amerindian territorial representations."[78] There is no reason to reject out of hand the quadrangular notion of space common in Ancient American thought. Why not try to pencil back in what has been erased?

Inside territorial borders, clan groups established limits between themselves. This is true even for the capital city. These fissures within Qosqo are related to divisions between panakakuna. Essential to the central Andean nation is the panaka and the ayllu, which continued to exist despite the importation of the European notions of province, nation, and republic.

Moreover, just as essential as these concepts are, they are also obscure because of contradictions in the chronicles that lead to a divergence of opinion between canonical anthropologists. It does not fall under our purview here to offer a definition of the panaka acceptable to experts working in different disciplinary fields. That may be impossible. We simply need to set down some parameters to infer more or less what the panaka means with respect to the nation.

A panaka in and of itself can be a nation in the sixteenth-century sense, but groupings of panakakuna, interfaced with each other, can constitute a nation in a somewhat different sense—the way the nation is viewed today. The issue of the panaka is paramount to Tawantinsuyo's organization because it was the way Qosqo was configured. Essentially, the panaka are ayllu of royal families. On top of that, as Zuidema indicates, "the organization of the Inca Empire as a whole was an extension and extrapolation of the system of organization of Cuzco." Both the capital and the empire refer to the same social organization, yet the two terms refer to two different functions of that organization, one endogamic and the other exogamic. Each Inka's descendants formed a panaka, with the exception of any son who in his turn became an Inka, which would imply the need for him to form his own panaka.

Because the Inka had to form his panaka with his wife (or wives) who bore his children, one could interpret it, as Zuidema does, "as being an indication of the matrilineal nature of the panaca."[79] Accordingly, while to all outward appearances Inka succession appears to be patrilineal, panaka arrangement was matrilineal. Given that this kind of kin group formed after the Inka received the *maskaypacha*, or royal tassel, some might argue that matrilineal power was after the fact. Chapter 4 looks at the gender aspect. For now, we must assert there is more to this than gender or lineage. Each panaka did not simply represent a particular Inka's descendants. In reality, these panakakuna embodied the organizational structure of Qosqo, which again is an issue of space and territoriality.

There were ten panakakuna, one for each Inkan ruler, with the exception of Wayna Qhapaq (the 11th) and his two short-lived Inka sons, Waskar and Atawallpa.[80] John Howland Rowe clarifies that the panakakuna for these three could not form in the confusion resulting from the civil war being waged between the two sons.[81] Wayna Qhapaq's panaka, we can theorize, could not be formed because Atawallpa or Waskar could not be in it if either were to be Inka. Both holding pretensions to the royal tassel, neither was at liberty to organize his father's panaka. Zuidema admits with caution that

Wayna Qhapaq had something of a panaka, but that it was not integrated into Qosqo's structure.[82] It seems the ten panaka existing at the time of the imposition of Spanish power were divided equally between the two moieties, Hanan Qosqo and Urin Qosqo, "Qosqo from above" and "Qosqo below or of the south."

The number ten, however, seems to suggest that each ruling Inka did not form a panaka; that despite that accepted principle, other structures of organization existed. Ten constituted a special number for the Inka, and their empire was divided up by means of decimal structures. Such structures could be applied to mita work brigades and to apportionment of military squadrons, brigades, and even armies. Regarding the former, Davies explains that the ideal structure allocated ten thousand inhabitants to a kuraka and then subdivided ten times, with each new group also divided into multiples of ten.[83] The divisions, Rowe explains, were given form by terminology: hundreds, *pachaka;* thousands, *waranqa;* and tens of thousands, *hunu.*[84] At some point, these multiples became "ayllukuna," a term whose meaning and size could vary, or as Rostworowski and Morris put it, "which had numerous and puzzling usages."[85] It makes sense that the same decimal structure applied to military service and to the mita system. It is easier to count men on a work gang or in a military squadron than it would be to count people in ayllu families because with births and deaths, the final census tally would be forever changing. The decimal system's usage does not end there. We can detect it in the mythology.

As Sarmiento de Gamboa writes, Manqo Qhapaq was said to have brought ten ayllukuna with him to Tambotoco. This chronicler illustrates that each of these ayllukuna held in esteem a *waka,* or sanctuary, which corresponded to it. Almost as an aside, he continues, it was the ayllukuna "that each Inka elected for his company" (que cada inga elegía para su compañía). It is as if Sarmiento reveals the ten panaka existing already in the time of Manqo Qhapaq "as those of his lineage and ayllu affirm" (según afirman los de su ayllo y linaje).[86] If this were so, each of the nine consecutive Inkakuna would have picked a waka and perhaps one of the remaining nine ayllukuna. The Inkakuna were already divided into panakakuna when they arrived in Qosqo, or there were already ten panakakuna when they arrived, which they then appropriated. Because of these possibilities, the eleventh, twelfth, and thirteenth Inkakuna would have had quite the task taking on the decimal system of organization in order to form a panaka.

Wayna Qhapaq's two sons—begotten of two different wives, each of a distinctive etnia that formed a noteworthy epicenter, Qosqo and Quito—should have been the representatives of the twelfth and thirteenth panakakuna, but instead drove Tawantinsuyo to civil war. This panaka fragmentation was still a hot subject seventy years later for Garcilaso. Because he originated from a different panaka, he felt compelled to write of "Atawallpa's tyranny and cruelty" (la tiranía y crueldad de Atahuallpa) (*CR*, I, xxiii). The need to use this kind of terminology to describe what happened reveals the inutility of the panaka-evading notion of "Indian" that the Spanish projected onto Andean peoples.

The panakakuna already formed, and the difficulty of forming new ones in the context of divergent nations clashing in some cases and coming together through reciprocity in others, gives us some inkling of the cultural whirling undergone by these nations in the period right before the advent of the Spanish. These processes reveal the interplay between some of the elements of the nation described in chapter 1. These include fluctuating territories and the boundaries between them, religions in contact and the favoring of certain deities over others, the projection of lineage through panakakuna, and the importance of armies. Chapter 4 returns to additional features of the panaka, with respect to gender. Now we turn to another essential element of the nation, as mentioned in chapter 1: the role of language.

A Problem of Language: an Andean Toltecayotl with a Twist

Chapter 1 cites the primary role of language in the shaping of nations. This is because legends, myths, history, literature, laws, trade, and even religion are transmitted with language, and a language held in common, containing these elements, fosters community. As noted, language and culture constitute one of Hobsbawm's forms of protonationalism. When there is a thrust to achieve a more cultivated form of expression, the nation can then elevate itself vis-à-vis other nations, or perceive itself as doing so. Chapter 2 reveals how Toltecayotl was an ideal to which learned people in Anahuac aspired. This nation-forming ideal was cultural and linguistic, the Nahuatl tongue constituting its core. Siméon's *Diccionario* reveals the richness of meanings inherent in the word "Nahuatl": it denotes the idea of sounding good or producing a good sound, and it connotates the virtues of wisdom, astuteness, and abilities or skills.[87] There was a comparable ideal in the Andes embodied in the Qheswa language, described by Inca Garcilaso de la Vega as the "General Language" and known to postcontact people who speak it as *Runa Simi*, "the

People's Language." While there is a parallel linguistic ideal among Nahua and Inkakuna with respect to Nahuatl and Qheswa, no flawless symmetry of approach exists to apprehend the respective language usage in the two regions because they were different. For example, important Mesoamerican groups adapted the alphabet quickly after the Spanish arrival, while Andean groups took more time to do so. Why would be this be so? One reason has to do with script. Another may relate to the attitude toward language. This is a complicated question to resolve, because while the New Philology aids our comprehension of Mesoamerica, we have no similar methodological tool with respect to the Andes. Because we are curious about the ideal of an imperial language, which had no proper name to refer to it and its relationship to an also unnamed cultural ideal, we will give greater attention to it than we did in the previous chapter to the imperial language of Nahuatl.

Garcilaso never called the General Language by the glottonym (the name of the language) generally in use today, Qheswa. In contrast, other early seventeenth-century authors such as Guaman Poma de Ayala use it, although infrequently. One instance occurs when Guaman differentiates between "Castile's tongue and the general one Qheswa" (la lengua de Castilla y general de *quichiua*) (*PNC*, 771 [785]; his emphasis).[88] There is difficulty with our translation's attempt to render Guaman Poma's meaning. There is room for discussion because of Guaman Poma's imperfect dominance of the Castilian language, which may have caused him to omit the definite article before "general" or insert the preposition "de" before "Quichiua." In the first possibility, Castile's tongue finds its parallel in the General Language, which means that Qheswa is not used as a glottonym, but as an ethnonym or demonym. In the second possibility of its use as an ethnonym or demonym, "general" could serve as an adjective to "Quichiua," making it a glottonym. Perhaps this confusion is cleared up in another place, however, when he refers to "la lengua de la castellana y quichiua ynga, aymara, poquina colla, etc" (*PNC*, 11[11]; see also 10[10]). In this instance, the reference clearly refers to a language called "Inka Qheswa," or more precisely, Inkan Qheswa. Guaman Poma's tenuous embrace of the glottonym and Garcilaso's avoidance of it do not make the language, acclaimed as the medium to transmit the cultural and religious ideal of the Inca State, any less important for Andean culture. The enigmatical lack of a proper name for the language, however, slows down our efforts to define the nation in obvious terms as would be the case for

England and the glottonym English, or for Spain and the glottonym Spanish, for example. This section attempts to shed some light on the problem.

It is well known that Qheswa was the Inka language, even when not called by this name. Despite the absence of a glottonym by which to refer to it, the language was held up as a means to promote good government. In an often-cited passage from the *Royal Commentaries*, Inca Garcilaso explains that for good government, the Inkakuna ordered "all their vassals to learn the language of the court, today called the General Language. To teach it they put Inkan teachers of rank in each province" (todos sus vassallos aprendiessen la lengua de su corte, que es la que hoy llaman lengua general, para cuya enseñança pusieron en cada provincia maestros Incas de los de privilegio). One of the implied benefits of the General Language is that when taught to subdued people who were "bellicose, ferocious and fierce" (belicosa . . . feroz y brava) (*CR*, VII, i), it brought them into the fold and elevated them. This was an important unifying factor in a heterogeneous linguistic environment.

Quoting Blas Valera extensively, Garcilaso recognizes that other nations, such as Puquinas, Collas, Urus, Yuncas, or Yungas, each spoke a distinct language (*CR*, VII, iv).[89] As can be seen in Willem Adelaar's map, these cultural entities still existed during the sixteenth century (see map 7). These nations—"nations" is the word Garcilaso uses—could all become refined, as they were taught to speak a lingua franca, which fosters harmony, goodwill, and good government: "With this skill, the Inkakuna domesticated and united such a variety of nations holding opposing idolatries and customs such as the ones who were then subjected to their Empire. With this tongue, they brought so much unity and friendship that [people] came to love each other as brothers." (Con este artificio domesticaron y unieron los Incas tanta variedad de nasciones diversas y contrarias en idolatría y costumbres como las que llegaron y sujetaron a su Imperio, y los traxeron mediante la lengua a tanta unión y amistad que se amavan como hermanos.) (*CR*, VII, i) This argument explains away the quilted dispersal of Qheswa and offers a reason to provide for its continued diffusion. Garcilaso's take on the importance of the role of this language, increasingly known from the second half of the sixteenth century by the glottonym Qheswa, was generally accepted by linguists such as Bruce Mannheim, who called it a "medium of communication among the diverse peoples who were incorporated into the state."[90] Thus, it is evident that the ideal had to do with elevating but also standardizing the culture of Tawantinsuyo and providing it with a lingua

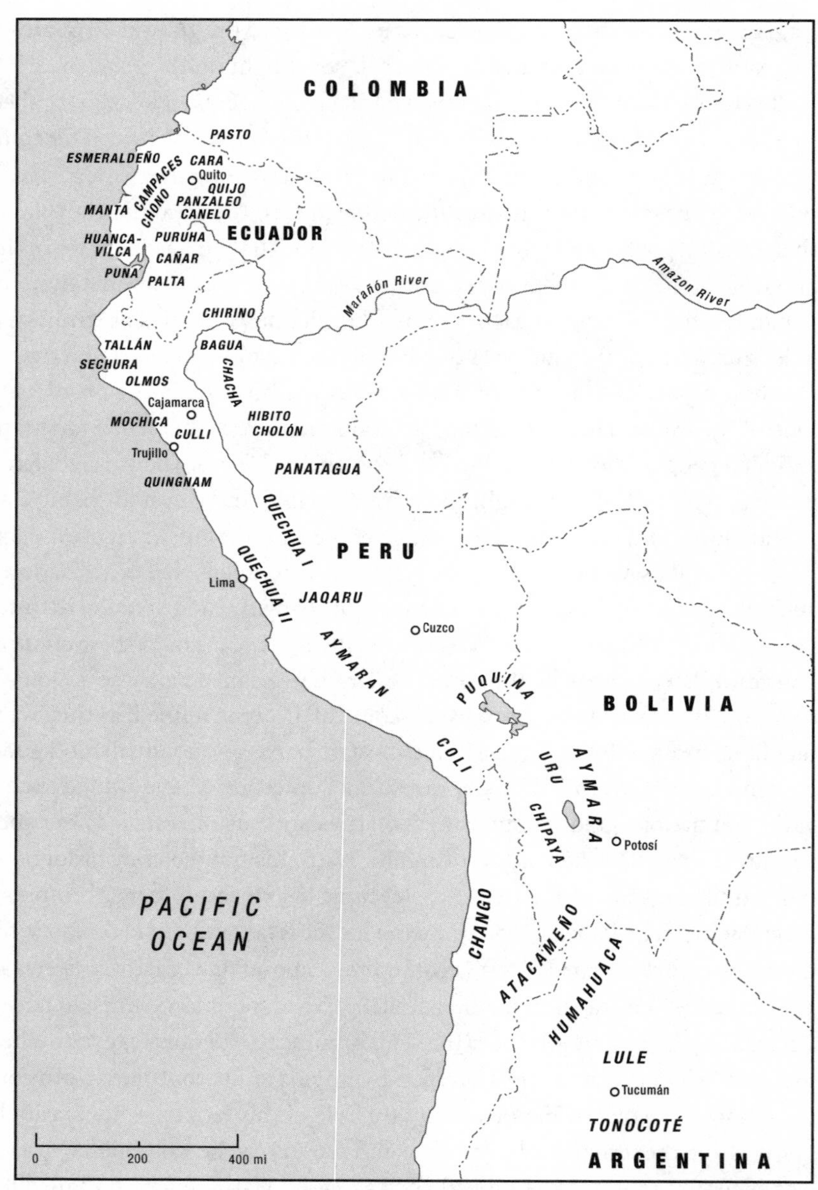

MAP 7. Approximate distribution of indigenous languages of the Andes in the sixteenth century. From Willem F. H. Adelaar, *The Languages of the Andes* (New York: Cambridge University Press, 2004), 166.
Map by Erin Greb Cartography.

franca. This latter aspect moves the Inkan ideal of a national unitary language unconnected to etnia closer to what would become the post-Enlightenment de-ethnicized model of the nation or at least closer to a pan-etnia such as, for example, "Spanish," "French," or "English." We will look at more of the "civilizing" attributes of Qheswa, but first other details warrant discussion.

What is this General Language and where did it come from? On the one hand, we no longer need the rhetorical strategy deployed by Garcilaso. On the other, linguistics and archeology have given us much more knowledge than could have ever been imagined by the great chronicler. Alfredo Torero explains that during the Formative Period, from 3000 to 200 BC, there were contacts between regional languages, some becoming more favored and others less so, until those "favored" "eliminated" or "absorbed" those more restricted.[91] This reality is an aspect of the whirling cultures described above. In those remote times, Torero isolates the linguistic grouping he describes as proto-Qheswa, derived from paleo-Qheswa. Such nomenclature refers to the time when the urban epicenter of Caral was thriving, from 2600 BC which, to offer a point of comparison, is around the time the Egyptians constructed their first pyramids at Saqqara. From that point on, Torero describes "the progression of proto-Qheswa from the north-central coast toward the north-central mountains and the central coast and mountains of Peru" (la progresión del protoquechua desde la costa norcentral hacia la sierra norcentral y la costa y la sierra centrales del Perú). Much later, around the middle of the first millennium during the Wari-Tiwanaku horizon, ancient Qheswa divides into Qheswa I (Huáyhuash) in the mountains and Qheswa II (Yúngay) on the coast.[92] During Inka times, the people of the highlands of Apurímac and Urubamba spoke Qheswa II. It and other variants eventually extended north, reaching into Colombia, and south to Tucumán in present-day Argentina. As part of their imperial strategy, the Inkakuna diffused Qheswa IIB and C, known also as Chinchay and described by Mannheim simply as "southern Peruvian Quechua" (see map 7).[93] Torero explains that the Spanish detected variants of the "General Language," which they sometimes called a "corrupt Qheswa" (quechua corrupto), erroneously thought to have radiated from Qosqo.[94] This was Garcilaso's viewpoint. We now know that Qheswa was diffused from the coast and evolved into distinct varieties in the different regions where it extended its reach because of the soft boundaries between multiple dialect continuums. It is hard to determine the number of variants, but they exist and they are not "corrupt." It is safe to say that within the larger divisions of Qheswa I and Qheswa II, several dozen varieties exist. After Spanish occupation was established, the Chinchay variant, sometimes called Pastoral Qheswa, was further diffused as part of the evangelization process.[95] It even came to be a printed language, as the catechism and other documents were translated into it.[96] It was Tawantinsuyo's official tongue, later an important vehicle of evangelization, and today, with Aymara and Guarani, it is still a widely spoken language. It has been used as a medium of poetic expression by poets such as José María Arguedas, Ranulfo Fuentes, Víctor Tenorio, Ch'aska Anka Ninawaman, and others.

The Inkakuna's Private Language and the Inkakuna's Acquisition of Qheswa: a Theory

It seems counterintuitive, but the General Language was not the Inkan ancestral tongue. Garcilaso also refers to a private Inkan mode of expression. This means the nación was not given form by one sole language. He spells outs its positionality in relation to the Inka court and to the Empire:

> The Inkakuna had another private language that they spoke among themselves, which the other Indians did not understand, nor was it legal for them to learn it since it was a divine language. [It] has been totally lost, because since the specific Republic of the Inkakuna has disappeared, so too has this language perished.

> Los Incas tuvieron otra lengua particular, que hablavan entre ellos, que no la entendían los demás indios ni les era lícito aprenderla, como lenguaje divino. Ésta . . . se ha perdido totalmente, porque, como pereció la república particular de los Incas, pereció también el lenguaje dellos. (*CR*, VII, i)

Garcilaso is not the only chronicler to reveal the existence of a private language in use among Inkakuna. The Mercedarian Martín de Murúa, roughly contemporary to him (and to Guaman Poma de Ayala) discusses a kind of school one Inka ruler ensconced in his home in Qosqo. He tells of four learned men who each taught a particular subject, one of whom was a language instructor: "The first teacher began by teaching the Inka's language, which is the private one that he used to speak, different from Qheswa and Aymara, which are the two General Languages of this kingdom" (El primer maestro enseñaba al principio la lengua del Ynga, que era la particular que él hablaba, diferente de la quichua y de la aymara, que son las dos lenguas generales de este reino).[97] From an objective and non-theological perspective, we can state certainly that this private language was not divine, as Garcilaso suggests the Inkakuna held it to be. The Inkakuna likely applied a veneer of divinity to their language of origin, a tactic that added to their mystique. Garcilaso and Murúa could not talk of the origins of this language because they did not have the field of historical linguistics, which benefits us greatly today.

This brings us to the realization that the Inkakuna spoke Qheswa, the "General Language," as well as the "Private Language" they brought from their ancestral homeland. In neither case does the ethnonym (the name of the people) coincide with the glottonym (the name of the language the people spoke). Additionally, if the "General Language" was the speaking ideal for everybody from educators and soldiers on down, the "Private Language" was reserved for members of the Inkan panakakuna. There was a ranking of languages within the nation and the elite language was shrouded in mystery, hence Garcilaso's calling it "divine." If the Inkakuna came from Tiwanaku, centered at Lake Titiqaqa (or Titicaca) in the south, as Garcilaso recounts, then they may have had a form of Aymara, called "Aymar Aru" in that tongue, as their primordial language. This is the view of Torero and of a nineteenth-century intellectual whom we will get to shortly. Torero cites Paccaritambo as the point of origin of the Inkakuna. He designates their language as "Aru Cundi," which may have become, what he calls after Garcilaso, the "'private language' of the Inkakuna" ('idioma particular' de los incas).[98] Another reasonable and additional scenario besides Aymara is the one that Waldemar Espinoza Soriano proposes. He argues for Puquina, because he believes they came from Tiwanaku (see map 7). Jan Szemiński has discovered a Puquina document imbedded in Juan de Betanzos's chronicle that he proposes as the first proof of the Inkan secret tongue. Rodolfo Cerrón-Palomino also supports the Puquina hypothesis in a recent book, *Las lenguas de los incas*.[99]

Either Aymara or Puquina in their origins may have derived from a kind of proto-Aymara, which Hardman theorizes was the lingua franca during the period of Tiwanaku-Wari expansion. Espinoza Soriano, who was writing around the same time as Hardman (but as a historian, not a linguist), supposes that the Tiwanakans spoke Puquina and that the Inkakuna came from there. Torero accepts the idea of Puquina-speaking Tiwanakans, although he calls the language "proto-Puquina."[100] It may or may not be relevant, but at one point Guaman Poma de Ayala interestingly claims that the "Puquina

Collas were also of the Inka class" (poquina collas también fue casta de yngas) (*PNC*, 85[85]). This is a little strange, as the Inka conquest of the Collas is legendary. So there may be some ancestral meaning in this Guamanian assertion. Torero, however, rejects outright the possibility of Puquina being the Inkakuna's furtive language.[101]

Hence, there are two competing ideas about the secret tongue: Aymara, or some form of it, and Puquina, which may have descended from proto-Aymara. The Inkakuna and their complex relationship to language obscure our understanding of the role of language in the nation. This is an issue linguists, ethnolinguists, and archaeologists must resolve. Here we can simply state that the early nation-building-minded Inkakuna migrated to Qosqo and, unsurprisingly, brought their language of origin with them, which gradually became their private language as they adopted the more locally significant Qheswa. The difficulty of proving the Inka language of origin was Puquina or any other language resides in the fact that, as Inca Garcilaso is aware, few people could speak the private language after the Inkakuna's demise. At the onset, they were decimated by European diseases that outran the conquistadors on their march south along the mountain range and that radiated inland from their coastal contacts. Then the process of disintegration that began with the demise of Wayna Qhapaq continued with the subsequent civil war between Atawallpa and Waskar, and with Pizarro's taking of Cajamarca, Qosqo, and Pachakamaq. The process continued with the isolation of elites in the last Inka capital of Vilcabamba, and with Spanish executions of principal Inkakuna, such Atawallpa and Thupaq Amaru. Few versed in the language survived. Garcilaso, though he descended from Inka Thupaq Yupanki and his sister consort, Mama Oqllo, admits that he cannot speak it and does not use it (*CR*, bk. II, xvii).[102] If the people who speak a language die, the language then becomes extinct.

The key to unlocking the private-language mystery may become apparent after the ambiguities associated with the mysterious Jesuit chronicler Valera are cleared up. Disputed papers that came to light in Italy during the twentieth century reference testimony from the kuraka (local chief) Mayachac Azuay, who talks about a secret and sacred language known only to *amautakuna* (sing. *amauta*), or wise men, the *akllakuna* (sing. *aklla*), or virgins of the sun, and other elite keepers of culture (such as poets). This language was not codified in khipukuna as was Qheswa. Sabine Hyland explains that it was represented in "woven textiles along with images in jewels and small objects."[103] These textiles were known as *quilca*, or *qelqa*, when meaning was inscribed on them. The guardians of these planes of expression therefore were not khipukamayoqkuna, the traditional male keepers of the khipukuna, but the *qelqakamayoqkuna* who resided in the *akllawasi* (pl. *akllawasikuna*). As a consequence, this private language may have been, or became, gynecocentric.[104] It may have been passed down in the domestic sphere from mother to child while the men increasingly used Qheswa in the public sphere for matters of state, reciprocity, and good living. Alternatively, perhaps Mayachac Azuay's language was yet another being stirred into the linguistic melting pot of the Andes. This cannot be proven or disproven with the present state of knowledge regarding these contested documents. However, the fact that the Inkakunas' private language disappeared with them offers another reason to conclude it was the language of their ethnic nation of origin, as it was not spoken by others from outside the Inka group who would have been able to carry on with that linguistic medium. This trajectory still does not explain, however, why they would relegate their own ethnic language to the domestic sphere where the qelqakamayoqkuna resided, while simultaneously appropriating Qheswa for the public sphere where the khipukamayoqkuna resided.

To conjecture about Qheswa and its relationship to the private language, we must turn to a curious circumstance in Inkan history as related by Inca Garcilaso. We have stated the Inkakuna did not call the General Language by any other name. But curiously, Cieza de León, Guaman Poma de Ayala, and Inca Garcilaso talk about a group from Andahuaylas distinct from the Inkakuna, whose ethnonym surprisingly was Qheswa! (See map 6.) Cieza de León, writing fifty years before Garcilaso, talks of these "Qheswakuna, [a] very ancient nation" (Quichuas nasción muy antigua) (*CP*-1*era* XC, fol. 115v, p. 254). Guaman Poma, referring to both the society of late antiquity as well as the colonial *visitas,* or inspections, which provided him with first-hand experience, comments on the existence of "Qheswan Indians" (yndios Quichiuas), and in the case of the visitas he mentions "Qheswa ayllu" (allo Quichiua) (*PNC,* 267 [269]; 676 [690]). In another place he talks about "the province of the Aymaraes and Qheswakuna" (la prouincia de los yndios Aymarays y Quichiuas) (*PNC,* 431 [433]). Again, Qheswa is used as an ethnonym for that ancient nation, but not as a glottonym for that nation's language.

Who were these Qheswakuna? Garcilaso goes into some detail as he explains how Qosqo's rulers brought the Qheswakuna into the Inka fold.[105] What the author reveals about Inkakuna and their relationship to Qheswakuna is just as interesting as what he does not say about it. He explains that the Inka Qhapaq Yupanki sent his brother Awki Titu as emissary to two provinces called Cotapampa and Cotanera, "both of the nation called Qheswa" (ambas de la nación llamada Quechua) (see map 6).[106] Later, regarding their integration into Tawantinsuyo, Garcilaso will refer to this region as the "province called Qheswa" (la provincial llamada Quechua) in the Cuntisuyo district (*CR*, III, xii; IV, xxv). Guaman Poma's mention of these people who are constituted as an ayllu substantiates Garcilaso's insistence on them in his text. That all three chroniclers use the term Qheswa (albeit with different spellings) as an ethnonym seems to confirm the Qheswakuna's existence as an ayllu, province, or nation. Guaman Poma's use of the term "ayllu" to talk about a people Cieza and Garcilaso call a "nación" says something about how European terminology supersedes Andean terminology. The progression from ayllu to nation here is not unlike the path from altepetl to nation discussed in the previous chapter.

Regarding Qheswa submission to the Inkakuna, Garcilaso offers an unattributed quote that reproduces a Qheswa-centric voice. In it, the Qheswakuna collectively say, "We desire it to see ourselves free of the tyranny and cruelty to which the Chankakuna, Hancohuallu, and other surrounding nations have been subjecting us for many years" (lo desseávamos por vernos libres de las tiranías and crueldades que las naciones Chancas y Hancohuallu y otras, sus comarcanas, nos hazen de muchos años atrás) (*CR*, III, xii). This knowledge did not issue solely from the oral tradition, or the khipu archives. Garcilaso knew these provinces from firsthand experience because, he explains, Cotapampa became the repartimiento of a Spaniard from Seville, Don Pedro Luis de Cabrera, and Cotanera, for its part, became the repartimiento of Garcilaso de la Vega, the chronicler's father (*CR*, III, xii). The term repartimiento means distribution, and repartimientos were forced-labor encampments, like encomiendas, that may have been forerunners to the hacienda system.[107] That would have been the fate of the Qheswakuna. Aurelio Miró Quesada fixes the date for Garcilaso's father's acquisition of the Cotanera province at 1543, a license authorized by Peru's Governor, Vaca de Castro.[108]

Garcilaso's version of events does not present the Qheswakuna as being more "civilized" than the Inkakuna. To be sure, the verb he uses to characterize this union between the latter and the former is *reducir,* "to subdue" or "to overpower." He recapitulates, "The Inkakuna went about subduing the provinces on both sides of the Amancay river, of which there are many that are contained under this proper name Qheswa" (Los incas anduvieron reduziendo las provincias que hay de una parte y otra del río Amáncay, que son muchas y se contienen debaxo de este apellido Quechua) (*CR*, III, xii). The people called Qheswakuna acquiesced easily so they could be protected from Chankakuna, who were also invested in conquering them. Cieza recounts that he personally interviewed Chankakuna and they told him they had indeed conquered the Qheswakuna (*CP-1era*, XC, fol. 116v, p. 254). Most likely for reasons of protection, the Qheswakuna allowed themselves to be incorporated wholesale into Tawantinsuyo. The narrative, cultural, and ideological frame in which Garcilaso recounts these matters has Inkakuna moving along, expanding their dominion, and purportedly bringing "civilization" to the people. As part of the edifying process, the Inka elites diffused the language for which Garcilaso offers no glottonym, but which we now call Qheswa. He also speaks of the Inka conquering a people to whom he assigns the ethnonym Qheswa, seemingly setting up an incongruity, a paradox, and a mystery.

As in Anahuac, in Tawantinsuyo there were horizontal and vertical forms of cultural appropriation and veneration, although this occurred in a subtler way regarding the Inkakuna. As noted, Chichimeca and Mexica descended from the north to the heart of Anahuac and openly and proudly appropriated the Nahuatl language and the ideal associated with it. When a Chichimecatl leader like Xolotl accepted the followers of the Topiltzin into his ranks, they were embracing the ideal of Toltecayotl because they began to adopt the language and culture of the Tolteca. The assimilative process for Inkakuna is similar, but two differences are apparent. First, they technically migrated north toward Qheswa-speaking territories, not south as did the Chichimeca and Mexica. Second, Inkakuna did not openly admit they were picking up the Qheswa language or adhering to an ideal we might call Qheswaness. Interestingly, the Qheswakuna are subdued, but Garcilaso does not describe them negatively, as he had described the Wankakuna as dog worshipers.

If there were a people named Qheswa, and we now call the General Language Qheswa, this begs the question as to what language the Qheswakuna spoke and if they brought it to the Empire. This question is interesting because if their language was the one we now call Qheswa, and Cieza, Guaman Poma, and Garcilaso called them by the ethnonym Qheswa, it suggests that Inkakuna were not Qheswakuna, raising questions about the cultural condition we can call Qheswaness. Additionally, if the Inkakuna spoke Aymara or Puquina as a private language, and we know they also spoke the General Language, then perhaps they adopted this latter language as they folded the Qheswa people into Tawantinsuyo. What Garcilaso does not dare say is what the nineteenth-century essayist Clorinda Matto de Turner hypothesized in response to a question posed to her in 1887 by the president of the Society of Archeology and Linguistics in Qosqo: "If the Inkan conquistadors were Aymaras, why did Wayna Qhapaq's empire speak Qheswa, which is to say, a language that was neither of the conquering people nor of the people being conquered?" (¿Por qué si los conquistadores incas fueron aimaras, el imperio de Huayna-Capacc hablaba la quechua, es decir, un idioma que no fué del conquistador ni del conquistado?)[109] Matto gets right to the point when she focuses on the Qheswakuna.[110] We will return to Matto, but here we need to discuss the answer to the question posed by the president of the Society of Archeology and Linguistics, which may have to do with the Inkan subjugation of the Qheswakuna. After absorbing the Qheswa nation, the Inkakuna appear to have learned the language spoken in the Qheswan provinces, which was also the language spoken in Pachakamaq, and it became the official form of expression throughout Tawantinsuyo. The priests of Pachakamaq speaking this language would have only added to its prestige. This idea of Inkakuna appropriating the General Language is strengthened when we realize the Qheswakuna were absorbed during the reign of the fifth Inka, Qhapaq Yupanki (*CR*, III, xi, xii). Torero seems to associate Qheswa's diffusion with Pachakamaq's religious and economic expansion.[111] Pachakamaq was conquered later under the reign of the Inka Pachakuteq, the ninth sovereign, whose conquering general was also named Qhapaq Yupanki. There may have been some confusion between the homonymous leaders, the latter the brother of Pachakuteq and the former, the son of Maita Qhapaq. Moreover, if we take into account Hardman's hypothesis that the Inkakuna spoke Aymara as a public language until they conquered Pachakamaq, there may have been a long process from the fifth to ninth Inkakuna, in which Qheswa was slowly being installed as an imperial language.

This appropriation of Qheswa is still curious, as the Inkakuna seem to avoid elevating their own ancestral language to this vaunted level. This is the paradox described by Matto de Turner. To begin, we must take from Garcilaso at face value the existence of a non-public language. As stated, Murúa, someone residing in a different geographical region, confirms this. If we consider this to be their original language, then we must assume they assimilated to the Qheswa language. If this is the case, we must then ask where they got this language, and consider that it may have initially come to them from the group of peoples who called themselves Qheswakuna. We must concede, though, that with respect to Inkakuna, the Qheswa ideal, if there was one, was subtler, its contours more difficult to discern than was the Nahua ideal of Toltecayotl.

A Third Language: Qosqo's Pre-Inka Tongue

If there was an Aymara- or Puquina-rooted Inkan language of origin, and there was the imperial language Qheswa subsequent to it, what was the tongue spoken in Qosqo before the Inkakuna arrived there? Garcilaso mentions this third language only in passing when he alludes to "Qosqo's language" (la lengua de Cozco) (*CR*, VII, iv). The answer has to do with Aymara, which like Qheswa, has remote origins. If the Qheswa language (but not the glottonym "Qheswa") came into being on the central Peruvian coast, proto-Aymara appeared on the southern Peruvian coast. Alternatively, according to Espinoza Soriano, it came to the lands now known as Peru from Coquimbo (Chile) or Tucumán (Argentina) during Tiwanaku's apogee.[112] To give a further example of the complexity of determining the lines of development, Cerrón-Palomino postulates that Aymara comes from the Central Andes and that it arrived in the Qosqo area with the Wari State.[113] Such a trajectory seems plausible, and Cerrón-Palomino appears to be correct in arguing for an Aymaran linguistic foundation in Qosqo, which does not discount an ancient coastal origin coeval to the apogee of Caral. He reasons that the toponym Qosqo itself comes from Aymara.[114] Regarding proto-Aymara and its relationship to the Inkakuna, Covey concludes that the Inkakuna built their imperial society on top of Wari ruins.[115] So if the Wari spoke proto-Aymara, it makes sense that the inhabitants of Qosqo spoke some form of Aymara before Inkakuna arrived there. Torero paints a historical-geographic map in the mind of the reader. He locates proto-Qheswa as being developed in the Formative Era in the present-day departments of Ancash, Huánuco, Pasco, Northern Lurín, and Northern Lima, while he sees proto-Aru as developing in the present departments of southern Lima, Ica, Southern Junín, Huancavelica, Ayacucho, and perhaps even, he suggests, Apurímac and Qosqo.[116] If Torero's suggestion of including Qosqo in the proto-Aru orbit makes sense, then it would also make sense that the same Aru-derived language was Qosqo's language before the Inkakuna brought in Qheswa. We can certainly agree with Proulx, who, referring to a later period, reports that Qosqo was one of two strongest areas of contact between Qheswa and Aymara (Cochabamba was the other).[117] This presupposes that long before the Inkakuna adopted Qheswa, they were migrants (like the Chichimeca in Mexico) who journeyed to the Qosqo region. The multilingual environment of Qosqo would have allowed for a push and pull between the different languages.

Hardman theorizes that Aymara and Puquina coexisted with Qheswa in the Inkan capital before the time of the Inka-Spanish war.[118] She suggests that Aymara, what she calls Jaqi, was the Inka's lingua franca until Pachakamaq was conquered.[119] This view seems to align with Torero. Cerrón-Palomino expands on Hardman's notion of trilingual Inkakuna this way: "From being Puquina speakers originally, the Inkakuna later became Aymara speakers, and only in their final expansive stage did they learn Qheswa, a language that came from the east of Qosqo." (los incas, de hablantes de puquina originariamente, devinieron en aimarahablantes posteriormente, y solo en su etapa expansiva final aprendieron el quechua, lengua que provenía del este del Cuzco.)[120] This all sounds plausible if we accept his, Hardman's, and Garcilaso's assertions that Inkakuna of the later period came to be trilingual.[121]

To conclude, based on the chronicle, Matto de Turner's essay on the topic, and other documents and recent research by ethnolinguists, we are suggesting that this General Language was most likely the third chronologically to be spoken in Qosqo. It may be that it, the Inkan ancestral language, and Qosqo's pre-Inka tongue were such an integral part of the elite social fabric that, as Hardman concludes, "the entire Inca court would for a while be trilingual."[122] This should not be surprising because, as Cerrón-Palomino suggests, there were three and perhaps four General Languages of Peru; along with Aymara, Puquina, and Qheswa there was Mochica, spoken by the aforementioned Chimú, located on the northern coast.[123] At any rate, the pre-Inkan language of Qosqo did not seem to have a long-lasting impact on the linguistic fabric of Tawantinsuyo the way Qheswa did. Puquina is now an extinct language and Aymara is predominant in Bolivia. In Qosqo, even today, Qheswa can claim to be the prominent, along with Spanish, of course, and with the tourist industry's ubiquitous English.

Verticality: The Power of Manqo Qhapaq

Language, naturally, is not an empty shell. It is filled with cultural content that comes from religion, history, myth, legends, and experiences that result in idiomatic expressions and sayings. Cultural ideals are related to these factors and to the language expressing those ideals. Before returning to the fascinating case of the Inkakuna's horizontal appropriation of Qheswa, we must first comment on their establishment of a cultural paradigm that their descendants and the people their descendants conquered could revere as a vertical source of ethnic pride. Where Mexica and Chichimeca told a story of a southward emigration to the center, where they then commingled with Tolteca peoples who elevated them, Inkakuna told a story of northward emigration from Lake Titiqaqa to a center that they would then enlighten. According to Garcilaso de la Vega, they were ordered to "proceed from good to better, cultivating those beastly folks and converting them into men so they could be capable of reason and of any good doctrine" (procediendo de bien en mejor cultivassen aquellas fieras y las convirtiesen en hombres, haciendoles capaces de razón y de cualquiera buena doctrina) (*CR,* I, xv). Garcilaso, just like his Mexican contemporary Alva Ixtlilxóchitl, is sculpting a history. In both narratives, the favored dynasties, be they Inkan or Tetzcocan, are represented as preparing the path out of polytheism toward Christianity. This "sculpting" has earned Alva Ixtlilxóchitl the criticism of various scholars,[124] Garcilaso, perhaps somewhat less so, at least on this issue.

Just as a theological aside, it is conceivable that the sculpting was more of a polishing than of quarry work. This might be the case since certainly the Inti, or sun deity, reigned supreme in the Inka pantheon, and Huitzilopochtli, while not all-powerful in the company of the Centzonhuitznahuac (the stars), Quetzalcoatl, and Tlaloc, was without exaggeration a primary deity for the Mexica. He was perhaps the first among equals. As mentioned, the Inkakuna allowed some conquered nations to retain some of their deities, but prohibited others, such as those associated with animals. The reduction of the Andean parthenon is a small step toward monotheism. A comparison of Tloque Nahuaque (Lord Up Close and Far Away), a primary unifying Tetzcocan deity, and Pachakamaq, an analogous homogenizing deity, is a topic for another time.[125] What the chronicles, or analyses of them, do not discuss, and what is interesting here for twenty-first-century scholarship, is that Inkakuna themselves may have become relatively more "civilized" when they stealthily appropriated the Qheswa language, although, again, they did not call it by that name. Ironically, this would make them more like Mexica or even the Celts and Visigoths, who learned the language of the cultured elite in the lands they were occupying/invading—Nahuatl in the case of the first, and Latin in the case of the latter two.

When Inkakuna came to the center, they were not too far from the font of ancient Wari power. In the foundation story offered by Garcilaso, four Inka men and four Inka women came north looking for a place where their golden rod would sink into a sunbaked ground (*CR*, I, xv). This was a necessary symbolic step for introducing the institution of agriculture, signifying a place where they would establish their capital. A similarity can be found here with the Mexica, whose experiences established a home-signifying symbol, the place where they found a preordained eagle perched upon a *nopal* eating a snake. There is also a similarity with another important group: the K'iche'.

Both the Inka and the K'iche' nations had four founding fathers who took wives, or tried to take wives, forming four conjugal pairs. Both thought the stories involving four sets of conjugal pairs were important enough to allow them to become the founding narratives for their nations. While the K'iche' had Balam Quitze, Balam Acab, Mahucutah, and Iqui-Balam, the Inka recounted numerous variations of stories surrounding Ayar Manqo and his consort Mama Oqllo; Ayar Cachi with Mama Cora; Ayar Uchu with Mama Rahua; and Ayar Auka with Mama Waco. Of these, Ayar Manqo, despite representing a people who may have still been at the tribal level, became the first Inka king, taking the name of Manqo Qhapaq. He became a legendary leader, much the same as the K'iche' Balam Quitze (or Balam Acab), the Mexicatl Tenoch and the Chichimecatl Xolotl. Garcilaso conveys how Inka Manqo Qhapaq builds the temple of the sun that Inka Yupanki later majestically reconstructed (*CR*, III, xx). Because of these foundational narratives, people who live in Qosqo during all Inka reigns, and especially after Inka Yupanki, can turn their eyes back vertically to the first Inka ruler, who was said to descend directly from the sun and who sunk his golden staff into the soil where he would establish the Inka capital. The social and religious sway of this vertical construction feeds into the pride of the Inka clans, or panakakuna, each of which claimed a vertical connection to that great moment.

Horizontality: More on the Inkakuna's Appropriation of Qheswaness

Besides a vertical relationship between Inkakuna and Manqo Qhapaq/Mama Oqllo and with Hanan/Urin Qosqo, a relatively hidden horizontal relationship intersects with Manqo's verticality, which has to do with language. Garcilaso de la Vega refers to "Quechua" neither as a toponym nor as a glottonym but as a gentilic noun, or ethnonym, that as mentioned, designated the people from a pair of provinces, Cotapampa and Cotanera, "both of the nation called Qheswa" (*CR*, III, xii). Most likely, the nación quechua resided in the present-day administrative division known as Cotabambas. This toponym is probably a Spanish corruption of "Cotapampa" already occurring during Garcilaso's time. He emphasizes "that wherever the Indians say *pampa*, which is plaza, the Spaniards say *bamba*" (que donde los indios dicen *pampa*, que es plaça, dizen los españoles *bamba*) (*CR*, VII, iv). We can conclude that the Spanish invasion caused a linguistic evolution from Cotapampa to Cotabambas. Garcilaso used the term "Qheswa" in a very limited sense, whereas in the postcontact, postcolonial, and now post-Independence sense, the ethnonym can be understood as a demonym with pockets of the demos residing in Peru, Ecuador, and Bolivia. But here we are talking about an earlier denotation, limited to these two provinces.

Being Qheswa provinces, it appears that Cotapampa and Cotanera could logically be considered two places where what we today call the Qheswa language was firmly grounded. We now know, as previously discussed, that it had origins on the coast long before Inka times, though this information was not available to the Inkakuna themselves. What was available was a familiarity with the geographic locations of Cotapampa and Cotanera (in the Andahuaylas region) and a cultural association with them through the language, a possibility Porras Barrenechea does not rule out.[126] This possibility could be considered controversial. In 1910 Max Uhle affirmed that the toponyms Cotapampa and Cotanera were formed with common Aymara words. Cotanera, for example, could be derived from *qoto*, lake; *qota-naira*, eye of the lake.[127] Hence, it is difficult to ascertain which elements came from Qheswa and which ones from Aymara, two languages long in contact. Regarding origins and place names, a substantial number of them denote Aymara origins, and often are covered with a Qheswa veneer. Cerrón-Palomino establishes how even words sounding Qheswa-like, such as Ollantaytambo, are actually Aymara-Qheswa compounds.[128] There appears to have been great social and ethnic movements prior to the advent to the Inka Empire. The peoples who spoke Qheswa and Aymara and other languages were on the move. Regarding the Qheswakuna, Garcilaso explains that in Andahuaylas province, Chanka nations by the name of Hancohuallu, Utunsulla, Uramarca, Uillca, and others displaced Qheswa peoples from their lands or button-holed them into little districts so they could extract tribute from them. This was information he may have acquired from Cieza de León (*CR*, IV, xv).[129] In the context of the Chanka war against the Qheswakuna, Garcilaso divulges that under the appellation "Qheswa" came "five great provinces" (cinco provincias grandes), but that it was precisely "the Qheswakuna designated as Cotapampa and Cotanera" (los Quechuas de los apellidos Cotapampa y Cotanera) who were the Inka Wiracocha's allies in the Inka war against the Chankakuna (*CR*, IV, xxiii; V, xxii).

The sovereign Wiracocha shows his gratitude to the Qheswakuna by making them into Inkakuna—by conferring the title of "Inka" on them, reconfiguring their identity. The Inka lord "ordered [the Qheswakuna] to wear their hair cropped, the *llautu* as a headdress, and with their ears bored out like Inkakuna, although to a lesser degree" (les mandó que truxessen las cabeças tresquiladas, y el llautu por tocado y las orejas horadadas como los Incas, aunque el tamaño del horado fue limitado) (*CR*, V, xxiii). Here we have the three symbols used to identify the royal social class: the *llautu*, the cropped hair, and the extended ears. Garcilaso explains the first this way:

> The Inkakuna wore in their hair as a headdress, a braid that they called *llautu*. They made it of many colors and the length of a finger wide and even a little thinner. This plait went around the head four or five times and appeared as a crown.
>
> Traían los Incas en la cabeça, por tocado, una trença que llaman *llautu*. Hazínla de muchas colores y del ancho de un dedo, y poco menos gruessa. Esta trença rodeavan a la cabeça y davan cuatro o cinco bueltas y quedaba como guirnalda. (*CR*, I, xxii)

That the Inkakuna would share this symbol of royal prestige says much for the expansive fluidity of their concept of nation. There are various possible ways to explain this.

Perhaps the Qheswakuna had made some kind of secret deal with the Inkakuna. The latter could expect aid for which the former were duly compensated in terms of prestige. Quite possibly the upstart Inkakuna realized that the Qheswakuna held useful military and superior cultural capabilities, and accordingly afforded them these honors. If indeed there was some kind of unstated recognition of cultural superiority, then this might explain why the Inkakuna began to assimilate to the language of the Qheswakuna. Garcilaso, as emphasized, adds to the mystery when he refers to Qheswa solely as a province or nation. Again he uses it as a demonym, but not a glottonym.

González Holguín alludes to this sense in his *Vocabulario*, when he defines the expression "Qquechhua runa" as "el de tierra templada," "Qquechhua" itself signifying "temperate land."[130] *Runa* is the generic word for people in Qheswa; thus the expression means "people of the temperate valley." The Corregidor of the Abancay Corregimiento, responding to a questionnaire (*informaciones*) wrote in 1586 that "this province is called Qheswa by a generation that used this name, which denotes 'temperate land'" (esta provincia se dice *Quichua*, por una generación que se nombró deste nombre y que quiere decir 'tierra templada').[131] Perhaps Qheswakuna themselves referred to their language as Qheswa, and this is one reason the Inkakuna did not refer to it as such, although scholars have not yet ascertained this. It does make sense that if Inkakuna "conquered" Qheswakuna and then announced that they appropriated those peoples' language, they might lose prestige, especially if it was recognized that another language was superior to their own primordial one. Therefore, they took Qheswa as their own and—at least after the Conquest, but perhaps before—deployed the imperialistic term "General Language."

The Inkakuna may have also been attracted to the Qheswakuna's language for its perceived greater aesthetical possibilities. Although writing some seventy years after the initial Spanish penetration and referring to the language in a colonial context, Garcilaso alludes to the language's capacity to allow people to express themselves with greater beauty and sophistication. He explains: "It makes them sharper of mind and more docile and more able to learn whatever it is that they want to learn; from barbarians they are turned in men who are more political and urbane" (les hace más agudos de entendimiento y más dóciles y más ingeniosos para lo que quisieren aprender, y de bárbaros los trueca en hombres políticos y más urbanos) (*CR*, VII, iv). One thing Garcilaso is suggesting here, perhaps as rhetorical strategy to preserve the language, is that this language would make an excellent medium for evangelization during the colonial era. It is also evident that he understands the sophistication of the language and its potential for turning rough folk into polished rhetoricians.

The next section further explores the idea of Qheswa as a tool for evangelization. From Garcilaso's vantage point, which harkens back to late antiquity, the language epitomized greater politeness of expression, a form to mold a greater profundity of thought. This does not seem to be mere posturing on the part of Garcilaso. One of his late-nineteenth-century bilingual readers, Matto de Turner, concurs, describing the three primary attributes of the language she, following the sixteenth-century friar-linguists, now openly calls Qheswa. In this fashion, she extends the name of the etnia from which the Inkakuna seem to have appropriated it to the language, while at the same time calling it "a single sonorous and rich language" (un mismo idioma sonoro y rico).[132] By calling the tongue of Cotanera and Cotapampa (which she spells Catonera and Suttupampa) a single language, she hints at its unity and its transformation into the Inkakuna's lingua franca. By referring to its richness, she alludes to the language's multiple syntactical and word choice possibilities. As a literary figure, she may have employed the adjective "sonorous" to refer to the language's resonance. As a linguist, she might have been referring to the voiced quality of many of its words. In 1887 Matto de Turner was inducted as a corresponding member into the prestigious Society of Archeology and Linguistics, an induction that, by its very occurrence, suggests the society's members held her views of things Andean in esteem. Their interest in both Archaeology and Linguistics suggests a sharp turn toward historical linguistics in an attempt to understand the nation of the past and consequently to extrapolate back 350 years to the point of the initial Spanish penetration into Tawantinsuyo.

This brings us to still another reason that the Inkakuna may have assimilated to the Qheswakuna's tongue. Whereas González Holguín offers the meaning of "temperate valley" for the word "Qquechhua,"[133] Matto submits another she derives from Villar, whose 1897 *Lexicología keshua: Uirakocha* was published the same year as the first part of her two-part essay on the Qheswa language. The theory Villar and others were advancing, as discussed by Matto, is an etymology of the word Qheswa that was not "temperate valley," but *quehuit* (to twist) and *ichu* (straw) which, when combined, could mean "straw rope" (soga de paja). Such a meaning could connote "invention or industriousness of those people [from Cotanera and Cotapampa]" (invención ó industria de aquellas gentes [de Cotanera y Cotapampa]). She derives this conclusion from Villar's *Lexicología keshua: Uirakocha* and the work of a certain Father Mossi.[134] González Holguín does define *Qqueuini* as "torcer hilo o soga" (to twist thread or rope) and he even cites this activity as constituting a profession, *qqueuiycamayoc,* "he who knows how to twist well" (el que sabe bien torcer).[135]

This twisted rope etymology of "Qheswa" brings to mind an elaborate device constructed with knots and twisted strands of strings in different colors: the khipu, which for Inca Garcilaso "means to tie and knot" (quiere dezir añudar y ñudo). The knots on colored chords denoted semiotic meaning frequently related to accounting (*CR*, VI, viii, ix). Some might theorize that the khipu served as a semiotic device that recorded the stories of the great battles of history.[136] This apparatus is a kind of meta "twisted rope," for its knots are twists of a rope that is already twisted in the braids that give it form. It is a chord twice twisted, once to make the rope and again to twist the rope into a khipu. Such an instrument was in use long before the people of the Qheswa provinces might have used it. It was utilized by the Wari, as discussed, and it existed as early as Caral. The fact that "Qheswa" could mean "temperate land" could imply that the Qheswa people, their ancestors, or other early speakers came from the coast—possibly Caral. That it could also mean "straw rope" associates the members of the group with the khipu.

The Qheswakuna did not originate the Qheswa language, but they may have been especially adept at constructing khipukuna and/or employing them to narrate beautifully rendered literary or historical stories. Even more likely is that they had developed the khipu into a finely honed instrument for keeping track of *ayni* (reciprocal labor) and *mita* (labor tribute) obligations, which would have been of great interest to the Inkan bureaucrats. In another book, *Lingüística nacional,* published three years later, Villar asserts that this device was "developed among the Qheswakuna to its highest degree of perfection" (avanzado en los kechuas a su mayor grado de perfección).[137] If indeed the Qheswakuna were the most advanced in khipu art during the Inkan rise to power, this may have factored into their close association with the Inkakuna, who became the best khipukamayoqkuna in the land.

Perhaps the subjugation of the Qheswa provinces was not a lightning-bolt enterprise. A nonobjective reading of the chronicles might suggest that the Inkakuna forged their state with a succession of rulers, each one conquering additional neighboring nations. Yet this is not likely the case. Covey weighs in on this matter, suggesting that processes began at least during Wari times and gradually gave shape to Andean governing practices. Even as Tawantinsuyo began to expand, the changes did not occur in the manner of a lightning bolt striking the ground. More likely, Covey concludes, "the full imposition of Inka state administration in many parts of the Cusco region required several generations as the state effected the transition from indirect to direct control."[138] The idea of commandeering the language also known as "Qheswa Simi" for their own use may have come slowly to the Inkakuna, with the process spanning more than one generation.

The Inka mechanism for language diffusion was achieved by moving conquered peoples to Qheswa-speaking provinces while concurrently moving Qheswa-speaking elites to conquered provinces, some to teach that language. These boundless migrations of peoples were called "mitmaq," and Garcilaso describes them as "exchanged Indians" (indios trocados), meaning "'transplanted' or 'newly arrived'" (transplantados o advenedizos) (*CR*, VII, i). Certainly, moving non-Inkakuna into well-established Inkan territories while also moving Inkakuna to newly conquered lands had the desired effect of Inkanization. This is true even if some of Garcilaso's stated goals of moving mitmaqkuna were to thin out overpopulated areas (social engineering), to move farmers to fertile soil (greater agricultural output), or to move bellicose resisters from their home territories to the Inka heartland (military strategy) (*CR*, XII, i). The unstated goal behind all or many of these efforts was Inkanization, signifying a thrust toward cultural homogenization. A large part of this process constituted what we might call Qheswaization. We return to an important quotation, here expressed more fully:

> Among other things the Inka kings invented to promote good government in their empire was to order all their vassals learn the language of the court, today called the General Language. To teach it they put Inkan teachers of rank in each province.
>
> Entre otras cosas que los Reyes Incas inventaron para buen gobierno de su Imperio, fué mandar que todos sus vassallos aprendiessen la lengua de su corte, que es la que hoy llaman lengua general, para cuya enseñança pusieron en cada provincia maestros Incas de los de privilegio.

Garcilaso offers two reasons for such linguistic policies in the Empire. The first benefit is to avoid "so many interpreters who are needed to understand and respond to such a variety of languages and nations as there were in the empire" (tanta muchedumbre de intérpretes como fuera menester para entender y responder a tanta variedad de lenguas y naciones como havía en su Imperio) (*CR*, VII, i). The second benefit, given that people can better communicate with each other, is that they come to know each other, and social relations become softer. That is to say, "different peoples blend together as if they were of one family and clan, overcoming the aloofness that comes from not understanding each other" (se amassen uno a otros como si fuessen de una familia y parentela y perdiessen la esquiveza que les causava el no entenderse) (*CR*, VII, i).

Garcilaso does not say it, but if the Inkakuna learned Qheswa, they probably initiated this policy of mitmaq themselves, sending Inka nobility to Cotapampa and Cotanera and bringing Qheswa speakers from Cotanera and Cotapampa to the Inka court in Qosqo. This would provide the opportunity for Qheswa speakers to Qheswaize Qosqo and for Inkakuna to go to the Qheswa provinces for a kind of study abroad, immersion-based language learning. After their positive experience and the successful Qheswaization of Qosqo, they then continued to deploy the mitmaq system throughout Tawantinsuyo, inversely disseminating Qheswa from the capital to the four suyos. In line with what Covey hypothesizes for governmental structures, Qheswaization most likely took various generations and was still occurring upon the appearance of Spaniards on the scene.

To conclude this line of inquiry, a parallel between Tawantinsuyo and Anahuac can be established. If Inkakuna, for whatever reason, learned Qheswa and dispersed it throughout their empire, we can be sure they thought it was a better, a more beautiful, or a more useful language than their own, or that it was politically or strategically expedient to do so. Qheswa then becomes something like Nahuatl. Chichimeca and Mexica appropriated Nahuatl as the language of learning, and then in future generations disseminated it in their conquests as they diffused Toltecayotl. The Inkakuna, in the same fashion, appropriated a language associated with, if we concur with Villar and Matto de Turner's reasoning, the khipu; then as an aesthetically superior language, disseminated it among the ethnic nations they were folding into the texture of Tawantinsuyo. By analogy with the idea of Toltecness, we can suggest the condition of Qheswaness. However, while the Mexica publicly wielded the original Nahua term for Toltecness, Inkakuna did not use the term we are suggesting here to describe their cultural accomplishments. Unlike the word "Toltecayotl," "Qheswaness" is a neologism we derive from the etymology of the glottonym "Qheswa" and the khipu device possibly related to the glottonym, relationships regarding Inkan linkages of power that have been inadequately studied. The neologism is necessary for readers in our time to understand the complexities of cultural aspirations during the period of late antiquity. Much the way the Inkakuna did not have a term for "colonization" yet engaged in it, they did not have a term for Qheswaness but they aspired to it.

Why might the Inkakuna not have freely divulged the fact that their private language was actually their language of origin, or that there had been a language in Qosqo before they arrived there? A probable answer lies in the truth they would not have liked to admit, which perhaps they did not even remember in their collective memory: that there remained some vestige of Wari culture and society in Qosqo before their arrival that did not need or desire to be "civilized" by them. Indeed, because we know the Wari had a developed version of the khipu, it may have also been that the Qheswakuna, because they were associated with it, learned it from the descendants of the Wari leadership, and as postulated, passed it along to the Qheswakuna. This would go against Garcilaso's Manqo Qhapaq story based on oral tradition. In that vertically oriented narrative, Manqo Qhapaq and Mama Oqllo come from Lake Titiqaqa to civilize "barbarian" tribes across the southern Andes (*CR*, I, xv). The lineage they established continued the civilizing process through the following generations. Regarding Inkakuna and their language, they would not have wanted to admit that Qheswa was more sophisticated than their primordial language, perhaps a form of Aymara or Puquina. Such an admission would have gone against their civilizing narrative. Therefore, unsurprisingly, they would have glossed over this aspect. Although they were not in power for enough time to erase those origins, there remained enough clues for Garcilaso to integrate those strands into his account. As with the Chichimeca of Tetzcoco, the Inkakuna of Qosqo were probably less sophisticated than the original inhabitants of the city and the Qheswakuna as well. However, they were unlike the Chichimeca, who openly and proudly admitted the details of their cultural journey, because they suppressed this upstart reality in favor of a confected narrative glorifying their attainments, their empire, and what was now their language.

A Pause: Qheswa, Aldrete, and a Theory of Language and Empire

We continue to ponder why, if the Inkakuna had an ancestral language, they would take the trouble of learning another province's language. Villar, the late nineteenth-century linguist, puts forth the theory that each province had its own language. Conversely, in his 1890 *Lingüística nacional,* he proposes that Aymara and Qheswa were dispersed heterogeneously, and that the language of the Qheswakuna "should have been the same one as Qosqo's" (ha debido ser idéntica á la del Cuzco).[139] This theory might explain why imperialist peoples would diffuse the language of people they were subordinating, but it would not explain Garcilaso's admitting three languages, and it especially would not reveal what the private language was. This is curious, as Villar openly refers to Garcilaso's *Royal Commentaries* (III, xii). If we reject his theory on these grounds, we must ask: what would compel the Inkakuna to embark on such a political and social program, to adopt for themselves the language of a people they conquered and then disseminate it to the four corners of their empire?

This is a thought-provoking question, because after Spaniards arrived in the lands they called the Indias Occidentales, they would be confronted with a similar query regarding their own linguistic policies as they proceeded with their multipronged invasion.[140] Some felt they should impose Castilian on Andean peoples in their efforts to govern and evangelize. One Renaissance erudite who thought in this vein was the philologist Bernardo Aldrete. Others, such as the Jesuit priest Blas Valera, felt priests could and should learn Qheswa because they would have greater success in converting conquered peoples to Christianity. The first case could be regarded as an interest in Hispanization, and the second, in Christianization. These, as discussed in chapter 2, are two of the three prongs of proto-nationalism, precisely the two isolated by Hobsbawm. In this section, we review the particulars with an eye toward establishing two concepts of the nation with respect to language, the Spanish-centric optic and the Qheswa-centric one. In chapter 4 we look back at the Nahua-centric one, but from a perspective that also considers gender. Well known is Nebrija's *Gramática de la lengua castellana* (Grammar of the Castilian language) (1492), in which he asserts to the queen the importance of Spanish for the empire.[141] Less known is Aldrete, who had contacts with Inca Garcilaso.

As historian Durand suggests, it appears Garcilaso had in his library Aldrete's *Varias antigvedades de España, Africa y otras provincias* (Various antiquities of Spain, Africa, and other provinces) (1614).[142] For his part, in his *Del origen y principio de la lengua castellana* (On the origin and beginning of the Castilian language), Aldrete referred to the Inkan scholar's etymological study of the proper noun "Peru."[143] Durand concludes that these contacts probably occurred around the year 1600, while Garcilaso waited for *La Florida del Inca* (1605) to appear in print.[144] Both erudites were residing in and around Córdoba, and it does seem probable they knew each other personally. Whereas Garcilaso was fixated on the Andes, Aldrete, naturally, departed from Iberian realities in his approach to language. Aldrete is valuable here because he assists in our understanding the issues at stake with respect to language diffusion and empire.

In *Del origen y principio de la lengua castellana*, Aldrete discusses the conquering Visigoths on the Iberian Peninsula. He explains why they learned the Latin being spoken there instead of imposing their own Germanic language.[145] With a somewhat flawed logic resulting from a non sequitur, he states, "Being a more bellicose and simple folk than being ambitious, they were concerned with preserving the Latin language more than extending the use of their own" (siendo gente mas belicosa, i senzilla, que ambiciosa, procuraron antes conservar la lengua Latina, que estender la suia propia).[146] The inverse is true of the next invasion of Hispania, the Moorish one. Mignolo, making plain Aldrete's complex syntax, expresses the Renaissance author's argument thusly: "Castilians under the Moors lost not only their language, but sometimes their religion, and often their lives." The Moorish and Visigothic invasions of the peninsula were not the only ones. Certainly before them, the Romans had overrun it. With at least three massive invasions since the Classical era, Iberia can be considered a controlled environment in which to study the relationship between empire and language, and it is especially useful to prescribe successes in the post-1492 enterprise, when the thrice-conquered people embarked upon their own conquering plans.

While Umayyads and Romans imposed both their language and their religion, there remained an intriguing difference between them. Mignolo explains this difference and how it might have appeared to Aldrete. Whereas Romans invaded and occupied the entire territory, the Moors did not, leaving "significant portions of the peninsula in which people were able to preserve their sense of territoriality, by preserving their religion, Christianity, and their language, Castilian."[147] What Aldrete is getting at is the need to coordinate territoriality with the limits of the diffusion of language and religion. Territory, language, and religion must be perfectly aligned, and the borders, both conceptual and spatial, must correspond with each other for the "nation" to thrive. The Romans succeeded because they imposed their language and their religion on the totality of the Iberian Peninsula (albeit not at the same moment, for assuredly we are talking about two waves of religions conversion, one polytheistic and the other monotheistic). The Arabs eventually failed because they did not conquer the entire peninsula.

Why must language and territoriality coincide for a conquest to succeed in a cultural sense? Without a doubt by 711, Iberians were not solely descended from Romans. They were already blending with Celts and with Goths. It was this hybrid type of people with a Christian identity, sometimes called

Celtiberos in Spanish, upon whom it eventually fell to carry out the *Reconquista*, or Reconquest, of the Iberian Peninsula from the Moorish emirates. While the first thrusts of the Reconquista during the eighth century were probably accomplished by soldiers who spoke a Vulgar Latin tongue, as the centuries progressed, and the language evolved, the majority of later generations of soldiers, through the last battles in 1492, mostly spoke a language recognizable as medieval Spanish. The *Poem of the Cid* (circa twelfth century) is an emblematic example of Reconquest literature written in Spanish, from the middle of this period. The Moorish invasion ultimately failed due to their incomplete conquering of the Celtic-Gothic-Roman Iberians, leaving themselves open to a military backlash. Aldrete writes of the post-711 reality on the Hispanic peninsula:

> The general loss of Spain would also have been a loss of the [Castilian] language, if those Christians, who by God's bountiful mercy escaped from the hands of the Moors, had not with great valor undertaken such a glorious enterprise such as turning back those who had become so powerful. If they had failed, the language would have been lost.
>
> La pérdida general de España fueralo tambien de la Lengua, si aquellos pocos Christianos, que por gran misericordia de Dios se escaparon de las manos de los Moros, i fueron los que con gran valor acometieron tan gloriosa empresa, como tornar a echar de donde auian hecho tan poderosos, no la vbieran conservado.[148]

Thus, Aldrete is not so concerned with the local ethnic nations inhabiting the Iberian Peninsula—the Andalusians, the Basques, the Galicians, and the Castilians. He is concerned with the nature of the empire comprised of all of the above as a political entity united by Catholicism and Castilian Spanish.

Aldrete found it unsettling that the lessons of Iberian history and language acquisition were being lost on the Spanish Empire as it conquered the New World. For if Romans, Inkakuna, and Mexica imposed Latin, Qheswa, and Nahuatl, respectively, on their recently conquered subjects, so too should Spaniards impose Castilian on their newly conquered Andean and Nahua subjects. The logic from a European perspective, Mignolo suggests, is that the Romans imposed Latin on the Iberian Peninsula, which was a conduit for Christianity, just as the Spanish imposing Castilian on the New World would install a conduit for Christianity.[149] Aldrete was an imperialist, but he was not so small-minded he could not draw lessons from the histories of the Mexica and Inkakuna while developing his theory of empire and language. In *Del origen y principio de la lengua castellana,* he is cognizant that in the Inka Kingdom "there is a great diversity of languages, so many indeed, that they cannot be counted" (ai gran diuersidad de lenguas, i tantas que no tienen numero).[150] One example to corroborate Aldrete's view is the 1586 *Descripción de la tierra del corregimiento de Abancay* (Description of the Corregimiento of Abancay), in which the Corregidor Niculoso de Fornee comments on the towns of Zurite, Guarocondor, Anta, and Puquibra. He writes of these towns, "All or most of them have different languages, but the one they speak is the general one" (todos o la mayor parte tienen diferentes lenguas, pero la que hablan es la general).[151] We hereby see that Qheswa was so rooted that it resolutely continued to function as a lingua franca a decade after the conclusion of the Forty-Years War that consolidated Spanish power in the central Andes. In the face of such linguistic diversity, the Inkakuna, Aldrete reasons, saw to it that "their courtly language of Qosqo be introduced" (su lengua cortesana del Cuzco se introduxesse). Aldrete mentions Wayna Qhapaq as the gran proponent of Qheswa's diffusion, and in this he draws parallels between Inkakuna and Mexica.[152] Mignolo puts this in perspective: "Aldrete found these examples extremely useful. The expansion and colonization of language by the Incas and Mexicas supported his thesis that the vanquisher always inflicted its language upon the vanquished, as did the expansion and colonization of language by the Spaniards." This is not to say Aldrete was open-minded with respect to the question of Inkan and Mexicatl languages. It cannot be clearer, as Mignolo reminds us: "Aldrete was interested in establishing the Greco-Roman tradition in language and the Holy Roman legacy in religion. Aldrete did not doubt a particular distinction and rightness in such legacies, and he never doubted that such a distinguished linguistic and religious tradition should be expanded to the Spanish dominions in the Indies."[153] This is fascinating because Aldrete developed his theory while meditating on Iberian military and linguistic history. It is even more so because the history of late antiquity peoples also influenced him.

This strand in his thought, as Mignolo evinces, is derived mainly from his reading of the Jesuit José de Acosta's *Historia natural y moral.*[154] Father Acosta's book not only influenced Aldrete, it also had an impact on his colleague and fellow member of the Córdoba circle, Inca Garcilaso de la Vega. It is important to note first that Aldrete likely had conversations with Garcilaso in the Cathedral of Cordoba and perhaps in the Jesuit college in that city.[155] As Durand suggests, he was undeniably one of the few people Garcilaso trusted to read his unpublished manuscripts.[156] In book three of *Del origen y principio de la lengua castellana,* Aldrete reveals in a footnote his debt to the *Royal Commentaries,* which "remain unpublished, but as a gracious gesture, [Garcilaso] has shared with me" (aun no está impressos que por hazerme gracia me a comunicado).[157] This confirms that, besides drawing on Father Acosta, Aldrete also drew on the chronicler from Qosqo.

In his conversations with Garcilaso, the philologist may have found intriguing Garcilaso's solid views on the value of Qheswa in the Inkan subjugation of the Andes, which he might have compared to Nahua expansion in Anahuac. What is compelling is that the parallel between Romans, Inkakuna, and Mexica does not hold water in linguistic terms, because neither Mexica nor Inkakuna diffused the original language of their ethnic nation, as Romans did and Castilians were doing. Aldrete does not comment on this circumstance and may not have even realized it, because Garcilaso does not openly admit it. The Mexiça, originally Chichimecatl and Nahuatlized slowly over multiple generations, certainly diffused Nahuatl as their tributary state expanded. They did not spread their own Aztlanish language, but instead the language they learned from descendants of the Tolteca. Likewise, although a relatively unknown fact, the Inkakuna did not spread their own ethnic language, but indeed spread the language of a people whom they had conquered, the Qheswa nation. Aldrete might not have been comfortable with such a possibility as he developed his theory of language and empire.

Despite the inaccuracy of his view on diffusing the language of ethnic origin with respect to Mexica and Inkakuna, what might be called the Aldretean principle is certainly applicable to both regions. That is to say, language and territoriality must coincide for a nation to be strong and to resist conquest. With respect to Perú, if the Inkakuna had been able to more thoroughly Qheswaize their realm of Tawantinsuyo, the ayllukuna that had aligned themselves so readily with the Spanish may have pondered this from a different angle and taken a different tack. The Inkakuna, of course, could not have imagined an invasion by people such as the Spanish, but they did understand that for national cohesion, language and territory had to be aligned. Thus they had embarked on their policies of mitmaq migration and language diffusion. They understood the Aldretean principle intuitively, even though they never could have known who Aldrete was—he was from another world.

On Blas Valera, the General Language, and the Colonial State

There is more to say on what we are calling here the Aldretean principle. We have discussed Qheswa and the Qheswakuna during late antiquity. Here we are interested in the same process during the early modern age, and especially as analyzed in the writing of the Jesuit priest Blas Valera, as cited in Inca Garcilaso's *Royal Commentaries.* Valera, whose work remained unpublished during Garcilaso's time, some of it lost forever, was converted into an authority by Garcilaso, who quoted profusely from his papers.[158] Markham, reviewing what was available at the dawn of the twentieth century, concludes that Valera was "by far the greatest of the clerical authors."[159] Indeed Markham puts Valera at a higher value than the chronicler writing in the company of Aldrete in Cordoba, Spain. He explains: "Unlike Garcilasso [*sic*], instead of going to Spain when he was twenty, he worked for Peru and its people for thirty years, devoting himself to a study of the history, literature, and ancient customs of his countrymen, receiving their records and legends and the older *Amautas* and *Quipucamayocs* who could remember the Inca rule, and their lists of kings."[160] Although of mixed heritage like Garcilaso, unlike the *Royal Commentaries* author, Valera found himself in a precarious situation by remaining in Peru. He was charged with fornication, a diversionary ploy to hide the fact that his ideas were considered subversive. He then found himself in a Jesuit dungeon being flogged each and every week, finally having to escape from the country to avoid the inquisitional bonfire.[161]

Perhaps one of the reasons Father Valera was considered a threat to the social fabric was his intense interest in the General Language. As Valera was of dual heritage, it should come as no surprise that Markham refers to "his perfect mastery" of Qheswa.[162] Because he could move about freely in both Qheswaphone circles and in the priestly class, Valera was uniquely qualified to understand the General Language as spoken by both native speakers and priests concerned with evangelization.

Why is the diffusion of the General Language an important topic for the colonial era? The answer, from the perspective of that era, has to do with Hispanization and Christianization. From the perspective of the twenty-first century, the answer includes those two nation-building thrusts, but also the colonial language realities and policies that both reflected and inverted the Qheswa ideal of Inkan times. As we saw with our analysis of Aldrete's theories on empire, Qheswa's incomplete diffusion plays a primary role in understanding the evolution of the concept of Peru. As Mannheim notes, although the Inkakuna worked tirelessly to impose the General Language as the official language of empire, "it did not achieve linguistic hegemony during Tawantinsuyo's brief existence, even in the immediate vicinity of the Inka capital, Cuzco."[163] Moreover, as previously noted, the diffusion of Qheswa did not become a linguistic priority until at least the Inka Wiracocha, who reigned until 1432, just one hundred years before the Spanish invasion. There simply was not enough time to diffuse Qheswa comprehensively and thoroughly throughout the empire. If we take the Aldretean principle regarding language into account, we can more fully understand the destiny of Tawantinsuyo.

When Spaniards came, the first thing they did was decapitate the Inka leadership, allowing their government to fall into disarray. Because of the region's linguistic heterogeneity, it would not take long for imperial linguistic policy, as well as that strand of protonationalism to crumble along with it. Writing in the last quarter of the sixteenth century, Blas Valera comments on the loss of Qheswa's privileged position. He writes, "All the City of Trujillo's limits and many other provinces in Quito's jurisdiction are unfamiliar with the General Language that was spoken; and all the Collas and Puquinas, content with their own languages, scorn Qosqo's." (Todo el término de la ciudad de Trujillo y otras muchas provincias de la juridición de Quitu ignoran del todo la lengua general que hablavan; y todos los Collas y los Puquinas, contentos con sus lenguajes particulares y propios, desprecian la del Cozco.) (cited in *CR*, VII, iii) This was pro-Qheswa rhetoric based on imperial practice that was coming up short during the colonial period. It was now, however, a rhetoric with a basis in colonial-era reality. Torero, studying the period documentation pertaining to El Collao and Charcas, finds "a weak introduction of Qheswa, at first glance, surprising" (una débil implantación del quechua, a primera vista sorprendente).[164] Regarding Puquina, Torero notes that in 1575 Viceroy Toledo could still call that language one of three "general languages." This all suggests that Valera got it right in both cases. Regrettably, just a century later Puquina had all but disappeared from the documentation.[165]

Furthermore, even where Qheswa is remembered and employed, Blas Valera laments, "it is so corrupted that it seems almost like it is another language" (está tan corrupta que casi parece otra lengua diferente). It could be that Valera was misinterpreting the varieties of Qheswa he was encountering. We discussed above the error of calling variants of the language "corrupt Qheswa." What this means from Valera's vantage point is that the Iberians may have effectively slowed down the royal Inka pro-Qheswa policy of lingua franca. He concludes,

> That confusion and multiplicity of languages that the Inkakuna, with such attention to detail, tried to resolve, has risen again to the degree that today among the Indians there are more language differences than there were in the time of Wayna Qhapaq, their last emperor.
>
> Aquella confusión y multitud de lenguas que los Incas, con tanto cuidado, procuraron quitar, ha buelto a nascer de nuevo, de tal manera que el día de hoy se hallan entre los indios más diferencias de lenguajes que había en tiempo de Huaina Cápac, último de Emperador dellos. (cited in *CR*, VII, iii)

Father Valera fears the loss of Qheswa, because without it the arduous task of evangelization becomes even more difficult. He may have exaggerated to a degree, because, as linguist Mannheim writes, "the Spaniards recognized its potential as a lengua general (lingua franca) for administrative purposes and especially for proselytization, and consciously promoted it as a vehicle of linguistic homogenization."[166] Valera tried to frame his argument in terms of Evangelization practice, but he was commenting on the situation resulting from an incomplete saturation of Qheswa, which allowed other languages to bubble back to the top of the linguistic surface after the murder of Thupaq Amaru.

In the documentation approving the translation into Qheswa of *Declaración copiosa de las cuatro partes mas essenciales y necessarias de la doctrina christiana* (A copious declaration on the four most essential and necessary parts of Christian doctrine) by the Saint Robert Bellarmine, a Jesuit who became cardinal and a central figure of the Counter Reformation, we find some letters by another Jesuit, Father Luis de Teruel, who resided in Peru. Father Teruel praises the translation, and proposes more Qheswa-language instruction among the clergy. One epistle states the following:

> And it is true that what can be seen in some towns because of not preaching to the Indians, nor catechizing them in their original language pains the heart. They forget what they knew, if they knew anything, and they do not perceive what one says, because they do not understand the Spanish language, not being able to perceive in it the profound mysteries of the faith.

> Y cierto es mucho de sentir lo que [en] algunos pueblos se ven por no predicar a los Indios, ni catequizarlos en su lengua original[. O]lvidan lo que sabían, si sabían algo, y no perciben lo que se le dize, por no entender la lengua Española, no ser capaces de penetrar en ella los profundos misterios de la Fé.[167]

Hence among the Jesuits there was an awareness of the need to preach the Gospel in Qheswa Simi.

Valera, one of the few Jesuit priests born in Peru, seemed to sympathize with the Inkan Empire, and he may have lamented the General Language's loss because he truly believed it to be a superior and sublime mode of expression.[168] Naturally, given that he was clergy, he may have been truly concerned about the difficulty of evangelization in such a multilingual environment. The latter of these two possibilities offers him a rhetorical strategy to preserve and continue to diffuse the formerly imperial tongue: "There was no one who remembered such a suitable and necessary thing to preach the Sacred Gospels" (no huvo quién se acordasse de cosa tan acomodada y necesaria para la predicación del Santo Evangelio) (cited in *CR,* VII, iii). What Valera is arguing is that if Qheswa is lost, so too is the best avenue for converting Andean folk to Christianity. Valera is not proposing a pro-Qheswa policy on a whim. He asserts it is indispensable for the preaching of the faith. Garcilaso quotes him again: "It is impossible that Peru's Indians, in this time of linguistic fragmentation, could be instructed in the faith and in good manners, unless the priests know all the languages of that Empire, which is impossible." (Es impossible que los indios del Perú, mientras durare esta confusión de lenguas, puedan ser bien instruídos en la fe y en las buenas costumbres, si no es que los sacerdotes sepan todas las lenguas de aquel Imperio, que es imposible.) He concludes that for priests who want to preach the Gospel, "only Qosqo's language, however it is known, could be of much use" (solo la del Cozco, como quiera que la sepan, pueden aprovechar mucho) (cited in *CR,* VII, iii). Valera was not a voice in the wilderness, because numerous religious and temporal authorities concurred. He was an idealist wanting further Qheswaization, even though there seems to have been some of that going on.

There is a certain logic to these kinds of arguments regarding the General Language, for certainly it would be easier for a small number of Spaniards to learn it—or even for them to learn several local languages or Viceroy Toledo's three general ones—than for a large number of Andeans to understand the urgency to learn Spanish. One possible strategy to help bring about conclusive adhesion to Qheswa as a medium of diffusion in the Catholic realm is to translate the Gospel into that language. This did not happen during the colonial era because Spaniards perceived the Andeans as being without letters. During the late colonial period, in the wake of the Thupaq Amaru independence movement, the Spanish authorities made Qheswa illegal to such an effect that Charles Walker terms what happened "cultural genocide"—what we might call ethnocide. Nevertheless, as noted by Walker, they ultimately failed, and Inkan dress, songs, and dramas survived.[169] It was not until the dawn of the twentieth century, when Matto de Turner received a subvention from the American Bible Society, that someone was able, at long last, to translate all four of the Gospels into Qheswa. Still, it must be stated that the Hispanist arm of the colonial apparatus won out. There are many intricate reasons for this. We can simply state that Bernardo Aldrete's apple does not fall far from Blas Valera's tree. Because the Spanish were not able to completely eradicate Qheswa (nor was that their goal), Peru, at least outside the coastal cities, remains just as Andean as Spanish. Conversely, if during late antiquity Qheswa had been better preserved, resistance to Spanish and Criollo rule may have evolved into a more coherent project. But that was not the case.

In the 1981 census, only 24 percent of Peruvians admitted to speaking Qheswa, a percentage that dropped in the 1993 census, which reported Qheswa speakers at 16 percent.[170] Needless to say, after scores of Qheswa speakers were wiped out during Peru's internal conflict of the 1970s and 1980s, they were not necessarily open to revealing they spoke the language. Specifically, as the Comisión de la Verdad y Reconciliación (Truth and Reconciliation Commission) reports, approximately seventy thousand people died in Peru, 75 percent of whom spoke Qheswa, Aymara, or Amazonian language.[171] In the post-war period, many people moved to the coastal cities and began to shed their linguistic and clothing-style identities. In a way, some of the attitudes about language enshrined in Spanish colonialism have survived until today.

From Old Structures to New Ones

One of the features of imperialist strategies is the reallocation of power to new geographic spheres. A surging Tenochtitlan may dislocate the center of a disintegrating empire, as was the case with Tollan, although clearly the Spanish completely redesigned Tenochtitlan in accordance with their norms, making it a satellite in yet another imperial constellation. At the same time, with the passing of one hub of authority to another, the ritual, economic, and geographical vertex is displaced. The same is true in the Andes. From the Formative Period to the moment the early Inkakuna began their period of migration, the cultural, demographic, and economic epicenter of the Central Andes was the Titiqaqa Basin.[172] With shifting power structures, the rise and decline of the Wari, and finally the Inka triumph, that center gravitated to Qosqo. Unsurprisingly, power became even more fluid after the 1530s. While Qosqo retained some of its prestige as the seat of the former empire, Lima became the new bureaucratic center of the viceroyalty (*NU*, 131), forcing Qosqo into a subordinate relationship with it. One of the strategies of the European sixteenth century was to build up its own ethnic centers, thereby suppressing other centers such as those of the Nahua or the Inkakuna.

If the Spanish assigned a nomenclature to New Spain, a proper noun overtly linking Tenochtitlan to the intercontinental empire, they embarked upon a different strategy when it came to the heart of the Inka domain. While expanding their kingdom, another more subtle phenomenon, as alluded above, was unfolding. Villamarín and Villamarín describe it this way: "Most of the chiefdoms annexed by the Inka Empire reemerged with chiefdom-like structures during the period between the empire's collapse and the Spanish imposition of control, indicating the level of adaptability to change in social and environmental conditions that this form of organization had."[173] This resurfacing of the polity attests to the potency of the ethnic nation. It also suggests a reordering of things as post-Inkan alliances were formed (*NU*, 135). Therefore when Titu Yupanki, one of Manqo Inka's captains, began to besiege the new capital of Lima, Governor Pizarro was able to call on various *kurakakuna* for assistance. In *Nacimiento de una utopía* (1988), Manuel Burga lists them as the Wanka kuraka, kurakakuna from Pachakamaq and Lurigancho, and the kuraka Condor Wacho from Huaylas (*NU*, 141). The latter had a direct link to the Governor. The kuraka from Huaylas was the mother of Pizarro's concubine, Inés Huaylas Yupanki, and the grandmother of his daughter, Francisca. Not all power flowed directly from Inka elites to the Spanish.[174] Other ethnic nations were involved.

As discussed, Spaniards were concerned with space in defining the new national provinces. We touched on "provinces" previously in this chapter and we turn back to this idea here. In Cieza de León's narrative, he sets out to trace the "demarcations and divisions of the Peruvian provinces" (la demarcación y diuisión de las prouincias del Perú) (*CP-1*[era], fol. 4v, p. 9). While Cieza does look over indigenous communities, and takes it upon himself to explain the "rites and costumes that the Indians formerly had since antiquity" (ritos y costumbres que tenían antiguamente los indios), he is also interested in the who, how, and where of the newly founded Spanish cities (fundaciones de las nuevas ciudades que se han fundado de Españoles) (*CP-1^{era}*, fol. 4v, p. 9). Each new Spanish city, as discussed with the formation of San Sebastian in Urabá, reorders space.

Cieza de León is not the only one who considered Peru a province. In a "Dedicatory Epistle" to Prince Phillip, who was at that moment en route to England for his nuptials to the Catholic Queen Mary I, Agustín de Zárate applies this same appellation. He refers to Peru as "that province" (aquella prouincia) of Spain (*HDC,* iiii). This same imperial ranking becomes even more prominent in the reworking of the title for the 1577 edition of his masterpiece, *Historia del descvbrimiento y conqvista de las provincias del Peru,* to include the notion of "provinces." Regarding other locations, Zárate writes of the "prouincia de Chili," and as previously reported, "la prouincia de Popayan" (*HDC,* 8 overleaf, 4). Consequently, the notion of Peru can be "province" or "provinces" plural, yet does not clearly connote a diversity of ethnic groups: the large mass of interconnected territories designated as "Peru," a proper noun based on an error of communication, Garcilaso explains, was inhabited by diverse peoples who were all reduced to the category "Indians" (*CR,* I, iv).[175]

Demarcation of provinces, a fluidic process, can be a superficial way to look at governed entities, because on the inside of these districts operated real mechanisms for defining, guiding, and even controlling people. For Mexico, as will be seen below, the repartimiento often followed the pre-Hispanic communal structures established by the coatequitl. This was not necessarily true for Peru. The tenth of the *Ordenanzas de la Real Academia de Lima,* published in 1685 (just about a century after Inca Garcilaso and Guaman Poma started to craft their monumental works) allows elections, but not with what we might call a democratic spirit. First, it allows elections for the positions of regidor, or council member, and alcalde, or mayor, but it prohibits "heathen Indians" (Indios infieles) from running in the election.[176] Second, Christian "Indians" can run for these positions as well as for a third: notary, or khipukamayoq (Escribano ó Quipocamayo).[177] It would seem here that democratic elections might be possible for at least Christianized Andeans, yet a sinister aspect to this becomes apparent upon investigation. The fifth and sixth ordinances prohibit *caciques principales,* which is to say kurakakuna, from participating in the elections. The ordinance has two telling elements, which read as follows:

Item. Said mayors must be advised that for said offices of mayors, aldermen, and other officials, they are not to nominate neither the primary kuraka nor his second.

Iten, los dichos Alcaldes han de estar advertidos, que para dichos oficios de Alcaldes y Regidores, y demás oficiales, no han de nombrar al cazique principal, ni segunda persona.

And the other:

Item. I order the kurakakuna not to involve themselves in the elections for mayors and aldermen and other officials of the Republic, nor should they circulate getting out the vote for one person or the next.

Iten, Mando a los caziques principales, no se entremeten en las elecciones de los Alcaldes y Regidores, y demas oficiales de la Republica, ni andan procurando votos para ningunas personas.

These elections were to take place each and every year! Finally, the eighth ordinance holds that the elections are not to be ayllu-specific, that one mayor must represent different ayllukuna, or parcialidades, which do not coincide with the contours of his own etnia.[178] One way to look at this legislation might be to see the initial stages of democracy. Another might be to recognize this as a way to rip power away from the hereditary kurakakuna. Yet another is to conclude that these policies either did not take into account what we call ethnicity, or that it attempted to weaken what we call ethnicity. Still another is to realize that because the election was convoked on a regular basis, commoners who won and then rotated out the next year would be prohibited from accumulating the kind of sway needed to represent an ethnic nation before the colonial authorities. All of this took place in the context of forced migrations reminiscent of the mitmaqkuna, suggesting that the Spanish were coopting imperial Inka policy and practice for their own purposes. Concurrently, the Spanish directly appointed kurakakuna from the plebeian classes, described by Guaman Poma as "false primary kurakakuna" (falsos caciques principales) (*PNC*, 762 [776]). The facts that the alcalde could not be from his own ayllu and that colonized nontraditional kurakakuna exercised power accelerated the separation of political power from the ethnic nation.

It is interesting to compare the Andes to Mesoamerica. First and foremost, it must be emphasized that Tawantinsuyo was a patchwork of perhaps two hundred etnias. Interethnic contact occurred at the highest levels of the social hierarchy as well as at the mitmaq level. We will concentrate on the upper echelons of society in our discussion only because there is more documentation. Nevertheless, we can consider at least one example from the working classes. Murra cites the practice of salt miners being relocated some eight-days walk from their ethnic communities to work. Because mitmaq workers came from far-flung areas, it is fitting to describe their settlement as "multiethnic." Later on, as Tawantinsuyo expanded, those walking days would need to be extended to cover as much as two months. Apparently it was not just male workers crossing ethnic boundaries, as women made such treks too. Murra, referring to sixteenth-century church records, writes that "spouses are listed as coming from very far away."[179] Because in both late antiquity and Hispanic times multiethnic civic structures were created and were fluid, we can infer transculturation processes in both place and time.

Speaking in general terms, one of the differences between the forced migrations imposed by Inkakuna on subject peoples and those imposed by Spaniards is that the former discerned and embraced the notion of ethnic communities reciprocating their efforts, while the latter simply moved peoples according to imperial economic exigencies. People could better preserve their ethnicity under the Inkakuna than they could under the Spanish. José María Arguedas, the novelist-ethnographer, recognizes the brilliance of an Inka policy that balanced the "maintenance of the personality of the regional cultures and the imposition of the fundamentals of Inkan organization" (mantenimiento de la personalidad de las culturas regionales y la imposición de los fundamentos de la organización incaica).[180] This was, of course, not the case during the Spanish era.

If the Inkakuna could distinguish the kinds of roots in communities that could be modified from those that were millenary and eternal, the Spanish were unaware of these matters. Kenneth Andrien explains the profound negative effect of migration in that postcontact era: "Pulling different communities into larger towns in some cases separated ethnic confederations or even split ayllu. This in turn weakened the reciprocal ties of allegiance between *kurakas* and their people." He offers as an example the case of Yauyos, where "over two hundred separate villages [were congregated] into only thirty-nine new settlements."[181] This type of reorganization is nothing less than a remodeling of the nation from the bottom up. The results are devastating for the individual cultures. Today, for example, there remain fewer than a thousand speakers of Jacaru, mostly women, as the men are generally more bilingual.[182] In this process, the kuraka is separated from his people in a two-pronged effort: the physical separation of him from his ayllu and the prohibition against him participating in temporal power.

There were efforts to protect indigenous groups. As discussed regarding Muñoz Camargo, and as Fernando Fuenzalida Vollmar underscores, the Spanish and the blacks were prohibited from buying indigenous lands; they were also prohibited from sleeping within the pueblos de indios.[183] Zárate, perhaps referring to the New Laws of 1542, explains that the use of the Andeans to transport silver was discontinued: "After executing the royal ordinance, the Indians did not have to carry" (despues que en ejecucion dela ordenança real no se cargan los Indios) (*HDC*, 13). However, we know these kinds of efforts were not the primary forces at play in the new colonies, nor were they entirely respected.

In her archival digging, Susan Ramírez discovers the repercussions of these types of laws in the people. In the documentation found regarding the case of one Don Juan, the kuraka of Collique, she finds that he was a kuraka in the style of the "old ones" and accordingly garnered the respect of the people. Ramírez stresses that a kuraka whose position was based on the reciprocity tradition did not have substantial wealth. He "distributed goods . . . as much for his own self-interest as for the material benefit of his people." While these hereditary leaders had little means at the time of their death, through the system of reciprocity they had enhanced their reputations as "good, generous, and able provider[s]." These traditional kurakakuna were poles apart from the postcontact ones, "who were being elevated to the position by their current Spanish overlords."[184]

There is some dispute about the number of panakakuna at the time of the advent of the Spanish horizon of power, culture, and bureaucracy. We discussed previously the number of panakakuna as being ten, and chapter 4 goes into the structural and anthropological reasons for this. However, not all researchers versed in these matters accept ten as the number of panakakuna existing before the Forty-Years War. David Cahill, departing from Zuidema and Rowe, suggests that there were twelve panakakuna, each related to an equal number of Inka houses, each in turn descended on the female side from one of the twelve Inkakuna on the official list. The extraordinary coincidence between this number that in its dyadic form equals twenty-four and the *veinticuatros*, described by Cahill as "a Spanish civil and ecclesiastical body that derives from a synonym for the composition of a peninsular *cabildo*," culminates in a form of "Incan and Spanish cultural accommodation." This can constitute evidence, as reported by Cahill, that some variant of panakakuna "formally extinct, was still in operation during the late colonial period in Cuzco."[185] The survival of colonial panakakuna may have been linked to women more than to the earth. Hence, they were transportable.

Zárate shows how the Spanish tried to cover over that which came before with their very existence, but could not really achieve this. Nonchalantly, he discloses that "the homes and buildings in which the Christians now live are the same ones the Indians had, although a few are repaired and have additions" (las casas y edificios en que oy viuen los Christianos son las mesmas que los Indios tenian, aunque algunas reparadas y otras acrecentadas) (*HDC*, 17 overleaf). The matter-of-fact way the author makes this statement shows how the Spaniards' practice of simply appropriating homes was viewed as "normal." There is no mention of the pain the former residents must have suffered when evicted, or what they might have felt when they walked by their former abodes, especially if members of family or friends who lived in those residences perished in the violence committed by the conquistadors. In his text, it is stated just is as it is, as if there is nothing more to say about it, and he changes the subject in the next clause of his very long sentence.

By 1542, Andrien tells us, there existed an astounding number of 467 encomenderos.[186] Each one controlled and represented a social unit, from fragments of the ayllu to the mine, farm, house, or other place of labor exploitation. Moreover, as he spells out, the Viceroy Toledo ordered all "Andean communities be resettled into large Spanish-style towns, called *reducciones*." Much like a social engineer, Toledo took processes begun at the onset of the Forty-Years War and accelerated them until he had reorganized the subordinate *reducciones* into a whopping "614 administrative districts, or *repartimientos* headed by a kuraka and an appointed town council of Andean elders." We know these repartimientos neither respected the traditional ayllu as they brought ethnic groups together nor did they respect the Andean vertical pattern of exchanges.[187] We equally discern from later legislation, as just considered, that the Spanish appointed the elders as a way of dismembering traditional modes of organization.

The early twentieth-century historian José de la Riva-Agüero takes from his reading of Cieza de León two types of Andean leaders who exercised some power after the Spanish annexation of Peru. The first was the *orejón*, a provincial governor of Inkan stock who managed to maintain power for himself and his offspring, propagating a line of hereditary elites. There was some confusion between this orejón class and other, lesser officials who "imitated the example of the orejón governors and then held on to their offices in perpetuity" (imitaron el ejemplo de los gobernadores orejones y se perpetuaron en sus oficios).[188] The Spanish could then take advantage of this confusion and insert "elected" alcaldes, who would chip away at true hereditary privilege.

The idea of a world upside down, now made famous by Guaman Poma's expression, results from very real conditions. Burga offers two examples. For instance the mitmaqkuna, Qheswa-speaking peoples the Inkakuna had imported into newly conquered lands, found that after the imposition of Spanish power, they could avoid paying duties by not reconnecting with the etnia of origin. In addition, as Burga points out, surprisingly many would become *yanakonakuna*, or hacienda Indians, a form of virtual servitude found to be preferable to the duties imposed on ethnic groups. Burga calls this a "process of feudalization" (proceso de feudalización) while Immanuel Wallerstein rejects the category "feudal" for cash-crop labor, even if it was forced, because in the imported hacienda system lay the kernel of the market-economy system (*NU*, 131).[189] Quickly after Inka omnipotence crumbled, as noted, the concept of providing labor to the state was slowly transmuted under the colonial administration into the concept of paying tribute in kind, and as Burga underscores, in money (*NU*, 133). Noteworthy among other aspects of this sea change is that the smaller groups folded into the imperial Inka structure found themselves freed up as the Spanish wreaked havoc on the Inka-imposed structures. This triggered the polities to sprout up again, at least for the short while, in an ever-changing web of post-Inkan alliances (*NU*, 134). One aspect of the coloniality of this is that to Spaniards, all the people they were conquering were Indians and nothing more.

The shift from old to new realities was not necessarily a peaceful one, and this section must take into account the violence required to force the kind of transformation desired by the metropole, as well as consider the difficulty in gaining perspective to fathom it. The chronicler of South America, Cieza de León, was genuinely unnerved about the violence, which was generalized. He alerts us to the truth that "not a few [Spaniards] went to extremes committing treason, tyranny, robbery, and other errors" (no pocos se extremaron en cometer traiciones, tyranías, robos, y otros yerros). Writing about the violence is not to explain why it happened in newly conquered lands. There is some kind of manifest destiny inherent in the Spanish thrust into these lands. Cieza writes, "Being their king our undefeated Emperor, those rich and abundant kingdoms of New Spain and Peru were populated" (siendo su rey y señor nuestro inuictíssimo Emperador, se poblaron los ricos y abundantes reynos de la nueva España y Perú) (*CP-1era*, fol. 4v, p. 9).[190] It goes without saying that these lands were "populated" by the Spanish. Chapter 2 discusses populating and depopulating with respect to the views of Hernán Cortés and Bartolomé de las Casas. In this chapter, we also saw this with the Colombian polities. *Poblarse* where there are already *poblaciones* implies different people coming together, with the favored group trying to blot out the other groups already residing there. As discussed, Cieza de León is aware of the problem of depopulating, and he makes reference to it on Pearl Island. Here it is as if the violence is permissible if committed for the greater good—the expansion of Castile.

As in colonial texts by Cieza de León and Cortés, Guaman Poma views Spanish immigration as a movement of "poblarse" (populating) (*PNC*, 393 [395]), a process his family had previously lived in an intra-Andean, precontact, mitmaq sense (*PNC*, 59 [59]), here applied to early modern migratory movement. Like Las Casas in the Mexican context and Cieza de Leon in the Colombian one, Guaman Poma observed the process of *despoblarse* in Peru. But for him it went beyond medical epidemics and the violence of the initial Spanish thrust. Because of the priests, he notes, "there is depopulating going on and the Indians of this kingdom are finished" (se despuebla y se acauan los yndios deste rreyno). To bolster his argument about Spanish cruelty, he offers the example of one priest who was prone to applying urine, salt, and chili pepper (*ají*) to people's skin, causing many to die (*PNC*, 581 [595]). And every so often he attributed depopulation to the process of *mestizaje*, as certainly the offspring of Spaniards and native women would necessarily be nonindigenous. He concludes, "Towns are depopulated, the Indians are finished, and the mestizos multiply" (se despuebla los pueblos y se acauan los yndios y multiplica mestisos) (*PNC*, 929 [943]). This idea of preserving the "Indian" nation was primary in Guaman Poma's thought.

We should not, however, fall into the trap of thinking that all the Spanish *pobladores* were "white" people or that the process was dualist, working itself out between Spaniards and "Indians." Guaman Poma is aware of unique ethnicities, Spanish, black, indios, and his primary concern, the mestizo. He was aware that one man with the original 160 conquistadors was a "negro congo." Subsequently, there were "mucha gente de españoles" and "muchos morenos," he reveals (*PNC*, 391[393]). He construes in a worldly way the diverse groups changing the face of Peru. Guaman Poma was acutely aware of diversity. We talk more about mestizaje in chapter 4; here we should simply emphasize that Cieza de León was aware of this process and Cortés saw it as a positive thing, while Guaman Poma and Las Casas before him were alarmed by it.

The Resilience and Transculturation of Late Antiquity in Postcontact Society

Not all the ayllukuna were destroyed, nor were all ethnic units completely disestablished. Some elements survived and resisted change. When Burga studied the towns of Mangas and Chilcas in the present-day province of Bolognesi during the early 1980s, he found an open wound depicted in the pageants performed there by the townsfolk. In these spectacles, primary episodes of the Spanish invasion are acted out. In Chilcas, for example, Burga observes that on the surface the sole objective of these pageants is "having fun and getting drunk" (la diversion y embriaguez). Upon deeper scrutiny, what they are doing is depicting, for example, the sleepless night the Spaniards endured on the eve of Atawallpa's capture (*NU*, 93). Furthermore, in Mangas, Chilcas, and other towns, dual politico-ethnic structures exist that seem to have survived from the Tawantinsuyo period. In Mangas, for example, there is Cotos, the Hana Barrio whose Guaris people tend to be relatively powerful in the municipal socioeconomic fabric. Conversely in Allaucay, Ura Barrio inhabitants, the Llacuaces, tend to be at an economic disadvantage to the Guaris (*NU*, 32).

This Hana and Ura division represents the survival of the pre-Hispanic dualistic form of social organizing which, if gender differences are taken into account, easily splits into four, the organizing principle of Tawantinsuyo. Besides the space-planning concept of four playing out in towns and cities, divergent strands of mythologies survive to bring the precontact past to the present in different ways. To get to how these mythologies respond to space, we can look at the Incarrí cycle of myths. Arguedas penetrates these myths and comes to social conclusions. One example of this appears in his essay on "Mitos quechuas poshispánicos" (Qheswa post-Hispanic myths) where he concludes that the myth of Incarrí finds, in some manner, its origins in

Juan Santos Atawallpa, who led a pro-Inka rebellion during the eighteenth century. More recent scholarship puts the origins as early as Guaman Poma de Ayala (see below).[191] The myth of Incarrí—a term formed, Arguedas tells us, by combining the words "Inca" and "rey"—is compelling because it explains the origins of contemporary social order, superimposed on its pre-Hispanic foundation.[192] Yet while its literary trajectory is somewhat difficult to substantiate, given its oral nature, Arguedas was able to document its path through at least at one stage of its multifaceted development. In Q'ero, a relatively isolated community in the province of Paucartambo near Qosqo, he finds little Spanish influence in the myth of Incarrí. This legend is a creation myth, not so different from those recorded by the early chroniclers of Peruvian history.

In the version from Q'ero, there is essentially one humanity that descends from the sun. In other communities, Puquio, Quinua, and the Vicos Hacienda, the myth assumes Spanish and Christian characteristics, incorporating either the Spanish king himself or elements from the Bible. As the story goes, Incarrí's head is inevitably separated from his body at the moment of contact and the Andean peoples are subjected to Spanish rule. Incarrí's laws are no longer respected. In some versions, hope remains of reuniting the head with the body. This is true as presented in the oral histories recovered from Puquio and Quinua. In another case, there is fatalistic acceptance of the duality of "indios y mistis," the latter representing the not-always-white ruling class. Arguedas hypothesizes that this division into two humanities, one precontact and one post-, embodies the ethnic division so characteristic of Peru. Although there are flaws in some of the techniques that helped to recover these myths—that is to say, some of the recorders did not speak Qheswa—the general tendencies of the inquiry are illuminating, reflecting what Arguedas terms "cultural and social dualism."[193] Finally, and this brings us back to space, Gordon Brotherston recognizes that the survival of the myth is not just a story. The multidisciplinary scholar explains the symbolism of the Incarrí, "whose head and body—capital and four limb-provinces—wait to re-unite, or [could represent] the female anatomical landscape which places the head in Quito, the navel in Cuzco . . . and the uterus in Tiahuanaco."[194] The 1532 event still holds spatial and social meaning for today's Andean people.

The idea of the resurrection of the Inka, now called the Incarrí cycle, takes on two primary versions that Burga calls contrapuntal. Simply stated, the main idea suggests two concepts of the nation. In the early chronicles written by Spaniards, they garroted Atawallpa. In later chronicles such as

Guaman Poma's, they decapitated him.[195] For this reason Mercedes López-Baralt has described Guaman Poma as the "first author of the Incarrí cycle" (primer autor del ciclo de Inkarrí).[196] For Spaniards, Atawallpa was killed and that was that. In the narratives beginning with Guaman Poma, because Atawallpa's cadaver was not destroyed—notwithstanding his being garroted or beheaded—the Sapa Inka could be resurrected. This is Incarrí (*NU*, 123–25). Here, we have two opposing views of the nation, as a Spanish colony or as the rebirth of Tawantinsuyo. The latter oral tradition would survive into the twentieth century, when Arguedas would study it.[197]

Returning to Burga's investigation into the town of Mangas and the co-ethnic pageants performed there, these act out the ancient encounters between the Guaris and the Llacuaces. It seems these events were probably pre-Inka, and could therefore be the archived memory of occurrences in the fourteenth century or before. What is their importance? Burga forms a hypothesis that these "encounters" deal with family relations among the noble class as well as the moment of organization of the ayllukuna (*NU*, 40). Thus, there is a cultural link between that which came before and that which exists now.

In these mountain pageants, some dimensions could be described as religious and/or political. Regarding the former, Andean and Christian rites are fused or superimposed (*NU*, 89). Regarding the latter, the most compelling event in Andean history is reenacted: the encounter between the Sapa Inka Atawallpa and Captain Francisco Pizarro. In the Ancash region, Burga finds that the elites in the small towns have come to identify with the Captain, while the disadvantaged masses continue to gravitate more toward the Inka (*NU*, 54, 96). As the colonial era advanced, Burga discovers there was less identification with Guaris, Llacuaces, or other affiliation, as they all blended into the category "Indian." While this suggests the development of a pan-ethnic solidarity, it also reveals that the Spanish reduction of all ethnic groups to "Indians" changed how Andeans viewed themselves, although this process remains incomplete. In light of these persistent realities, we can be sure there was no lightning bolt conquest, and not everything changed when the first Hispanics arrived in Peru.

Another aspect of national updating can be found in civic spaces, which also went through a transformative process. While it is certain the street layout has pre-independence origins, and perhaps even precolonial origins dating back to the time of ayllu formation, the nomenclature has changed. Burga observes that the Qheswa street names have given way to evocations of the

War of Independence or the war with Chile. The street that divides the upper moiety from the lower one, "Chaupi calle," is now called "calle Comercio" (*NU*, 57). The symbolism of the new designation is inescapable: both ethnic groups must come together on the border in the free-market system where money, not ethnicity, is the guiding force. Burga concludes that the Utopian message of these history plays—what he calls the Andean Utopia—is less vital than it was during the colonial era (*NU*, 99), but their continued importance in small-town life indicates a continuity from the precontact past, through the colonial past, to the national present.

All times and peoples start to come together in the idea of Peru. In some of these carnival plays, the pre-Inka, pre-Hispanic, Conquest, Colonial, and Republican eras all become fused, for example, when Burga observes in one *Masha* dance the unfurling of Peruvian flags updating the past into present reality (*NU*, 44).[198] This is not so unlike the twentieth-century *testimonio* of Gregorio Condori Mamani, when he confuses the War of the Pacific with the War of Independence. The past erupts into the successive pasts until it arrives at the present. The reality studied by Burga resurfaces with a twist in Arguedas's *Todas las sangres* (1964), in which the *misti* landowner comes to feel closer to the mestizos and indigenous, who are also rooted in the land, than to the coastal Creole elite allied with the forces of globalization embodied in a "Consortium."

It is helpful to remember that the colonial period's racial categories were not totally rigid, nor were they purely biological. While the concept of race did not exist, notions we would consider "racial" could be fluid after time. Flores Galindo describes the changing process:

> In colonial society a man could occupy a predetermined place because of his caste and another, very different because of his income. Understanding this last point requires considering that as colonial society unfolded in time, the initial identification between white-colonizer and Indian-colonized began to fade.
>
> En la sociedad colonial un hombre podía ocupar determinado lugar por su casta y otro, muy distinto, por sus ingresos. Entender esto último exige considerar que a medida que transcurría el orden colonial se fue desdibujando la identificación inicial entre blanco-colono e indio-colonizado.[199]

And certainly, as this colonizing process unfolded, the insurgent mestizo class began to exert itself to the detriment of Spanish and "Indian" castes that began to lose ground. These tendencies survived and thrived in the post-independence age.

We cannot talk about Spaniards, "Indians," and people of hybrid heritages without talking about transculturation. The Qheswaphone Guaman Poma de Ayala, for example, must operate within the Holy Roman Empire. When he tries to communicate with the king, he must do so in the Spanish tongue, and ergo must acquire some degree of European culture. He rebels and he denounces, but he does so from within the medium of the Spanish language to the degree he is able. He gives and he takes. As Fernando Ortiz counsels regarding these types of processes, "We should study both sides of cultural contact and consider this integral phenomenon as one of transculturation" (debemos estudiar ambos lados del contacto y considerar ese fenómeno integral como una transculturación). What Ortiz describes here is a universal phenomenon, and as such it explains what was happening in Peru.[200] The Spanish side of the process is well known from the canonical chronicles—Guaman Poma reveals the inverse of it. The product of Guaman's effort must be understood as hybrid, neither entirely here nor there, but in both spheres at once. As Camilo Fernández Cozman explains it, three stages can be isolated: deculturation, creative incorporation, and recomposition in language, literature, and worldview, incorporating both the original and invading cultures.[201] Accordingly, to present an inclusive critique of colonialism and strategies used to resist it, we must adequately grasp all elements. Our present interest resides in ferreting out pre-Hispanic structures and behaviors, as they certainly have the potential to be just as important as the Hispanic ones.

CHAPTER FOUR

GENDER AND EXPANDING ETHNICITY

In this book I am discussing different nation-forming ingredients and, in doing so, continue to find the need to work against the grain of commonplace notions of the nation in our time that consider it to be a postracial place of citizenship where men and woman of all stripes are equally included. The ideal of a postracial and postgendered nation is alluring, but it seems few places in the world have truly achieved such a goal. The relationship between the ideal and reality constitutes a paradox. In *Between Woman and Nation* (1999), Alarcón, Kaplan, and Moallem posit that "at the core of the modern nation-state, a contradiction is set in motion insofar as there is denial of sexual or racial difference or both, and simultaneous universalization of difference."[1] There can only be inequality if some people deny the identities of other people. Identities are contested categories, as are nations. Simultaneously denying and affirming contradictory appreciations of the nation in dissimilar frameworks muddies the waters and obfuscates the true nature of the nation.

Although it does not have to be, the relationship between gender and the nation is a particularly perplexing one. In her 2015 collection of essays provocatively titled *No hay nación para este sexo* (There is no nation for this sex), editor Pura Fernández denudes the oft-stated given of the post-Enlightenment nation as a place for everybody. She argues that during the nineteenth century the utopian triad of liberty, equality, and fraternity "was conceded in its unilateral application to one same dominating sex" (solo era concebida en su aplicación unilateral a un mismo sexo dominante).[2] Fernández is not alone in her view. Research on the role of women in the nation is lacking. As late as 1993, Women's Studies scholars Kaplen and Grewal observed that year's annual conference of the Modern Languages Association offered many talks on "gender," "geography," and "nation." But these researchers "were powerfully struck by the fact that there was very little theorization of the relationships among these historically grounded terms."[3] This is a substantial deficiency because, to state the obvious, at the most basic level it is the relationship between geography, men, and women that gives form to the nation. However, there survives some kind of mainstream view that women's experiences are embodied in the experiences of men. Nira Yuval-Davis takes notice that even many mainstream scholars, such as Clifford Geertz and two others mentioned in this book, Eric Hobsbawm and Anthony Smith, "have ignored gender relations as irrelevant."[4] She takes note of the Oxford reader, *Nationalism,* edited by John Hutchinson and Smith, which positions women as entering the national arena in the modern era. It is hard to imagine how an ahistorical premise such as that could inform such a prestigious publication. Seemingly in exasperation, Yuval-Davis refers to women when she exclaims: "they were always there and central to its constructions and reproductions!"[5] She reminds us, "It is women—and not (just?) the bureaucracy and the intelligentsia—who reproduce nations, biologically, culturally and symbolically."[6]

Smith, Hutchinson, and Yuval-Davis are talking about nations closer to our time, but the nations contemporary to us are built on the backs of previous configurations. Just as women are an integral part of our lives today, so too were they integral to the lives of the men and women during late antiquity and the early modern era. Yuval-Davis's assertion that women "were always there" is an eternal truth. Consequently, despite the positive gains achieved, what can be said about women in our time can often be true for earlier periods; the human condition may change, but human nature, with its gendered relations, seems to be a constant. Despite being integral to all societies during the Encounter, women were left out of history, or were often reduced to sexual objects (see further on in this chapter). These objects could be referents erased from history. Whether erased, objectified, or allegorized, women's place in these societies needs to be acknowledged. Women need to be represented as the flesh-and-bones beings they are, with brains and feelings, and with social purpose. As we will see in the following pages, the role of pre- and postcontact women was intimately interwoven with the fabric of ethnic configurations of naciones as they came in contact with other naciones.

There has been some research on Amerindian and Spanish women during the period that flows from late antiquity to early modernity, such as Schroeder, Wood, and Haskett's edited volume *Indian Woman of Early Mexico,* Vega's *La poligamía española en el Perú* and "La prostitución en el incario," and Maura's *Women in the Conquest,* among others. In this chapter, I examine the role of women in the processes of horizontal and vertical cultural formation. We see the symbiosis of ethnicity and gender in these late ancient relationships appropriated by the early modern operators that came after.

It is important to first consider gender as it intersects with ethnicity and power in diverse cultural settings, including Nahua, K'iche', Moche, Inkakuna, and the Colombian polities. Discussion of each group concludes by taking stock of women's interactions with transatlantic colonial actors, whether they result from love, lust, power, or the violence that seems to be inherent to human behavior. Yuval-Davis calls to mind three varieties of result: those where mixed-heritage offspring isolated into a "separate social category," as happened in South Africa; as part of an "'inferior' collectivity," as with the enslavement of Africans in the Americas; or as part of a "'superior' collectivity," as occurred between conquistadors and aristocratic hereditary lords in Mexico.[7] Here we are interested in the third category, as that is the realm of the chronicles and other early modern documents of the Americas, but we should not forget there were multifold exogamic relations that resulted in babies being thrust into the second category, the "'inferior' collectivity," especially when they came into the world as the product of the licit and illicit liaisons occurring between Spaniards and everyday *runa* and *maceualtin,* their new vassals. Elites, however, are easier to trace because they left behind a well-paved paper trail.

Women were not simply passive receptacles of the violence and ensuing hegemony. Women were also actors. One woman, variously called Doña Marina, La Malinche, and Malintzin, is a case in point. It is violently debated whether she was an active collaborator in the subjugation of

Mexico-Tenochtitlan to suit her own ends, a traitor, or a founding figure of Modern Mexico. Jean Franco, for example, argues that in a case like La Malinche, the feminine becomes identified with "the constitution of hegemony, a hegemony that after the violence will be secured by loving words."[8] But we should not judge Malintzin too harshly. It is not as though she behaved solely in accordance from greed, or lust for power. She had been given as a slave by a Nahua group to the Tarascans, who then "gave" her to Spaniards. She passed through three "nations." It is as if she were a present in a three-way gift exchange. There was a horizontal flow back and forth between these nations, each based on local vertical tradition and practice, and within each she gave and received. Despite this complicated system formed by vertical and horizontal pressures, Malintzin skillfully liberated herself from slavery and, in the process, became the mother of one of the first mestizos in Mexico, Martín Cortés.

While some investigators, such as June Nash, have looked at the power of gender relations in pre-Columbian and colonial situations, others have given these kinds of associations the short shrift. This is unfortunate, because (the statistical cliché being unavoidable) our societies from the ancient past to the present day have been roughly half-male, half-female. In the lands eventually known as Latin America, gender relations were often intertwined with ethnic relations, as in the case of Malintzin. To offer just one more of a thousand postcontact examples, in her detailed discussion of Paraguay, Paola Domingo states that throughout the sixteenth century, "the assiduous frequentation of indigenous women by the conquistadors was, without a doubt, one of the principal characteristics of the province of Paraguay" (la fréquentation assidue des femmes indigènes par les conquistadores fut sans nul doute l'une des principales caractéristiques de la province du Paraguay).[9] The same could be contended for other regions, with minor exceptions. It is logical and inevitable that women played a key role in defining nations, and in a mestizo way, this is especially the case for early modern societies. What may not be apparent is that gender's role is not simply a "Spanish" importation into the Western Hemisphere; it was a primary agent of ethnic flows before the Europeans' arrival, and then became a primary factor in multidirectional and multilayered indigenous-Spanish relations.

But what is gender? The well-known feminist theorist Judith Butler explains: "Gender is the repeated stylization of the body, a set of repeated acts within a highly rigid regulatory frame that congeal over time to produce the appearance of substance, of a natural sort of being."[10] The idea here is that gender is something learned and passed on from generation to generation. It can be cultural, and thus not some isolated force affecting certain constituencies and not others. As Irene Silverblatt explains, "Gender ideologies overflow male and female identities to infuse the fabric of social life."[11] We could make this assertion stronger and add that they permeate the entire fabric of our existence. Therefore, as Silverblatt goes on to say, in order to adopt a critical stance regarding how society works, we must "see gender as a highly complex social construction."[12] In this chapter I look at gender as correlated to ethnicity primarily, but also to class and power. Sets of "repeated acts" served to direct and redirect power. This is not the only way to approach gender, but this way helps us fathom how nations are composed in terms of the primary determinants of ethnicity and gender.

The preceding two chapters surveyed several perspectives on the nation. One of the primary foci for horizontal contact consisted of men from one etnia taking women from another. Shifting border ontologies would have been less dynamic if women had not been involved, although in some instances, men may have been exchanged. There have been cases, such as one in Teotihuacan, of a husband who may or may not have been from another ethnic group being brought in to marry a daughter of the patriline.[13] More frequent was the giving of women, sometimes construed as *dádivas,* as gifts. The following section attempts a rereading of a number of early colonial chronicles in light of the natural and social sciences including modern historiography, anthropology, and archaeology, along with DNA testing. We do this as a step-by-step analysis into the workings of mestizaje while considering how the roles of men and women differed in this process.

ETHNICITY AND GENDER AMONG THE NAHUA

A good place to begin a discussion of gender in Mexico is with Nobel Laureate Octavio Paz, who in his controversial but deeply thought *Laberinto de soledad* suggests the male view of women is tempered in Mexico by a masculine vanity inherited from both Spanish and indigenous peoples. Without question, men were dominant in governance in the pre-Hispanic, the colonial, and in the post-Independence periods. However, there have been certain cases of female rulers, such as one depicted in the Codex Nuttall,[14] and furthermore, as Bruhns and Stothert point out, "high-born women often achieve positions of power in both public and private spheres."[15] These kinds of role models call out to be taken into account, but here the focus is on how males used females to accumulate political power within their nations. As Nash observes, "The origins of male dominance and its ideological support in human history is a cause for speculation and research."[16] The process occurs when men in dominant roles use women as tools, commodities, or sources of labor. There are multiple throngs of control. This leads to perplexing questions regarding the mechanisms of dominance which may never be absolute, as women were, are, and will be active agents struggling against male dominance.

As evident, ethnicity constituted a potent determinant in both positive and negative ways. Ethnic affiliations were so pronounced that they often survived after Spanish penetration. Bernardino de Sahagún's informants hold to precise ethnic stances in their narrations of yore. Fernando de Alva Ixtlilxóchitl's defense of Tetzcocan uniqueness is another example. Charles Gibson has noted this phenomenon, and Sara Castro-Klarén emphasizes that even an astute organizer such as the Viceroy Mendoza (1535–50) could not subdue what she calls the "the desire for ethnic separation" (deseo de separación étnica).[17] Bruhns and Stothert tend to think that even in Teotihuacan, "the vast majority of marriages were between people of linked lineages within the same socioeconomic group, or perhaps between members of different segments of the same lineage."[18] Westerners sometimes find these propensities to be perplexing. José Joaquín Blanco finds it incomprehensible that "even in defeat, the Indians continued to fight among themselves, and, far from regarding themselves as ethnically and culturally united against the invaders, they insisted on their local identities, their traditional enmities (such as Mexica against Tetzcocans)."[19] The Conquest can be explained in no other manner, because Cortés played on the desire for ethnic separateness as part of his strategy. James Lockhart finds ethnic pride to be deep-seated: "Even when local conquered groups and intrusive migrants were no longer discernibly distinct in language and culture, they retained a tradition of separate origin" (*NAC*, 27). Gibson sees these boundaries as powerful, and suggests that the very idea of a "Triple Alliance" between Mexica, Tepaneca, and Acolhuaque reveals the potency of the Tepaneca and Acolhuaque identities. In spite of the Mexica's boundless military might, he concludes, they failed "to dominate Valley affairs absolutely or to exterminate the tribal concept" (*AZ*, 22).

One way boundaries could be porous, though, was through interethnic conjugality. These liaisons were exogamic in nature, forged among two or more kin groups. Gender becomes the point of intersection. I say "gender" here because, despite biology's important role in the physical creation of hybrid lineages, it was the cultural aspect, Butler's "set of repeated acts," that made it necessary for women's expending their social and political capital to cross altepetl boundaries. Gibson seems to deny and accept simultaneously the importance of these interethnic gender contacts. He asserts, "Miscegenation was a factor of limited importance in preconquest history" (*AZ*, 22). This implies that the peoples of central Mexico tended to maintain their distinctiveness. Yet he theorizes that marriages linking Mexica rulers, or tlatoque, with other dynastic groups "might eventually have obliterated the non-Mexica tribal jurisdictions entirely, but they were still far short of this result at the time of the Spanish conquest" (*AZ*, 38). The first case would tend to make ethnic exceptionalism a significant feature of life; the second suggests cross-cultural gender relations as integral to politics. In Anahuac cross-ethnic mating practices we see strategies designed for accumulating temporal and cultural power. This proves that despite distinct ethnic identities, the barriers between them were porous. To demonstrate this, we should now discuss the relationship between Nahua men and women, the role ethnicity played, and how Spanish men later incorporated some of those behavioral patterns.[20]

From Endogamy to Exogamy: Gender's Role in Horizontal Appropriation

In pre-Hispanic Anahuac, societies organized themselves according to dualities. Davies finds that the Mexica favored two monarchs, two clerics, two merchants, and so on. Sometimes the duality was multiplied by a factor of two, creating a political standard in which there were two pairs of monarchs (*AZ*, 24). This principle was so primary, one could conclude that these social structures were organized through dualities, their subordinate microdualities, and the guiding macrodualities superior to them. One famous expression of this dualist understanding of the cosmos resulted from the conflict between the legendary leaders Topiltzin and Huemac, along with their theological incarnations Quetzalcoatl and Tezcatlipoca. Although these binary structures were not always informed by gender, they often were. In actuality, Mesoamerican cosmology is grounded in Ometeotl, an androgynous construct. As Miguel León-Portilla points out, it is precisely from Ometeotl that the origins of "humanity" emerge.[21] These, as Alfonso Caso reminds us, take the form of the divine couple, Omecihuatl (the feminine) and Ometecuhtli (the male). Etymologically speaking, the female term is created by coupling *ome*, meaning "two," with the word for woman, *cihuatl*. For the masculine, the *ome* is joined with *tecuhtli*, meaning lord or nobleman. From there, as Caso explains, different androgynous beings and pairs are derived: Xochiquetzal-Macuilxochitl, Xochiquetzal-Xochipilli, Chalchiuhtlicue-Tlaloc, among others.[22]

Lockhart confirms that Nahua social frameworks were organized by "symmetries and reciprocal relationships" (*NAC*, 76). One primary relationship of this type was the one between a man and a woman. Even though, as Klor de Alva puts it, Sahagún's informants had to operate within the colonial system that forced them through "fear and/or the manipulation of the moral conscience" to see and talk about themselves as the Other, we can glean much about Nahua notions of gender relations from the informants.[23] Sahagún's sources relate that even the "barbarous" Teochichimeca—the extreme Chichimeca—espoused monogamy. This dualist gender coupling was so sacred there were few adulterers. When such misbehavior was denounced, the guilty parties were caught, brought before the ruler, and then executed by bow and arrow (*GH/FC*, 10:172). Lockhart does find evidence, however, that some groups did accept multiple unions (*NAC*, 110, 205). Bruhns and Stothert theorize polygamy increased because of tribute demands; women were being required to weave more cloth, so much that female slavery increased to meet those demands. Women were so enmeshed in this tax and commercial system, at least under Mexicatl rule, they had to adapt strategies and learn techniques in the family's kitchen to keep up with their public demands. For Bruhns and Stothert, this pressure had a negative impact on domestic life. They write, "It is known to have led to an increase in disharmonious relations within the family compound."[24] Despite Lockhart and Bruhns/Stothert's findings, data on such polygamous unions is fragmentary and unreliable because, logically, the Nahua would not want to reveal to their interrogators polygamous practices their new rulers considered unchristian.

Regardless of whether monogamous or polygamous, the union of a man and a woman from different groups formed a basis for an expanding community rooted in ethnicity or co-ethnicity. Exogamic unions are common to various nations and may seem, therefore, unremarkable. Well known to any student of the Renaissance are the international alliances forged through intraregal marriages. Yet if in other nations exogamic conjugality represented a limited gain for the moment (think of Henry VIII), in Anahuac the practice was a standard feature of royal life for groups in the valley.[25] Just as the Mexica expanded their influence through wars and coercion, at least in the early dynasty (see further in this section), they also saw transethnic connubiality as a way to gain the prestige and power they eventually earned. Cross-cultural mating practices were basic before Cortés's arrival, and they remained so well after.

Hernán Cortés, an educated man, would have been familiar with intra-European royal mating practices, and he was able to perceive these kinds of Nahua customs after arriving in Mexico. In his "Second Letter" to Carlos V, he paraphrases various tales of intercultural mating he heard about in his conversations with Moctezuma. In them, the Mexicatl ruler refers back to legendary times, when Chichimeca and other nomadic groups immigrated into Anahuac. Moctezuma recounts the story of "a lord whose vassals were all his" (un señor cuyos vasallos todos eran), perhaps even referring to Topiltzin, who left some followers in the valley. When he returned, he discovered that those he had left behind had married the local inhabitants. They had forged *generación,* and thus, pueblos (*CDR,* 52a; 60a). Considering the double meaning inherent in the noun "pueblo," those Nahua colonists not only had created a "town," but also a "people," a first step in the nation-building process. This mixing was both general and extensive. It was biological, political, and social. The Dominican friar Diego Durán refers to "the Mexican nation" (la nación mexicana) and appreciates that the Tenocha found themselves "getting mixed up with the rest of the nations in their dealings and in their conversations" (mezclándose con las demás neciones en trato y conversación).[26] Davies reminds us that early on, the Tenocha linked themselves to the Culhuaque and to the Tepaneca (*AZ,* 41–48). We now study these bonds, focusing on the role of gender in them.

Rounds maps out three stages in Mexican history: predynastic, early dynastic, and late dynastic.[27] The predynastic phase has to do with Tenocha residency in Aztlan, Tenoch guiding his people through their vicissitudes in establishing Tenochtitlan, and the naming of the first tlatoque. During the early dynastic phase of the royal narrative, this group extended their temporal and spiritual power. Blood mixing was necessary to achieve the required lineage for a tlatoani, or supreme ruler. The Mexica needed to associate with women from other nations to achieve their expansionistic goals, and women openly collaborated in this strategy. The *ne plus ultra* of mestizaje was the political and spiritual policy for electing the first three tlatoque of Tenochtitlan during the early dynastic period. It is revealing that these rulers were not of pure Mexicatl blood. Such was the case of the first tlatoani, Acamapichtli (1372–92?). Durán tells us this young fellow was the son of Opochtzin, "señor de los mexicanos" and Atotoztli, "señora de Culhuacan,"[28] a significant union because the bride was from Culhuacan (see map 3). This city held special importance because it was one of the few where the original Toltecatl dynasty continued to function.[29] The Tolteca came to be revered by the Mexica as a mother culture, notwithstanding their different origins. By selecting the biethnic Acamapichtli for the highest honor known, the Mexica infused the archetype of the Tolteca into the person of the tlatoani.

By melding their bloodlines with the Culhuaque, the Mexica horizontally appropriated Toltecayotl, or Toltecness. As emphasized in chapter 2, this ideal implies subsuming the heritage of Tollan with its artisans and wise men. A horizontal linkage of this kind, when achieved, conceded the authority to harvest Toltecatl spirituality, including deities such as Quetzalcoatl and Tezcatlipoca. This tradition, appropriated first horizontally and from there vertically, is reflected in their very name. When Europeans appeared on the scene, they were told the supreme rulers were known as the Culhuaque-Mexica, reflecting the twofold legacy from Aztlan, their site of origin, and Tollan, the capital city of the Tolteca, now incarnate in Culhuacan. This kind of usage is documented in various places (*HV*, 67a, 79a; *OH*, 2:124). While the journey from Aztlan (vertical, given its nation-derived legendary fiber) may have denoted success at overcoming tremendous adversity, it was the initial horizontal social contact with the descendants of Tollan that then gave the Mexica a *felt* vertical bond to the exalted traditions of Quetzalcoatl and Tezcatlipoca. Laying claim to a "superior" ethnic group's past conferred greater spiritual authority.[30] On other occasions, Mexica bonded horizontally with neighboring groups solely to acquire temporal power. Such horizontal mobility implied that the bride left her own group and moved to the group of her husband.[31] They pursued such unions, by way of illustration, with the Tepaneca. By importing mates for their rulers from other centers, they generated a multiethnic power base.

The Mexica elected their second tlatoani in the person of Huitzilihuitl (1391?–1415?), the son of Acamapichtli. Yet since we do not know which of his father's wives (there may have been as many as twenty) was his mother, difficulties persist in precisely ascertaining his lineage. We can only affirm that Acamapichtli was half-Mexicatl and half-Culhua, and therefore Huitzilihuitl was one-quarter Mexicatl, one-quarter Culhua, and one-half unknown on his mother's side. For his part, Huitzilihuitl married four times, the first two to princesses who were Tepaneca. His second nuptials were celebrated with Miahuehxochtzin, a niece of Tezozomoc, the influential ruler of Azcapotzalco. We know Miahuehxochtzin was of Tepanecatl blood (which, in turn, was probably a mixture of Tepanecatl and something else). Their son Chimalpopoca (1414?–26?) would have to be considered one-half Tepanecatl (Miahuehxochtzin), one-quarter unknown (Huitzilihuitl's mother), one-eighth Culhua-Toltecatl (Opochtzin), and now only one-eighth Mexicatl (Atotoztli). Through these horizontal connections, the Mexica began to improve their social fortunes. As their bloodlines diluted, paradoxically, their sway increased.

By choosing to associate with the Tepaneca through arranged marriages, the upstart Mexica positioned themselves to usurp the most coveted political position in Anahuac. While they continued paying tribute (literally) to the great city of Azcapotzalco, now royalty from that urban center came regularly to Tenochtitlan with gifts. The political import of royal mestizaje cannot be underestimated. What was at stake was power itself. They accumulated Culhua spiritual authority via Acamapichtli, who was half-Mexicatl and half-Culhua. They accumulated temporal power first through Chimalpopoca (half Culhua-Mexicatl and half-Tepanecatl), and then finished the task with Itzcoatl's military successes in Azcapotzalco.

The exogamic political maneuvering that characterized this phase was not particular to the Mexica. Chronicler Diego Muñoz Camargo, whom we meet in chapter 2, confirms the Tlaxcalteca, non-Aztec Nahua, likewise used women to forge relations. In Tlaxcala, leaders gave their daughters to lords and powerful men, who accepted the ones they wanted (*HT,* 197). Alva Ixtlilxóchitl, another historian of our acquaintance, also records the practice in Tetzcoco. He recounts that Tzontecomatl, an Acolhua, mated with Quatetzin, of Toltecatl stock. Later, after Nopaltzin entered into wedlock with Azcaxochitzin, "granddaughter of Topiltzin, the last King of the Tolteca" (nieta de Topiltzin último rey de los tultecas), a process started whereby "they all began to intermarry" (comenzaron a emparentar los unos con los otros). For Alva Ixtlilxóchitl, an era of perpetual peace and conformity began. A number of subsequent intercultural marriages are named in the pages that follow (*OH,* 2:18, 21, etc.). It seems interethnic mating was more of a pattern than a collection of isolated occurrences.

While the emerging Mexicatl dynasty accumulated power by blending with women from other nations, women seem to have been divested of some degree of their power. Nash, discussing this process, hypothesizes that these marriages were "an assertion of control and dominance over the women whom they took in marriage from the neighboring kingdoms."[32] Such a hypothesis takes for granted that the brides coming into the ruling house did not accumulate any power in the emerging "Aztec" power structure as their power in the previous power structure was diluted. This may not have necessarily been the case. They may have lost some power when they left behind their ethnic group, but given the matriarchal vectors of power during the Toltec apogee, and given the Mexicatl policy of assimilating to Toltecayotl, the brides may have gained some power based on their cultural authority transferable to the group they were entering. Either way, it is clear that gender was subordinated to ethnicity in the wake of imperial designs. However, the interethnic model made possible by the exchange of women was not to remain dominant.

It is probably no coincidence the reign of Itzcoatl symbolized the early period of the Mexicatl Empire, the beginning of the late-dynastic phase, and the abandonment of the primary policy of hybrid tlatoque in favor of endogamic relations. This is the point for Nash, "that an agnatic royal lineage can be said to have been established."[33] The sixth through eleventh tlatoque descended from the son of Itzcoatl (fourth tlatoani) and Atotoztli, known also as Huitzixochtzin, the daughter of Moctezuma I (eventually the fifth tlatoani). For the most part, it is not taken into account whether Atotoztli, a woman, exercised power as tlatoani for some time after her father's death in 1468, a possibility Bruhns and Stothert consider, or if she simply served as a kind of regent.[34] It seems likely she was the tlatoani without the ordinal number, or she held authority along the lines Europeans would describe as a king's regent, because the next ruler after Moctezuma I was her son, Axayacatl, who may have been born in the same year her father died. Since there are some discrepancies regarding when Moctezuma I's reign ended and Axayacatl's began—either 1468 or 1469—there is reason to believe Atotoztli did rule as tlatoani for a short time. If Davies is correct and Axayacatl was nineteen years old when he ascended to power,[35] then Atotoztli may have exercised authority just between 1468 and 1469. Alternatively, if he were somewhat younger, she could have served as regent to Axayacatl for a longer interval. Whether or not she held title as tlatoani, it cannot be disputed that she did exercise significant political influence as the daughter of Moctezuma (1440–68/69), as the wife of Tezozomoc (son of Chimalpopoca) and the mother of the next three successive tlatoque, Axayacatl (1468/69–1481), Tizoc (1481–86), and Ahuitzotl (1486–1502). As evident, the late-dynastic phase abandoned filial succession in favor of fraternal succession. Rounds construes this transition as an undertaking to expand internal "mobilization of political support for the throne."[36] The late-dynastic Mexica could afford internal power-building precisely because they were now politically connected in the Valley.[37] This differed from the early dynastic phase, when they had to reach outside their peer group to accumulate power.

While the men in these relationships were commonly considered the "source of lineage" (*GH/FC* 10:1), the women, because they organized marriages, as Inga Clendinnen concludes, became the guardians "of interfamilial alliances."[38] This gender power was shared not in terms of equality, but in terms of reciprocity. The blending of etnias through gender relations had the effect of large-scale nation building. As Eduard Calnek observes, the upshot of frequent "interdynastic marriages . . . was that *pipiltin* everywhere in the Valley of Mexico were closely related to each other by ties of kinship."[39] Even polities that tended to be enemies were blood linked. Alva Ixtlilxóchitl refers to the Acolhua Nezahualcoyotl's aunts, some of whom were Mexica, while others lived in Tlaxcala (*OH,* 2:51, 54). Such ties among the nobility formed an overarching system of linkage between the diverse altepeme that ever so steadily were becoming support struts of a well-oiled machine of empire, suggesting, in the process, the possibility of outgrowing the ethnic nation model, a possibility truncated with the arrival of Cortés and his minions. Some of these endogamic and exogamic modes of doing things would endure for years after the so-called "Conquest."

Early Modern Society and the Persistence of New World Forms

The renowned Spanish historian José Antonio Maravall writes that when the men of the Renaissance began to contemplate the men and women they encountered on the other side of the Atlantic, they began to notice that "the anatomic differences between them were slight" (las diferencias somáticas entre ellos eran escasas), and that cross-fertilization between them was possible. Once that realization had been made, they then took a great step toward understanding a unified human species.[40] Maravall makes this assumption by reading chroniclers such as Pedro Cieza de León, who saw both Spanish and indigenous peoples as descending from Adam and Eve.[41] This might have represented a big step forward, but the European invaders did not get to the top of the stairs of human comprehension and compassion, a postracial accomplishment still not attained in our time. Racism persists, as do ethnocidal wars in the Balkans, the Middle East, the Sudan, and Rwanda, and as does the legacy of ethnocidal wars in Guatemala and Peru, where women suffered and still suffer mightily. Nor was taking an Amerindian woman as big a step as Maravall implies, as a Conquistador would have been more likely to rape or take as a concubine a woman who was not of Spanish or Christian origin than one who had emigrated from the Old World. Additionally, he probably would not have thought well of an indigenous man taking a European mate.[42]

This brings us to an essential paradox as pondered by Franco. She writes that it is difficult to "understand" how "this exogamous system operated so efficiently despite the cultural gap between Spaniards and the indigenous."[43] One way to understand this is that Spaniards simply appropriated horizontally age-old practices in use in the Indias Occidentales. They took the women because it suited them, and because the traditions for them to do so were well established. It all seemed "normal" to Amerindian men. It was their horizontal fluidity and the gendered norms that brought women to the table that opened the floodgates of mestizaje. There was a coloniality to this situation that, if measured, reveals that all things were not equal in these relationships. We turn again to Franco, who puts it this way: "Women were passed around freely between the indigenous and the Spaniards and between Spaniards and Spaniards, though of course no Spanish women were presented to indigenous allies."[44] The coloniality indicator tests positive when a situation is inverted. Indigenous women could flow to Spaniards and between Spaniards, but it would have been unthinkable for Spanish women to flow to indigenous men.

Additional clarification is helpful here regarding what could be called the gender factor. Certainly, men's evaluation of female beauty, their sizing up of women based on physical traits, is common to most cultures, and there is nothing earth shattering about recognizing that in and of itself. Violence against women seems to be a trait different cultures hold in common, and have across the ages. However, when men are conquering a people of a different ethnic background and become aware of aspects of its sexual booty, it leaves the realm of violence against individual women and moves into an even darker area of male behavior: colonialist cross-cultural violence against women. In other words, when gender-based violence is based on racial difference, it becomes violent two times over, because the violence is committed by men against women, and by men of one race against women (and men) of another. When this complicated aspect of human behavior comprises one of the cogs of international colonialism—Guaman Poma de Ayala's concern—it associates with ethnocide, a sinister mode of destruction of entire nations. It wreaks havoc on women, their children, the men associated with them, and the cultural structures that guide them. It goes beyond violence against women, but includes that primary aspect as it becomes violence against nations.

Awareness of women and etnia as a method of control was paramount from the time of Christopher Columbus's first voyage. From his familiarity with Portuguese colonial practices in Guinea, the explorer understood interethnic mating to have two political purposes. The first was to use indigenous women to keep the Spaniards obedient to the Crown. The second was to use them as a bridge to the people being colonized (*TD*, 56). Little by little, this gendered practice became a third rail for the locomotive of colonialism. Cortés, like the Admiral before him, knew the attraction between a man and a woman could be used as an interethnic instrument of conquest and control, engendering a larger political unit. As mentioned, he observed and heard about these kinds of practices among the Nahua. He quickly assimilated exogamic practices because they served his interest. As pobladores followed conquistadors, they quickly redoubled their efforts in the practice of taking mates from other ethnicities.

The Spaniard in the Indies did distinguish himself somewhat from the Englishman when he commingled with autochthonous women, as he would with any other "vassal" of the Spanish Crown. This he did with greater zeal and sense of entitlement than he would have in the Old World.[45] As a result, the honorific ideal of the *cristianos viejos,* or Old Christians, melted away into multitudes of *cristianos nuevos,* or New Christians. Any student of *Siglo de Oro* literature knows it is pervaded by an obsession with *pureza de sangre*, or blood purity.[46] As Paz explains, the honor of the Spaniard was a religious notion associated with purity of lineage.[47] The so-called Conquest, whose stated mission was to create cristianos nuevos, diluted this notion, the diffusion of the faith achieved through mestizaje. Marvyn Bacigalupo explains that the higher niches of Nahua society were assimilated first, as the native elites filled the gap between Spanish authorities and autochthonous masses.[48] Soon, besides mestizos, there were mulattoes and zambos, because—we cannot forget—Spaniards brought slaves from Africa with them. A clear-cut partition between the pueblos de indios and pueblos de españoles, Indian towns and Spanish towns, began to blur. Whether through legal wives, clandestine concubinage, or outright rape, the number of people with dual and even multiple birthrights grew. From the first contact between Cortés's men and the cultures of Anahuac, the inevitable process of ethnic blending overwhelmed pureza de sangre guidelines. Ethnicity, however, must not be taken solely in its biological sense. Ethnic mixing could take place on various levels: religious (Christianization), political (Hispanization), economic (slavery, capitalization), cultural (oral-lettered hybridization), and social (godfathership, marriage, concubinage, or rape). Habitually, these forces worked in tandem to provoke further cultural and biological agglutination. This chapter focuses on the attitudes, norms, and practices that favored mestizaje.

During the initial Spanish penetration and immediately after, slavery, alongside concubinage, rape, and those rare cases of marriage, contributed to the first postcontact wave of interethnic gender relations. Before the Spanish had appeared in Mexico, Las Casas reports in the *Brevísima relación de la destrucción de las Indias,* they already had abused some women in the Caribbean (*TR,* 1:23, 31). Columbus had instituted such practices. To set up the institution of slavery within the ken of the European world, the admiral and his shipmates drew on Spanish experience in the Canaries, as well as Portuguese experience in Guinea.[49] When Cortés and his men and women (there were several, such as the legendary María de Estrada) arrived in Mesoamerica, they quickly recognized the indigenous practice of slavery hinging on ethnicity.

In *Historia verdadera de la conquista de la Nueva España,* Díaz del Castillo offers some details. On the coast, Spaniards heard the Fat King of Cempoal complaining that the Mexica took his people's sons and daughters for sacrifices or slavery (*HV,* 88a). Spaniards grasped the implications when those slaves were women, and immediately began to participate in local practice, accepting eight Totonac lovelies. They were received explicitly to forge generation (*HV,* 97a). By doing so, the Spaniards established links on a political level, a mantle that hid and satisfied more personal needs. After Cempoal, the Spaniards marched on Tlaxcala. After three savage battles, the Tlaxcalteca opted for peace with the invaders. How did they plan to achieve it? Without hesitation, women are offered "so that with their offspring we could become relatives" (para que de su generación tengamos parientes). The women came from Tzompantzingo at first. Then the tetrarch Xicotencatl the Younger sent four others—old and low-standing, to Bernal Díaz's mind (*HV*, 129a, 135a). To the Spaniards' joy, feminine hordes were to follow. How could the Tlaxcalteca arrive at the decision to give up their women so decisively? The answer is a simple one. When Cortés, viewed by some huehuetlatolli as an incarnation of the deity Quetzalcoatl, arrived on the scene in Tlaxcala and defeated the Tlaxcalteca in those brutal battles, Xicotencatl the Elder surmised that he and his men had come from where the sun rises. The legendary Nahua leader Topiltzin, who represented Quetzalcoatl, had disappeared to the east. As a result of the confusion regarding Topiltzin/Quetzalcoatl/Cortés, the decision was made, as recounted by Muñoz Camargo, that "they must mate with us, and we will all be one" (han de emparentar con nosotros, y que hemos de ser todos unos) (*HT*, 192).[50]

This giving and receiving was extensive. Díaz underscores the plentiful female bounty the Spaniards accepted (*HV*, 146a). The Tlaxcalan historian Muñoz Camargo corroborates Díaz's version of events, relating that more than three hundred beautiful women slaves were given to serve Malintzin alone, a fate better than the sacrificial death, for they had committed crimes against the Tlaxcalan state (*HT*, 195, 196). There is perhaps some hyperbole here regarding the numbers, as often is the case in these colonial documents. Nevertheless, the essential practice of allotting women across ethnic boundaries from one nation to another can be verified in numerous sources. The act of giving to cement relations seems to have been general. When the ruling council of Tlaxcala saw that the women slaves got along well with Spaniards, they saw fit to allow their daughters to mate and get pregnant; accordingly, generación would follow with the very valiant men (*HT*, 196–97). Outside sources corroborate intercultural allegiances associated with Tlaxcala's submission. The Chichimeca-Acolhua historian Alva Ixtlilxóchitl confirms that the Tlaxcalteca requisitioned for the Spaniards "many other damsels" (otras muchas doncellas) (*OH*, 2:214). He, Díaz del Castillo, and Muñoz Camargo were not the only chroniclers to document these practices.

A cursory look at Cortés's "Second Letter" reveals he openly accepts this custom. In his march from Cholula to Tenochtitlan, he mentions receiving female slaves, "esclavas," three times. The first instance occurs in Guasucingo, where he receives a few women and clothes (*CDR*, 48a). Later the lords of Amecameca/Chalco offer him up to forty, unambiguously written in the original Spanish as the feminine "esclavas," not "esclavos" (*CDR*, 49a). Finally, he arrives at Iztapalapa, where again he receives "some female slaves and clothes" (algunas esclavas y ropas) (*CDR*, 50a). Nowhere thus far does the Conquistador make any attempt to justify the acquisition of these women. True to his writing style, he omits most local color and details, preferring explanations of his grandiose military strategies. During those passages, he is explicit about who said what to whom and the meaning of what was said, while also providing a detailed justification for the war, long before the polemic between Las Casas and Ginés de Sepúlveda. No rationale is given for obtaining "esclavas." Cortés merely inserts himself into a horizontal nation-forming tradition, common in Anahuac since time immemorial.

Díaz del Castillo states that Cortés would normally receive these women with a happy face, but always with a condition: "but to take them, since as we are saying, we are brothers, there is a need that they do not have idols in which they believe and adore" (mas para tomarlas, como dice que seamos hermanos, que hay necesidad que no tengan aquellos ídolos en que creen y adoran) (*HV*, 97a). At this juncture, the confluence of Christianization and temporal power comes into play. The newcomers accepted the women as a political tool in accordance with Nahua custom but, modifying that custom, they demanded they first be Christianized. A first step toward achieving Hobsbawm's "proto-nationalism" is thus established.

After passing through Cempoal, Tlaxcala, and Cholula, the Spaniards finally arrived in the Mexicatl capital. The male-female structural dynamic is clearly evident. Díaz indicates that Moctezuma had two legitimate women and various "amigas" (*HV*, 184a). He comments on Moctezuma's practice of marrying off his female friends to his captains. Upon the arrival of the Spaniards, the tlatoani extended this practice to the newcomers. Díaz himself held the autochthonous women in high regard. At an early stage in his narrative, he proclaims Doña Marina to be a very excellent woman, and a good translator to boot (*HV*, 70a).[51] He remembers asking Moctezuma for a woman. The tlatoani granted his request, and with the wink of an eye, she became Doña Francisca (*HV*, 209a).

Did Spaniards acquire their women through traditional means? Initially yes, but after the fall of Tenochtitlan, they simply selected the ones they wanted, the white or pretty ones, or the ones with the yellow bodies (*GH/FC*, 12:122). In the earlier Guatemala manuscript, the noncanonical one Rolena Adorno points out, Díaz had admitted that they actually branded some women with a "G" for *Guerra* (*HV*, 669b).[52] As one can imagine, this supreme moment of procreation was not a happy bacchanal for all. This may have been so distasteful that Díaz suppressed it for subsequent versions of the *Historia verdadera* to render the notion of "just war" more palatable.[53] Sahagún's informants report that as Tenochtitlan fell, the Tenochan women smeared themselves with mud, dressing themselves in rags to appear ugly (*GH/FC,* 12:122). Díaz does not refer to these episodes. He inverts them, claiming the women of Tenochtitlan truly wanted to be with Spaniards, not with their fathers and husbands (*HV,* 416a). Such manipulation of fact obscures the story of women during the fall of the capital city.

If Nahua women were sexual objects for Spanish men during the moment of initial penetration, later they could become a source of wealth. Nahua matrons from the patrician classes were targets for greedy peninsular and later mestizo men. Like their male counterparts, noblewomen held rank, owned property, and took part in family decision-making (*NAC,* 139). There are a number of examples of this practice. An interesting case can be found in the two Diego Muñoz Camargo figures, father and son, the chronicler and the governor of Tlaxcala (who were the son and grandson of the Conquistador of the same name).[54] Both entered into conjugal unions with Tlaxcalan noblewomen. Through such relationships, the two men accumulated immense estates and wealth, so much so that the Crown expelled them from Tlaxcala.[55] The men were not the only social and economic actors; the women were also capable of initiating and provoking social movement. There are other examples. Bruhns and Stothert mention the female members of Cuauhtemoc's family in this regard, who "proceeded to marry a series of Spaniards to keep the family property."[56] Davies brings up Moctezuma's daughters, who also married "well-born Spaniards."[57]

Labor law, irrespective of earlier legislation to promote separate guilds for Spaniards and the Nahua, eventually admitted the latter into the Spanish guilds. Such inclusiveness paved the road for continued mestizaje. This was so much the case that the guilds of the seventeenth and eighteenth centuries reacted against Nahua-Spanish mating practices (see *AZ,* 401). Racial blending did not only arise through marriage or concubinage. Asunción Lavrin documents assorted cases of premarital sex, adultery, and rape that often crossed ethnic lines.[58] The indigenous elders of Mexico City sent a petition to the king in 1574 in which they begged for separation of "pueblos," for otherwise "many children are born out of wedlock" (nacen muchos hijos adulterinos).[59] To summarize, sexual encounters took place in the forming New Spain at moments and under conditions unthinkable in Spain. This occurred, as Adorno reflects, despite the fact that much "Inquisitorial activity concerned sexual behavior."[60] Lavrin recognizes that "the Church had to bend and accommodate its theoretical norms to the social reality."[61] Horizontal matching up was encouraged, while the multiplicity of indigenous nations—as Octavio Paz reminds us—was negated by New Spain.[62] For Gibson, "New colonial modes of organization displaced the tribal concepts" (*AZ*, 30). Horizontal mating between Spaniards and Nahua was defined by an overwhelming vertical element originating in Europe. Such elements were a pride (exaggerated, according to Benassy-Berling)[63] in lettered culture and, beyond any doubt, in fifteen centuries of Catholic religion. Nahua culture—originally "Oriental" and diverse—began moving toward a Western religious, social, and economic ideal.

As with other aspects of postcontact society, the impact of Spanish norms on Nahua marital and mating practices is not thoroughly documented. However, we can distinguish two kinds of human relationships; consanguineous and affinal. The former represent blood relatives who were ancestors (parents, grandparents, and beyond) or descendants (children, grandchildren, and so forth). Consanguinity is vertical because it implies moving backward (parents, grandparents) and forward (children) in time. In mythological or legendary terms, consanguinity connotes ethnic pride. At one point in his history, Motolinía mentions that when a man marries a woman he had to do so with someone from his own "gentilidad" (*HI*, 99a). That would imply conjoining within one's own peer group. When Muñoz Camargo describes the marriage of Doña María Luisa Tecuelhuatzin, the tlatoani Xicotencatl's daughter, he remarks that she had to respect the norms of her "gentilidad" (*HT*, 197). This awareness of gentilidad, or lineage, shows that verticality continues to guide the proto-national idea, even when submerged by the coloniality of the early modern era.

Motolinía observes the presence of certain wise men—called *licenciados* in Spanish—who were knowledgeable in conjugality, and in "consanguinidad y afinidad" (*HI*, 99a). Serge Gruzinski verifies that native matchmakers continued to ply their trade after Spanish power had begun to take root.[64] This idea of gentility, a vertical notion constructed around the idea of *gens*, would be an ethnocentric posture. Such vertical substance may have only been relevant for the pipiltin, exogamic relations being formed only when politically expedient. Lockhart does not find wide-ranging evidence of a concern for lineage in postcontact Nahuatl legal documentation (*NAC*, 59).

There is, however, a set of terms that denote "household." This concept is defined more by living together than by "family" (*NAC*, 72). In Nahuatl, the term for sibling could also refer to cousins, the one for grandparents to great aunts and uncles, and the one for grandchildren to great nieces and nephews. Terminology that refers to people who, in the European sense, would be on the family's periphery brings them to the center. That said, horizontal behavior (to whom she would be married) took form in accordance with vertical custom.

Affinal bonds are those resulting from marriage. Spouses are immediately brought into the household. This interethnic horizontality implies moving not back or forward in time (as with verticality), but moving spatially outward into the community, moving into other communities, or bringing an outsider into a particular household. From his study of Nahuatl source material, Lockhart finds several terms that "embrace both lineal and collateral relatives." He documents affinal kin (in-laws, for example) being described with consanguineous language. The connections broaden, as kin terminology was applied to nonrelatives (of the same age) such as "neighbors and acquaintances" (*NAC*, 75, 78, 89). Such practices reveal a relatively open and communal system intertwined with horizontal social interaction regulated by vertical bloodlines. When verticality and horizontal gender linking coalesce, we get to the crux of nationness.

Lockhart concludes that lineage solidarity might not have been as primary as the calpulli (groups of households) and the altepetl (groups of calpulli) (*NAC*, 82). Chapter 2 explains that it was precisely the diluting of lineage that allowed the tlatoque to accumulate power. This could be understood as a mode of strengthening the tlatoani's individual calpulli and the altepetl over which he ruled. Because lineage ultimately was not as important as "household," there was an opening that could allow for interethnic mating practices.

Both monogamy and polygamy were additional factors defining Nahua mating practices, which were formal. Cline concludes that the Nahua entered into conjugal relationships that were permanent. Nevertheless, "divorce" was possible under Nahua traditions and "so was marriage to more than one wife simultaneously."[65] Such customs allowed for horizontal acquisition if the partners were of different ethnicities. Motolinía observes native practices allowing for one man forging generation with numerous women. We have broached the topic of Moctezuma's polygyny. After the defeat of the tlatoque, Motolinía comments, the lords continued to have innumerable women, some enjoying as many as two hundred. Having multiple wives, Cline theorizes, "was an index of status for men."[66] When the friars tried to articulate to the Nahua that polygamy went against Christ's teachings, they responded, "the Spaniards also have many women" (también los españoles tenían muchas mujeres) (*HI*, 98a). Despite some limited Spanish monogamy, as Motolinía notes, both the Nahua nobility and the Peninsular colonists had so many women among themselves the common man found it difficult to find himself a partner (*HI*, 95a, 97b). Even the religious, who were supposed to be celibate, were keeping mates. Leonard explains: "Throughout Spanish America, as in Spain itself, the rules of many monastic orders so far relaxed that numerous members lived outside convent walls and maintained illegal families and dependents in private houses."[67] However, the non-religious were the most egregious. Anthropologist Esteva-Fabregat provides the somewhat shocking detail that a friend of Bernal Díaz "had thirty children in three years, while another had fifty."[68] For Cline, this polygynous quandary for the Church persisted despite large-scale baptisms and secular legislation prohibiting polygamy.[69]

As can well be imagined, innumerable Nahua noblemen were wiped out in the wars of late antiquity, the invasion, and the turmoil that followed. Given the subordinate condition of Nahua females, a continued pattern of inter-ethnic commingling resulted. Nahua noblewomen held assorted and varied privileges. They may have even sought out Spanish men "in order to defend their inheritance" as Blanco maintains, or they may have been vulnerable to love or marital interest from working-class men from Spain who sought to improve their social station.[70] A prime example is Alva Ixtlilxóchitl's family tree, as both his father and grandfather were Spaniards. The same kind of heritage informed Muñoz Camargo's situation. Moreover, not all men were looking to settle down, and it was common to have other designs, some of which were less than honorable.

While it has been plainly documented that the conquistadors and Nahua nobility reached across ethnic lines for their mates, such practices among the lower strata are more difficult to ascertain. It does appear, conversely, that with the upheaval stemming from the plagues, the carnage of war, and the severity of colonial life, this increasingly was the case. Such disorientation could only facilitate unions between the mestizos, creating mestizos of mestizos, breaking down still further the ancient ethnic groups. Lockhart describes this period as one of "great demographic storms that swept through the indigenous population" (*NAC*, 82).[71] Nathan Wachtel labels this catastrophe as a "destructuration" that reached close to 90 percent on the central Mexican plateau.[72] This turmoil resulted in part from the brutality of the conquistadors, the diseases they brought with them, and directives issued by the new colonial government, such as the ethnic reshuffling among the lower classes through resettlement, the *congregación*. Gibson determines that these programs "resulted in new associations of peoples derivative from separate 'tribes'" (*AZ*, 28). Haskett arrives at the same conclusion from analyzing economic data. He finds that men and women from remote areas were assembled together as slaves, a common practice until the late 1540s. In his thorough analysis of labor and social forces in a 1548 Taxco slave inventory, he discovers that of thirty-seven couples, only thirteen were from the same place of origin. In contrast, the partners in twenty-five unions had "come from different towns and regions, indicating marriage after they had been brought together in the slave cuadrilla."[73] Before its demise, Central Mexican slavery reorganized by the Spanish, then, had a palpable impact on notions of ethnicity.

The Church had its parallel role in breaking down ethnic barriers. Intercultural mating may have been encouraged as a Christian guard against kinship relations. A severe form of blood proximity was incest, which was naturally banned under Christian doctrine. The Church hierarchy was so troubled about marriage within clan groups that—as Lavrin reports—it "had a carefully designed system to judge the degrees of proximity and rule on dispensation requests."[74] This became a bailiwick of the Church, because ethnic groups before the Spanish invasion often were restricted to one locality, a town or city, allowing for centuries of inbreeding. This was especially true for the lower strata, where political exchange of women across ethnic lines may not have been as prevalent, except perhaps in cases of slavery. One way to correct this problem was to tolerate contact between the Nahua and the *peninsulares*. Gibson concludes that "city life promoted miscegenation." Spaniards moved out of Tenochtitlan's center while the Nahua migrated toward it. In general, "Indian and Spanish dwellings became steadily more interspersed" (*AZ*, 368, 376). Lockhart concurs, commenting on "the Spanish civil population that almost immediately began to spill out of the cities." There were also economic reasons for blurring the lines between the pueblo de indios and the pueblo de españoles. Lockhart writes, "Communities of humble Hispanic people, including small agriculturalists and stockmen, petty traders, and muleteers, soon grew up inside many Indian towns." The movement also went in the opposite direction, as the Nahua progressively looked to Spaniards for employment and for protection (*NAC*, 3, 4, 113). Contact between Spaniards and the Nahua was comprehensive in the central areas of Mexico.

The Occidental-Oriental synthesis inherent in the abstraction Cortés-Malinche. An incomplete sentence, an unfinished concept. Due to confusion originating from the fact that Malinche translated and gave voice to Cortés, both the Tlaxcalteca and the Tenocha called Cortés "Malinche" (*HV*, 143a). The irony of this is that another duality is formed, reflecting Ometecuhtli-Omecihuatl, the divine couple personifying the formation of the nation. With Cortés and Malinche, that duality was the new political entity known as New Spain, which was part Castilian, part Nahua, and included elements from their peripheral cultures. From this fountain sprang Martin Cortés, the first representative of what Vasconcelos would later dub *La raza cósmica*, that is, the cosmic race, the first of those whom Paz would then call "los hijos de la chingada."[75]

To look at the Mexica under a contemporary microscope, they could be a nation in the modern sense, although not necessarily in the Western spirit. Smith enumerates five conditions to form a nation in an Eastern or "ethnic" sense.[76] They are historical territory, shared idea of patria, legal equality among members of the community, and common values. With a few restrictions, Smith's characteristics are all present under the Mexicatl model. Obviously, legal equality is impossible in any hierarchical culture. Furthermore, not all groups were included in the nation. The Tlaxcalteca, despite being Nahua, were not embraced because of their distinctive values, territory, narratives, and patria. The Totonaca were not considered part of the body politic, though they suffered under the imperial tribute system. They did not share a common notion of patria, had different territory, etc. Still, the provocative question remains: would the Totonaca and the Tlaxcalteca eventually have become "nationalized" by the Mexica if Spaniards, their African slaves, and their allies—the Tlaxcalteca themselves—had not overrun Mexico-Tenochtitlan when they did?

The Nahua concept differed from Smith's Western model, because an individual could not belong to whatever nation he or she desired.[77] (The present author is not convinced of the contention that this has been possible, even in our time.) Applying Smith's theory, the Mexicatl ideal would be non-Western, because it was organized according to ethnicity both in intent and in practice. Nonetheless, consequent on an expanding notion of ethnicity, Mexicatl practices did encourage fusing with other autochthonous groups and, ultimately, with Spaniards. Their *res publica* approached Smith's Western model. Beyond doubt, not all transethnicizing (forgive the neologism) resulted from interethnic blending. Economic factors also intensified the process. Haskett has found cases, such as one in 1607, where a Nahua individual suddenly proclaimed himself a mestizo to petition exemption from repartimiento service.[78] Haskett's self-appointed mestizo was not an isolated case. Jackson argues that the colonial categories "did not reflect social or cultural realities" and that individuals could consciously change "their behavior to be able to move to another and usually higher racial status within the caste system." Protean behavior implied cultural modification. Jackson continues: "Indios could change their mode of dress, learn to speak Spanish, move to a city or away from their place of birth, take up a profession generally not associated with the indigenous population, and be reclassified as mestizos."[79] Such transethnicizing—the direct and independent adoption of another etnia's culture—could be the most immediate form of horizontal annexation. Such practices do not indicate the individual could be a totally free cultural agent, at liberty to transethnicize at will. Cultural, political, religious, and economic forces limited possibilities. Jackson begs us to remember the caste system itself played a powerful role.[80]

The Nahua continued to practice interethnic connubiality after Tenochtitlan's defeat to preserve their status in a new social order. Without a time machine, they had no way to foresee a future that would bring the relative annihilation of their proud culture's outward aspects. Spaniards, like the Nahua, continued to commingle interethnically, but for their own reasons. Repeatedly, they took indigenous women to satisfy their primal urges. Women came to have value as commodified bodies as well as objects of sexual pleasure.[81] Often, as with their military experiences in Tlaxcala, Spaniards took women to forge alliances that would work to their advantage. Occasionally they would take an indigenous bride at the urging of the Church. Others unscrupulously tried to marry into Nahua nobility to enhance their own economic station. It appears love had little to do with such political, religious, and economic use of gender.

THE MAYA REGION: WOMEN AS MERCHANDISE AND WORSE

Some things stated about the Nahua in chapter 2 also describe the Maya, as with the adhesion to quadripartite concept of spatial divisions. The Nahua-Chichimecatl view is not so different from the *Popol Wuj* in this regard. The Nahua calpulli was imported into Mayan lands or both sectors mutually influenced each other. There are religious borrowings too. The Toltec Quetzalcoatl makes his appearance at the Classic Chichen Itza, now known as Kulculcan, and for his part Kulculcan appears in the K'iche' *Popol Wuj* as Gucumatz. The Grandparents appear in both Nahua and Mayan theologies. The Grandparents as venerated in both regions —Xpiyacoc and Xmucané in Ki'che' and Cipactonal and Oxomoco in Nahuatl— represent a creative dyad formed between a man and a woman. Despite the commonalities of dualist, quadripartite, and cosmogonic thought, different histories, narratives, and languages separated individualized Nahua and Maya groups, as well as unique ethnic identities that fostered separate cultures, despite their belonging to what is sometimes called the Mesoamerican cultural complex.

At the dawn of the early modern era, a good number of Nahua groups had been fusing into Triple Alliance, while the Maya remained divided into individual polities with distinct identities and languages: the Ixil, the Yucatec, the K'iche', the Mam, the Kakchiquels, and various others. In his book *Maya Conquistador,* Restall shows that the Maya actually considered themselves to be conquistadors, because they were often at war trying to conquer each other. Unlike the distinct Nahua-speaking nations, each of the Mayan nations had its own distinctive language. In fact, there were thirty-one Mayan languages that descended from a common trunk.[82] To make several points regarding gender, we return to the *Popol Wuj,* perhaps one of the best-known pieces of Native American literature, and to the *Brevísima relación de la destrucción de las Indias,* one of the more graphic depictions of the violence that transpired during the sixteenth century.

One distinction between the Nahua and the Classic Maya was that sporadically among the latter, a ruler was capable of marrying his sister, which was, as Bruhns and Stothert point out, "a means of keeping the throne within the immediate family." One instance can be found in Pacal II, who ruled Palenque from AD 615–83.[83] We will later turn to the Inkakuna, who categorically participated in these kinds of endogamic relationships in the official sphere.

However, unlike Inkakuna and the case of Pacal, the Maya mainly, like early dynastic Mexica, preferred exogamic relationships to expand power. The *Popol Wuj* offers interesting information in this regard for the K'iche' (see map 1).

In the sacred text, the divinities Tohil, Avilix, and Hacavitz instruct the K'iche' to bring them the blood of other peoples. One way to do that would be through sacrifice. Another would be for the other etnias to bring their lineages and embrace the K'iche' divinities (*PV,* III, x). These early "tribes" could yoke their bloodlines to the K'iche' through conjugal ties. This theology becomes concrete when the sons of Balam-Quitze, Balam-Acab, and Mahucutah, three of the four founding rulers of the nation, take their consorts from the peoples they conquered (*PV,* IV, vi). The K'iche' broaden their natural base by strengthening their intraethnic bonds. We are told the three Houses of K'iche' are likewise united by the women crossing over from one house to another (*PV,* IV, vii). This practice of mating with a partner of parallel lineage or of a neighboring ethnic group, given its concomitant transcultural characteristics, is part of the process we call horizontal appropriation. It is as if the woman's body was the place where cultural osmosis took place.

Alongside culture, there is an economic element to these exchanges. This is especially true for members of the original royal families depicted in the *Popol Wuj* in which the wives, sisters, and daughters seem to hold a monetary value (*PV,* IV, viii). This is not unusual. Archaeologists Papadopoulos and Urton explain that not only objects could acquire value. They assert that the human body can hold "an exchange value—all its own."[84] These kinds of grids of value held meaning for the K'iche', and would hold meaning for Spaniards when they arrived. They allowed for nation-blending while concomitantly inserting women into commercial circuits within and between nations both before and after 1492.

Horizontal journeying is empowerment through spatial maneuvering, easily achieved through conjugal bonds. While the men were the obvious beneficiaries of this process, the entire nation, including the women and children, gained advantages from these arrangements. By marrying "across," one could at the same time be marrying "up" if the second group held some type of advantage. This linking of contemporary etnias for political purposes is different from what we recognize as a vertical quest: the direct adoption of spiritual, religious, cultural, or historical notions from a nation's own past. These stories of interethnic mating are paramount, because they establish a horizontal pattern of multiethnic gender relations from which the origins of

Mesoamerican royalty would emerge. They also, in some small way, dilute the power of the fortress of ethnicity.

The diverse groups of Maya came into intense and protracted contact after 1524, with one of the more aggressive cultures contemporary to them from the Old World. Unsurprisingly, Spaniards were not as curious about Mayan culture as they were about extracting wealth from Mayan lands, and failing at that, they turned to extracting wealth from the people themselves. Consequently, as with other nations in the hemisphere, the K'iche' nation suffered massive cultural damage during the prolonged K'iche'-Spanish war. However, they successfully resisted extermination, and today retain many of those cultural traits, albeit in modified forms. That is why the passage from late antiquity to the early modern is so important to our understanding of these matters.

Bartolomé de las Casas, despite the apparent hyperbole and striking discursivity of his *Brevísima relación,* provides graphic descriptions of the events he witnessed or heard about that comprised the Encounter. He recounts how the Lord of K'iche', probably Tecum Uman, came out to meet the Spaniards "with trumpets, timbales, and many parties" (con trompetas y atabales e muchas fiestas). From this, we can surmise the Lord greeted the Spaniards with a spirit of hospitality. However, Las Casas continues, when the intruders were told there was no gold, a tyrant "ordered that they be burnt alive" (mandólos luego quemar vivos). The tyrant was probably Pedro de Alvarado, who went from being Cortés's right-hand man to a primary conquistador in his own right. Las Casas laments, not only were many K'iche' burnt to a crisp, but "all those provinces" (todas aquellas provincias) were incinerated too (*TR,* I:82–85). As part of that violence, numerous Maya were sold as slaves. Las Casas reports that they were sometimes bartered for "wine and oil, and vinegar, and for bacon, for clothing and for horses" (vino y aceite y vinagre, y por tocinos, e por vestidos, y por caballos) (*TR,* 1:102–3). As with other geographical areas, the inverse reorganizing trends of poblar and despoblar were present. Annis reports Alvarado populating five new towns on the shores of Lake Quinizilapa "with captives and slaves who had been rounded up during the wars." There was no acknowledgement of cah structures, as people from all over, including blacks from the Caribbean, were thrown together.[85] This reality was dreadful for all Maya, a proud people who lived structured lives, but it was especially egregious for the women.

In the violence of the Conquest, late-ancient notions of interethnic mating took on new dimensions, new pathways given form by the violence of the moment. Gender certainly entered into the picture of the Conquest because a female slave could catch a hefty price. One who was pregnant could fetch an even higher amount. Las Casas divulges the existence of a particularly evil Spaniard who had boasted to a priest of how "he worked wherever he could to get many Indian women pregnant, so that, selling them as pregnant slaves, they would garner him a higher price" (trabajaba cuanto podía por empreñar muchas mujeres indias para que, vendiéndolas preñada por esclavas, le diesen más precio de dinero por ellas) (*TR*, 1:106–7). It seems men could just pluck women right off the street for the simple profit of it. Such a story denotes the existence of a mass rapist who was at the same time nothing more than a crass capitalist.

While Las Casas's text used hyperbole as a rhetorical device, making it an inadequate source in the quest for objective history, there are other genres of sources. Modern science can fill in the gap as it sheds further light on those seemingly far off events. There has been DNA testing among the Maya by Nick Patterson and his team of scientists, revealing a connection to the Mozabite people, who today reside in Algeria (they are Berbers).[86] One plausible explanation for this seemingly implausible connection is that the DNA was deposited by slaves, owned by Spaniards, who originated in the Maghreb. Another explanation, following Leo Garofalo, is that some conquistadors already had some African blood before they left the European world. He recognizes mixed-heritage people already living on the coast of West Africa during the fourteenth century. He encapsulates that for some scholars, "creolization happened for many people before they moved to the Americas or Europe."[87] If so, the Mozabite DNA suggests that the transethnic violence women were subjected to was happening in the Old World even before the transatlantic migration. However, if those genes are from slaves owned by Spaniards (also a likely possibility), the presence of these genes, along with conquistadors' genes, suggests additional sexual violence committed by the conquistadors and their slaves against Mayan women. It may be counterintuitive, but certain transafricans, as Gerhard and Restall put forward in separate articles, were something like "black conquistadors."[88]

Interethnic sexual encounters, violent or not, led to greater heterogeneity among the later generations. Regarding heterogeneity among the Maya, a group of geneticists headed by Mao mapped out three additional groups, Aymara/Qheswa from Bolivia, Qheswa from Cerro de Pasco (Peru), Nahua from Guerrero (Mexico), and Maya from Yucatan. These researchers concluded: "The Mayan sample shows substantially more heterogeneity than do any of the other samples characterized in this study."[89] Mao's group's conclusion that there was a high degree of mixed ancestry for the Yucateca only strengthens our awareness of high level of sexual violence during the sixteenth century and after in that particular region. The Maya suffered a particularly violent, sexualized encounter with the Spanish, surpassing what the Bolivian Aymara and Guerrero Nahua (but not the Cerro del Pasco Qheswa) suffered. Much more remains to be learned about these diverse DNA trajectories.

Nevertheless, the Maya were quite adept at preserving layers of their culture. Robust resistance to Spanish (soon to be Ladino) culture is already apparent in the sixteenth century. The *Popol Wuj* itself is one example, a text put to script at the midpoint of that century, but hidden from Spanish speakers until the eighteenth century.[90] As discussed in chapter 2, Barbara Tedlock notes the survival of the *calpules,* the Mesoamerican way of organizing clan life. George Lovell also describes this phenomenon. He explains even after the Spanish reorganized the Highland Maya by means of congregating people into pueblos de indios, they continued to organize themselves in accordance with "pre-conquest domestic lines Spaniards called *parcialidades.*" He continues, "These were social units of great antiquity, organized as patrilineal clans or localized kin affiliations, and usually associated with particular tracts of land."[91] These precontact modes of association were hardy, and not easily overcome by Spaniards. Lovell concludes, "*Parcialidades* would preserve their aboriginal identity by continuing to operate socially and economically as separate components rather than merging to form a corporate body."[92] Chapter 2 discusses Rigoberta Menchú's description of the four candles put out during ceremonies in the 1980s. These represent the four parcialidades directly derived from the quadrangular notion of space as represented in texts such as the *Popol Wuj.* Such practices suggest the hardiness of Mayan nations in the face of prolonged and stubborn Hispanic pressure to give in.

THE NORTHERN ANDES: THE POLITIES OF COLOMBIA

The lands eventually known as Colombia did not have a unified cultural complex, although there were affinities in norms of succession for rulers and the intense interest in gold working. The cultures of late antiquity constituted an unordered patchwork of what the Spanish called *señoríos,* chieftainships, and what we call polities. We now survey several of them, including Zenú (or Sinú), Urabá, and Guaca, from the perspective of gender relations. This section looks at the internal power composition of these polities in the frame established by Cieza de León's chronicle, and offers context with secondary sources such as Bruhns and Stothert, Rappaport, Cummins, Gordon, and Villamarín, as well as DNA test results.

Cieza de León, like his countrymen, had a keen interest in the women he encountered while penetrating deep into the South American continent. This, of course, results in a masculine bias, but it also resulted in the collection of details about the women and about the cultural practices associated with them. Cieza's masculine bias does not set him apart from other chroniclers of the time and indeed, it puts him into a category Strasser and Tinsman describe as "World History," which "commonly centers its analyses on domains of life in which men are primary actors, be it patterns of trade and labor exploitation, or empire building and state formation."[93] Opening up the field of "world history" implies the exigency of taking male-centered bias into account with respect to gender relations. During a time when it would have been unthinkable for women to cultivate the historiographical genre (even the determined Sor Juana, one century later, was not so daring), male authors remain a primary source of information.[94] Here we take one small step to address these blank spaces in the quest for a gender-nuanced view of things.

Gender Relations, Hereditary and Shared Power

The origins of the Zenú, a lowland culture of the Caribbean region of what is today Colombia, go back to the beginning of the second millennium. While those remote origins are foggy in time, we know a number of things about this culture at the beginning of the Hispanic age. One has to do with gender. Of three paramount rulers, one had an extremely powerful wife, the Lady of Finzenu.[95] This female sovereign was transported on a sort of royal palanquin in a gynecocentric retinue. Bruhns and Stothert describe the litter as being "supported by serving women who let her walk on them if she had to move about on her own."[96] Thus, females had a role to play in the brokering of power. Female-centered governance was not common in the Americas, yet it was not unheard of. We have already touched on Atotoztli who, as the daughter of Moctezuma I and the mother of Axayacatl (the fifth and sixth tlatoque of the dynasty) ruled Tenochtitlan either as tlatoani or as regent to Axayacatl. We consider the phenomenon of female leaders among the Moche in the next section, and in *La Florida del Inca,* Garcilaso de la

Vega describes in relative detail the *cacica*, the Lady of Cofachiqui, in the lands that eventually became South Carolina. That paramount ruler held sway over a province of the Mississippian culture, probably near present-day Camden, South Carolina. She aided Hernando de Soto, giving him provisions from the few remaining after a pestilence. Spaniards were greatly impressed with her, and she is admired for her elegance and poise, not so much for her physical beauty.[97]

Thus, the Lady of Finzenu had female colleagues, and by all odds was relatively contemporary to the Lady of Cofachiqui and the cacicas of Moche, even if she was not aware of them. Like them, she presided over a relatively large territory. Indeed Finzenu, the capital of the ruler of the same name, "was the most extensive city in the area."[98] This was a culturally and geographically significant matriarchal polity. Le Roy Gordon, drawing on Juan de Castellanos's epic poem, *Elegías de varones ilustres de Indias* (Elegies of eminent men of the Indies), describes the city itself as being sophisticated, with a center plaza surrounded by twenty "communal or multifamily" dwellings, each of which "had three or four smaller buildings nearby."[99] These features suggest a sedentary culture, hierarchical, with a female locus of power mixed with three male radii. The female-nuanced Zenú elite offer an interesting point of comparison with the people of Urabá, another ranked lowland society, to whom we now turn.

This discussion must begin with the family. Juan and Judith Villamarín see a generally polygamous region that included the Cauca valley, as well as coastal Ecuador and Colombia.[100] Regarding succession, the Uraban hereditary leader's position passed from father to a son begat in the primary wife, who herself maintains a certain authority. While a patrilineal custom exists in the trajectory of the paramounts among the Urabá, the principal wife's role suggests a parallel matriliniarity that allows for a bilateral system of governance.[101] This is not unlike the gendered division of power seen among the Inkakuna. Cieza de León provides details about the level of organization attained by the Uraban people, yet does not specify which of the sons the potentate engenders with his principal wife will succeed him. That is to say, we do not know if primogeniture was a factor. When the paramount dies, Cieza tells us, he is interred—after a ceremony of great imbibing, it seems—with his arms, a quantity of chicha, and a few women, who are buried alive (*CP-1^{era}*, fol. 20v, p. 46). Later, Cieza describes this same custom around the polity of Guaca. There, chicha was given to "the most beautiful of their women" (las más hermosas de sus mugeres) to get them drunk before interring them with the paramount leader (*CP-1*^{era}, fol. 24v, p. 56). While Cieza does not elaborate on which women were consigned to the grave with the patriarch, we can infer whom they might have been and what form their function might have taken in this arrangement. Presumably, women still able to broker power were not entombed. If the first wife could no longer broker, she might have been sacrificed, perhaps according to her own wishes. If the second or third wives could remarry, or if they were still the sisters of the paramount leader, they likewise might have avoided the living burial. We return to the Guaca momentarily.

Cieza offers another remarkable clue about the Uraban people: "they marry their daughters to their brothers" (cásanse con hijas de sus hermanos) (*CP-1*^{era}, fol. 20v, p. 46). Since nieces conjoined with their uncles, we can surmise that this ethnic group did not forge bonds with other groups through marriage, a widespread practice employed in the Mayan polities. The absence of such practices suggests an endogamic system limited not only to the group, but also to a small subset of that group, the leader's family. Such a system is reminiscent of the practices of the late-period Mexicatl dynasty, and as will be seen, it parallels leader selection customs among the Inkakuna.

These details suggest the presence of an urbanized community living a more or less sedentary existence, with a hereditary elite interested in preserving its power through the practice of uncles marrying their nieces. However, without horizontal appropriation through gender, the avenue toward *supra-etnia* creation was not taken. Urabá elite power was primary, in broad terms, as Mary Helms suggests, because its "activities helped to unite all members of society into a single polity; perhaps also into an integrated economic whole."[102] Consequently, the emphasis was on polity building, expanding the borders of the political and ethnic nation without adopting intraethnic modes of appropriation.

After the peoples of Urabá, Cieza jumps down to Guaca, the dominions in the Antioquian region of the great Nutibara, a man who "had many wives" (tenía muchas mugeres) (*CP-1*^{era}, fol. 23 [xiii], p. 52). This fits what we know about the region. Grace Burbano Arias explains that during the sixteenth century in and around Santa Fe de Bogotá, another highland location, polygamy was common.[103] We do not know if Nutibara had wives from other ethnic groups, such as from the peoples living along the Abibe Sierra. We are aware of what Cieza tells us. The Nutibarans married, they did so of their own will, and the son born of the wife became the heir. If the couple bore no child, then the son of the husband's sister became heir (*CP-1*[era], fol. 23v, pp. 53–54). This pattern insures that both men and women share in power, even if it is automatic. In this manner, a predetermined succession through the female's family gives her ironclad access to power. Again, the power of succession lying in the hands of the paramount's wife or sister suggests a cultural affinity with practices among the Urabá, and (as we will see) the Inkakuna. The development of polygamy may have allowed for greater wealth and, in the case of rulers such as Nutibara, enabled him to accumulate assets from each of his wives' families, thereby broadening the reach of his political authority.

Thus, polygamy is associated with power. This is important because, as Rappaport explains, in the three regions of "Bogotá, Quito, and Popayán, a fixed political hierarchy defined the political jurisdictions of social units. Individual rank was determined by genealogical distance from rulers." These hereditary practices did not extend to all of the lands making up present-day Colombia. For example, Rappaport underscores, "there were 72 Pijao caciques, their supreme rulers chosen apparently by consensus." The Andakí's "caciques enjoyed only very restricted political authority."[104] Quito, certainly, had been under Inka dominion, the last Sapa Inka Atawallpa actually being from there. Bogotá and Popayán had not come under Inka domination, suggesting an intermediate ranked position between Pijao/Andakí and Quito/Qosqo. Building on Verdesio's notion of alternative forms of organization, we can posit that Pijao and Andakí power sharing implies a more democratic form of governance.

Slavery as an institution, obviously, also affected women. Abuse of this kind did not begin with the Spanish. It was customary in late antiquity. Women from the Antioquia area, for example, when captured as slaves, were often impregnated by their captors, who we can imagine were of another etnia.[105] Chronicler Cieza de León states that along these northern valleys, lords, who for him were Caribs but for Humboldt were likely Urabás, Zenús, and Guacas, captured female slaves as war booty, doing what they wanted with them.[106] When children were born of those unions, they treated them well, fattening them up until they could be eaten in a hearty feast:

> They searched in their enemies' lands for all the women they could find; once taken to their homes, they made use of them as they would their own; and if they got them pregnant, they raised the children as

> if they were a gift until they reached the age of twelve or thirteen, and then being good and fat, they ate them with great gusto.
>
> Buscauan de las tierras de sus enemigos todas las mugeres que podían: las quales traydas a sus casas, usauan con ellas como con las suyas propias: y si empreñan dellos, los hijos que nacían los criauan con mucho regalo, hasta que auían doze o treze años, y desta edad estando bien gordos, los comían con gran sabor. (*CP-1^{era}*, fol. 24 [xiii] [*sic*], p. 54)

In other cases, male slaves are captured and then given to the victor's female relatives and neighbors (sus parientas y vezinas) to produce more offspring, and thus more meals (*CP-1^{era}*, fol. 24v, p. 55). Norms of slavery and polygamy allow us to anticipate the kinds of interactions late-antiquity Colombian women had with early modern Europeans.

Spanish Voyeurism: Women in the Crosshairs

We have talked about a type of nascent anthropology cultivated by the chroniclers. While less concerned with scientific truth than modern anthropology, the sixteenth century did bequeath upon us considerable information about South American societies of that time. One of the compelling aspects for the invaders was the women—their physical attributes and their openness about sexuality—at least in some ethnic groups. The beauty of the indigenous women was juxtaposed with what Pablo Rodríguez Jiménez appropriately describes as "an irreparable deficit of Spanish women" (un irreparable déficit de mujeres españolas).[107] Centuries before the Geneva Conventions (1949) and the Declaration on the Protection of Women and Children in Emergency and Armed Conflict (1974), without women of their own kind, and with the power of gunpowder and horses, it is unsurprising Spanish men would turn their sights on Amerindian women. When Cieza de León wrote about the physical traits of the women he came across while descending the continent, he sometimes ranked them, as Bruhns and Stothert suggest.[108] The chronicler finds this to be an essential subject worthy of discussion. Describing the areas surrounding San Sebastian, near the coast, he describes the local leaders as "fine looking" (dispuestos) and "clean" (limpios). He brazenly adds, "Their women are of the beautiful and loving types that I have seen in these Indies where I have walked" (sus mujeres son de las hermosas y amorosas que yo he visto en la mayor parte destas Indias donde he andado) (*CP-1^{era}*, fol. 19 [ix], p. 43). Descending south along the cordillera, he comes to Nutibara's domains. He rates the women there of superlative beauty ("las mugeres más hermosas") (*CP-1^{era}*, fol. 23v, p. 53). This frequently repeated idea implies two things, one explicitly, and the other implicitly. Regarding the former, the women were beautiful, an aesthetic asset. Regarding the latter, because Cieza did not speak the local languages, "loving" would not likely have been of the spiritual or intellectual type, but more of the physical type. Hence, without stating it, the stage is set: pretty women, not afraid to express themselves physically, opening the door to transatlantic mestizaje.

The titillation a sixteenth-century male reader might have felt upon surveying the litany of half-naked women being subjected to Cieza's scopophilic gaze might have helped make Cieza's book a market sensation, turning him into a source for other chroniclers.[109] But reading turns into drudgery for twenty-first-century readers actually interested in trying to locate those women in their respective ethnic groups—the interest of this book on the formation of Latin American nations. For this reason, we should not engage in a detailed overview of his rankings of natural beauty and state of dress, especially given his penchant for hyperbole in these matters. On more than one occasion, he is prone to a lack of clarity, as in his description of a people separate politically from Guaca although of the same language group. This leaves us ethnically estranged from those conditions. On top of that, he may have been blind to class differences. At times he contradicts himself. In one sentence, he states, "These [people] walk naked like the others" (andan desnudos estos como los demás), and then in the next, he adds, "The women cover themselves with ponchos" (las mugeres andan cubiertas con otras pequeñas mantas) (*CP-1^{era}*, fol. 24 [xiii] [*sic*], p. 54). One possible explanation for the contradiction is that Cieza jumps from common people not permitted to wear the sophisticated garb of the ruling class to elites who were sumptuously robed. This is possible because he also talks of señores in the context of clothing, "señores" being the Spanish term for lords. Clothing descriptions and stages of dress can be taken as anthropological data, but they also suggest on Cieza's part a certain fixation on objectifying the women that he came across.

Appraisals of the feminine form are not mere literary constructions to delight the reader, although they may have done that in the case of the early modern male reader. These aesthetic assessments went hand and hand with the behavior of Spaniards, who took the women they desired and did what they wanted with them. This becomes evident if one reads between the lines of Cieza's text. Inquisitively, if we compare Cieza with Guaman Poma de

Ayala, we can garner additional information. The latter, as the final section of this chapter discusses, implies that women were often agents of their own destiny in these matters.

Whether women were active agents of erotic entanglements, targets in sexualized warfare, or some degree of both, the sexual and power chaos of the period can be documented biologically using genetic data. Gabriel Bedoya and colleagues compare ratios of mitochondrial DNA (mtDNA) and Y chromosome lineages to determine racial admixture in Antioquia, perhaps even including some of the descendants of the great Nutibara. Bedoya and his team confirm what we know from the chronicle: there was "a biased pattern of mating" in favor of Spanish men at the moment of initial contact of European and Antioquian peoples.[110] Their genetic research validates information from the chronicle and offers a more nuanced, even statistical, perspective. Because individuals receive two sets of chromosomes (twenty-two, plus an X or Y marker to denote sex), one from each parent, the ethnic composition of a person's ancestors is now possible to determine (females have two X chromosomes, males have an X and Y).[111] In addition, the mother transmits mtDNA mutations to her children, both male and female.[112] The study's results show that Y, or male, chromosome lineages for people in six Antioquian towns founded by Spaniards—Marinilla, Peñol, Santuario, Carmen, Guatapé, and Granada[113]—were 94 percent European, 5 percent African, and 1 percent Native American, while mtDNA lineages were shown, by contrast, to be 90 percent Amerindian, 8 percent African, and 2 percent European.[114] These ratios evince the noteworthy situation of Spanish male and indigenous female ancestry, with the exclusion of Spanish women and indigenous men from DNA lineages. The data offers an unclouded view of human relationships, and proves the substance of Cieza de León's narrative. It reveals that Antioquia's present-day inhabitants descended from European men and Antioquian women who came together during the 1500s, confirming what we strongly suspected about the Spanish invasion. It confirms that there was violence against women, who had to develop survival strategies, such as linking up with men who would perhaps guarantee their inheritance, their stability, and their hope to have lives free from violence. We can hypothesize that if large numbers of families were being formed (by rape, active agency, concubinage, or marriage) with conquering males at the head of a unit that included conquered females, then the gendered power differential would become ethnically tinged, a key attribute of the coloniality of power.

The Bedoya study reveals another social phenomenon. The initial burst of admixture between conquistadors and indigenous women did not last beyond the initial period of cross-Atlantic intercourse. This is true primarily for the obvious reason that the local population was decimated in the aftermath of the initial epidemics and the subsequent wars of penetration. Burkholder and Johnson report that in Tunja, in Colombia's eastern Andes, as a case in point, the population fell by about 80 percent in the first hundred years of Spanish presence.[115] Referring to the area in and around Antioquia, Peter Wade rightly proposes "that the demographic and sociocultural erosion of the indigenous element led to many Indians being assimilated into the ranks of the *libres* and mixing with other racial types."[116] Even if the mother or father dies afterward, once a child has been born, depending on if he or she receives indigenous or Spanish upbringing, the child moves more or less toward the reconfigured emerging Hispanic cultural center achieved with laws, peer pressure, and survival instincts. Additional factors must be considered. One of these is that Spanish males continued to immigrate into the Antioquia region. Another is that, as the Bedoya team points out, "as colonial society became consolidated it increasingly discouraged new Spanish immigrants from marrying natives." They then had to turn to mestizas who, given their one-half or more Spanish blood, could be afforded a higher station in colonial society than people of indigenous extraction could. Mestizos certainly also transmitted Amerindian mtDNA markers, as had their indigenous feminine forbears. This process advanced rapidly. The Bedoya study cites a 1675 census in the Aburra Valley that registered some three thousand inhabitants "of which 18% where white, 56% mestizo, 9% native, and 17% African." The findings suggest that these ratios, coupled with discrimination, would later aid in the establishment of a class system that would deny "access to higher education or government office" to people of Amerindian or African ancestry.[117] The Bedoya study understates what this meant to people on the ground when it asserts, "These circumstances are likely to have made even more difficult a continuing incorporation of Amerindian women into the Antioquian population."[118] We can affirm that people who were originally at the flashpoint of the cultural clash were pushed further into the periphery of colonial society, because Iberians continued to immigrate as one century unfolded into another.

One might ask, if indigenous women's impact yielded to mestiza women, why would we even be curious about them? The first and primary part of the answer lies in their coming from a tradition that paved the way for a new mestizo society. We could hypothesize there must have been some familiarity with the custom of exchanging women across ethnic lines for the Antioquian women to participate so fully in the process, willingly or unwillingly. We can also hypothesize the women brought something of their cultural heritage into the relationship as Spanish men did. Such integration is a centrifuge of expanding nationality, derived from pre-Hispanic patterns of ethnic mixing and from Spanish men's interest in indigenous women. However, given the ruling Colombian classes' tendency to be endogamic, we must consider the opposite hypothetical possibility: the lower classes were also endogamic. If this were the case, then their interaction with Spaniards would have gone against their culture and would have been an even more painful process than if they had been exogamic. Of course, the possibility exists that elites were endogamic, and commoners, exogamic. Whatever the case, we know enough interethnic mating took place to create a brand-new kind of nation.

When we combine modern biological science with sixteenth-century historiography, we arrive at a notion of the mass sexual encounter. The DNA testing showing combinations of more than 90 percent Spanish male and more than 90 percent Antioquian female, given the sample tested, suggests that a widespread intercultural mating spree ensued during the first half of the century, regardless of whether late-ancient mating practices were open or closed. While we have not been able to determine the relationship between dynastic succession and the large-scale interethnic mating that came to pass, it is clear that the women of antiquity were open to female leadership. Besides the Lady of Finzenu, there was also the Cacica Gaitana from the region of Timaná, Huila, who during the same time frame led the people of the Upper Magdalena River Valley against the Spanish onslaught. Such courageousness and leadership may have something to do with matriarchal traditions that met Spanish patriarchal ones head on. It is also possible that the existence polygamy in these regions might have aided individual Spanish men in having multiple sex partners.

THE PERUVIAN COAST: FOREIGN WOMEN IN THE MOCHE WORLD

Because there is limited media transmitting ancient cultural horizons' heritages, it can be tedious to ascertain the level of political organization as well as the kind of gender arrangements giving form to them. Additionally, the evidence can be contradictory, or its meaning can be obscure. Archeologists, for example, are not of the same mind on the level of political sophistication or on the degree of integration of the Moche settlements on the northern Peruvian coast (see Mochica area, map 7). Archeologist John Verano sums up the debate by explaining that for some scholars, Moche culture functioned in coordination with a large state whose capital was at the site of Moche; for others, a state-level organization was not achieved until Moche IV (AD 450–550), its capital at Pampa Grande in Lambayeque; for still others, politically, it did not go beyond a loosely linked confederation.[119] There is also a gendered aspect to this.

If in South Carolina, Finzenu, and Timaná there are glimpses of female rulers, on the Moche coast we find a female ruling class based on centuries-long tradition that may have accepted interethnic mixing. The encounter with these women is documented in Cieza de León's chronicle. What is interesting here is not merely the development of statecraft, but at what level women become involved in a statecraft. Prior to the eighth century, women were rarely represented in this culture's art, Alana Cordy-Collins explains. She then traces the insertion of the feminine form into their artistic paradigms.[120] She observes that spiked-lipped women appear in Moche V artwork (AD 550–800). For Luis Jaime Castillo, the tombs of the High Priestesses discovered in 1991 at San José de Moro date from a similar period.[121] This priestess must have become even more vital, as her image is more frequent than any other. Castillo detects a direct correlation between the apogee of her iconography and the appearance of tombs for high-powered women.[122]

Because few women appeared in the Moche archaeological record before that time, and certainly none with a labret, one can begin to suspect these women were foreigners. Additional scrutiny reveals women with similar ornamentation from further north. Cordy-Collins finds evidence of this in two proto-Ecuadorian cultures, La Tolita (600 BC–AD 400) and Jama-Coaque (350 BC–AD 400). Even if we do not know exactly why these lovely protopunkers came to the Moche region on the Peruvian coast, we do know they had what it takes to interface with the men there, allowing them to be ascendant enough to appear as part of the visual discourse painted on pottery (see figure 3). Their musical instruments, drums and conch-shell horns, indicate public power. Eventually, as Cordy-Collins suggests, they may have had a role in so altering "the Moche tradition there that it ceases to be recognizable as such in the archaeological record." Cordy-Collins hypothesizes two possibilities: one, these northern women "maintained an independent power base that endured for centuries," or two, they slowly become part of Moche administrative structures.[123]

Cordy-Collins tends to favor the second possibility in her assessment of what happened, and she offers none other than Cieza de León as support for the hypothesis that these women evolved into the sixteenth-century señoras of matriarchal Moche culture.[124] Cieza comments on the Spaniards encountering these cacicas on the coast. He uses the term "cacicas" interchangeably with two others, "capullana" and "señora" (*CP-3^{era}*, fols. 25–26, pp. 69–71). "Señora" is the feminine form of señor, meaning lord, and "cacica" is the feminine form of the Taino word "cacique," meaning hereditary lord.[125] This is quite remarkable, first because he documents female rulers who were most likely hereditary, second because he uses the word "señora"—a title reserved for Spanish women, but not indigenous women, unless they were rulers—and third because their leadership, according to the archeological record, does suggest an ethnic immigration that reorganized Moche culture. Few references to lady rulers appear in the record documenting the encounter. In the previous section, we mentioned the Lady of Finzenu from the lands that became Colombia. We have similarly consulted Inca Garcilaso, who tells of one in Book 3, chapter 10 of *La Florida del Inca*: the Lady of Cofachiqui, who ruled over a polity in lands now southeastern United States. The Ladies of Cofachiqui and Finzenu were roughly contemporary to the Moche *capullanas* described by Cieza de León. The kuraka Condor Wacho from the Huaylas area was a cacica during the time of the Spanish founding of Lima. As mentioned in chapter 3, she became Francisco Pizarro's *de facto* mother-in-law when the conquistador took her daughter the ñusta, or princess, Quispe Sisa (called Inés Huaylas Yupanki by the Spaniards) as a concubine.[126]

Cieza not only offers clues to what became of the spike-lipped ladies of Moche culture, he comes right out and admits the seductive sway they held over the conquistadors. When one Pedro de Halcón de la Cerda met one of the *capullanas*, he fell hopelessly in love with her: "The more he looked at her, the more he became lost in love" (mientras más la mirava, más perdido estava de sus amores). This poor Halcón became so enamored of the *capullana* that, upon the Spaniards' departure, "he lost his mind and went crazy" (lo qual sintió tanto Halcón, que luego perdió el çeso y se tornó loco) (*CP-3^{era}*, fol. 25, p. 70; fol. 26, p. 73). Undoubtedly, manifold encounters between Spanish men and Amerindian women sparked the men's passion. But this one seems to be especially noteworthy.

FIGURE 3. Labretted Lady.
Courtesy of Museo Larco (013311).

Thus, in terms of gender, the situation with the Moche was poles apart from that in other locales, where the Spanish were equally excited by the women, but generally dealt with the men to obtain them. For a comparison with more traditional male-female relations, we can consider Tumbes, where Spaniards first arrived in the lands they ended up calling Peru. Chronicler Agustín de Zárate reports that the paramount leader of Tumbes was greatly feared by his subjects. He seems to have had a cherished female retinue he jealously guarded so much that any sentinel who protected his house had to undergo surgery to have both his nose and his genitalia removed (*HDC*, 8). Because the Tumbes people were to the north of Lambayeque, where the Moche horizons unfolded, and because we are talking about a later time, when the Iberians arrived, not Moche IV or V, there are gender-informed reasons why the patriarchal Tumbes people might have viewed women differently from the way the Moche did. However, a word of caution is necessary. When Zárate observed the gender relations of South American peoples, he doubtlessly projected European cultural understandings onto them. In this, he coincides with other Spanish historians, as Silverblatt remarks, viewing "the world they conquered only through the categories and perceptions that their culture provided."[127] Nevertheless, he does offer some valuable information about the area of Tumbes populated by a people who had been conquered by the Inkakuna during Pachakutiq's reign and consolidated into Tawantinsuyo during Thupaq Yupanki's.

The Moche, then, offer a unique case, removed from those more patriarchal practices of the Tumbes, Nahua, K'iche', and Nutibara traditions, but perhaps not from the señoras of Cofachiqui and Finzenu. This case shows how beauty and refinement were so potent they could cause a Spanish man to go insane with desire. It also shows that some kinds of men desired active, powerful women, which goes against the stereotype of men finding passive women attractive. If this story is true, the same may have happened earlier, during Moche V, when the Ecuadoran women came and entranced the Moche ruler (or rulers), so much so that he (or they) shared power or even gave it up. There may have been ethnic mixing, which seems plausible, or the labretted ladies may have arrived with their male subordinates, allowing for a closed endogamic system to persevere in the midst of teeming ethnic diversity. Either way, those labretted ladies then garnered a place in the public sphere, and consequently, in the archaeological record. Unfortunately, in all of this there is no mention about the Moche women who were originally there, and who probably lost both their men and their political prestige after the arrival of the labretted ladies. We can imagine this was not a happy time for them. Thus, gender and ethnicity played decisive roles in the allotment of power.

This all changed after the encounter. Positions of power of this nature, as Bruhns and Stothert suggest, would later be lost after the establishment of Spanish sovereignty, owing to the Spanish distaste for women in the public sphere.[128] The great feminine line of power in Moche would eventually disappear along with the masculine ones in Tumbes and other locations in the ways described in chapter 3. In the end, the capullanas would become nothing more than "Indians," their memory preserved only in chronicles and ceramic figurines.

THE CENTRAL ANDES: THE INKAKUNA

We now move south, from the areas occupied by Chibchas, Nutibarans, Tumbens, and the Moche to the central Andes, what Covey has called the Inka heartland. During the time of the Encounter, the polities of the north were being folded into Tawantinsuyo, as just hinted regarding Tumbes, and the polities of the center were already integrated, many of them deeply so. One of the differences between the polities of the northern cordilleras and coast and the Inka state further south was the political complexity of the latter. Villamarín and Villamarín succinctly contrast the two types of systems: "Passage from chiefdom to state involves intensified centralization of power, great inequality between population sectors, expanded scale of labor appropriation by elites, increased administrative and labor specialization, codification of law, and a formal juridical system."[129] Covey considers the complexity of Inka organization in the context of agriculture. The transformation of valley-bottom lands for maize production involved massive investments in state infrastructure—not only for the terraces and canals for growing crops, but also for storage structures, a road system to bind the area to the capital, and administrative buildings for governing the local population.[130] It was the transformation from polity to state that allowed for massive public works projects across vast geographical spaces, such as the Inka road and *tambo*, or inn, system. Such a network allowed for policies favoring, to a degree, cultural homogenization. Another word for "homogenization" in the central Andean context is Inkanization, the spreading of Inkan culture to the smaller polities as they were incorporated. Both women and geography were integral to this process. Such complex organizational expansion finds its roots in a dualist structure, but not exclusively so.

Dualities, Trinities, Panakakuna, and Ethnogendered Quadripartition

It is well known that Tawantinsuyo comprised four suyos, each one representing a district. The numbers four and, as we will see, two and three, were organizing principles of Tawantinsuyo along with gender-informed distributions. Referring to the four suyos, Inca Garcilaso gives their geographic identifications and then states, "These are the four limits that the Inka kings lorded over" (Estos son los cuatro términos de lo que señorearon los Reyes Incas) (*CR*, I, viii). This quadripartition was also apparent on a micro-level, and was reflected in the capital Qosqo, or Cuzco. The Inka capital at the time of the coming of the Spanish was divided into upper and lower moieties, constituting an alternate form of organization. Hanan Qosqo and Urin Qosqo reflected a makeup that was different, but not entirely so, from the Nahua altepetl. Four, naturally, is divisible by two. However, if there was a possibility of rotating altepeme in Central Mexico suggesting some degree of equality, at least among three of the four sectors, it seems one moiety in the Andes held power over the other, hence the denominations "upper" and "lower." This type of organization was not limited to the capital. Flores Galindo explains that these kinds of dualities could be found in any town or city and were reflected in a macro sense in the Empire. Each duality was comprised of two moieties "opposite and necessary to each other" (opuestas y necesarias entre sí).[131] This type of symmetry was not necessarily an Inka innovation, and may have survived from the Wari horizon or earlier.

Again, the number four is also apparent. Sarmiento de Gamboa reports that in early Qosqo, the town of Acamama had four districts or neighborhoods, numerically and spatially related to the four cardinal directions. Quinti Cancha was the *barrio de picaflor,* or hummingbird neighborhood; Chumbi Cancha, where the weavers were; Sairi Cancha, a tobacco neighborhood; and Yarambuy Cancha, probably an ethnically mixed neighborhood, which perhaps even served as a mestizo sector. María Rostworowski posits that "Yarambuy" is not a word from Qheswa, but from Aymara.[132] This suggests a non-Qheswa district or perhaps a heterogeneous one. If this is so, and it seems to be, it is just further evidence that Qosqo's language may have been Aymara before Inkakuna arrived there. We discuss the fourth sector as mestizo sector further on in this section.

There were two types of collective units known in Tawantinsuyo, the ayllu and the panaka. Whereas ayllu standards are relatively well understood (their configuration still survives), the structure and origins of the panaka has stirred much debate. We know each panaka identified with a particular Inka. Porras Barrenechea describes the panaka as a particular "Inka's descendants, akin to European institutions of nobility" (descendencia de un Inca, equivale a las instituciones nobiliarias europeas).[133] Some commentators view the panaka as having a patrilineal organization. Others, like Rostworowski, see it as having a matrilineal one. It is this possibility that interests us here.

The origins and social organization of Qosqo are reflected in its mythology, which likely had some basis in fact.[134] Inca Garcilaso's *Commentaries* makes evident that the famed Andean duality was organized not so much in terms of God and man, but of gender (with divinities and humans expressed as such), not unlike what we have seen in Mesoamerica. While Westerners might tend to focus on duality in terms of mythology, the Inka with the Inti, or sun, and the Qoya with the Mamakilla, or moon, dualities also formed between Inti-Mamakilla and Inka-Qoya, all four pairs constituting different angles on the foundation of Inkan spirituality and political organization. The first Inka-Qoya pair, Manqo Qhapaq and Mama Oqllo, is primordial. Most strikingly, the central duality is organized as male-female and sun-moon. Silverblatt convincingly argues in her book that "spheres of gender" were the guiding light of political design in Tawantinsuyo.[135]

Garcilaso explains that Mama Oqllo and Manqo Qhapaq founded Qosqo, which was divided into moieties. Manqo Qhapaq founded the upper half, Hanan Qosqo, by populating it with people he rounded up in the valley, whom he then refined with his teaching. Mama Oqllo did the same with the lower half, Urin Qosqo (*CR*, I, xvi). Garcilaso offers further details, revealing a gendered division of labor. While Manqo Qhapaq taught the men "how to break and till the soil and plant the grain, the seeds and the vegetables" (como romper y cultivar la tierra y sembrar las miesses, semillas, y legumbres), Mama Oqllo imparted to the women "feminine trades, to spin and weave cotton and wool, and make clothing" (los oficios mujeriles, a hilar y texer algodón y lana y hazer de vestir) (*CR*, I, xvi; also VII, viii). Thereby arises an incongruity. If Manqo Qhapaq founded and ruled Hanan Qosqo, which logically must have men and women residents, and if Mama Oqllo founded and ruled over Urin Qosqo, which logically must have women and men residents, did he solely train the men of Hanan Qosqo and she solely the women of Urin Qosqo? Did she go to Hanan Qosqo to educate the women there, and he to Urin Qosqo to train its men? It is clear from archaeology that Manqo Qhapaq and Mama Oqllo did not actually teach agriculture and sewing, two hallmarks of "civilization" that can be verified in the Wari culture from which the Inkakuna sprung. Garcilaso, of course, did not have the access to archaeology that enhanced our understanding after the late nineteenth century. We can suppose that two early Inkakuna probably made enough advances in the development of the Inkan form of governance that oral history immortalized them as the first Inka and the first Qoya.

Bruhns and Stothert argue for an awareness of women's power in Andean life because the ayllu's ancestors came in female-male pairs, because they had some control of the land, and because of their roles in textile production and religious activity.[136] They were also guardians of languages maintained in domestic spheres, such as the Inkan private language discussed previously, but which could serve as an element of prestige as well as a code system for delicate military and political communications. There was also a divine aspect to this. In his history of the Andes Kenneth Andrien explains: "Before the expansion of Tawantinsuyo many indigenous religious traditions established parallel lines of descent for men and women, with males descending from a panoply of male-oriented gods and females from roughly an equivalent number of female-oriented gods." He goes on to caution that within Inkan expansionist modes, "the Sun god (Inti) and his descendant the Sapa Inka were clearly superior to their female counterparts."[137]

It appears that subsequent Inkakuna and Qoyakuna both exercised authority in a parallel sort of way, much like the first male and female rulers, according to Garcilaso. Historian Francisco Hernández Astete, after reviewing some divergent takes on this in historiography, concludes that whatever the case, female power was always associated with male power and that each acted as the other's opposite and complement.[138] Hernández Astete goes on to examine clues about this complementarity in the chronicles, and he offers some startling information. He suggests the Inka did not necessarily marry the Qoya on the day he took the royal tassel, but during the previous Inka's reign. He goes on to offer cases when the Inka exchanged one Qoya for another and cases where the Qoya changed Inkakuna, one of these resulting in an Inka (Wayna Qhapaq) complementing a Qoya who was not his sister, but his mother.[139] This suggests the Qoya was not the Inka's consort so much as a complementary operator working in tandem with the Inka, who was her complementary operator.

The essential gendered division of labor is borne out in the historical, anthropological, and archaeological record. Often, men and women participate in complementary activities for the greater common good. Bruhns and Stothert explain how the Canelos Quichua adults are interested in spiritual perfection, the men indulging in shamanism and the women imparting spirits into the pottery they make. There is also a division of labor in agriculture, with men "clearing gardens, and women restor[ing] it by planting domesticated plants."[140] Silverblatt discusses this gendered duality in terms of everyday life, which for her was of paramount interest: "The pairing of women with the making of cloth and men with the plowing and bearing arms was a critical part of the construction of Andean personhood."[141] These kinds of roles imply a complementary function of men and women.

Qosqo's design, however, is more complicated than mere moieties. As mentioned earlier, Zuidema offers at least three possible ways to represent organizational structures by means of panakakuna and the ceque lines, a system of ritual pathways emanating from Qosqo into the different regions

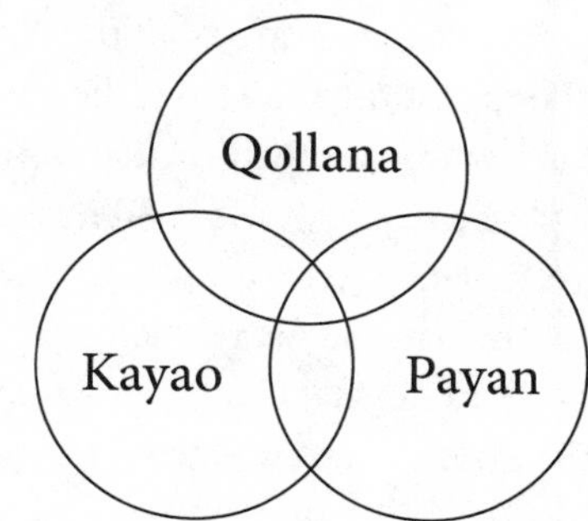

FIGURE 4. Endogamic and exogamic clusters: Qollana, Kayao, Payan. *Drawing by author.*

of Tawantinsuyo. Integral to these are divisions by means of tripartition, quadripartition, quinquepartition.[142] These are derived from the distinctive possibilities that different combinations of interethnic marital bonds provide. There is nothing extraordinary about tripartition and quadripartition. To take a well-known example, the Holy Trinity existed in medieval thought and reflected a European mindset that had difficulty admitting a fourth continent beyond Europa, Asia, and Africa. Medieval thinking also allowed for the quadripartition of the world. Adorno mentions the thirteenth-century Ebstorf map from Germany, "in which the inhabited world is inscribed on the crucified and resurrected body of Christ: the head, feet and hands occupy the four cardinal directions, and the navel of Christ is the center of the world."[143] Andeans also used three and four as organizing principles, and, as Walter Mignolo has recognized, they saw Qosqo as a belly button, the center of the cosmos.[144] These kinds of divisions from an ethnic or regional perspective, when compared with other cultures in the world, are unremarkable. However, they do reveal how the Andeans themselves viewed the cosmos and how the Europeans could superimpose their worldview over that of the Andeans.

Three ethnic clusters acted endogamically and exogamically, the former mating strategy being a closed ethnic circle, the latter being open. These groups were Qollana, Kayao, and Payan (see figure 4). Both the Qollana and the Kayao encouraged endogamous activities, but when they functioned as exogamic groups, a third hybrid category was born in the Payan. This tripartite relationship may have been something like the three houses of K'iche' discussed above, although we know more about the Andean case. Referring to it, Tom Zuidema explains that the men from the primary Qollana would tend to select their primary wife from their own group and their "subsidiary wives" from the Kayao.[145] The result would be that the Qollana pretenders were Inka men, the non-Qollana wives were Kayao, and their offspring were Payan. Silverblatt looks at these interayllu relationships outlined by Zuidema and puts another spin on the same data. She views them as conquering and being conquered, as "a three-tiered ranking structure when 'male conquerors' produced an intermediary descent group, symbolized as their children from secondary marriages with 'female subjects.'"[146] Men, not women, "could enter into secondary marriages with 'conquered' women and thus be founders of intermediary descent groups." Therefore, "gender became the trope through which power was expressed and articulated."[147] What Silverblatt is getting at, it seems, is that there was a form of gendered subordination to this process, although it must be stated that this was nowhere near as significant as the one that would come to pass after Spanish infiltration. If Silverblatt is correct in terms of power, Garcilaso's idea of complementariness comes into question. The issue of gender is a reasonable one to pursue, as is the ethnic or clan one.

The Payan were a primary mixed group, and the other areas of the chart represent other diverse combinations ethnically possible. Because Zuidema is a structuralist with roots in Claude Levi-Strauss, he argues that the complex relationship between these three groups could give rise to a number of quadripartite structures derived from the flow of women from the Payan and Kayao groups to the Qollana group. Therefore, one quadrant would be occupied by the Qollana, another by the Kayao, another by Qollana-Kayao engendered Payan unions, and the fourth possibly by Kayao-Payan engendered Payan unions. The fourth could also be like fourth quadrant in Acamama, the heterogeneous Yarambuy Cancha sector. Multiple possibilities are apparent for the formation of the grid.[148]

There are four ayllukuna. The Qollana ayllu would have been the most ethnically pure, as Inkakuna took their primary wives from this group. On this subject, as Zuidema sets it forth, the principal wife was so "because she was his kin within the fourth degree."[149] By crossing over the demarcated ethnic line from Qollana to Kayao, a cross-border relationship is forged. Cahill substantiates these types of interethnic unions still existing in the mid- seventeenth century. They were between people from the ayllu Hanan Qosqo Qollana, who were purely of Inka heritage, and people from the ayllu

Hanan Qosqo Kayao, who were of the *runa* classes, meaning commoners. Links between the two groups engendered a third hybrid Qollana-Kayao ayllu, or Payan.[150] The notion of endogamic forces forming the hub of power, and exogamic ones arising in greatly varying degrees from the other three sectors and interacting with that hub of power in a quatrilinear scheme, creates parallel and hierarchical structures informed by gender and ethnicity and suggests the organizing principle of Qosqo and, consequently, of Tawantinsuyo.

José María Arguedas is best known for a series of novels including *Deep Rivers,* the untranslated *Todas las sangres,* and *The Fox from Up Above and the Fox from Down Below.* He participated in great debates about education in the newspaper *El Comercio* during the 1950s. His anthropological fieldwork in Puquio, Lucanas, in the Department of Ayacucho detects the same type of quadripartite configuration, although enduring a process of transculturation.[151] He finds a quadripartite ayllu system with the same associations of ethnicity and hybridity, albeit with some startling differences. First, Qollana, Chaupi, Pichqachuri, and Kayao comprise a tetrad of ayllukuna. Noticeably, two of these names coincide with Zuidema's Qollana and Kayao, suggesting a kind of "national" idea that goes beyond local municipalities. Second, the ayllukuna have ethnic significance, although Hispanic, misti, or mestizo becomes an ethnic group. Arguedas understands the ayllukuna as brotherhood pairs, Qollana and Chaupi, Pichqachuri and Kayao. Each aims for "a certain uniformity in social composition and in its economy" (cierta uniformidad en la composición social y la economía). Interestingly, "Chaupi" means that which is in the middle of everything, imparting an interesting meaning to the pre-Hispanic "Chaupi calle" (Chaupi Street) in Mangas, mentioned in chapter 3, which may have divided the two moieties there. With respect to Arguedas's towns, what is remarkable is that of the four ayllukuna, the pair continuing what was the primary ayllu pair in Qosqo is now the one with the highest degree of mestizaje, the Qollana and the Chaupi.[152] We might infer from this that Spaniards mixed with the inhabitants of the most prestigious ayllu after they arrived. Conversely, the other pair, consisting of the Kayao and Pichqachuri ayllukuna, would have been the lower-level dyad if Puquio's pre-Hispanic organization coincided with Qosqo's. However, Arguedas tells us, in the Hispanic era it sustained "a most high percentage of indigenous population" (altísima proporción de población india).[153] What is not totally clear, if the parallel is true, is how could it be that the "secondary wife giving"

Kayao ended up not with a more mixed, but instead with a more ethnically pure Andean extraction? A credible supposition holds that when Spaniards arrived, they took their women from the most prestigious ayllu, the Qollana. In this fashion, ironically, what had been the most "pure" ayllu became the most mixed and, ultimately, the most transatlantic. The former secondary-wife-giving ayllu then became abandoned by both Inka and Spanish elites, preserving, ironically, a purer autochthonous culture.

Arguedas's work finds its corollary in the historian Manuel Burga's *Nacimiento de una utopía* (1988). When Burga studies Mangas and Chilcas in the present-day province of Bolognesi during the early 1980s, he finds a counterintuitive result. In Mangas, "an ancient Chinchaysuyo town," a more "pure" Qheswa language is preserved in the town's women, who are monolingual, and less so in the town's men, who tend to be bilingual (*NU,* 29). The town has a dual structure that survived from the Tawantinsuyo period. There is Cotos, the Hana Barrio whose Guaris people tend to be landowners of small cornfields and who tend to be more educated. The obverse of Cotos is Allaucay, whose Ura Barrio inhabitants, the Llacuaces, tend to be herdsmen and women who are likely to be monolingual Qheswa speakers. This is a curious partition of the town—half-bilingual in the upper moiety, while the lower moiety remains monolingual.

Burga is quick to point out that the division of the population into two halves is not, strictly speaking, physical or geographical (*NU,* 32). This is not to imply that Cotos was not subdivided geographically. This moiety resides at a higher elevation and to the south, while Allaucay resides at a lower elevation and to the north (*NU,* 33). The more powerful moiety is located in the geographical south, closer to the direction whence came the Inkakuna. The other moiety, the weaker one, was further away, to the north. This special/cultural mystery begins to reveal itself with the knowledge that the divisions are acquired by paternal affiliation (*NU,* 32). Burga does not go deeply into details, but what interests us here is the idea of a paternal affiliation not associated with a specific geographic half. This implies that men may take wives from their own half, or from the other half, or wives may take husbands from their own half, or from the other half. In the Masha dance, the Mashakuna come from Cotos and the Lumtsuyekuna from Allaucay (see figure 5). Masha semantically means "son-in-law," and Lumtsuye means "daughter-in-law." As Burga concludes, the dance symbols come to "ritualize matrimonial alliances between the two neighborhoods" (ritualizan las alianzas matrimoniales

Figure 5. Masha: Cajista de Allaucay. From Manuel Burga, *Nacimiento de una utopía: muerte y resurrección de los incas* (Lima: Universidad Nacional Mayor de San Marcos/Universidad de Guadalajara, 2005 [1988]), 70.

entre los dos barrios) (*NU*, 47). A *Hana Barrio* man obtaining a mate from *Ura Barrio* would echo imperial Qosqo, where a Qollana-to-Kayao marriage celebrated a relationship between the two ayllukuna, forging a larger micronational structure. With any other combination, there would be less of an echo.

Burga finds a similar pattern in Chilcas with two barrios, *Hana* and *Ura*, Umpay and Kihuillan, respectively. As in Mangas, one is better off economically than the other is, and like in Mangas, the more fortunate one is *Hana Barrio.* Getting back to that counterintuitive result, Burga suggests that in Mangas, where the presence of Qheswa is strong, the memory of the quadripartite structure is lost. In contrast, in Chilcas, whose inhabitants hardly use Qheswa names, a vague memory remains of the ancient quadripartite way of apportioning (*NU,* 35). Burga only mentions this in passing and does not attempt to explain it. One possibility is that the present-day Qheswa-speaking peoples were originally the more mixed group, and thus subjected to Hispanic transculturation with lesser intensity. Even so, they originally may have had less access to elite education, and thus are less aware of ancient cosmology. The group that speaks less Qheswa now may have been the group with access to elite knowledge that was more on the stage of Hispanization processes during the colonial era. If Aymara- or Puquina-speaking Inkakuna elites could learn Qheswa, a culturally superior language (see chapter 3), then it makes sense that the Qheswa-speaking elites in Mangas could learn Spanish, a superior medium in locally constructed canals of power. That formerly privileged group went through a more intense process of transculturation, but may have retained the memory of the basic structure of late-ancient Inca teaching.

This is meaningful because we are not simply speaking of ayllukuna or ethnic groups in a vacuum, as each group exists in a larger power structure. In Mangas, the *alcalde de varas* was from Cotos and the regidor from Allaucay; the next year they would rotate. Burga suggests it may not have always been this way, and the structure might have been fixed (nonrotating) in the past. We learned previously what Hispanic legislation (such as that archived in the Odriozola Peruvian manuscript collection) did to soften local governmental norms. Burga suggests the rotation may have come "as a consequence of the ancient ethnic order deteriorating" (consecuencia del deterioro del antiguo ordenamiento étnico) (*NU,* 38). Either way, whether it rotated or not, the two positions of authority were shared between neighborhoods. This structure suggests a municipal organizing template that, if repeated in other towns (as it was in the aforementioned Chilcas), could imply a broader range for this model. This configuration—rotating or not—is preserved in festivals such as the Masha holiday, which symbolically represents the mythological coming together of Guaris and Llacuaces. Dancing and singing, despite sector-specific interpretation, has curious national implications, especially when the sector-specific symbols are relinquished in favor of Peru's national banner (*NU,* 47).

Arguedas and Burga's research aides in extrapolating back to social and political structures before Pizarro's arrival and in hypothesizing how those structures were modulated after the advent of the Spanish. Anthropological research helps us to read back in time, to fathom that which came before and to decipher the present while simultaneously documenting the way the nation of late antiquity survives in fragmented form under Hispanic influences spread out over a wide geographic plane.

This type of apportionment, as defined by Zuidema for late antiquity and verified by Arguedas and Burga as still surviving, evinces a quadripartite arrangement organized into two moieties. This brings to mind Zuidema's concern discussed in chapter 3. If there were five Hanan Qosqo Inkakuna and five Urin Qosqo Inkakuna, maybe Rowe is only partially right when he suggests that because of the civil war, Waskar was unable to create an eleventh royal ayllu or panaka.[154] Structuralist Zuidema seems to be suggesting that with the dyadic ayllukuna, five in all, the addition of one more panaka would break the scheme. In *Ceque System in Cuzco,* he expresses extreme doubts about the relationship between lists of Inkakuna and the panakakuna, because they do "not take into account that the panaka together appeared to form a structural part of a particular form of organization which was that of Cuzco."[155] He admits some evidence for an eleventh panaka, the Tumibamba of Wayna Qhapaq, "but in the context of the organization of Cuzco expressed in the ceque system, only the panaca of the first ten rulers have to be taken into account."[156] Zuidema is interested in the structural function of the panakakuna—as opposed to the dynastic one—because if "the rulers of Cuzco were in actual fact not rulers of one dynasty but the personified chiefs of social groups, the material about these rulers can then be used outside its historical context in order to throw light on the position which these social groups occupied in the organization of Cuzco."[157] If so, this would be a system of succession completely different from ones employed in Europe. What Zuidema does not say, but what he might have been thinking, is that such an arrangement, upon adding an eleventh panaka for Wayna Qhapaq, would need to append not one more panaka, but two. That could have only happened if Waskar had defeated Atawallpa and Pizarro and this alternate universe had turned north or west instead of south, allowing Tawantinsuyo to develop on its own terms, with Waskar forming the twelfth, not the eleventh, panaka.[158] The other hypothesis, perhaps a wild one, is that precisely because of the ten-panaka structure in Qosqo, Wayna Qhapaq may have become even more interested in Quito than simple imperial intentions. There he could have established the panaka system and added two panaka, his own and Atawallpa's. It is not our intention to resolve this issue here. However, it should be acknowledged that Tawantinsuyo, like any other nation or empire, was defined by complementary and sometimes even opposing representations.

Whether the quadripartite makeup was defined ethnically or dynastically, it was what gave birth to the quatrilinear suyos.

Exogamic and Endogamic Marriages: In and Out of the Elite Panakakuna

There were assorted modes of reciprocity in Tawantinsuyo.[159] Along with the interpanaka relations discussed in the previous section, strong links were forged between the Inka elites and elites from outside the quadripartite panaka system. Such relationships are of an exogamic nature. These unions served to strengthen Tawantinsuyo's expansion, and the unions themselves were strengthened with gifts. Rostworowski explains that women could be among the "things" given as a form of "generosity," along with clothing, luxury items, or coca.[160] To that list, Hernández Astete adds corn and chicha beer, as well as precious metals.[161] He describes these "things" as *dones,* or gifts.[162] Thus, and this is Hernández Astete's contention, women could be considered dones, called *dádivas* in other areas.

Covey finds early interethnic conjugal unions between Inkakuna and elites from the towns of Sañu, Oma, and Taucaray. He suggests an inherent subordination occurring with these kinds of practices. In his words, "wife-giving polities appear to have been subordinate to wife-taking polities as the Inka state formed." Yet this does not imply that the wives themselves were completely subservient to their husbands. Covey cites the description of one of these matrons as a cacica, and other cases of women actually seeking out these alliances.[163] Through these marriages, the wives gained power in the Inka political and religious structures, and accumulated prestige in their home ethnic groups. In addition, sometimes Inkakuna married their relatives off to other groups, as in one case narrated by Father Martín de Murúa, where a daughter was given to a Cuyo Lord (Cuyo Qhapaq).[164] These kinds of relationships are confirmed in Juan de Betanzos, who knew the Inkan culture well. This chronicler writes that the Sapa Inka would offer women as an element of a reciprocal exchange: "Inka Yupanki ordered a gathering of kurakakuna and lords who . . . had served him and he granted them numerous favors, giving them clothing, women from his lineage." (Inga Yupanqui mandó juntar los caciques y señores que . . . le habían hecho servicio y les hizo numerosas mercedes, dándoles ropa, mujeres de su linaje.)[165] Unambiguously, this giving of women is a primary mode of advancing interethnic relations and extending power.

What kinds of power did these elite associations wield? First, loyalty from amalgamated etnia would be expected. Second, there was an economic benefit, "additional labor tribute," another obvious gain cited by Covey.[166] These local leaders may have been strong-armed into these alliances, but owing to the millenarian familiarity with the custom of reciprocity, they could have expected, in turn, benefits for the local polity.[167] Even inside the patchwork of Tawantinsuyo, the Sapa Inka could not just order the construction of a road or the payment of duties. He first had to be "generous." Interethnic marriages served as a pathway to forming subsequent reciprocal development.

These give-and-take practices were so ingrained that they survived into the colonial interval. Without making an explicit reference to ethnicity, Susan Ramírez explains how even during the postcontact period, "a curaca often received gifts of women, who would expand his immediate household by having more offspring and thus encourage subjects of other lords to marry into the local curaca's service and embolden others to ask the curaca for protection or help in return for their labor."[168] An implicit interethnic meaning resides in this type of reciprocal arrangement. Each kuraka would speak on behalf of one ethnicity, or even a microethnicity, differentiated from the other etnia represented by other kurakakuna. Each exchanged woman brought a plentitude of her ethnicity to her new household, a process occurring before and after contact with Spaniards.

Not all marriages were interethnic or interpanaka. Some special ones, endogamic, were intrapanaka—so much that the Inka had to marry his sister, or in one aforementioned case, his mother. Inca Garcilaso recounts that since the time of Manqo Qhapaq, Inkakuna have conjoined with their sisters. Manqo Qhapaq, the first Inka, married Mama Oqllo Waco, his sister. The second Inka, Sinchi Roq'a, who was also Manqo's son, married his sister, Mama Oqllo, known to some as Mama Cora (*CR*, I, xxv). Consequently, the Inka's mother was also his aunt.

This is at variance with the early dynastic Mexica and other Mesoamerican nations, who tended to marry interethnically, but not unlike Pacal II in Palenque, who married his sister. According to Garcilaso de la Vega, Qhapaq Inkakuna married their female siblings in order to "preserve the purity of the blood line and so that the male heir belonged to the realm by mother just as much as by father" (conservar la sangre limpia y por que al hijo heredero le perteneciesse el reino tanto por su madre como por su padre) (*CR*, I, xxv). This was justified because the Inka descended from the sun, and the Qoya, the moon (*CR*, I, xxv). Some historians such as Riva-Agüero, who came of age during the apogee of late positivism, have questioned the authenticity of this closed-lineage system. For him, common sense dictates that "after a few centuries the race would have become sterilized" (después de algunas generaciones, la raza se habría esterilizado).[169] This is perhaps not quite true, but we do know that incest leads to homozygosis, which in turn can lead to health problems such as decreased fertility or problems with a child's immune system.

The peregrine chronicler Guaman Poma de Ayala recounts that well into the colonial era, a brother and sister named don Cristóbal Sari Thupaq Inka and Doña Beatriz Quispe got married and were able to get a dispensation to do so from Archbishop or second bishop Don Juan Solana, with the authority of Pope Julius III. In a matter-of-fact mode, Guaman Poma explains that both were the children of Manqo Inka and his mother Cusi Warcaya Qoya (*PNC*, 443[445]). This practice tended to create a hermetic system, closed to the outsiders, not prone to mestizaje. When Inkakuna did cohabitate outside the royal lines, as Wayna Qhapaq did, problems of succession surfaced, such as Atawallpa from Quito challenging Waskar for the royal tassel. Even though a coterie of Inka nobles did evidently commingle with Spaniards after their defeat—the historian Inca Garcilaso de la Vega is a famous result of those unions—the Inkakuna through Thupaq Amaru I (assassinated 1572) continued to marry their own sisters. This closed system for rulers in Tawantinsuyo contrasts with the open one they had outside their ethnonational power structure and with the early dynastic Mexicatl—one that deliberately had them forming bonds outside their ethnic group. The hermetic architecture of command inherent to the Inka model negated horizontal appropriation and accentuated vertical reaffirmation.

Fear of Mestizaje: Guaman Poma's Conflicted Approach to Female Agency

Conquistadors and their successors felt entitled to manage all aspects of their colonies. These included spiritual, political, economic, and social matters. Both Church and State had their roles in defining every detail of the new hybrid society in formation. As can well be expected, and as explored previously, Spaniards held a great interest in women and they observed indigenous practices in this regard that they then put into play. Riva-Agüero gives us a flavor of the time. He writes, "In the tumultuous disorder of the Conquest, when the unbridled polygamy of the native princes was still in mind, basic concubinage was very accepted and public, and even proper in the eyes of both Spaniards and Indians." (En el tumultuoso desarreglo de la Conquista, reciente aún el ejemplo de la desenfrenada poligamia de los príncipes autóctonos, el simple concubinato era muy aceptado y público, y casi decoroso a los ojos de todos, así españoles como indios.)[170] Paradigmatic to this situation is Gonzalo Pizarro's stance toward woman and his blatant disregard for the institution of holy matrimony. Upon his researching of the Conquistador Francisco de Caraval, Wilfredo Kapsoli consulted the chronicle of Juan Cristóbal Calvete de Estrella, where he found a revealing episode about the character of Pizarro, who wanted the wife of a certain "Frutos." He sent Frutos to the mines so that he could "better enjoy his woman" (gozar mejor de su mujer). Later fearing a revenge of honor, he ordered the husband's death, which was achieved with some difficulty.[171] Such commonplace attitudes regarding women during the colonial interval could only be detrimental to women's well-being, and certainly to the well-being of the men who were lovingly associated with them (fathers, brothers, and husbands).

As suggested, precontact realities continued to guide the contours of colonial society. This brings us back to Guaman Poma de Ayala. This wandering scholar was from a family of mitmaq that had participated in the Inka system of forced migration. After the Conquest, his family remained uprooted. What may have provided Qheswa-centered stability in Inkan times became a source of litigation and even upheaval in the postcontact era.[172] Because he had a millenary heritage, because his family was mitmaq (from Huánuco), because he read sundry books from Spain, and because he ended up a migrant himself, he became a keenly honed observer of cultural mores.[173] Indeed, Raquel Chang-Rodríguez describes him as a "seasoned traveler, suffering pilgrim, and ideal informant" (viajero experimentado, peregrino sufrido e informante idóneo).[174] He was able to document many things in many places from an ethnocentric vantage point, including his observations of ethnic blending and what that implied for the nation, he called, of "Indians." It is the implication of what sexualized reality meant for the nation that Guaman Poma's prose leaves the realm of mere description and becomes discursive, expositive, and even argumentative. He becomes polemical about what was happening and what it meant.

To set the stage, so to speak, in his thousand-plus-page epistle Guaman Poma talks about female domestic servants as *yanaconas* and *chinaconas* who unwisely come under the authority of Spaniards:

> The *yanaconas* and *chinaconas* are lazy because they are taught by the Spanish men and women to be that way after they bring them in as *yanacona* [male servant] or houseboy, or *chinacona* [maid], housekeeper, cook, baker, or steward. In this way, they get lost, they become very big whores, and they give birth to mestizos. This is the way the towns become unpopulated. Indians come to their end and mestizos multiply.
>
> Son holgasanes *yanaconas, chinaconas* porque les enseña los españoles y españolas, trayéndole por *yanacona* [criado] o po muchacho o *chinacona* [criada], ama o cosenera, panadera, despensera. Y ancí se pierde y se hazen muy grandes putas y paren mestisos. Y ancí se despuebla los pueblos y se acauan los yndios y multiplica mestisos. (*PNC,* 929 [943]; brackets in the original)[175]

Guaman Poma is horrified that his people—not just the people of his ethnic nation of Huánuco or his adopted mitmaq nation of Huamanga (now Ayacucho), but all people of Andean extraction—will simply cease to exist if the women continue to procreate with Spanish men.[176] His view is not so unlike the aforementioned one expressed by the Nahua elders, who wrote to the king begging for separation of pueblos because of the children being born out of wedlock. Guaman Poma takes this a step further and frets about mestizaje.

His awareness of the history and realities of Spaniards and their descendants in Peru brings him to his anti-mestizaje stance.[177] He explains that in the moment of initial contact with the Inkakuna, the Spanish began taking their women. He offers the example of Atawallpa and his retinue: "Right before their eyes, they took their women and daughters, and damsels with their evil thoughts" (a uista de ojos les tomauan sus mugeres y hijas y donzellas con sus malos opinions) (*PNC,* 399[401]). Guaman Poma's censure of abuse does not end with Spaniards forcing Andean women into acts and situations that result in the birth of mestizo babies.

There is a darker side to this question with respect to a woman's right to act in her own right. While Guaman Poma blames Spaniards for prostitution in the Andes, he sometimes sees these women as agents themselves, as the word *puta* sometimes implies. When Guaman Poma says women "get lost, they become very big whores," the expression translated from the original Spanish phrase formed with *se* is ambiguous. One meaning of "se hazen muy grandes putas"—"they become very big whores"—is self-agency, which occurs if the *hacerse* has inchoative active meaning akin to "they become," implying the women themselves "made themselves into," as if they were agents of their own activity. Another meaning is derived when the phrase "se hazen muy gran putas" is read as the *pasiva refleja* (passive meaning achieved with *se*). In that case, the phrase simply signifies "they are made into"—that the women's prostitution was imposed by Spanish men. The *se* construction in *se hazen* adds ambiguity to the phrase's meaning, as we cannot be sure if Guaman Poma meant it as the *pasiva refleja* or as the *se incoativo*.

The possibility of the *se* being the *se incoativo* is very real and is no mere generalization, or theorization, on the part of Guaman Poma. Adorno has surveyed the specifics of various cases of this nature offered by the author: the beautiful indigenous women in the town of San Cristóbal; Juan Quille's daughter; the kuraka Juan Apo Alanya's wife; the false accusations leveled at Diego Chusqui Llanqui by his spouse, so she could become free of him and become a puta; and the most egregious of them all, the passes made by the friar chronicler Martín de Murúa toward Guaman Poma's own wife.[178] Some of these women may have taken Spanish partners of their own volition—which seems to be the case with a number of them—as reflected in the *se hazen* with inchoative meaning, but other cases, such as the advances the Murúa made toward Guaman Poma's wife, would have been what we today call sexual harassment, or worse.

Regarding self-agency, Guaman Poma adds other clues, as when he recreates a "conversation of the Indian whores" (conuersación de las yndias putas) in which they say they will not stay (*morar*) with *mitayos*, but rather with Spaniards, miners, encomenderos, priests, scribes, mayors, and kurakakuna (*PNC*, 717–18 [731–32]). Unquestionably, Spaniards, miners, encomenderos, priests, scribes, mayors, and kurakakuna had disposable incomes, while mitayos did not. Without out a doubt, there were cases of self-agency on the part of women. Juan José Vega considers the possibility that many of the akllakuna initially saw the Spanish men as a way to escape from the akllawasi. These women may have actively pursued the conquistadors. But, he adds, "all of them would end up abandoned, mistreated, and even denigrated with their children in their arms" (la totalidad de ellas acabarían abandonadas, vejadas, y hasta infamadas con hijos en los brazos).[179] This sets the stage for the widespread disoriented mestizos that Chang-Rodríguez calls attention to and that Guaman Poma documents.[180]

The chronicler Cristóbal de Molina anticipates this darker side of connotative meaning with respect to the nation. He writes in 1552 about how "loathsome a thing it was when these women walked about publicly committing clumsy and dirty acts" (cosa aborrecible andar las mujeres públicamente en torpes y sucios actos).[181] It may be that these women were prostitutes, or as Burga suggests, that the Spanish prostituted them (*NU,* 123), or that simply Andean attitudes toward sex were not as prudish as were the Catholic Molina's. Guaman Poma's use of the word "putas" from a traditionally masculine perspective does suggest he viewed these women categorically as social actors in their own right. However, and this is what is important for the concept of the nation, the focus seems to be more on the act of consorting with the enemy than on the "immoral" actions of sex workers, although there was some acknowledgement of that too. Adorno describes this political self-agency as "free collaboration with the colonizers" (colaboración libre con los colonizadores).[182] However, in just about every place Guaman Poma uses the descriptor "puta," it comes in the context of priests, corregidores, and kurakakuna who have a primary role in women's conditions and in whose company the women "get lost." This would be the second meaning: the women are "made" whores by the Spanish men.

There is another facet to this. Who were the Spanish men interacting with Andean women? They were none other than the "judges, corregidores, and parish priests" (justicias y corregidores y padres de las dotrinas). Inevitably, they were men in positions of power. Their social station gave them even more than the power over women common in the traditional gender relationships that occur within one heterogeneous ethnic group. These officials went about and would "force themselves on the married ones and devirginize the damsels" (fornican a las cazadas y a las donzellas los desuirga) (*PNC,* 504 [508]).[183] The newborn mestizos resulting from Spanish men raping Andean woman had as their fathers figures of authority. What would be the psychological effect of this reality of class and racial difference installed in family memory?

Guaman Poma gives priests special attention, and as we move across the pages of his text, we learn how priests would disguise themselves at night wearing traditional garb, entering the homes of *doncellas,* looking at their private parts, and finally "devirginizing" them. The result would be more "mestizos, children of priests" (mestizos, hijo{s} de saserdotes) (*PNC,* 391

[393]). When Viceroy Toledo mandated that the boys, not girls, would be moved into the *doctrinas,* or collative curateships, the priests did not respect the ordinance, and they continued to bring in both boys and girls. Predictably, Guaman Poma warns, they bring in the latter, "to have mistresses close by and to have a dozen kids and to multiply mischievousness little mestizos as well as making those unmarried girls work" (para tener de serca mensebas y tener una dozena de hijos y multiplicar mesticillos y hazellos trauajar a las dichas solteras) (*PNC,* 446 [448]). The chronicler certainly felt "moral" revulsion at such behavior, stemming from his ardent Catholicism, but he felt a concern for the nation too, both of which bring about the overriding consternation expressed in his writing.

He was not alone in his distress, and other Andeans voiced similar anxieties. From the perspective of these voices, priests forcing themselves on their women were egregious acts. In a 1625 memorial signed by fifteen elders, they censure a cleric, Doctor Alonso Mejía, parish priest in Qollana de Lampas, for more than twenty reasons they enumerate one by one. In item number fourteen, for example, they censure Father Mejía for taking from *un yndio casado* named Diego, his wife, Barbola, and then publicly living with her. In the very next item, it is sworn that Father Mejía brings unmarried women into his home so that they might spin and sew. After he picked the one he wanted, he would accuse her of stealing so that "putting her into his bed, he forced her, and in this way he took advantage of all of them" (mitiéndola en su cama la forsaba, y desta manera se aprobechó de todas).[184] Therefore, countless women were coerced, and others may have simply been seduced by a more secure lifestyle. Whatever the case may be, Guaman Poma felt revulsion about an indigenous woman being with a Spanish (or black or mestizo) man, because inevitably the offspring is mixed, implying the perdition of indigenous people and culture (perdiciones de los yndios) (*PNC,* 446 [448]). We do know, however, that Guaman Poma also felt revulsion at the thought of the kurakakuna who sent the men away into the night so they could then make forays into the men's abodes and force the women (*PNC,* 718 [732]). Thus while ethnic dilution was a big concern for him, so was the treatment of women by all men, Andeans and Spaniards. In either case, the abuse of women by men of any stripe—a feminist concern—or women's abuse of the nation—a concern for the nation—was at the forefront of his social anxiety.

CHAPTER FIVE

MIGRATIONS, TRADE, AND OTHER HUMAN INTERACTIONS

As we strive to comprehend the naciones of late antiquity, the traditions and practices that drove them, and the colonialism that began to move them into the early modern era, we must also look at the interactions between them, resulting from migration and trade before 1492, as well as how they were impacted by the subsequent inauguration of the first truly worldwide connections. As seen, migration was a shared experience among many naciones, and the trade between them reconfigured them from the borders in. These processes became even more extreme during the early modern era as new kinds of migrations were introduced and distances became even more accentuated. Even though, as Stephanie Kirk cautions, "little circulation of people, goods, and ideas existed between the hemispheres in the early modern period," which is to say, throughout the Americas and between the English and Spanish spheres of influence. Both hemispheres were being increasingly linked with their respective metropoles in Europe, and the southern one with Asia.[1] But those transoceanic trade routes did not develop spontaneously. They grew out of, and were fed by, existing networks in the Americas and in Europe.

Certainly, these exchange processes were not brought to the extreme level seen in today's information-mad world, but without them, today's "globalization" would probably have a very different footprint. This section begins with knowledge about the earliest known peoples and their migrations, and later concentrates on trade during late antiquity and then during the early modern, with a discussion of how the former merged into the latter.

Human migration and the transportation of cultural articles have defined the human condition since Homo sapiens first migrated from Africa. The further back we go in time, the more difficult it is to trace those movements. A group of scientists working on a "Genetic Atlas of Human Admixture History" enumerate an assortment of sources germane to our task: "Diverse historical, archaeological, anthropological, and linguistic sources of information indicate that human populations have interacted throughout history, because of the rise and fall of empires, invasions, migrations, slavery and trade."[2] Modern science sheds more light on those seemingly far off movements. Ancestries are neither direct nor uninterrupted. As another group of geneticists reminds us, "most human populations derive ancestry from multiple ancestral groups."[3] We have corroborated these types of interactions in previous chapters with the study of mitochondrial DNA and Y chromosome lineages. Human interactions take place when people come together for whatever reason, be it the slave trade, goods, markets for goods, imperialism, military alliances, mutual cooperation, or horizontal cultural appropriation.

A research group headed by Nick Patterson completed DNA testing on some Mayan people from southern Mexico, revealing a genetic relationship to three distinct groups: the Surui people of Brazil, Mozabites related to the Berbers in North Africa, and Spaniards of Northern European heritage.[4] Northern European genes could suggest the presence of Basques, who we know traveled to Mexico with Cortés (*HV*, 244a). The genetic link with the Surui suggests shared generic Amerindian genes that originated with the three great Bering migrations occurring over what is today the Chukchi Peninsula, the most eastern point in Siberia to the western shore of Alaska, then a land mass now called Beringia. For linguists Sicoli and Holton, the first of three important migrations across the Beringia landmass between North America and Asia (40,000–15,000 BC, 14,000–12,000 BC, and 12,000–9,000 BC) is the one now "associated with the greatest distribution of language and cultural groups across North, Meso, and South America."[5] Language and cultural distribution can only happen if there is cross-human distribution forging

DNA connections. Some artifacts exist documenting movement, such as the ten-thousand-year-old Clovis arrowheads descending the west coast.[6] For José Sandoval and a team of researchers, the people who would become the first Peruvians arrived in the late Pleistocene, that is, some twelve thousand years ago.[7] Because human migration in the Americas has a long and varied trajectory over millennia, there is still much to learn.

If people were moving, they were presumably moving with their things. Later they were involved in trade. Comparative archaeology shows some artifacts from one location coming from another. Indeed, "chemical characterizations" can link an object found in a particular site with the site of its provenance.[8] People also remembered routes of migration and the means by which they had engaged in trade. Some of this information was transmitted orally and was captured by Spaniards in their writing. Thus, the colonial chronicles aid in the process of discovering that which came before.

These processes constitute a structure described by Richard Lee (referring to Braudel) as a "plurality of social times" that gives form to a social arc called the *longue durée*.[9] This unfolding of the human story has to do with nations, not always with the content of the master narratives of nations, but generally with the real-life, everyday interactions taking place between them. Laura Doyle has described these interactions as instances of "inter-imperiality," but many of them were simply between polities and even smaller human groupings. Either way, cultural development in the Americas is and has been a millenary process. From the "Old World" perspective of Europe, Asia, and Africa, however, the Western Hemisphere is generally construed as secondary. Doyle corrects our understanding of the Western Hemisphere and the positionality of the world to it. She writes: "The data increasingly establish, among other things, that many systems we call modern emerged in a period typically designated medieval and that they did so not in the European West but in the global South and East, among Asian, Islamic, and African states, and to some extent in the pre-Columbian states of South America."[10] We would add, most certainly, Mesoamerica, to Doyle's assertion. Here we look at Amerindian nations as their own centers, developing on their own in relation to their neighbors and their neighbors' neighbors, and later, as they begin to interface with European and African priests, merchants, encomenderos, corregidores, and slaves.

This chapter, will not focus so much on the longue durée but on migrations, to a degree, and on trade in the development of processes that resulted in what

Immanuel Wallerstein describes as the World-System. As seen previously, naciones looked to their past to strengthen vertically their identities. But when they entered into contact with adjacent naciones as well as naciones from further afield, they underwent a transformative process by horizontally sharing elements between cultures. Prior to 1492 no trading system in the Western Hemisphere was truly global, but with time, the scope of contact expanded, clearing the pathways eventually to form and blend into the arteries of the World-System.

We are specifically interested here in the development of the World-System from the vantage point of the Western Hemisphere. Of course, the World-System also had origins in Africa, Asia, and Europe and between those continents, but for our present purposes, we are first interested in the coverage and contact occurring within and between Anahuac, Tawantinsuyo, El Quiché, and Kwe'sx Kiwe Wala, and from there how they interacted with Spaniards. A multiplicity of origins/trajectories were coming together before contact with Europe, and ultimately they were connected globally, as the Eastern and Western hemispheres were coupled together in trade, religion, and language. Trade, also known as exchange, is quite simply, as Braswell and Glascock put it, "the transference of goods, services, or information between individuals and groups."[11] Papadopoulos and Urton spell it out this way: "Valuable objects or commodities are circulated by people, whether commercially exchanged in a market economy or as part of gifting in a nonmarket context, and are often deposited–or even destroyed–with the dead."[12] People themselves could be objects of trade. As noted, the K'iche' Maya depicted in the *Popol Wuj* assigned value to their sisters and daughters (*PV,* IV, viii). Papadopoulos and Urton have written: "In certain times and places, the exchange and use of human slaves was every bit as real as the exchange and use of gold, jade, silver, feathers, shells, or whatever else was valued."[13] Parallel to the indigenous slaves and peons of the Western Hemisphere, the trafficking in Africans would eventually reach the four corners of the globe. Millenary routes can be difficult to detect so long after the fact, but the flow of information sometimes was codified in pottery or other surfaces that can be traced out with archaeology, for example. Additionally, routes of late antiquity were observed by Spaniards, and thus some of them are documented in the colonial-era chronicles.

Intense interethnic and international commercial networks existed in the Americas before the arrival of the Europeans. These networks are known, but they do not usually serve as a starting point in discussions about long-distance trade during the sixteenth century. The Colombian essayist William Ospina in a book about mestizaje in the Americas enumerates some of these pathways in the Western Hemisphere:

> The labor of the men of Puerto Hormiga, on Colombia's northern coast, found on the Mississippi river delta; cakes of salt in the form of loaves of bread from the Muisca utilized in Peru; ritual objects of gold from the Chibcha found among the Inkakuna; the way in which the languages of Amazonian peoples are related to languages of the Caribbean, events multiplied in the collective memory of each people, are proof of long pilgrimages, of mutual influences, of established trade.
>
> La labor de los hombres de Puerto Hormiga, de la costa norte colombiana, encontrados en el delta del Mississippi; los panes de sal de los Muiscas utilizados en el Perú; los objetos rituales de oro de los Chibchas, encontrados entre los Incas; el modo como las lenguas de los pueblos amazónicos están emparentadas con las lenguas del Caribe, hechos que podrían multiplicarse con la memoria de cada pueblo, son prueba de largas peregrinaciones, de influencias recíprocas, de comercios establecidos.[14]

Clearly, we can see various mini-World-Systems interacting with each other. Muiscas and Chibchas, for instance, are important Colombian nations linked in trade with Inkakuna. Other examples abound. In this chapter, we discuss the Amazonian origins of Neolithic Cuban and Puerto Rican Taino peoples, salt as an international trade product, and a particular type of seashell valued in trade. These linkages respond to "value," described by Papadopoulos and Urton as "a social construct . . . defined by the cultural context in which it is created."[15] The cultural context produces value on an artifact relative to the value the article is perceived to have in another cultural context, which encourages trade between peoples.

Why would we be interested in trade during late antiquity? If these interethnic precontact commercial networks had not existed, Spaniards would not have been able to "milk dry," so to speak, peoples such as Mexica and Inkakuna. Ralph Bauer describes these networks as forming by "interregional cultural contact, exchange, and migration." The interchange of both commercial and cultural items is one of the activities in which empires engage.

He puts this matter into perspective for Mesoamerica: "The highly developed cultures the Spaniards encountered in the Central Valley [of Mexico], marked by intensive maize production with trade and surplus extraction that sustained a hierarchical urban lifestyle with a highly developed division of labor, enabled the Spanish to set up a colonial system of surplus extraction on the back of the Aztec system already in place."[16] The same is true for other regions. As Christian Fernández comments, the second part of Inca Garcilaso de la Vega's *Royal Commentaries* has much to say about commercial ties between Spain and Peru.[17] Chapters 2 and 3 of this book show how naciones were reorganized in power-accumulating maneuvers that continued to hold importance after Cortés and Pizarro. Chapter 4 looks at how gender and ethnicity intersected in the formulation and strengthening of naciones. Here, I look at additional ideological and social constructions that define nations, but also discuss other pressures that go against the nation, move away from it, expand it, or simply do not consider it at all.

ANCIENT AMERINDIAN WORLD-SYSTEMS

Well before 1492, there was a Mesoamerican center of commerce, a central Andean one, a Southern Andean one, and others emanating from the Amazon basin, the northern Andes, the circum-Caribbean, and the Mississippi basin. (For Mesoamerica, see map 2.) Unmistakably, there are grounds to recognize that these systems came in contact with each other, perhaps prospering from their mutual interactions. To use geographic categories familiar to the reader, early Mexicans engaged in transactions with Nicaraguans and Panamanians, who looked to Ecuadorians and Colombians, who in turn looked to Peruvians, who then turned their sights on the Chileans.[18] Early Brazilians had dealings with early Venezuelans, and even migrated to Venezuela and from there, cultural diffusion moved out into the Caribbean. We call this culture Arawak whose famous subgroup, the Tainos, encountered Columbus.[19] If one nación came into contact with another, its culture filtered into the other's culture, and vice versa, at the point where the trade was made. Therefore, we can say that one nación's border overcomes the limits of another nación's border as horizontal cultural exchange flows between them. This activity transpires where groups are contiguous and where trade arcs are expanded.

An awareness of these kinds of circuits allowed the Cuban anthropologist Fernando Ortiz to come up with his now canonical theory on transculturation, which posits cultures bumping into and then modifying each other.

Ortiz studies the extension of the so-called bifurcated tubes used for smoking tobacco and for inhaling *cahoba,* which may have been a specially prepared tobacco. Ortiz, who published his *Contrapunteo cubano* in 1940, was able to study colonial chronicles published in the nineteenth century—including Fernández de Oviedo, Las Casas, Columbus, Sahagún, Ramón Pané, Bernabé Cobo, and others—to trace the diffusion of a culture that used bifurcated tubes to smoke or snort tobacco, snuff, or cahoba. He also was able to take advantage of the discoveries being made in the newfound field of archeology, and he poured over new research published by Max Uhle, Henry Walter Bates, Jules Crévaux, and the Cuban Alvaro Reynoso. What people were discovering, and what Ortiz himself found out, is that certain cultural affinities extended from Hispaniola Island to the Orinoco River in Venezuela and Tiwanaku (the cultural horizon on the Peruvian-Bolivian border between the seventh and eleventh centuries).[20] Arawak culture probably originated in Amazonas State in Brazil, moved up toward Venezuela, and then became a Neolithic force in the Caribbean, overrunning the Paleolithic Siboneyes (also known as Guanajabibes), Ortiz tells us.[21]

Not all migrations ended up in Cuba. For example, why would the *Popol Wuj* include among its primary deities Juraqan, "huracán" in Spanish or "hurricane" in English (*PV,* I, i)? We know that "huracán" is a Taino voice.[22] It seems unlikely that the word could have entered into the K'iche' language just two decades after the Spanish-Tlaxcalan invasion of Guatemala in 1524, with enough force to be codified in an early script configured in alphabetic text between 1554 and 1558.[23] The Spanish may have brought the word with them, but it does not seem likely it could have moved into K'iche' religion to refer to a primary deity so quickly as to appear in the *Popol Wuj.* The word may have gone directly from Venezuela to Guatemala, or by means of the Caribbean to Guatemala. Human migrations brought with them cultural exportation from the old lands, cultural importation to the new lands, and the leaving of cultural elements behind that were no longer useful in the new milieu (the give-and-take process of transculturation).

The K'iche' incontrovertibly engaged in non-elite and elite production and trade of goods. Carmack, culling various sources, observes that mats, called *petates,* were manufactured along with "nets, bark clothing, maguey-fiber cloth, cotton cloth, pottery, leather goods, and wooden tools." By reading the *Popol Wuj,* he discerns the existence of elite artisans who carved wood and special precious stones. They decorated ceramics, worked with metals, and produced writing. While all these products were generated in Q'umarkaj, "some of the resources used in the elite crafts came from outside Quiché."[24] We know K'iche' elites were somehow connected to (derived from, some would say) the ancient culture of Teotihuacan, and perhaps also of Tollan.[25] The very fact of both a K'iche' name (Q'umarkaj) and a Nahuatl name (Utatlan) for the ancient capital bespeaks of the influence coming to Guatemala from central Mexico. Ruud Van Akkeren, drawing on Las Casas, conjectures that marketers from Q'umarkaj acquired gold and silver jewelry in Oaxaca or in the Mixtec region.[26] Central America was deeply connected to the rest of Mesoamerica.

Without question, Mesoamerica had intense and well-worn trade routes. As far back as the Olmeca (roughly 1800–250 BC) there is evidence of cultural exchange. Richard Lesure observes, "Figurines in the Olmec style appear at widely separated sites, often alongside stylistically distinctive figurines."[27] Chichen Itza has left many traces. One trace can be found in numerous obsidian artifacts obtained at the site. Archaeologists Braswell and Glascock studied these artifacts through "visual attribute analysis and neutron activation analysis."[28] They found 75 percent of these artifacts originated in central and western Mexico in the present-day states of Mexico, Hidalgo, Puebla, Veracruz, and Michoacán, some of them at a distance of 1,200 kilometers. The other 25 percent of the obsidian artifacts came from places like El Chayal, Ixtepeque, and San Martin Jilotepeque in Guatemala. Long before the exchanges in obsidian and jade that we will see with respect to Teotihuacan, the routes of maize profoundly changed numerous Amerindian cultures.

Maize originated in Mesoamerica and slowly made its way down the Pacific coast, becoming ceremonial in the central Andes (Chicha) and even replacing manioc (yucca) in some areas for "bread" making.[29] Additionally, there is the curious phenomenon of Nahua-sounding place names in northern Peru, such as in Jequetepeque, where archaeologist Verano notes similarities between local Moche visual discourse and Maya and Central Mexican patterns. He cites Moche-Mesoamerican commonalties in depictions of prisoners, one-on-one warfare, the combatant's heavily ornamented dress, and "the use of short range weapons."[30] Is Verano commenting on a mere coincidence for two cultures not in contact? Perhaps not, because evidence of trade also exists. Raúl Porras Barrenechea culls from the historical record and recounts a revealing fact. When Conquistadores Núñez de Balboa and Pizarro were interrogating a fellow named Tumaco in Panama, he drew for them in the sand the image of a llama, that emblematic animal of Peru.[31] This shows that an Amerindian in Panama was aware of livestock common in the central Andes.

The peoples known as the Maya and the Nahua constituted two apexes of the Mesoamerican cultural complex. That complex reached far south into lands that became Nicaragua and El Salvador. The former, for example, was invaded from the north by epigonal Toltecatl peoples known as Nícaros. Before them, though, a Classic Maya people known as Chorotegas had arrived, and before them, Chibchas from the south, from the lands that eventually became Colombia. McCafferty explains that Santa Isabel, an early Postclassic site, reveals a primarily Mesoamerican composition including "Oto-Manguean-speaking Chorotega for the Early Postclassic and the Nahua Nicarao for the subsequent Late Postclassic periods." He concludes, "the residents of Santa Isabel probably predate the arrival of the Nicarao and had some affiliation with the Chorotega, but also probably with the preceding Chibcha group."[32] Additionally, the Lenca people lived in present day El Salvador and Honduras. While Lenca origins are unclear, they did build a trading hub on the Pacific coast during the Classic period, and tellingly, they could boast both northern and southern cultural traits. In a brief article, Woodward lists them: "Mesoamerican traits include agricultural and religious practices, the use of wooden swords with obsidian and cotton armor for war, and a calendar of eighteen months of twenty days each. Poisonous weapons and the panpipe, however, are characteristic of South American cultures."[33] Central America, we can say, was a great melting pot in which cultural exchange broke many barriers by flowing from north to south and, needless to say, from south to north.

These kinds of contacts perhaps began as early as 6000 BC. This conclusion is reached by comparing the burial patterns of the Vegas peoples, who resided on the Santa Elena Peninsula, with those at the settlement at Cerro Mangote in Panama.[34] Art history documents these kinds of movements. To offer an example, the ninth-century Teotihuacan culture of central Mexico shows evidence of distant trade, either directly, or more likely, taking advantage of intermediaries and their networks. Consider the mask made of greenstone shown in figure 6. If we compare this greenstone mask to another like mask from the same period and place, we can see a covering on the surface not indigenous to Mexico, but to Ecuador or perhaps the Caribbean.

Figure 6. Teotihuacan mask. WAM no. IL.2002.3.44.
Courtesy of Walters Art Museum, Baltimore.

Figure 7. Teotihuacan mask with Spondylus covering. WAM no. IL.2002.3.46.
Courtesy of Walters Art Museum, Baltimore.

In figure 7, the bright orange *Spondylus* seashell covering sharply contrasts with the mask in figure 6. There are some four-dozen species of Spondylus, but we will mention three: *Spondylus princeps, Spondylus calcifer,* and *Spondylus Americanus.*[35] The first two can be found on the Pacific Coast in warmer waters, the third in the Caribbean. Because Spondylus cannot be indigenous to inland areas, its use in Teotihuacan indicates it must have been transported from distant shores. As Charles Kolb finds, in the Preclassic period various varieties of Spondylidae "were transported from the Gulf and Pacific coasts into central Mesoamerica during the Formative or Preclassic." He notes that conveyance of these items "apparently intensified during the Classic period."[36] Finally, he theorizes a half dozen each of Pacific and Gulf coast trade routes.[37] Spondylus shells should be considered, Mary Beth Trubitt states, as "prestige goods," which serve "for adornment and display, money and wealth, status markers, and ritual use."[38] The longer the distance, the more prestige these types of goods could add to an elite's standing.

Data in the chronicles suggests Pacific exchange routes. We turn again to Cieza de León, who seems to have written about every detail regarding the Spanish experiences in South America. In the early stages of the Spanish in Perú, Pizarro remained inland where there were crops of corn, Almagro returned to Panama with some gold that had been taken, and the pilot Bartolomé Ruiz began to explore the coast. At one point, as they were moving out to the high seas, they ran into a balsa, a large wooden raft that may have been from Tumbes (*CP-3^era^*, fol. 12). These pre-Hispanic balsas are so sturdy and basic to the fishing industry off the coast of Peru and Ecuador that they are still in use in our time. According to Dorothy Hosler, "these balsa rafts were capable of making two round trip voyages between coastal Ecuador to the coasts of west Mexico."[39] The chronicler Francisco de Xérez describes a ship capable of long-distance travel. He notes that it was a 30-ton vessel for carrying people and merchandise, adding that it "had tall masts made of very fine wood, cotton sails of the same size, in the manner of our ships" (Traía sus mástiles antenas de muy fina madera y velas de algodón del mismo talle, de manera que los Nuestros navíos).[40] Cieza de León recounts that the men and women of that first balsa encountered by Spaniards were transporting both spun and raw wool (*CP-3^era^*, fol. 12). In the earlier chronicle, Xérez offers a complete description of the cargo. He starts off by observing that their persons were adorned with silver and gold, and then he formulates a list:

> crowns, diadems, belts, articles to be worn, and leg armor, breastplates, little pincers, bells, handfuls and strings of beads, rose-colored silver objects, and mirrors adorned with the above-mentioned silver, and cups and other drinking vessels; they brought many wool and cotton blankets, and shirts, *aljuras, alaremes,* and many other types of clothing, all of it tailored lavishly in burgundy, blue and yellow, red silks.

> coronas y diademas y cintos y ponietes y armaduras como de piernas, y petos y tenazuelas y cascabeles y sartas y mazos de cuentas y rosecleres y espejos guarnecidos de la dicha plata, y tazas y otra[s] vasijas para beber; traían muchas mantas de lana y de algodón, y camisas y aljulas y alcaceres y alaremes y otras muchos ropas, todo lo más de ellos labrado de labores muy ricos de colores de grana y carmisí y azul y amarillo.

He then mentions a small scale to weigh the gold.[41]

In the episode mentioned in Chapter 4 when Pedro de Halcón de la Cerda meets one of the capullanas, some fifty of these balsas surround the Spanish ship (*CP*-3*era*, fol. 26, p. 73). While Cieza only mentions recently sheared and spun cotton as the cargo, the chronicle alludes to the fact that the ships patently had a trading function besides military use. Hosler cites earlier researchers who in the 1920s, 1960s, and 1970s discovered and "maintained that metallurgy was introduced to Mesoamerica from either Central America, South America, or from both regions possibly via a maritime route." She builds on their research and concludes, "The data strongly support the idea that knowledge of metallurgy was introduced by Ecuadorian voyagers to peoples living in west Mexican ports."[42] Besides exporting South American metallurgical skills, the balsa traders undoubtedly dealt in Spondylus shells found "in dispersed deep water pockets from coastal Ecuador to southern Sinaloa, Mexico."[43] John Murra remarks that Spondylus "does not live in the cold Pacific waters south of the gulf of Guayaquil." From the archaeological record, he is able to observe that Spondylus was used early and widely "in the highlands as far south as Chile and Argentina."[44] Ecuadorian traders may have navigated all the way to the Mexican coast, or they may have plied their wares with intermediary traders, who then entered into exchange with still others who eventually had dealings with the Teotihuacanos. Evidence of fine stone and shell workshops has been brought to the fore in Teotihuacan by various researchers.[45] Spondylus may have also come from the Caribbean; in that case, it would have been of the *Americanus* variety. The unique combination of the greenstone and Spondylus must have made this an especially coveted treasure. Without long distance bartering, this sought-after and culturally revealing *object d'art* would not have been possible. These routes continued to be plied throughout the Classic and into the next period.

During the late Postclassic, we have intense exchange of objects, both luxury and everyday items. As discussed in chapter 2, Gibson observed that life in Anahuac was characterized by "refugee movements and some systematic administrative insertion of peoples of one tribe in the area of another" (*AZ*, 22–23). People were not the only items circulating. Haskett, in a short article, explains that the hereditary merchants known as *pochteca* were associated with Mexico-Tenochtitlan and had extensive trade links. He illustrates: "From the Chaco Canyon area of New Mexico to Guatemala, *pochteca* exchanged processed goods for precious feathers, stones, and other items which fueled Nahua artisan production." While social standards did not allow the pochteca merchants to display their wealth publically, they did so within the confines of their outwardly appearing humble abodes. From the economic muscle they acquired from trading and acquisitions, they became "privileged to own property, have their own law codes, and sacrifice captives," even though they were not of the noble class.[46] Besides the pochteca, Van Akkeren reminds us, there were other merchants known as *oztomeca*, who dealt in precious metals and stones as well as feather work.[47] Robert Carmack brings up one issue regarding the pochteca in Nahua altepeme, not unlike their peer merchants in the amaq' of Q'umarkaj. They were given scant recognition in the chronicles.[48] More research is required to integrate those realities into both historiography and theories of the nation.

Linguist Alfredo Torero speculates that the Central Andeans may have dealt with Mexicans, but if so, that trade was more limited than what went on between the Peruvian and Ecuadorian coasts.[49] Moche excavations have yielded highland artifacts, as well as Chilean lapis lazuli jewelry and Ecuadoran Spondylus.[50] Another clue is the fine-line technique appearing in pottery toward the end of the Moche trajectory. As Luis Jaime Castillo suggests, "the late period appearance of fine-line ceramics may be the result of outside influences." These are detected in the funerary rites discussed with Chapter 4's labretted ladies. Castillo reports that two of the chamber tombs held respectively two and four pieces of the "fine-line style." He comments on the presence of Wari-inspired ceramics at Moche sites, evidence that the Wari coming from the south traded either directly with them or through intermediaries. However, Castillo provides further insight: "There is no tomb where the majority of artifacts are of foreign origin."[51] This suggests the Moche were not conquered outright, but they did engage in actual trade as part of larger hemispheric circuits. There also may have been migrations.

Charles Stanish explains what it means when the artifacts are ceremonial in nature. He emphasizes the need to distinguish ceremonial pieces from domestic ones when comparing two sites. As noted, Trubitt describes these ceremonial pieces as "prestige goods." She differentiates such items from "utilitarian and subsistence goods."[52] Utilitarian encompasses domestic goods. Stanish concludes that household objects tend to be local in nature, while nondomestic wakakuna or similar items tend to suggest exchanges between allied peoples. For example, at one site in what is today northwest Argentina, he finds "the nondomestic component in sites differs dramatically from the domestic component and that the former tends to contain considerably more exotic pieces." For its part, "household" refers to the economic realities that bring a group of people together in a domestic space and not to the lineage or kin-based ties associated with the concept of "family." Stanish concludes as follows: "Artifacts discovered in domestic contexts are superior in defining the resident population of the site."[53] Everyday culture can be studied emicly, which is to say relative to its internal structure irrespective of foreign influences. Inasmuch as these Moche pieces were non-household items, it would appear some form of long-distance barter took place, be it directed or market-based trading. Castillo argues that the Wari relics discovered in the Moche tombs signify that the Moche, hitherto a closed society, had opened to the outside world.[54] This view tends to be supported by the case of the aforementioned Gallinazo peoples, who served as laborers during Moche V.[55] The existence of the labretted ladies also leads to this conclusion.

Proto-Ecuadorans engaged with other pre-Peruvian horizons as early as the preceramic La Paloma site near Lima and the Aspero site further up the coast.[56] Cordy-Collins traces actual migrations such as the labretted ladies, who migrated to the present-day Peruvian department of Lambayeque. Even more evidence of an Ecuadoran or perhaps even southern Colombian connection comes with the discovery of a sheet-gold hollow figure in the Tumaco style that suggests interethnic trade.[57] Bruhns and Stothert write of Ecuador's Manteño people: "They were known as great maritime traders, plying the seas from northern Peru to southern Colombia and beyond."[58] The Ecuadoran connection is key, as there is a growing awareness of people from this region serving as intermediaries for commercial and religious exchanges, including Spondylus, exported to places as far away as the Central Andes and the Mexican coast.[59] As touched upon, evidence shows this Spondylus trade is relatively ancient. Covey suggests the Wari, who declined as a substantial refined society somewhere around AD 1000, traded other goods for it, bringing it into the heart of the Wari homeland in the central Andes.[60]

The patterns established by Spondylus peddlers, the labretted ladies, and the Teotihuacanos endured, and later peoples such as Mexica-Nahua, Chimú, and Inkakuna built on them. As discussed, cotton was an essential indicator of class and was directly linked to the market system. The hidden history of this market is that as empires expanded, they required more cotton. And who wove this material? Undoubtedly, women were the ones who bore the brunt of its demand, especially in the altepeme of Central Mexico, but in the ayllukuna of the Andes as well. As Bruhns and Stothert write, "local rulers who acquired cotton from the warmer regions of Mexico often issued this fiber to women who spun it to satisfy their tribute obligation." Lockhart provides insight: this cotton cloth, or *quachtli*, was so valuable it could serve as money to purchase slaves in Cuernavaca (*NAC*, 177). The inverse of this process is that as quachtli became valuable as tender, more of it was needed, resulting in increased female slavery to meet commercial and tribute demands. The presence of female slaves before (or after) 1492 should not be surprising. Hamilakis explains, "People's living bodies may be commodified and objectified as labor, material or art, or for sexual pleasure."[61] In the context of quachtli, women laborers were integral to this system, sometimes weaving so much for the state, at least in the Mexicatl sphere, that they had to develop domestic strategies to keep up with their public demands. Logically, men were not the only ones to engage in trade activity because the blankets, jewelry, and foodstuffs made by women could be used in negotiating marriages and in interethnic commerce. Specifically, women were long distance traders, who may or may not have followed their wares to their destinations. This is exactly what the anthropologists Bruhns and Stothert are talking about when they differentiate egalitarian tribal societies located in the Paleographic and Archaic periods from the hierarchical urban domains of the Preclassic, when women tended to lose out on power because of gender stratification.[62]

The stories of Columbus trading glass beads for gold are well known. Columbus's bartering was not something that developed solely from European traditions. Barter was also known in the Indies. Late-antiquity trading systems included both basic commodities and luxury items. Even the early chroniclers were aware of pre-Columbian commerce. If we can trust Cieza de León, and there is no reason why we should not on this issue, we can see how trade was carried out. Various groups near Popayán in Colombia mined salt from rivers that could surely be used for barter. Cieza discusses the salt mining carried out by extracting the mineral from the waterways. He explains that the Coconucos in Popayán especially used salt fonts, although their salt was "neither so much nor as good as Carthage and Anzerma's" (no tanta ni tan buena como la de Cartago y Anzerma) (*CR-1*^{era}, fol. 53v, p. 117). Hence, we can summarize that the Coconucos supported themselves by extracting salt from rivers, which they then inserted into networks for reasons of religion, profit, or culture climbing. The people near Santa Marta and Cartagena on the Caribbean Sea traded in hogs, fish, and salt, and included among their wares gold and clothing (*CP-1*^{era}, fol. 19v, p. 44). As for Antioquians, they traded in arrows and salt, the latter "its principal merchandise" (su principal mercadería). The town of Mugia, or Mungia, also traded in salt, transporting it through the mountains to acquire gold, cotton clothing, "and whatever else they had need" (y otras cosas de las que ellos han menester) (*CP-1*^{era}, fol. 30v, p. 68). This mineral was integral to the Andean diet, and some people, such as early Ecuadorians, used it for its medicinal qualities. Some pre-Hispanic salt mines are still in operation in Peru, for example in Maras. Today, the Maras mines are divided up into sections, each one seemingly belonging to one family. The individuality aspect may have been a postcontact modification. Whether they were collective or family based, the transactions mentioned by Cieza were carried out according to ancient trade patterns along the lines of the aforementioned maize diffusion, and simply broadened to include new routes upon contact with the Europeans.

Mary Helms, reviewing the literature, explains that the Spanish "found Muisca emeralds in Tairona, while Taironian sea shells adorned distant Muisca chiefs."[63] Despite his far-fetched proposal that the Ancient Peruvians migrated to the South American continent from the Platonic Atlantis (discussed in Chapter 3), Agustín de Zárate suggests they had "use of navigation learned from the commerce that they had with this great island" (vso de la navegacion aprendida del comercio que tenian con esta grande isla) (*HDC,* [5]). Despite his bias, Zárate must have observed commerce to make such a statement. The eminent lord Nutibara, who exercised control of a large polity in the Cauca region (at or near the present-day Medellín), annexed the Abibe region, perhaps for its gold. Because slaves, gold, and blankets were in abundance, these were the items likely traded.[64] Hermann Trimborn maps out diverse pre-Colombian trade routes, stretching from a region of Antioquia known as Buriticá, that traded gold for slaves, hogs, fish, salt, and cotton to the other regions of Colombia mentioned: Urabá, Zenú, and Guaca, as well as the north South American coast and Central America.[65] These are the routes to which Ospina was referring. Villamarín and Villamarín verify those tradeways and suggest that Nutibara and others like him participated in an exchange complex that included Antioquia, Central America, and the Colombian coast, as well as other lands that now form Venezuela. Along these trade routes "markets and fairs were held"[66] allowing diverse peoples to peddle their wares, most likely by means of barter.

Frederick Stirton Weaver notes that both Mexica and Inkakuna employed a tribute system to fund their empires.[67] Contributions could be exacted in the form of textiles, which brought women directly into the imperial system with unpaid labor, the coatequitl in Nahuatl, or mita in Qheswa. Commerce took place throughout the Americas, although varying in intensity according to time and place. At the moment of the Encounter, the Mexica were engaged in it, as Díaz del Castillo's emotional description of Tenochtitlan's market attests, while the Inkakuna, on the other hand, tended to concentrate on the well-being of the entire empire. Weaver explains that in Tawantinsuyo, "the movement of goods was almost exclusively either tribute or the transfer of grain from one region of the empire to another to alleviate the effects of crop failures."[68]

We turn once more to Stanish to look at these geographic regions in terms of trade and markets. He distinguishes between forms of exchange in the northern and southern continents: "Unlike Mesoamerica or even the northern Andes where examples of price-fixing markets and merchants can be found, virtually all cases of central Andean exchange are most profitably understood as types of administered trade."[69] Prior to the Inkakuna, a mercantilist economy thrived in the region today known as Ecuador. As Torero deduces from his study of Andean languages, the Inkakuna imposed an economic system that tended to annul the mercantilism common up until that point.[70] María Rostworowski and others characterize Tawantinsuyo's economy as a system of reciprocity. Steve Kosiba puts it this way: "The Inka economy was rooted in institutions of redistribution and labor management."[71] Nevertheless, whether reciprocity or mercantilism, tribute needed to be collected to fulfill diverse exigencies.

Reciprocal arrangements in contrast to redistribution (taxation, tribute demands) do not necessarily indicate what Stanish calls "a political hierarchy." Neither do they infer necessarily direct colonialism. However, if the reciprocal arrangement is coerced, then it could. In this form of redistribution, "political authorities manipulate traditional symmetrical relationships into unequal ones, setting up an economic system in which resources flow disproportionally to an elite group."[72] This was the case with Inkan expansionist procedures as they moved to incorporate new ayllukuna into their jurisdiction. As mentioned, Inkakuna offered presents to the regional kurakakuna and expected something in return. This would be the case if the Inka wanted to construct a building. He would offer presents before and after the construction, respectively as an enticement and as a reward. However, the gifts would not necessarily equal the value of the structure.

This kind of activity was one element of many. As previously discussed, one of the primary Inkan policies was to move people around within Tawantinsuyo. These mitmaq ensured revenues reached Qosqo. They were artisans from one area who produced articles to be traded with another, and they were farmers from one area transported to another, Garcilaso tells us, who would grow crops then stored in tambos to feed *chaskikuna*, or mail couriers. Without question, there was a great flowing of people from one area to another, some people involved in trade with neighboring areas.

In Tawantinsuyo, like in previous horizons, goods (ceremonial ceramics, textiles, foods) from other areas were highly prized. The interayllu exchange of cultural and culinary pieces was deeply ingrained into society. Murra explains how the "drive for access to exotic products was so strong that periods of strife were followed by years in which access was shared, no matter how tense the truce." Trade has been associated with the rise and fall of cultural horizons, even though some see this exchange as commerce, while others view it as having a more religious thrust.[73] Either way, the interethnic exchange created far-reaching networks before the Europeans' arrival on the scene.

In a passage examined in Chapter 4, chronicler Betanzos informs us that "Inka Yupanki ordered a gathering of kurakakuna and lords who . . . had served him and he granted them numerous favors, giving them clothing, women from his lineage" (Inga Yupanqui mandó juntar los caciques y señores que . . . le habían hecho servicio y les hizo numerosas mercedes, dándoles ropa, mujeres de su linaje).[74] Some of the kurakakuna came from faraway districts, and exchange between them and the Sapa Inka was a form of long-distance trade. Other exchanges were short distance. This representation of giving of women and things reveals the principle of reciprocity. Andrien explains that when the Sapa Inka could not conquer a certain area, he would try to integrate it into Tawantinsuyo's trade network. He writes, "The Inca settled for dispatching trading expeditions to acquire local exotic products, such as medicinal plants, feathers, wood, and Spondylus shells."[75] Even when the Inka nobility was able to integrate other ayllukuna into Tawantinsuyo, they did not reconfigure everything from the bottom up. As mentioned, Garcilaso, upon discussing the Wankakuna, explains that they were forced to give up their "man-idols," but not other types of representations. The gears of trade seem to have been left mostly intact. Covey explains, "The Incas left specialized merchants and preexisting exchange networks in place."[76] Regarding the local power, there was imposed a superstructure that reflected local avenues of administration, but that added new mega-arteries to collect, organize, and redistribute material and human goods. In a broad sense, as Burga paints it, the Inka "appears as the extension of the local kurakakuna" (aparece como la ampliación de los *curacas,* locales) (*NU,* 129). In this way the expanding nación, already a mix of Inkakuna, Qheswakuna, and others, becomes nuanced and no longer based on one sole ethnicity, but instead on an expanding ideal known as Tawantinsuyo.

Yacobaccio, Escola, Lazzari, and Pereyra trace out long-term movement in the traffic of obsidian in Northwestern Argentina. They discuss the existence of llama caravans "throughout the entire south-central Andes." In their study of obsidian traffic, they explain that by combining "ethnoarchaeological studies of present-day caravans" to archaeological data, ancient trade routes begin to emerge.[77] What they found is that obsidian was exchanged through a sizable swath of what is today Argentina, throughout the provinces of Jujuy and Catamarca. What they call "Zapaleri obsidian" was dispersed over highlands, lowlands, and the temperate valleys in between—dispersed between Tiwanaku, the Bolivian altiplano, and the Salar de Atacama in Chile, a wide range.[78]

It is fascinating to speculate on these emerging Amerindian exchange circuits. What would have happened if they had had been allowed to evolve as they served different naciones in contact with each other, instead of being engulfed by the expanding European World-System? What if there could have been a Maya resurgence or the emergence of new and surprising power that would build on old networks, but with youthful vigor exploring new and surprising trade routes and military grids? If they had been left to develop on their own, would Inkakuna have entered into direct contact with the Nahua peoples? While at present such speculation is more the realm of a good historical novel than scientific historical inquiry, tradeways were active and in some cases dynamic. Archaeology, anthropology, genetics, and even literature and legal documents not yet on the radar portend to reveal even more information. What we can be sure of was that the amaq' entered into exchange with distinct amaq', with the not so far away cah, and with the distant altepetl. The altepetl probably had only indirect contact with the ayllu, probably through intermediaries. In the language of sixteenth-century Spanish, naciones came into contact with other naciones, and generally they interacted. Sometimes one nación would greatly influence the other, and every once in a while, certain naciones ceased to be *behetrías* (see chapter 3), that is, they became empires.

THE EUROPEAN WORLD-SYSTEM

The World-System would not have been able to function in the Americas if it had not been first developed and perfected in Europe. There, kingdoms and nations may have tried to stem the advance of trade because it adversely affected local business, but they were not completely successful. William McNeill's classic *The Rise of the West* states: "Although most governments tried hard to manipulate the flow of trade and particularly of specie, the European exchange economy was never effectively caged within the separate compartments of rival political jurisdictions."[79] Commerce did not operate on one level, and there was not just one system. Writing about Thomas More's England, Sacks talks of two economic systems, the one "buying and selling for profit in large-scale regional, national, and international markets," the other relying on exploitation of resources in the forests, commons, and wastes; cooperation among neighbors or gift exchanges; and solely local engagement in a limited number of items among known traders and neighbors.[80] These two forms of market-based exchange systems, long and short networks, worked in tandem with more direct forms of resources reallocation, such as slavery. What is intriguing about Sacks's description of sixteenth-century England with two levels of trade is that it also describes the reality in the Andes and Mesoamerica, before 1492 and after. For instance, it could be compared to domestic and ceremonial contexts as outlined above by Stanish.

Not so dissimilar to Mesoamerican systems, the European one evolved out of the systems of Antiquity. The Phoenicians, the Greeks, and the Romans were all traders and colonizing cultures. The Romans conquered a wide swath of Europe, and the Germanic tribes also had long-distance impacts. The Romans, as archaeology reveals, had money, so capitalism's remote origins may lie in those cultures, although mixed with feudalism and other precapitalistic economic practices. The intense interest in "New World" gold resulted in part from the dependence on a moneyed economy during the Renaissance. It may be easy to link the rise of capitalism with the industrial revolution during the eighteenth century. An earlier benchmark came with the initial European incursion into Anahuac, Abya Yala, Kwe'sx Kiwe Wala, and Tawantinsuyo. José Ortega explains how this is possible: "When the Conquest began, the metropole was in a period of transition from feudalism to capitalism by means of monetary mercantilism, especially based on oceanic navigation and firearms." (Cuando se inicia la conquista, la metrópolis estaba en un período de transición del feudalismo al capitalismo a través del mercantilismo monetario, basado, especialmente, en la navegación oceánica y en las armas de fuego.)[81] Considering Columbus, where it all began, Morison explains that he was a wealthy man who had "business connections with one of the leading merchant-banker houses of Italy." He benefited from "several lucrative sinecures" and would eventually hold hundreds of slaves in Hispaniola. To get ahead in his time he needed "to follow the upward curve of merchant shipping to be a success."[82] Indeed, Columbus was very wealthy for the time, as the norm in Portugal was to have no more than a handful of slaves.[83] Here we come to the crux of the matter, because while slaves did not earn salaries, they were bought and sold according to the norms of supply and demand. Manning describes the enormity of the situation. Eventually, more than ten million Africans would be brought to the Americas in a world slave market that after 1700 would span five continents.[84]

New forms of feudalism would interface with this early modern stage of capitalism when the mita, the coatequitl, and other forms of obligatory labor were seen as a way to accumulate capital. Ortega talks about this as the introduction of "intensive labor" in the Americas.[85] A gold-standard, agricultural products, labor to produce them and markets to sell them, as well as entrepreneurial bonds, stocks, and money-based economies all help form an economic system recognizable as capitalism, where profit and industry (albeit preindustrial-age industry) were more and more controlled by the private sector. All of this affects the very nature of the Conquest and the institutions that would be put in place. These would include the Casa de Contratación, the Trade House in Seville, Spain that lasted until the eighteenth century.

From the get-go, Spaniards were businessmen. Initially, as Lockhart and Otte, and later Matthew Restall, have noted, the conquistadors did not consider themselves soldiers.[86] They were motivated by profit more than a desire to serve the Crown or the Church.[87] Lockhart puts it this way: "The conquerors were free agents, emigrants, settlers, unsalaried, and ununiformed earners of encomiendas and shares of treasure, and a great many other things that do not fit well with today's concept 'soldier.'"[88] Lockhart and Otte, as well as Restall, disclose how and why the Spanish forces did not constitute armies. They were more like adventurers. Restall has coined an accurate expression to describe them, "armed Spanish entrepreneurs." They came to the Americas to make money, and they established systems for their descendants and compatriots to follow in their footsteps. At least in the fifty or sixty years of the imposition of the colonial apparatus, they sought opportunity as free agents, Restall explains, "both through patronage networks . . . and competition with other Spaniards."[89]

As ever-expanding structures were developing in the Western Atlantic and Eastern Pacific communities, so too were they in the European World. Thomas More, writing of his beloved Utopians, relates that when they have enough for themselves, "they export into other countries, out of their surplus, a great quantity of grain, honey, wool, linen, timber, scarlet and purple dye-stuffs, hides, wax, tallow, leather, as well as livestock" (*YE,* 4:148–49). Here we have a basic description of the materiality of capitalism and its logic.[90] These Utopians, good-hearted Europeans in disguise, are not crass capitalists. They temper their capitalism with a desire to fuse charity into commerce. "Of all these commodities they bestow the seventh part on the poor of the district and sell the rest at a moderate price" (*YE,* 4:148–49). More with his Utopia was looking at ways of seeing the future, not at ways of being in the present. There were perhaps few Europeans offering up as charity one seventh of what they were trading, especially when, in the Indies, they owed what was known the royal fifth as well as the tithing required to support the Church being installed.

Wallerstein has written extensively on the creation of the first modern World-System, the Luso-Hispanic one, whose glory days persisted until both the Hapsburg and Valois empires declared bankruptcy in 1557.[91] This date comes just six years after the first English-language translation of More's *Utopia* in 1551 (the original Latin version appeared in 1516). There was something happening during the 1550s. Wallerstein's thesis is that because economic structures are more efficient than political ones, the European world has tended to move in that direction, encompassing the entire globe as other regions entered into its consciousness.

How was the early World-System perceived at that time? Antonio de Guevara's "Villano del Danubio" comments on the lands known today as Germany. He showcases a supposed Germano-Roman awareness of an international economy, representing how the early modern Spanish saw things. He refers to imperial commerce that integrated "merchants from Carthage, oil from Mauritania . . . , steel from Cantabria, spices from Asia, gold from Spain, silver from Great Britain, amber from Sidon (Lebanon), silk from Damascus (Syria), wheat from Sicily, wine from Candia (Crete), purple die from Arabia" (mercaderes de Cartago, azeyte de Mauritania . . . , azero de Cantabria, olores de Asia, oro de España, plata de Bretaña, ambar de Sidonia, seda de Damasco, trigo de Sicilia, vino de Candía, púrpura de Arabia).[92] Guevara does not mention the Indies, of which he certainly knew, as it would not have made sense in the fictional discourse of a Germanic plebian addressing the Roman Senate. His Teutonic character is aware of a world that extends from England, descending the western coast of Africa, crossing the Mediterranean Sea, passing through present day Italy, Greece, and the Middle East, and reaching all the way to the Silk Road through Baghdad. Furthermore, this wide-reaching "world" is not just a lesson in geography; it is a well-thought-out, diversified map of commerce.

Wallerstein is wise to recognize that the European world-economy was not the only world-economy. The Semitic peoples had an extensive trade universe. Dirk Hoerder brings that network into focus: "Emanating from eleventh-century Cairo, Jewish and Arab merchant connections spanned the seas and reached Arabia, the East African cost, India, and China."[93] Beyond the Mediterranean, as can be seen in map 8, and as Wallerstein reminds us, there was the Indian Ocean-Red Sea complex and the Chinese regional economy, as well as the buying and selling that occurred between Mongolia and Russia.[94] Unknown to Europeans, Asians, and Africans before 1492, these systems of trade were coetaneous with other systems operating across the Atlantic.

What was the nature of trade in the European economy? First, besides trade along land routes, Yun explains, "new fuel for seaborne trade appeared, such as Iberian and Bordeaux wines, salt from Ibiza, Basque iron, and little,

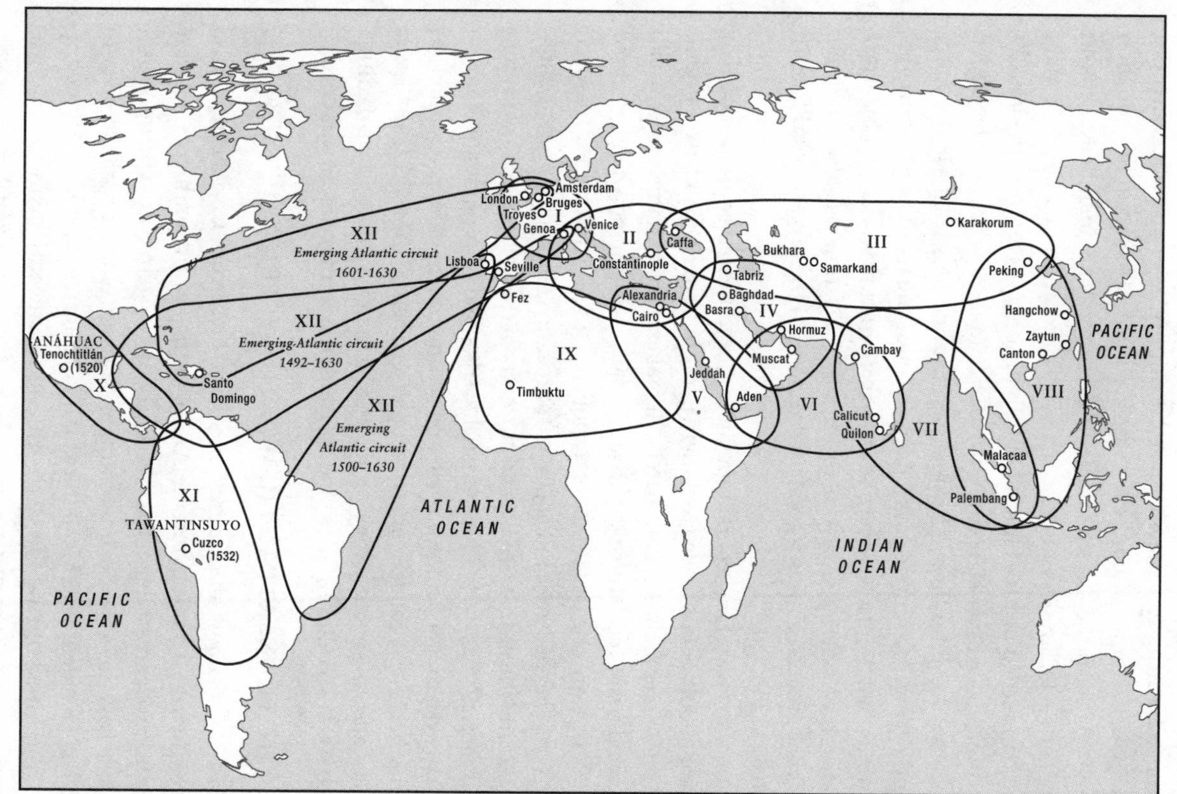

MAP 8. Sixteenth-century World-Systems. From Walter D. Mignolo, *Local Histories/Global Designs: Coloniality, Subaltern Knowledges, and Border Thinking* (Princeton: Princeton University Press, 2012), 28. *Map by Erin Greb Cartography.*

by little, Castilian wool."[95] Second, the European village began to diversify in terms of ethnicity, gender, and professions, slowly moving away from subsistence farming to a market-based economy, as cited with respect to More's England. Thomas Robisheaux sums up the people part of this equation this way: "By 1600 the classic village, if there was one, included far more women, cottagers, landless laborers, artisans, peddlers, and other dependent groups than settled heads of households living completely from the land."[96] What's more, as Weaver elaborates, because feudalism was underdeveloped and decentralized, it allowed for business innovations such as "the water mill, and new ways to rotate crops, design plows, and use draught animals," innovations that themselves were "drawn from distant lands."[97] Robisheaux concludes this description by explaining that migration was also a distinct part of that process, as was a greater openness "to the broader world" than previously suspected.[98]

Again, there were two general types of commodities, an actuality noted by Wallerstein. Bulk goods tended to remain in the local market and luxury items moved into larger realms of commerce.[99] It makes sense that the former would have a local basis, foodstuffs were used for subsistence, and what remained could not be transported far before it spoiled. Long-distance trade included dried spices, "pepper from India, ginger from China, cinnamon from Ceylon, and especially the nutmeg, mace and cloves from the Spice Islands of present day Indonesia,"[100] as well as nonperishable silks that Europe imported from the Asian system. Naturally, buying and selling things creates a market for fashion, what for the modern era is an interest in being "in style." It also spurs creativity, allowing makers, their products, and their vendors to leave tradition behind. And as Walter Mignolo has insisted, modernity has its underside.

THE TRANSATLANTIC WORLD-SYSTEM EMERGES

While we cannot know for sure if the circuits of the Circum-Caribbean, Central Mexico, Central America, and the Andes in the late fifteenth century were expanding, we can establish that the European system was expanding as it reached across the Atlantic, interacting with many of the circuits in place in the Indias Occidentales. McNeill explains, "Interregional European commerce intensified during the sixteenth and seventeenth centuries and was supplemented by an increasing volume of transoceanic trade."[101] For this reason, Mignolo calls the sixteenth century "the early global period."[102] James Casey puts it another way, stating that the early modern encounter with the Americas resulted in "opening up of a world economy."[103] Indeed, during the sixteenth century the world's trade routes became connected for the first time in history.

If there is any ambivalence toward recognizing the worldwide movement of people, products, and ideas originating in the wake of Columbus's voyages, three obvious factors document worldwide connections: religion, letters, and commerce. Regarding the first, there can be no doubt that Spain and Portugal were successful in spreading Catholicism around the world. For no other reason than the successes of evangelization are the numbers of Spanish- and Luso-American adherents to the faith so plentiful in our time. Latin America, the Philippines, and—to a lesser extent today—Goa, are still relatively Catholic regions of the globe.[104] The westward-moving Catholic religion represented a significant transplantation of culture, rushing to keep ahead of the eastward-moving Islamic thrust. As Mignolo explains, the cultivation of universals helped establish "the epistemological foundations of the practical project of Christianizing the World."[105] The darker side of this Christian project is the violence of the Conquest, and in the following decades, the quixotic quest for pureza de sangre (see previous chapter), which filtered into the Sacred Inquisition's trials and weeded out impure members of society who did not come from the heart of Castile.

Regarding the second, an adhesion to a lettered form of culture maybe less apparent, but the minute the uninitiated begins to dig into history, a large corpus of chronicles, poetry, legal briefs, anthropological interviews, proceedings of the Inquisition, and other forms of writing suffice to suggest an eagerness to document manifold facets of life. And of course, the lettered aspect of Christianity was inscribed in the Bible, Encyclicals, catechisms, breviaries, and other documents that gave form to Hispanic life. Some of the more educated Spaniards read books too, such as the *Amadís* series of novels. This literary thrust from the metropole became an integral part of life in the colonies. The title of Irving Leonard's classic *Books of the Brave* (*Los libros del conquistador*) says it all.

Regarding the third, as mentioned, Conquistadors saw their mission as a commercial enterprise. As stated in the introduction, Casey specifies that one of the features of the early modern period was the marking of the transition from feudalism to capitalism.[106] In Spain itself, Casey indicates that the rise of towns and a market economy paved the way to the Industrial Revolution.[107] This was not a local matter. The documents that came out of the Inquisition are the unintentional proof that the early modern period saw the establishment of a worldwide financial network. Consider the case of Manuel Bautista Peres, a "New Christian" brought before the Sacred Inquisition in Lima ostensibly for Judaizing. His insertion into history reveals a far-flung commercial network that, as Luis Millones maps out, ranged from Lisbon and Seville in Europe and Luanda in Africa to such places as Veracruz, Guatemala, Panama, Cartagena, Potosí, Santiago de Chile, Moquegua, Arica, and Ica.[108] His business connections reached three of the four known continents.

After the installation of the Spanish in the Western hemisphere, three distinct economic strains gave form to the early modern system. They were monarchical tribute-gathering efforts, early capitalism, and a blatant third arm Andrien categorizes as "the pillage/conquest economy."[109] Tribute gathering would institutionalize a human category known as *tributario*, allowing the monarchy to extract wealth directly from the people and bring it to Spain (see below). Early capitalism, mercantilist or not, can be traced back to the pre-contact pochteca, colonial *obrajes* (see below) and local and long-distance trade. As mentioned in Chapter 2, the chronicler Muñoz Camargo traded in "cattle, salt, slaves, cacao and other goods," all valuable commodities in local and regional markets. There was also plunder, which Wallerstein stresses, "is over time self-defeating, whereas exploitation within the framework of a single world-economy is self-reinforcing."[110] Despite having models such as Muñoz Camargo, the Spanish did not appear to grasp immediately that get-rich-quick schemes were ultimately untenable. Wallerstein determines, nevertheless, that pillaging evolved into production modes in the Spanish empire. He writes, "the harvest of bullion, wood, leather and sugar from the New World, which evolved during the [sixteenth] century from a gathering technique to a stable form of production using cheap labor and European supervision . . . *transformed* the social structure of the areas involved, incorporating them into the European world-economy."[111] It is unclear just how much the encomienda interfaced with the forming World-System, but there was a distinct possibility that it did in some degree. The tools at hand seem to have come from roots in late antiquity. Robert Keith explains how in Peru, for example, "communities produced a surplus which was collected by the Inca rulers and redistributed among their followers and dependents." Keith argues this system continued after the arrival of the Spaniards, except that "it was now the encomenderos who collected and redistributed the surplus with the result that they possessed a kind of monopoly of the economic life of Spanish Peru."[112] The question then arises: what did the encomenderos do with this surplus? They most certainly traded it. Readers of the chapter of Inca Garcilaso de la Vega's *Royal Commentaries* titled "De la hortaliza y hierbas" (*CR*, IX, xxix) or of Ricardo Palma's "Carta canta" would be familiar with the parable of the mitayos (encomendados) who had to bring the encomendero's melons to Lima, where assuredly they would go to market. Melons would have been consumed in Lima, but other products would have gone to Spain proper, Mexico, or the Philippines. We have mentioned salt, the pre-Hispanic product embraced in the colonial interval. Lisa DeLeonardis indicates that "salt was a valuable item, along with gold, cotton clothing, and maize that was paid annually to encomenderos."[113] Keith explains that the encomenderos, who were more powerful than any other Spaniards, at least in economic terms, "contracted with miners to operate their mines and with merchants to important Spanish goods with their capital."[114] Here we see concretely that the World-System was not solely interested in importing, but also in exporting.

This system moved toward capitalism. Wallerstein explains that feudalism has no place in the World-System, and therefore he rejects that label "for the various forms of capitalist agriculture based on coerced labor which grew up in a world-economy"[115] As the chattel system, despite a burst in potency, became less prevalent, forced labor based on debt developed. The debt-peonage model required money and, more importantly, loans, refocusing the "hacienda system." Credit and debt not only in agriculture, but also in industry and finance became institutionalized through a lettered culture that could transmit ideas and facts over long distances, forming the primary gears of the World-System.

This is not to say that there were capitalists a la Donald Trump, Carlos Slim, and Baruch Ivcher during the sixteenth century. There was an important difference. Wallerstein paints a picture of that somewhat hidden world: "The most curious aspect of this early period is that capitalists did not flaunt their colors before the world. The reigning ideology was not that of free enterprise, or even individualism or science or naturalism or nationalism. These would all take until the eighteenth or nineteenth century to mature as world views."[116] Religion and letters were the blanket that covered over those kinds of activities during the sixteenth century. But they were there, and the marketplace mentality was present from the first instant of linkage between the hemispheres.

From the earliest appearance of Europeans in this hemisphere, concerns for the market were paramount. Referring to the "Indians" he encountered,

Columbus explains, "They brought us parrots, balls of cotton thread, javelins, and arrows" (traían papagayos y hilo de algodón en ovillos y azagayas y otras muchas cosas) that were traded for the likes of "little glass beads and bells" (cuentezillas de vidro y cascaveles) (*TD*, 30). Columbus took these activities seriously, so much so that Beatriz Pastor has rightly argued his observations of the geographical features were primarily geared to their suitability for establishing trade: "Rivers are 'good' if they are 'large,' 'beautiful' when they are 'deep,' ports are 'marvelous' if they are 'useful,' perfect' if they are 'ample.'"[117] Such is the connotative use of language.

In a 1494 *Memorial,* Columbus suggests one way to make money with these newfound islands is by farming Spanish products there and then trading via partners in Seville. He recommends planting "wheat, barley, and vineyards" (trigos y cebadas e viñas) (*TD,* 151). Gold, logically, is added into the system. As we know, the Antilleans had small gold jewelry they probably had received in trade from other nations of the circum-Caribbean, such as those on the coast in the lands that would later become Colombia. In the case of this precious metal, he recommends charging it to "some merchant in Seville" (algún mercader en Sevilla) who can then use it to provision vessels in wine and wheat (*TD,* 152). Despite the failure of wheat to grow in the Caribbean, the intention to forge a transoceanic link with these areas is very clear. Before Columbus had sailed on his fourth voyage, the Crown established the Casa de Contratación, the House of Trade, which had two primary charges, regulating all transatlantic commerce and mapping out of the new regions being encountered.[118] The rates of growth were astronomical. Wallerstein stipulates the volume increased "eightfold between 1510 and 1550, and threefold again between 1550 and 1610."[119]

There were a number of activities used to engage people. The most egregious was what we would today call human trafficking, practiced along with plunder and extraction. As mentioned in Chapter 3, Cieza de León comments on Spaniards in the Pearl Islands who "have blacks and Indians from Nicaragua and Cubagua who take care of their livestock" (*CP-1^{era}*, fol. 14 [iiii], p. 31). It is not clear in Cieza's language, but the people from Nicaragua could have been from any one or all of the different naciones in existence there in the sixteenth century (see above). The same was true of the fishing communities that resided in Cubagua (today a Venezuelan island). The blacks could have come from any number of locations on the African continent. There was also the people-moving mita. Fuenzalida Vollmar explains that in Peru, each town had to give one seventh of its male population for four months of the year to the mines in Potosí and Huancavelica for mining operations.[120] Free labor was not the only element. As DeLeonardis suggests, even the *kamayoq* specialists for certain products could become mitayos, and distributed across wide geographical areas in the Andes because of their expertise. They served the pre-contact Qhapaq order and then the Crown. DeLeonardis studies the particular role of "Cachimayos (salt specialists) of the Pisco Valley," Qheswa speakers in an Aymara locale.[121]

There were other kinds of movement. Certainly the livestock on the Pearl Islands would be milked, butchered, or sold for profit. As is clear, the gold and silver from the forced labor system regarded as the fruits of a tribute economy passed almost directly into the world market. Mercantilism (local production sent to the metropole) coexisted with feudal-like practices (local production for local use) and the origins of market capitalism (at least in the regional realm, with Ecuador exporting salt and Mexico exporting quicksilver). The movement of people and things from the ancient cah, amaq', ñuu, altepetl, or ayllu was the crux of the colonial system.

In broad terms, as Wallerstein explains, "Mexico exported manufactures, luxuries, and slaves to Peru and received in return specie and mercury." After the northern Philippines entered into this system (the southern Philippines remained part of an Islamic World-System operating coetaneous with the Christian one), Mexico—surprisingly, given its northern geographic position in the triangle—served as an intermediary between the south Pacific islands and Peru.[122] Fuenzalida Vollmar fleshes this out when he explains that additional services were demanded, forcing the establishment of textile shops, transport networks, mail service, construction gangs (to repair bridges and roads), salt mines, and shepherds for privately owned flocks. Even water, firewood, and domestic service were provided for the *vecinos,* the citizens who could only be so if Spanish born. During the colonial era, flocks of livestock, textile shops (obrajes), salt, and even the salt specialists fed into the tribute system. This system, as Brooke Larson helps us visualize, "was a pillar of Spanish Colonial rule."[123]

Tribute itself, paid in cash or in kind, was yoked directly to the world market. In the latter instance, taxes could be paid in locally originated merchandise, such as textiles or ceramics, and in products of European origin, such as wheat, barley, sheep, and hen's eggs.[124] This system also represents the social and economic stratification of peoples. If the citizens of the empire were the vecinos, the noncitizens were legally designated *tributarios,*[125] or tributaries, which neatly explains their place in society. Thus, the system is simple; the payers existed simply to confer wealth on the vecinos, who reached up to insert themselves into the transoceanic network.

As is being suggested, if people did not have tribute to pay, they became the tribute themselves. With or without hyperbole, Las Casas reports in his *Brevísima relación de la destrucción de las Indias* that when Spaniards began ripping apart the fabric of the K'iche' amaq', its inhabitants were immediately required to pay tribute in slaves to their new lords. Those that did not have the resources had no other choice then except "giving them their sons and daughters, because other slaves they did not have" (dándoles los hijos e hijas, porque otros esclavos no los tienen). At this juncture, we are interested in how those slaves were used. Las Casas reports that they ended up in "ships filled with them to be sold in Perú" (navíos cargados dellos a vender al Perú) (*TR*, I, 90–91). There was accordingly an ethno-cultural aspect of this practice. People speaking Mam, K'iche', Kaqchikel, or other Guatemalan or Mexican language would leave behind their cah or amaq' and bring those identities to Peru, fusing with the transatlantic, transcontinental melting pot being established there. Not just the Maya were internationalizing Lima's culture. Keith determines that "the Indian population of Lima was drawn from as far away as Chile and Panama, and there were even a few 'Indians' from Portuguese Asia."[126] Indeed, even the mother of the Lima-based Saint Martín de Porres (1579–1639) came from Panama, and being an ex-slave, she may have even brought a slice of African culture with her.[127]

Sea routes between the northern and south regions of the Western hemisphere, and between it and Europe, may have been exploited by the Spanish, but local land routes combined precontact with postcontact knowledge. Two types of trade routes were utilized. Sometimes, as with the Inkan road system, new trade maps were superimposed over existing ones. Other times, as the linguist Torero notes with respect to the Cholón region, the Spanish invasion "broke down the ancient trade networks between the mountains and the jungle" (rompió las antiquísimas redes de intercambio sierra-selva).[128] New pathways were forged favoring Spaniards, not Amerindians. Under pressure from the colonial wave, forced modification of traditions and customs was not uniform. Almost any trajectory was possible.

As mentioned, gold and silver were integral to this new expanding economy.[129] Wallerstein explains that bullion circulated through Europe as a monetary base and served as a trade unit for increasing contacts with the orient.[130] After 1546 vast silver deposits mined from Potosí (in Bolivia) and Zacatecas (in Mexico) began to enter the European market.[131] As the year 1600 began to approach, a shifting in economic structure became apparent: the World-System would have been obvious even then to an acute observer. Bartolomé Yun describes the world circuit as a central Europe "whose questing merchants in Asia no longer spoke Italian but Portuguese and Dutch, and who paid for Asian products with the sweat, transmuted into silver, of the Indians of Peru and New Spain."[132] This New World subordinated to the old one in an emerging World-System was apparent long before our time, as we began to suspect from our reading of Guevara's *Relox de príncipes*. Thomas More's *Utopia*, written at the early date of 1515, describes Vespucci's New World intensely involved in long-distance commerce (*YE*, 4:52–53). By the time Adam Smith wrote *Wealth of Nations* (1776), exchange routes between strange places were crystal clear. Concerning mining, Smith describes this reality in succinct fashion: "Their market is not confined to the countries in the neighborhood of the mine, but extends to the whole world. The copper of Japan makes an article of commerce in Europe[,] the iron of Spain in that of Chil[e] and Peru. The silver of Peru finds its way not only to Europe, but from Europe to China."[133] Again, these were local and global processes. Texts that Restall, Souza, and Terraciano have collected attest to the fact that "Mesoamericans participated in a global money economy while also maintaining aspects of local trade."[134] The initial shock of the wars of conquest brought immediate and substantial globalizing thrusts with it. The Iberians took routes hitherto only used in segments to cover the long distance between Guatemala and Peru, for instance, and covered the distance in clearly delineated circuits.

Susan Ramírez explains that as the Andeans' economy, based on the production of cloth (*qompi*), was slowly replaced with the money-based economy of mercantile capitalism, they were then incorporated "into expanding global networks of unequal exchange."[135] There was a certain unevenness in the ways different places and regions were integrated. Larson offers examples of local *señoríos* asserting themselves, or not, during Inka and Spanish times. The Canas, Collas, Lupaqas, Pacajes, Soras, Carangas, and Quillacas were able to continue to distribute products from contrasting ecological zones, such as corn, potatoes, coca, *ají*, salt and even textiles, although, she cautions, not through commercial means. The Aymara-speaking *altiplano* served as "a strategic crossroads" through which silver, salt, textiles, potatoes, and other products passed. In contrast to those two strategies, the Pastos, Caras Puruha, and Canaris of the North Highlands remained isolated and did not engage in trade.[136]

As one of Francisco de Victoria's theses of "legitimate and valid titles" (títulos legítimos y validos) justifying indigenous submission to Spanish rule, the Salamancan theologian upholds the right of Spaniards to conduct commerce with Amerindians, exporting merchandise and importing gold or silver. "It is legal for Spaniards to trade with the Indians . . . exporting, for example, merchandise, importing from there gold, silver or other things" (Es lícito a los españoles comerciar con los indios . . . exportando, por ejemplo, allá mercancías . . . importando de allí oro, plata u otras cosas).[137] While there were radical defenders of human rights among the Dominicans (Montesinos and Las Casas) and protoanthropologists among the Franciscans (Sahagún and Motolinía), others like Vitoria and Cortés's Father of Mercy sanctioned the economic surge of Spanish expansion. Therefore, while letters and religion were making their mark, there was a commercial tinge, even among some men of the cloth.

There is a need for caution using the term "capitalism" in this colonial context. According to Stern's useful interpretation, "capitalist production bases itself upon the sale of labor-power for a wage, induced primarily not by political, social, or cultural coercions but rather by economic necessity." He concludes, "on *ayllu* lands, capitalist production was impossible."[138] This is because 1) the mentality of collectivism among the ayllu's inhabitants; and 2) Andean governance is one of tribute, so much so that even today the Peruvian internal revenue department is called the Sistema Tributario Nacional or Sistema Tributario Peruano. A taxpayer is a tribute payer. However, despite forced labor in the encomienda and subsequent debt-peonage on the hacienda, the patron of either system could reach up with their profits and touch the emerging World-System.

While the traditional ayllu may represent a capitalist-resistant structure, as people left the ayllu, they began to take up the ways of the city. There, they may have been able to earn a wage. This was true in Guaman Poma's time and continued to be a primordial factor in the time of Arguedas. Commenting on the twentieth century, Arguedas refers to a problem that certainly began right after the encounter; he refers to the *qepa ñeqen,* the younger generations who leave the traditional ayllu for the coast. When these qepa ñeqen return to the traditional community, the elders complain that they are no longer willing to fetch water for the fields, and they express themselves differently. While Arguedas was concerned with language and belief systems, it goes beyond saying there was also an economic aspect.[139] That aspect, as Stern stated, was based on need.

First, there were early qepa ñeqen who went to the coast, as well as the forming mestizo class, who began to participate in petite bourgeoisie activities, so much so that in 1549 King Charles limited the possibilities for mestizos holding public office (*NU*, 144). Both Andeans and blacks could be seen in the street.[140] Much of Lima's initial commerce, being limited to foodstuffs, construction, and the apparel business, was not global in nature. Later, as Irene Silverblatt has shown in her research on the Inquisition, it began to take on global dimensions. Predictably, capitalism developed along the Peruvian coastline. The early street names of downtown Lima attest to that (Plateros, Mantas, Moneda, Bodegones, etc.). In short, the trades ran the gambit, including lime-crushing mills, oven-firing brick mills, and pottery shops. There were grain mills and bakers as well as storefront tailor, silk, hat, and shoe shops. These were complemented by silver, iron, and gunsmiths near carpentry, tanning, and curing shops.[141] Women were involved in this commercial activity, especially as *curanderas* (medicine women) and bread and pastry makers. They ran *alhondigas*, where they sold grain (wheat and corn), flour, and wine.[142] *Pulperías* (general stores) and apothecaries had a presence.[143] Men and Women served as *taberneras* and *chicheras* (tavern keepers), and a number of women worked as *ambulantes* (street vendors) selling things like clothing, jewelry, jewel cases, and other accoutrements of dress.[144] Some women would have been seen selling bread and sponge cake on their front door steps, and carts bringing fish and other products from Callao would have been circulating through Lima's streets.[145]

Second, while the movement of goods, peoples, and even cultures and religions does not have to be predominantly capitalist in its origins, there was a budding capitalist link in certain regions of Europe during this time (as Wallerstein argues), and various Conquistadors saw their enterprise as a business venture which, as stated, was not expressed as openly as was the Christian dimension. Díaz del Castillo and other Spaniards saw their repartimientos as business enterprises. Such ventures, however, did not yet constitute full-blown capitalism.[146] Mercantilist structures were established and trade routes utilized (and in some cases, repurposed), establishing the groundwork for capitalism to begin to make inroads.

The colony also provided for a market economy, but it was an economy stymied by constant interference by a Crown and/or viceregal government. The products associated with a market within the Viceroyalty of Peru were wide-ranging. Durand mentions cloth, drumsticks, cordovan leather, blankets, sacks, hats, porcelain and glass objects, and saddles, as well as gunpowder.[147] In a "Memoria de bienes" for Francisco Domínguez in 1587, *pesos corrientes* and *reales al peso* associated with the sale of linens, sheep, and a slave are registered.[148] In some cases, the market itself was constituted by forced labor. The 1625 memorial signed by fifteen elders (mentioned in the previous chapter) describes how a parish priest, one Doctor Mejía, forced Andeans to go to market for him under extreme conditions. The result: "Two died of hunger in Anbar while transporting some hogs; three died in Lima whilst they were carrying two horses, chickens and bacon to sell" (dos murieron de hanbre en Anbar llebando unos puercos; tres murieron en Lima que llebaba don caballos y gallinas y tocinos a bender).[149] These transactions are indicative of a market economy, albeit a contradictory one, as the market on the surface appeared "modern," but the mitayos and slaves that turned the gears underneath were brutalized. In addition, constant governmental interventions impeded the free market. Fernando Silva Santisteban indicates that this was the case in 1548, when the Cortes de Valencia prohibited people in the colonies from purchasing products in Spain proper. At another point, the Crown prohibited the production of *paños,* or cloth, in Peru, favoring the exportation of raw materials from the colony to the metropole. This would be classic mercantilist posture for the imperial government to take, importing raw materials from the periphery to the metropole, where the finished product is assembled and perfected. Other times there was a downright solicitousness, because the original Peruvians were prohibited from working obrajes. An obraje, or wool mill, included all the stages of textile manufacturing, including dyeing, spinning, and weaving. Yet despite it all, the number of obrajes grew on the backs of the Qheswan and Aymaran peoples.[150]

Fuenzalida Vollmar makes manifest that as the population waned and as Spanish greed increased, growing pressure was put on indigenous communities for tribute in kind and in cash.[151] Viceroy Toledo put into effect a number of reforms and, in Andrien's words, "established the foundations for a network of regional markets, branching off from the trunk line running from Lima to Potosí." He clarifies the nature of these regional markets: "Potosí allowed producers and merchants to make fortunes supplying luxury goods, wine, brandy, and fish from coastal Peru, while sugar, coca came from inland centers such as Cusco, Chucuito, Tucumán, Paraguay, Santa Cruz, and Cochabamba."[152] Some indigenous communities got directly involved in these activities, while others "still resisted European modes of production."[153] While there was unevenness in the process, the ayllukuna that began to articulate more and more with Lima or other local ethnic nations found that their links to their heritage severed more and more. The horizontal forces favoring further Hispanization worked to the detriment of local cultural resistance. Local naciones would enter into transcultural transformations, and if Hispanization became predominant, these naciones would become reformulated as a kind of hybrid community, as we saw with Burga and Arguedas's research.[154]

The market was neither uniform nor did it provide favorable conditions to all. While an exchange economy had existed before the Spanish, and while the Toledan reforms greatly increased the scope of market activity, it could not be a free-market economy, per se, because not all could participate, and freedom of movement was not guaranteed. Freedom of movement, as discussed, is one the attributes of the "Western" nation Smith describes. Nevertheless, bullion, tobacco, sugar, and other products filtered into the European World-System. Wallerstein explains that Genoese, Dutch, Portuguese Jewish, and French men of commerce were involved in these dealings, while at the same time Charles V, as Holy Roman Emperor, was unwilling "to take a Spanish *nationalist* perspective and adopt a mercantilist policy."[155] Regarding the relationship between the free market and the Castellano-centric nation, there was a strange administrative paradox. "Instead of moving against foreign merchants–Wallerstein writes–Spain pursued the path of expelling Spanish non-Catholics, a self-destructive course."[156] The groups referred to are the Moors and the Jews. In addition, as Silverblatt establishes, during the seventeenth century this policy would turn the gears of the Inquisition against Portuguese New Christians resident in Lima.[157] These "Portuguese" were people of Jewish descent whose families had been expelled from Spain and who participated in far-flung trade networks from Lima.

Whereas, as mentioned, some encomiendas on the periphery may have actually paid a *sesmo,* or sixth, to their peasant workers,[158] it would be idealistic to think all could participate favorably and equally in the budding capitalist system. Wallerstein points out that the indigenous were forbidden to raise cattle, an economic activity more profitable than farming. This is no different from contemporary farmers in England, who were forced from the land by the enclosure movement in favor of cattle producers. As Wallerstein puts it, "Sheep ate men, in middle America just as in England."[159]

There was also a colonized of the colonized. If the Peruvian guilds were subordinated to European guilds, as Iñigo García Bryce argues, within the former there were also hierarchies.[160] He writes, "The rules of the Guild of Spanish Tailors prohibited master artisans from teaching their trade to slaves and excluded blacks and zambos from membership in its brotherhood." At other times, "attempts by Spaniards to limit the participation of Indians, blacks, and castas in the trades were unsuccessful." This was no mere cultural practice of factoring out or allowing in subordinated peoples, because market pressures were another element. García Bryce concludes his thought: "The attempts at exclusion by race often occurred at times of increased competition."[161] Hence, some people of mixed heritage actually participated in the trades and were eventually members of guilds. The involvement of all people in the colonial commercial enterprise was uneven because of market pressures, colonial hierarchies, royal intervention, and the impulse to suppress the local cah, ñuu, amaq', altepetl, or ayllu.

Despite all the economic forces working against the cah, ñuu, amaq', altepetl, or ayllu, even when multiple nations were folded into larger nation-state configurations upon independence, the feelings, impulses, and organizational tendencies of some of those late ancient naciones survive, and in some cases thrive. New forms are combined with them to reflect realities on the ground. Academies of indigenous languages have been established. Qheswa and K'iche' are two that come to mind. Important texts, indigenous or otherwise, have been translated and published, and even translated into millennial national languages. One such case is the *Popol Wuj,* updated recently into modern K'iche' by Enrique Sam Colop. Another is the avant-garde poet Cesar Vallejo's *Trilce*, recently translated from Spanish into Qheswa by Porfirio Meneses Lazón. Indigenous nations have held international conferences. In 1992 a K'iche' woman was awarded the Nobel Peace Prize for her work in Guatemala, now understood as a multiethnic political configuration that, in its postwar period, has been striving to introduce bilingual teachers in its many indigenous zones. Menchú, the awardee, herself was even a presidential candidate, an unthinkable possibility in earlier times. Perhaps the greatest sign of resurgent micronational identities is the recently renamed Plurinational State of Bolivia. New understandings of the nations of the past with respect to the nations of the present may be on the horizon.

NOTES

Introduction

1. Ward, *Decolonizing Indigeneity: New Approaches to Latin American Literature.* The third and final book of the trilogy, nearing completion, bears the working title *Everyday Coloniality and the Rise of Liberation Thinking: The Idealism of Humanism during the Long Sixteenth Century.*
2. Cameron, "Editor's Introduction," xvii.
3. Casey, *Early,* 1.
4. Casey, *Early,* 43.
5. Prak, citing Hobsbawm, delimits the Early Modern as before capitalism and after feudalism, *Early Modern Capitalism,* 1. However, in Latin America elements of the hacienda system survived into the nineteenth and twentieth centuries. It might be more precise to say the early modern represents the birth and advance of capitalism and the decline of the feudal, even if independence from Spain did not perfectly extinguish feudal elements.
6. "tribu," *Diccionario de la lengua castellana,* 4: n.p.
7. English-language usage in our time, for some reason, seems to vacillate between "tribe" and "nation," despite the connotative differences between them. Just to offer an example, Gover, a Pawnee and the Director of the National American Indian Museum, in his "Forward" to *Nation to Nation,* talks about "treaties between the United States and American Indian Nations," while in the very next paragraph he refers to "treaties with Indian tribes," xi.
8. I have tried to respect the spelling and diacritical marks usage of indigenous words, except with authors' names and titles for published works. The Inka Garcilaso's name appears as the Inca Garcilaso and Alva Ixtlilxóchitl's second last name appears with the accent mark, both as their names first appeared in print. I have decided to treat plurals of indigenous-language nouns as we treat Greek, Latin, and French borrowings in English. As we say phenomena, millennia, and tableaux for the plurals of phenomenon, millennium, and tableau, we can say Inkakuna for the plural of Inka, altepeme for altepetl, and Mexica for Mexicatl (regarding Mexicatl,

see Lockhart, *Nahuatl,* 51). Finally, while Inkan is clearly an adjective relating to things Inka, Mexican commonly refers to the modern republic, thus, for lack of a better solution to refer to precontact Mexica, I have used Mexical as an adjective for singular nouns, and Mexica as an adjective for plural nouns.

9. Competing phonetic spellings of Qheswa words have left behind an inconsistent mosaic of variants, such as Qheswa, Keshua, Qhichwa, and Quechua or Quichua. I use the spelling preferred by the Qheswa Simi Hamut'ana Kurak Suntur, the "Academia Mayor de la Lengua Quechua" based in Cuzco, Peru. Despite the K'iche' (Quiché in Spanish) referring to their language as *Qatzijob'al* ("Our Language"), I follow the model of K'iche' scholars Sam Colop and Valle Escalante, who spell the proper noun as "K'iche'." Nahuatl also has variants, and no system is perfect. I have used Siméon's *Diccionario de la lengua náhuatl o Mexicana.* For a brief discussion of the variants, Molina, Carochi, and the modern system, see Lockhart, *Nahuatl,* viii-x, and especially x.
10. As a result of ethnographic studies by Lockhart and others, we now know there was no lightning "Conquest" forcing indigenous societies into immediate subordination or extinction. Conversely, substantial elements of indigenous and African societies survived into the colonial era and beyond. As Restall explains, we use the word "Conquest" because Spaniards "doggedly insisted the Conquest was complete until it looked to them as though it was." *Seven,* 76. Where possible I try not to use the term, however the limitations of other terms such as "discovery" and "encounter" force me to use it from time to time.
11. Papadopoulos and Urton, "Introduction," 3.
12. J. Lee, *The Allure,* 42, for example. The divergence between Nahuatl singulars and plurals does take some getting used to, but Mexicatl is the singular and Mexica is the plural. Again, see Lockhart, *Nahuatl,* 51.
13. Mazzotti, *Coros,* 46–47.
14. Merrim, "The First," 61.
15. Adorno, *The Polemics,* 154–67.
16. Cortés, "¿Dónde está Tlaloc?" 341.
17. Cortés, "¿Dónde está Tlaloc?" 342–43.
18. Castro-Klarén adds that archaeology has been important over the last two centuries because it "proved crucial for colonial peoples engaged in the endeavor of 'inventing' a nation, and indeed, in deploying the ethnographic principle as a positive force on which to base their claims to legitimate struggles for self-rule." "The Nation," 171.
19. Pardo Bazán, "La Espagne de hier," in *La España de Ayer,* 32. The author gave this lecture in French. Later she translated it to Spanish.
20. Pardo Bazán, "La Espagne," in *La España,* 38.
21. Kirk, "Mapping," 977.
22. For more on the black legend, with bibliography, see Quilligan, Mignolo, and Rich, *Rereading.* For a defense of Spain against the Black Legend, see Carbia, *Historia.*
23. As noted by Greer, Mignolo, and Quilligan, "Introduction," 1.
24. Gadamer, *Truth,* 309–10.

25. Derrida, "Structure," 252.
26. Fabian, *Time,* 17.

Chapter 1

Epigraph: Salvatore, "Conclusion," 248.

1. Anthias and Yuval-Davis, "Introduction," 2.
2. Alarcón, Kaplan, and Moallem, "Introduction," 1.
3. I have used the term "Aztec" sparingly in this book for the reasons outlined by Thomas: "'Aztec' from Aztlan was not a word used in the sixteenth century (though it may have been in the thirteenth). It was made popular by the Jesuit scholar, Clavijero, in the eighteenth century, and then by Prescott." *Conquest,* xix; I have used the more precise ethnic identifiers "Mexica," "Acolhua," and "Tepaneca" (all plurals) to refer to the three primary players incorporated into the term "Aztec." As for the term "Anahuac," many of the peoples who lived in the valley, as Siméon notes—among them, the Mexica, the Xochimilca, the Chalca, the Tepaneca, the Culhua, the Tlahuica, and the Tlaxcalteca—were all able to call themselves anahuatlaca. Siméon, *Diccionario,* 28b.
4. A number of politico-cultural movements suggest many people still perceive racial, ethnic, and gender differences in our supposedly nonethnic nations of today. To name a few: *negritud,* diverse strands of *indigenismo,* Postcolonial and decolonial methodologies, feminism, and even Ni Una Menos and Black Lives Matter.
5. Unwittingly, in this expression, I have referred to the title of Mignolo's *The Idea of Latin America.*
6. Renan, "Qu'est-ce qu'une nation?" 55. All translations from French and Spanish are mine, except where otherwise noted.
7. Holt, "Forward," viii.
8. Renan, "Qu'est-ce qu'une nation?" 53.
9. Susan Neiman, "Change Germans Can't Believe In," *New York Times,* July 26, 2008, A27.
10. Hobsbawm, *Nations,* 14.
11. As noted by Hastings, *The Construction,* 2.
12. Anderson, *Imagined,* 41–49.
13. Hobsbawm, *Nations,* 14.
14. Hastings, *The Construction,* 3.
15. A. D. Smith, *National,* 40.
16. I draw on Restall ("Heirs," 244), Christenson (*K'iche'-English Dictionary*), as well as my own knowledge in naming these configurations.
17. Welsh, *The Four,* xix. Welsh's "Introduction," xix–xxviii, provides a helpful discussion of the difficulties with defining the British ideal.
18. Steven Erlanger, "'Brexit' Aftershocks: More Rifts in Europe, and in Britain, Too," *New York Times,* June 24, 2016, www.nytimes.com/2016/06/25/world/europe/brexit-aftershocks-more-rifts-in-europe-and-in-britain-too.html?_r=0 (accessed June 25, 2016).

19. Welsh, *The Four,* 201.
20. Weber, "Chiquitano," 195.
21. Northrup, quoted in Marriot, "Cultural Policy," 28.
22. A. D. Smith, *The Antiquity,* 1. Smith uses the French variant *ethnie*; here we will use, where possible, the Spanish form, *etnia.* No comparable term exists in English, as "ethnicity" has become predominantly a noun of classification.
23. "Naturaleza," *Diccionario de la lengua española,* Real Academia Española, 7:1063b; Chang-Rodríguez, "Coloniaje," 29–30.
24. Bonilla, "Etnia," 88.
25. Guaman Poma's *Nueva crónica* could just as easily serve in this role, although less known in the English-speaking world than the *Popol Wuj.*
26. Arias, "Kotz'ib," 8
27. López, "The *Popol Wuj,*" 84.
28. *Popol Wuj Online,* Folio44 recto. The word is spelled *amac* in Father Ximénez's transcription. The modern spelling is *amaq'.*
29. Geertz offers many of these same factors as primordial elements in society. He lists blood ties, race, language, region, religion, and custom—all of these contrary to civil sentiments. Geertz, "The Integrative," 109–16.
30. Holt, "The First," xii.
31. I do not intend to single out the K'iche' here. Peruvian chroniclers' depictions of the Inkakuna and their concept of nación, lineage, and ayllu surprisingly hold much in common with K'iche' concepts. See for example, *CR,* III, xii, IX, xxxi; Sarmiento, *Historia,* ch. xiv; included in Garcilaso, *Obras,* 4:219b, 220a, 219b.
32. Hannaford, *Race,* 5–6.
33. Corominas, *Breve diccionario,* 494.
34. Garcilaso, *Royal Commentaries,* 1:606–7.
35. On the recent recalculations of the period duration in which complex society developed in the lands later becoming Peru, see Haas, Creamer, and Ruiz, "Dating the Late Archaic."
36. Dore, "One Step," 38 (my italics); see also Holt, "The First," ix.
37. Holt, "The First," ix.
38. See Stanish, "The Revaluation."
39. Van Akkeren, "El Chinamit," 223.
40. Quiroa, "The *Popol Vuh,*" 467.
41. This is an argument specifically referring to Latin America, made by Deas, *The Man,* 77.
42. López sums this up by noting that the episodes of the *Popol Wuj* can "demostrar la procedencia e identidad de la nación kiché dentro de sus propio pasado y territorio." *Los* Popol Wuj, 50.
43. Previous three quotes from Goetz and Morley, trans., *Popol Vuh.*
44. Renan rejects these obvious national attributes as a result of his interest in fostering the multi-lingual, multi-national "confederation europénne." "Qu'est-ce qu'une nation?" 55, also 45–53, 54, 55.

45. I prefer the spelling of "Tiwanaku" instead of the Academia Mayor de la Lengua Quechua's preferred "Tiyawanaku," as the former has greater currency among scholars.
46. See Silverblatt, *Moon,* 72–73, 4n.
47. See Arguedas, "Mitos quechuas poshispánicos," in *Formación de una cultura nacional.*
48. Castro-Klarén, *The Narrow,* 267.
49. For Robinson, "nation-states are no longer appropriate units of analysis, in part because they are no longer 'containers' (if indeed they ever were) of the diverse economic, political, social, and cultural processes that are objects of study in the social sciences." *A Theory,* 88–89; See also Glade, "The State in Retreat"; Ohmae, *The End of the Nation State.*
50. Recent scholarship perpetuates this view. This is the case with Castillo et al., whose *Nación, estado y cultura* seems to forget Latin American nations did not magically appear when Napoleon invaded Spain. A similar issue could be raised with Colom González's *Relatos de nación: la construcción de las identidades nacionales,* whose very title implies constructing something. And with what would the nation be constructed? People, who despite their origins across four continents, did not miraculously appear in the wake of Hidalgo, San Martín, and Bolívar.
51. *Oxford English Dictionary,* online version, s.v. "nation," accessed September 1, 2006, emphasis mine.
52. Guevara, *Relox,* 81–82, emphasis mine.
53. Beckjord, *Territories,* 64.
54. On diverse indigenous experiences with English and Spanish colonialism, see Seed, *American,* chapter 1.
55. Mignolo, *The Idea,* 4.
56. Torero, *Idiomas,* 375.
57. Ward, *Decolonizing Indigeneity,* 1–33.
58. Curet, "The Taíno," 267.
59. Porras Barrenechea, *Pizarro,* 38.
60. Shimada cautions the Mochica did not achieve statehood until the Moche V period. He suggests the idea of "superchiefdom" before Moche V "is just as plausible"; *Pampa,* 261.
61. Sharer, "The Maya," 471, 479.
62. Dillehay, "Town," 266b, 267b, 271b, 274b, 275a.
63. Dillehay, "Town," 27b, 274a, 272a, 263b.
64. Dillehay, "Town," 275b, 273b.
65. For Shimada, *Pampa,* 17–18, "Mochica art is the only true pre-Hispanic narrative art south of the Maya territory." The fine-line drawings "are representational in nature, telling us stories about significant features and historical events in the real or mythical world." For Sharer, first examples of hieroglyphic inscriptions in what would become the Maya tradition date to the Late Preclassic period (400 BC–AD 100), the majority being in the southern area, that is, belonging to the so-called Highland

Maya. Sharer, "The Maya," 470. New research by Pohl, Pope, and Von Nagy, "Olmec Origins," suggests an even earlier point in time for the origins of writing.

66. Porras Barrenechea, *Mito*, 37, 31, 38.
67. Restall, Souza, and Terraciano, *Mesoamerican*, 8, 10.
68. Zuidema, *The Ceque*, 18.
69. Adorno, "Cultures," 43.
70. Adorno, "Cultures," 40.
71. Regrettably, because of space limitations, we will not be able to treat thoroughly the Chimú here. They, like other groups, represent an excellent case in nation formation. Topic reports on research and excavations showing Chimú working-class artisans as endogamous resulting in "cast-like kin groups" "directly attached to the royal court." "Craft," 146. For discussions of this area with respect to diversity, see chapters 3 (the section "Inkakuna, Chimú, and Their Precursors as Diversity in Time and Space") and 4 ("The Peruvian Coast: Foreign Women in the Moche World").
72. Mignolo, *The Darker*, 303.
73. Fernández, *Inca Garcilaso*, 154, 21n.
74. Husson, "Introduction." This work's authorship is in question. See Zevallos Aguilar, "Inkarri," 20.
75. Díaz Caballero, "El incaísmo," 103.
76. Burga, *NU*; Kapsoli Escudero, *El retorno del Inca*, 34–79.
77. Almeida, *Reimagining*, 22, 33, and 41.
78. Adorno, *The Polemics*, 9.
79. See Castro Arenas, *La rebelión de Juan Santos*; Villegas Romero, *El movimiento de Túpac Amaru II*. Juan Santos Atahualpa was also known as Atahualpa Apu Inka.
80. See Thomson, *We Alone*.
81. Mallon, *The Defense*, 48.
82. Klarén, *Peru*, 175–76; McEvoy, "Indio," 61–118.
83. Arroyo Reyes, "Entre el incaísmo."
84. Covey, *How*, 22–23, 121.
85. Covey, *How*, 36.
86. Mariana, *Obras*, 2: 477b.
87. Spellman, *European*, 1, 2.
88. Spellman, *European*, 8.
89. Erasmus, *The Education*, 27.
90. Erasmus, *The Education*, 37.
91. Erasmus, *The Education*, 23, 43, 37.
92. Spellman, *European*, 9.
93. Covey, *How*, 7, 56, 109.
94. Dore, "One Step," 37.
95. Portocarrero, *Rostros*, 190, 192, 193.
96. Rivers, ed., *Poesía lírica*, 79.
97. Cited in Courcelles, "Managing," 4.
98. Courcelles, "Managing," 4.

99. Erasmus, *The Education*, 6.
100. Royes, ed., *The Book of Chilam Balam*, 30–31.
101. Regarding these issues on the North American context, see Hinkelammert, "The Hidden Logic of Modernity."
102. These include Anderson, *Imagined Communities*; Bhabha, *The Location of Culture*; Hobsbawm, *Nations and Nationalism*; A. D. Smith, *National Identity*.
103. A. D. Smith, *National*, 20.
104. A. D. Smith, *National*, 14; italics removed.
105. See Rama, *Transculturación narrativa*; Cornejo Polar, *Escribir en el aire*; García Canclini, *Culturas híbridas*. A good review of recent debates with superb bibliographical references can be found in Moraña, ed., *Indigenismo*.
106. Restall, *Seven*, 51.
107. Schneider mentions "Don Pedro the Mexican Prince" as embarking with Narváez in *Brutal Journey*, 47. It does take connecting the dots to suggest Muñoz de Camargo tutored the Floridians Cabeza de Vaca brought back to Mexico. Miller, "Covert," 43, offers textual evidence Muñoz Camargo was among the Tlaxcalteca who tutored them, a fact mentioned by Gibson, "The Identity," 200. And we know Muñoz Camargo did his tutoring in 1538 (per Miller) or 1537 (per Gibson) and Cabeza de Vaca arrived in Mexico City after April 1536. Cabeza de Vaca, *The Narrative* f61v, 6n, and Adorno, "Introduction," 17. Otherwise the Floridians would have had to make it to Mexico City by other means.
108. Mignolo, *Local*, 1–9.
109. Anzaldúa, *Borderlands/La Frontera*, 3.
110. Mignolo, *Local*, xi.
111. On the *tocapos*, see Cahill, "The Inca," 129–30. Early commentators found the *khipu* to be confusing and unreliable. Zárate writes of "ciertas cuerdas de diversas [*sic*] colores añudadas." He concludes that while, "por aquellos nudos y por las distancias dellos se entienden," they do so only, "muy confusamente." *HDC*, "Declaracion," 5–6.
112. Mignolo, *Local*, 11.
113. Leonard, *Baroque*, 50.
114. See Leonard, *Baroque*, 50–52. Stephens provides comprehensive resources for this racial terminology, *Dictionary*, 224, 190, 17. These terms are subjective, and Stephens offers multiple definitions for many of them.
115. We use the term "chronicle" loosely here. Mignolo and Miller distinguish between *Instrucción y memoria*, the *Relación geográfica*, and the *Crónica*, of the three, the only truly literary genre. See Mignolo, "El mandato," 454–62; Miller, "Covert," 44–45.

Chapter 2

1. Some ideas developed in this chapter were presented in Ward, "From the 'People.'" Earlier drafts of several other portions of this chapter, as well as of Chapters 1 and 4, appeared in article form, Ward, "Expanding Ethnicity."
2. Díaz is not a trustworthy or objective commentator. This is especially true in his version of the alleged massacre of a considerable number of people from the altepetl

of the Chololteca. We can, however, divine his attitudes toward native people from his word choices. The only reference to indigenous nations as "nations" occurs in Chapter LXXXVI, when he is not referring to any nation in particular: "no tenían los Mexicanos, ni otras ningunas naciones."

3. Adorno, "Discourses," 246.
4. For an intertextual analysis of Díaz's arguments on Cholula, see Beckjord, "'Con sal.'"
5. Díaz's page numbers that end in an "a" refer to the "Remón" manuscript. Because some folios are mutilated, we refer to the earlier "Guatemala" manuscript with page numbers ending in "b." Variances of cited material will be identified with a footnote.
6. One time, in Chapter VII, he does use the term *países* when referring to some groups (it seems) in Cuba, but again, as in Chapter LXXXVI, without any cultural specificity.
7. In the second "Carta de relación," Hernán Cortés specifically distances indigenous peoples from "naciones de razón," thus clearly denying their nationness.
8. Gibson, "The Identity," 198.
9. Durán, *Historia,* 2:55; *HI,* 92a.
10. Cortés, "The Colegio," 95–97.
11. Adorno, *The Polemics,* 17.
12. As is the case with Domingo Francisco Chimalpahin Cuauhtlehuanitzin.
13. Whittaker, "Aztec Dialectology," 321.
14. For those who object to the inclusion of colonial chronicles into the category of Colonial Literature, we can accept them, per Mignolo's suggestion, simply as colonial texts. "Colonial" in this case refers to a chronology and a socio-economic environment that produced these "texts," preserved discourses archiving collective memory (see Mignolo, "El mandato," 453). It is worth considering the possibility of democratizing of our notion of what is literature to include the chronicle, *testimonio,* and oral expression.
15. Blanco "The Production," 112a.
16. Cornejo Polar, *Escribir,* 88–89.
17. The expression "horizon of understanding" comes from Gadamer. It is precisely from the fusion of the diverse horizons of understanding that we can form a horizon of interpretation. For example, see Gadamer, *Truth and Method,* 214, 317, 415.
18. Adorno, "Literary," 3.
19. Restall, "A History," 126.
20. Earle, "The Role of Print," 22, 25.
21. For a discussion of the *huehuetlatolli,* see Mignolo, *The Darker,* 93, 107, & 209.
22. Restall, *Seven,* xvi.
23. Davies, *The Aztec,* 241.
24. Davies, *The Aztec,* 8.
25. Gillespie, "The Triple," 233.
26. Klor de Alva, "Sahagún," 46.

27. Lienhard, *La voz,* 52.
28. Moraña, *Viaje,* 26.
29. Lienhard, *La voz,* 42; Adorno ("Literary") discusses the particulars of the censorship of Sahagún's works.
30. Bruhns and Stothert, *Women,* 161–63, have argued that because elites and nonelites alike quickly learned to write using the Latin alphabet after the Conquest, marriage brokers needed to consult the codices in their work. They do lament, nevertheless, that "women's knowledge has been lost." Bruhns and Stothert, *Women,* 158.
31. Besides Lockhart, *NS* and *NAC,* see Gibson, *TSC;* Cline, *Colonial;* Wood, "Pedro Villafranca"; Haskett, *Indigenous Rulers;* Horn, "The Sociopolitical"; and Schroeder, *Chimalpahin.*
32. Anzaldúa set up the paradigm for border thinking Mignolo brought to full flower, and has helped me develop my ideas on border osmosis.
33. Gadamer's *Truth and Method* got me thinking about horizons, and from there the application of an ethnic sense to them. In this study, the term "etnia" refers to any ethnic group, not just those traditionally looked down upon by European commentators. The Mexica and the Basques can both be described as etnia.
34. Moreiras, *The Exhaustion,* 14; For him, this "hermeneutic circle is a circle of hegemony." Moreiras, *The Exhaustion,* 15. Naturally, in the case of the Mexica this would indeed be a hegemonic circle, but it is not necessarily so, for it is theoretically possible for two equally powerful cultures to coexist side by side.
35. A. D. Smith, *National,* 43.
36. León-Portilla, *Toltecáyotl,* 13, as quoted and elaborated on in Mignolo, *The Darker,* 141.
37. A. D. Smith, *National,* 29 (his emphasis), 50, 36.
38. Siméon, *Diccionario,* 21a.
39. Horn, "The Sociopolitical," 21.
40. Restall, Sousa, and Terraciano, *Mesoamerican,* 5.
41. See León-Portilla, *La filosofía,* 181–82.
42. Restall, *The Seven,* xvii.
43. Earle, "Menchú Tales," 291.
44. Burgos, *Me llamo,* 227.
45. Tedlock, *Time,* 16.
46. Siméon, *Diccionario,* 306b; Bierhorst, *A Nahuatl-English Dictionary,* 225.
47. Siméon, *Diccionario,* 306b.
48. Leibsohn, "Primers," 169. Her italics.
49. Leibsohn, "Primers," 162, 176.
50. Siméon, *Diccionario,* 62b-63a.
51. Taylor, "Remapping," 1419b.
52. Maravall "La aportación," 524.
53. Rabasa, "Historiografía," 73.
54. Coe, *America's First Civilization,* 23, etc.; Coe and Koontz, *Mexico from the Olmecs to the Aztecs,* 16–17; Davies, *The Ancient Kingdoms,* 11. The Olmecs, of course,

constituted an earlier, non-Nahua cultural configuration, and there are other non-Nahua cultural configurations, such as the Mixteca and Zapoteca.

55. For Rocío Cortés, the Templo Mayor was formed by two pyramids of equal dimensions, one dedicated to Huitzilopochtli and one to Tlaloc, "¿Dónde está Tlaloc?" 343. Another interpretation is that Huitzilopochtli embodied Mexicayotl and, in an era when Teotihuacan was thought to have been Toltec, Tlaloc embodied Toltecayotl. Later, as noted by Rivera Domínguez, precisely these three deities—Tlaloc, Quetzalcoatl, and Huitzilopochtli—made themselves felt in novo-Hispanic conceptions of the Virgin and of the saints. "Conflicto," 82.
56. Mignolo, *The Darker,* 242, 243.
57. See Daneri, "¿Tloque Nahuaque o dios desconocido?"
58. See Davies, *The Aztec Empire,* 27.
59. Davies, *The Toltecs,* 167–71, 349–414.
60. Nicholson, *Topiltzin Quetzalcoatl,* 82.
61. The Olmeca were actually centered to the south, but their influence was felt in the central basin.
62. Lesure, "Figurine," 379, 381.
63. Meyer, *Teotihuacan,* 17.
64. Diehl, *Tula,* 14.
65. Clendinnen, *Aztecs,* 23.
66. A. D. Smith, *National,* 35–36.
67. Calnek, "Patterns," 52–53.
68. Clendinnen, *Aztecs,* 21.
69. A good place to begin would be Anzaldúa, *Borderlands/La Frontera.* Mignolo's *Local Histories/Global Designs* brings it all together and includes ample bibliography.
70. Cortés, "The Colegio," 95–97, and 100–101.
71. Mignolo, *The Darker,* 35, was referring to seventeenth-century European conclusions about indigenous peoples, but the paradigm he derives from his reading of Aldrete can also be applied to power structures of pre-Cortesian society.
72. "[René] Acuña establece que el título *Historia de Tlaxcala* es totalmente inventado y que el auténtico y único es *Descripción de la ciudad y provincia de la Nueva España y Indias del Mar Océano, para el buen gobierno y el ennoblecimiento dellas, mandada hacer por la Sacra Católica Real rey Don Felipe nuestro.*" Mignolo, "El mandato," 454; Rocío Cortés confirms this text was born as a *relación geográfica,* "The Colegio," 101, one of various subgenres in the general category "chronicle."
73. Niza's history has been lost. Cortés, "The Colegio," 96.
74. Miller, "Covert," 44.
75. Miller, "Covert," 45.
76. Gibson, "The Identity," 200.
77. Vázquez, in *HT,* 11–12.
78. Gibson, "The Identity," 200.
79. For a discussion of the indigenous use of the "don," see *NS,* 33; *NAC,* 513, 162n & 587, 6n.

80. Gibson, "The Identity," 201–3.
81. Mörner and Gibson, "Diego Muñoz Camargo," 564.
82. Gibson, "The Identity," 202.
83. Mörner and Gibson, "Diego Muñoz Camargo," 566.
84. Mörner and Gibson, "Diego Muñoz Camargo," 567.
85. In *Royal Commentaries,* Garcilaso writes, "este nombre *vecino* se entendía en el Perú por los españoles que tenían repartimiento de indios." *CR,* "Advertencias." The same was true for New Spain. See also Fuenzalida Vollmar, *La matriz,* 11–12; Keith, *Conquest.*
86. The *Historia de Tlaxcala* is a reworking of an early version of the *Descripción de la ciudad y provincia de Tlaxcala* (see Miller, "Covert," 41–42). The *Descripción* and the *Historia,* despite sharing many textual passages, were different works (see Mignolo, "El mandato," 452, 3n).
87. Those who lived in that "era" (*HT,* 97), "época" (*HT,* 108), or time (*HT,* 113).
88. Gibson, "The Identity," 200.
89. Miller, "Covert," 43. For more on this and on travel writing in Muñoz Camargo and Alva Ixtlilxóchitl in general, see Voigt, "Peregrine," 5, etc.
90. Miller, "Covert," 48.
91. *Oxford English Dictionary,* online version, s.v. "demonym," accessed February 6, 2017. The *OED* cites the first use of this word as occurring in *National Geographic* in 1990, and it was used recently in *The New Yorker.*
92. Horn, "The Sociopolitical," 27.
93. Davies, *The Aztecs,* 135
94. See Davies, *The Aztecs,* 163, 198.
95. Miller, "Covert," 47, 46.
96. Cortés, "The Colegio," 88.
97. Gillespie questions the use of the term *Triple Alliance* when referring to pre-Cortesian political relationships between Tenochtitlan, Tetzcoco, and Tlacopan. By using it, I do not mean to imply the three elements of this triadic power arrangement were equal to each other. The Mexica, needless to say, were preeminent. Davies (*Aztec,* 42–43) gives credence to the notion of a Triple Alliance. For Velazco, the alliance's origins can be found in Mexico-Tenochtitlan's military support for Nezahualcoyotl's return to Acolhuacan after the death of Azcapotzalco's tlatoani Tezozomoc. *Visiones,* 77. While there still may be a great deal to learn, there must have been a reason for Hernán Cortés to assassinate the tlatoque of precisely these three cities (*OH,* 1: 503).
98. On the Colegio, see Cortés, "The Colegio," 101.
99. García Loaeza, "Fernando de Alva Ixtlilxochitl's Texcocan," 220.
100. Brian, "The Alva Ixtlilxochitl Brothers," 201–18.
101. See Paz, *Sor Juana,* 65. The other great baroque figure of Mexico is Sor Juana Inés de la Cruz, dealt with in the subsequent section.
102. Kauffmann, "Figures," 37.
103. Ong, *Orality,* 8.
104. Mignolo, *The Darker,* 140.

105. Townsend, "Polygyny," 96; García Loaeza, "Fernando de Alva Ixtlilxochitl's Texcocan," 233.
106. Blanco, "The Production," 11b.
107. The idea of the chronicler translating millenary culture for Old World sensibilities comes from Julio Ortega.
108. Adorno, "Arms," 217, 219.
109. See Adorno, "Arms," 216.
110. See Adorno, "Arms," 210–13. Because of historians' and critics' efforts to insert Alva Ixtlilxóchitl into a binary paradigm, and because of philological mysteries surrounding his manuscripts (some now being resolved by Brian, "The Original Alva Ixtlilxochitl Manuscripts"), Nicholson describes the chronicler as "the number one problem child of Central Mexican ethnohistory." *Topiltzin Quetzalcoatl*, 113.
111. Or, "those barbarous proper-named nations."
112. On Alva Ixtlilxóchitl's Chichimecatl lineage, see Vásquez, "Introducción," *Historia de la nación chichimeca*, 59, 7n.
113. Siméon, *Diccionario*, 95a.
114. On Alva Ixtlilxóchitl's reconfiguration of the time line, see Velazco, *Visiones*, 43–126.
115. For the Spanish as a conglomeration of ethnic groups, see the next section below.
116. Mignolo, *The Darker*, chapter 1.
117. Mignolo, *The Darker*, 141.
118. Mignolo, *The Darker*, 141.
119. Another interesting field of study is the Spanish appropriation of Nahua food in Mexico and why that happened there and not in Peru, for example.
120. Paz, *El laberinto*, 28. Paz concomitantly comments on a gulf between Old and New World attitudes toward life, for example, when he contrasts the views of two playwrights from the Golden Age, Lope de Vega from Spain and Ruiz de Alarcón, from New Spain. *El Laberinto*, 30. Similarly, when we talk of parallels between Spanish and Nahua modes of being, we do so acknowledging there were also differences. The obvious ones were language, the nonformal elements of religion, etc.
121. Davies, *Aztec Empire*, 40.
122. A. D. Smith, *National*, 40.
123. Gott, "Latin America," 273.
124. Another of Bailyn's titles also suggests North America was a virgin territory: *Voyagers to the West: a Passage in the Peopling of America*, while another, written under the influence of Samuel Huntington, *The Barbarous Years: the Peopling of British North America* (2012), does allow for the presence of "people" from different continents (he includes Africa in the equation).
125. This is somewhat different from the nineteenth-century Alberdi's more nuanced assertion that "to govern is to populate" (gobiernar es poblar), which seems to have more with an educational policy. He clarifies, "poblar es educar, mejorar, civilizar, enriquecer, y engrandecer espontánea y rápidamente como ha sucedido en *Estados Unidos*." Alberdi, "Gobernar es poblar," 266. However, when he, writing

in 1872, likens what he is proposing to "what has happened in the United States" we cannot help but think of US government Indian policies.

126. Clendinnen, *The Aztecs,* 18.
127. Livi-Bacci, "The Depopulation," 199.
128. See Mignolo, "El mandato," 462.
129. Jackson, *Race,* 4.
130. Lockhart, Berdan, and Anderson, *The Tlaxcalan Actas,* 1.
131. Esteva-Fabregat, *Mestizaje,* 39.
132. For a slightly different interpretation of "nosotros" in Muñoz Camargo, see Miller, "Covert," 44.
133. Quijano explains that "coloniality of power is based upon 'racial' social classification of the world population under Eurocentered world power." "Coloniality," 171.
134. Alva Ixtlilxóchitl likewise uses the expression "nuestros españoles" several times in the *Sumaria relación,* as a point of comparison to the Tolteca, as different from the historical Chichimeca, and as enemies of the former tlatoani Quinazin's allies, as well as when "Nuestros españoles" were arriving in New Spain. *OC,* I, 274, 289, 546–47.
135. Adorno, "Arms," 116.
136. Leonard, *Baroque,* 172.
137. Galaviz, *Juana Inés,* 18.
138. Paz, *Sor Juana,* 179.
139. Benassy-Berling, *Humanismo,* 286–88.
140. Moraña, *Viaje,* 214.
141. See Benassy-Berling, *Humanismo,* 289.
142. Moraña, *Viaje,* 210–13.
143. Benassy-Berling, *Humanismo,* 309; Zanelli "La loa,'" 194.
144. See Moraña, *Viaje,* 32.
145. Nations as ethnic communities can still be seen in Spain, but it is polemical to view them as such. Herzog notes the presence during the twentieth century of "regional nationalists, who affirmed the existence of separate nations in each of the Iberian kingdoms and Spanish nationalists, who denied it." *Defining Nations,* 10. By describing these ideological differences, Herzog hints the etymological notion of the nation, and the early modern, post-1492 notion of Spain.
146. Paz, *Sor Juana,* 26.
147. On the wider European experience, see Lienhard, *La voz,* 22–23.
148. Las Casas (*Brevísima*) would later appreciate the five kingdoms of Hispaniola.
149. Vespucio, *Cartas,* 30–31.
150. Hobsbawm, *Nations,* 46–47.
151. Anderson, *Imagined,* 82–83.
152. Mignolo, *The Darker,* 46. Restall concurs, "there was no campaign to force natives to learn Spanish." *Seven,* 75.
153. Rocío Cortés explains the emerging interest in Hispanization: "in the face of the

Counter-Reformation and emerging social pressures in an established colony, colonial policies would turn to favor further the economic goals of colonization by Hispanicizing the natives." "The Colegio," 92.

154. Mignolo, *The Darker*, 46, 52, 53.
155. Mignolo, *The Darker*, 53, 59; Lockhart, *NAC*.
156. Acosta, *Historia natural*, 3, 5, 7.
157. Esteva-Fabregat, *Mestizaje*, 2.
158. Phelan reviews the mendicant's unheeded concerns (especially Mendieta's) on why the indigenous should not be Hispanized. *The Millennial*, 86–91.
159. Kauffmann, "Figures," 34. Italics removed.
160. Haskett, "Our Suffering," 448.
161. Ortiz, *Contrapunteo*, 260.
162. Las Casas, *Historia*, 1:22.
163. Mörner and Gibson, "Diego Muñoz Camargo," 561.

Chapter 3

1. Ospina, *Ursúa*, 36.
2. There remains much to do in addressing enduring colonialist attitudes enshrined frequently in scholarship, even in our time. For examples, see Ward, *Decolonizing Indigeneity*, 20–26.
3. For a further discussion of the inversion of the established and colonialist view of civilization as a decolonial methodology applied specifically to Alva Ixtlilxóchitl, see Ward, *Decolonizing Indigeneity*, 110–26.
4. The Maya had a script, but this was not fully understood until the twentieth century. See Coe, *Breaking the Maya Code*.
5. Verdesio, "Latin America," 341.
6. See Ross, "Historians," 121.
7. Hampe Martínez, "La misión," 112.
8. Ross, "Historians," 120–21.
9. Maddox, *Removals*, 24.
10. Wade, "Patterns," 4.
11. Pease, "Estudio preliminar," ix-x.
12. Rappaport and Cummins, *Beyond*, 1–3.
13. Juan and Judith Villamarín suggest the chronicles are valuable for their ethnographic information: "Despite sixteenth-century European biases, misunderstandings, exaggerations, and flights of imagination, the early works contribute substantially to our knowledge of contact-period South Americans, often with incisive and pertinent descriptions particularly regarding contrasts in political complexity of different groups." Villamarín and Villamarín, "Chiefdoms," 578.
14. Pratt develops the idea of a "contact zone" in *Imperial Eyes*.
15. Markham, *The Incas*, 3.
16. Markham, *The Incas*, 4.
17. Helms, "The Indians," 40.

18. Wade, "Patterns," 13.
19. Qosqo is the present-day Qheswa spelling, Cusco is the preferred Spanish-language spelling in Peru.
20. Londoño Vélez and Villegas, *Colombian Art,* 11–80.
21. Parsons, *Antioquia's Corridor,* 5; Gordon, *Human,* 33. *Webster's New Collegiate Dictionary* defines "cacique" as "an Indian chief" (203b).
22. Duncan, *Hernando de Soto,* 29.
23. Duncan, *Hernando de Soto,* 20; also Porras Barrenechea, *Pizarro,* 31–42.
24. T. L. Smith, "The Racial," 222.
25. Cieza's chronicle poorly distinguishes between the two San Sebastiáns, the first, San Sebastián de Urabá, and the second, San Sebastián de Buena Vista. The first, short-lived and more like a fort, was founded by Spaniards around 1515, constituting their first settlement on the mainland. The second, according to Cieza, was founded and populated by Alonso de Heredia. *CP-1*[era], fol. 20v, p. 46. Melo explains that this San Sebastián was founded by Heredia in 1535, "probablemente en sitio cercano a donde había estado San Sebastián de Urabá." *Historia,* 91. Both towns then would be at or near the present-day municipality of Necoclí. Since Sebastián de Buena Vista was abandoned after 1547, other towns of this name represent third and fourth attempts at founding a homonymous municipality. There was a short-lived attempt at Urabá by a *vecino* of Cartagena after 1550 or so and, according to Parsons, there was an early eighteenth-century San Sebastián on the Sinú river populated by both Spanish and indigenous peoples. Parsons, *Antioquia's Corridor,* 14; San Sebastián de Urabá was something of a Who's Who of the Conquest, with the likes of Alonso de Hojeda, Francisco Pizarro, and Vasco Núñez de Balboa passing through. Parsons, *Antioquia's Corridor,* 7–8.
26. MacCormack, *Religion,* 199.
27. Melo, *Historia,* 41.
28. Villamarín and Villamarín, "Chiefdoms," 598.
29. T. L. Smith states, "The Catíos lived along the Atrato, the Sierra de Abibe, and extended to the Gulf of Urabá." "The Racial," 222. The Embera people are sometimes known as the Cocó. The Emberá-Wounaan are thriving in present-day Darien province, Panama.
30. For a discussion of text, literature, orality, and weaving see Ong, *Orality,* 13.
31. Murra, "Andean," 77.
32. Helms, "The Indians," 40.
33. Lehmann, "The Moguex-Coconuco," 969.
34. Melo, *Historia,* 41.
35. Lehmann, "The Moguex-Coconuco," 973.
36. Troyan, *Cauca's Indigenous,* 8.
37. Mazzotti, *Coros,* 69.
38. Villamarín and Villamarín, "Chiefdoms," 579.
39. Covey, *How,* 206.
40. Lehmann, "The Moguex-Coconuco," 969.

41. Velasco, *Historia,* 287.
42. Lehmann, "The Moguex-Coconuco," 971, 972.
43. Rappaport, *The Politics,* 7.
44. Rappaport, *The Politics,* 18.
45. Calero, *Chiefdoms,* xi.
46. T. L. Smith, "The Racial," 232.
47. Sánchez-Albornoz, "The Population," 5; Wade, "Patterns," 13.
48. Wade, "Patterns," 13.
49. Porras Barrenechea writes: "La posición de Cieza es netamente contraria a los conquistadores y equilibrada para juzgar a los indios." *Fuentes,* 151.
50. Like with San Sebastián, Cieza does not always make his geographical referents precise in a geographic and political plane expanding so fast the Spanish had to scramble in their quest for toponymic nomenclature.
51. Pérez Fernández, *Bartolomé de las Casas,* 427. Cieza actually sent his manuscripts to Las Casas. On this and on Cieza and Las Casas in general, see Pease, "Estudio," xii.
52. Porras Barrenechea, *Pizarro,* 35; On the signifier "Indian" and how it negates culture, ethnicity, and even nationness, see Ward, *Decolonizing Indigeneity,* 26–29.
53. Moseley, "Structure," 2.
54. Bruhns, *Ancient,* 5.
55. Mann, "Unraveling," 1008. We will examine in detail the relationship between the khipu and the notion of Qheswa later in this chapter.
56. Zuidema, *Reyes,* 204.
57. Larson, *Trials,* 21.
58. Kauffmann Doig explains that the Chimú drew not only on the Moche, but also the Tiwanaku-Wari. "Los liberteños," 571–72.
59. Shimada, *Pampa,* 259.
60. García Bryce, *Crafting,* 23.
61. Menéndez y Pelayo, *Orígenes,* 2:153.
62. Durand, *El Inca,* 55–56.
63. It may say something about standard mentalities of empire that while I was writing this book, President Bush declared the president of the Republic of Iraq a tyrant and then used this depiction (true in several ways, but not others) to justify the invasion of that country.
64. Flores Galindo, *Obras,* 3.1:49.
65. I am thinking of Polo de Ondegardo. Porras Barrenechea explains that Polo was motivated by the "interés de implantar un buen sistema de tributación y por la idea de probar el justo título del Rey de España en las Indias." *Los cronistas,* 38.
66. While I use the term "Forty-Years War" to describe this period, many scholars continue to think of a one-year conquest despite its inappropriateness for many regions. That "the Conquest" took forty years in Perú has been suggested as early as 1993 by Mercedes López-Baralt: "Pues en el Perú la conquista no duró un año ni dos: entre 1532, el año que marca la captura de Atahualpa a manos de Pizarro, y 1572, fecha de la muerte del primer Tupac Amaru por orden del virrey Toledo, hay

cuarenta años de resistencia." *Guaman Poma,* 33–34.

67. Covey, *How,* 96, 190.
68. Rostworowski de Diez Canseco, *Historia,* 97. Covey renders the same idea: "The Inca state thus formed in a region characterized by a high degree of ethnic diversity." *How,* 10.
69. As mentioned in a previous note, despite giving preference to the spelling norms of the Academia Mayor de la Lengua Qheswa (Qosqo), we are respecting the spelling of authors' names as published, thus Inca Garcilaso and not Inka Garcilaso. The one exception is Zárate, who spelt his last name with an initial "C" with cedilla, but now is exclusively referred to with an initial "Z" in the spelling.
70. Sarmiento de Gamboa, *Historia,* en Garcilaso de la Vega, *Obras,* vol. 4, ch. 63, p. 266b.
71. The "Chancas" may have spoken Qheswa or Puquina or both. They seem to have been organized as Hanan and Urin moieties. Here I will use the Qheswa spelling to refer to them in the plural.
72. *CR,* I, v; Camayd-Freixas, "Enunciating," 113, also 115.
73. Murra, "Andean," 68.
74. Topic, "Craft," 150.
75. Murra, "Andean," 73.
76. As discussed in Murra, "Andean," 69.
77. Mignolo, *The Darker,* 301.
78. Mignolo, *The Darker,* 297.
79. Zuidema, *The Ceque,* 39; 7, 5n; 185.
80. Waskar was spelled Huáscar in Spanish; Atawallpa, Atahualpa; and Wayna Qhapaq, Huayna Cápac.
81. Rowe, *Los Incas,* 45.
82. Zuidema, *The Ceque,* 123.
83. Davies, *The Incas,* 170–71.
84. Rowe, *Los Incas,* 17; Murra, "Andean," 81.
85. Rostworowski and Morris, "The Fourfold," 780.
86. Sarmiento, *Historia,* ch. xiv, in Garcilaso, *Obras,* 4:219b, 220a, 219b.
87. Siméon, *Diccionario,* 305b.
88. Cerrón-Palomino notes that Runa Simi, like Qheswa, is a postcontact term that came into usage to distinguish it from *Castilla Simi,* language of Spaniards, "Sobre," 94–95.
89. Kauffmann Doig points out "Mochica" and "Yunga" were terms referring to the language spoken by the Moche people at the time Spaniards arrived. "Los liberteños," 576–77.
90. Mannheim, *The Language,* 64; Cerrón-Palomino, "Sobre," 89, attributes the source of the glottonym to Domingo de Santo Tomás.
91. Torero, *Idiomas,* 124.
92. Torero, *Idiomas,* 45, 47, 48, 127.
93. Torero, *Idiomas,* 51, 56, 89–90, 127; Mannheim, *The Language,* 64.

94. Torero, *Idiomas,* 54.
95. See Crowley, *Garcilaso,* 122; Torero, *Idiomas,* 90; Mannheim, *The Language,* 65; Durston, *Pastoral Quechua,* 38–49.
96. Mannheim, *The Language,* 65–66; and especially Durston, *Pastoral Quechua.*
97. Murúa, *Historia,* Libro II, cap. xii, p. 364. Linguists prefer different names for the Aymara language, especially in its historical trajectory. Hardman suggested Jaqi, Torero prefers Aru. Here I use "Aymara" to simplify reading, as it is the name with which most readers will be familiar. For Aymara and Qheswa diffusion geographically, see maps 6 and 7.
98. Matto, *Leyendas,* 91–92; Torero, *Idiomas,* 136; Sometimes it is difficult to ascertain Torero's intended meaning. On the one hand, he writes, "El estrato lingüístico más antiguo asignable al área cuzqueña y al linaje de los incas es, sin duda, el aru 'quichua' (o 'quechua,' para el cual estamos acuñando el apelativo de 'cundi' a fin de evitar la confusión que ha existido prácticamente desde el momento de la conquista española." *Idiomas,* 135. Because we now suspect Aymara was the substratum of Cuzco, the idea of some kind of Qheswa being the substratum is confusing. On the other hand, he contradicts himself when he corrects this confusion: "el 'idioma particular' de los incas sería básicamente una de tantas variedades del aru cundi" (136), which makes much more sense.
99. Espinoza Soriano, *Los incas,* 37; Szemiński, "Un texto," 379–89. Cerrón-Palomino, *Las lenguas,* 59, 217, etc., also argues for Puquina as the Inkan private language.
100. Torero, *Idiomas,* 157
101. Torero, *Idiomas,* 146.
102. Inka Thupaq Yupanki's sister consort, Mama Oqllo, bore him six legitimate sons. The fourth, Huallpa Thupaq Inka Yupanki. had two children with his wife, Cusi Chimbo, the *auki* Huallpa Thupaq Inka Yupanki and the *palla* Chimpu Oqllo, Garcilaso's mother. See Varner, *The Life,* 8.
103. Hyland, *The Jesuit,* 197.
104. Regarding women weavers, see Bruhns and Stothert, *Women.* Concerning the polemics surrounding Valera, see chapters 9 and 10 of Hyland, *The Jesuit.*
105. I have already discussed this relationship briefly elsewhere. Ward, "Modern Nativist Readings," 171–89. Because this issue is germane to the matter at hand, I must go over it again, albeit with a different perspective and with some other varieties of sources. We focus here on the sixteenth century and the time before the arrival of the Spanish, not as a problem debated in the nineteenth, as is the case with "Modern Nativist Readings."
106. Guaman Poma names this captain who subdued the Qheswakuna more fully as Auqui Topa Inga Yupanki, but describes him as the son of Qhapaq Yupanki. *PNC,* 154 (154).
107. On the evolution of structures toward hacienda, see Keith, "Encomienda" and Lockhart, *Of Things.*
108. Miró Quesada, "Cronología," 286.
109. Matto, *Leyendas,* 91–92; her italics and caps removed.

110. Matto, *Leyendas,* 96, for example.
111. Torero, *Idiomas*, 93.
112. Torero, *Idiomas*, 124; Espinoza Soriano, *Los incas*, 37; Proulx simply states that Aymara occupied the southern coast up to Lima and suggests concomitantly that "Aymara once occupied areas considerably further north that is presently the case." "Quechua," 92.
113. Cerrón-Palomino, "El aimara," 10; Isbell argues that proto-Qheswa was spoken in the Wari realm. "La arqueología," 199–220. His proposal, in this linguistic darkness, is at odds with most other research. If Qheswa was Cuzco's pre-Inkan language, why would they wait until the eleventh sovereign Wayna Qhapaq to declare it the general language? If Isbell were correct, it would throw out Garcilaso's statement, and Hardman, Torero, and Cerrón-Palomino's research. Obviously, more investigation is required.
114. Cerrón-Palomino, "El aimara," 11.
115. Regarding the development of the Incas from Wari stock, see Covey, *How*.
116. Torero, *Idiomas*, 48, 55, 124.
117. Proulx, "Quechua," 97.
118. Hardman, "Aymara," 627.
119. Hardman, "Aymara," 627.
120. Cerrón-Palomino, "El Nebrija," viii. In a sort of amateurish yet interesting book, Oblitas Poblete argued the Incas spoke Callawaya, a variant of Puquina. However, he argues that this stemmed not from origins of the Incas, but because the Callawaya people were great practitioners of medicine, a profession that allowed them to gain access to the Incas and share their language, which became the Inca's "secret language." See Oblitas Poblete, *La lengua*, 25–27.
121. Part of the problem is the terminology employed and exactly what is meant in the range of terms, including "official tongue," "private tongue," "secret tongue," and "maternal tongue."
122. Hardman, "Aymara," 628. For further discussion on the three Inkan languages with additional bibliography, see Cerrón-Palomino, "Estudio," xii-xiii.
123. Cerrón-Palomino, "El Nebrija," vi; Cerrón-Palomino, "Sobre," 88.
124. See Romero Galván, "Los cronistas," 284; J. Lee, *The Allure*, 193–228.
125. For further discussion, see Ward, *Decolonizing Indigeneity*, 125–26; See also Daneri, "¿Tloque Nahuaque o dios desconocido?"
126. Porras Barrenechea, *Fuentes*, 24.
127. Uhle, "La posición histórica," quoted in Cerrón-Palomino, "Examen," 93.
128. Cerrón-Palomino, "El aimara," 12.
129. Antawaylla in Qheswa, Andahuaylas in Spanish.
130. González Holguín, *Vocabulario*, 300.
131. Fornee, *Descripción de la tierra*, 27.
132. Matto, *Leyendas*, 93.
133. González Holguín, *Vocabulario*, 300.
134. Matto, *Leyendas*, 93.

135. González Holguín, *Vocabulario,* 307.
136. On the khipu, see Urton, *Signs;* Radicati di Primeglio, *Estudios;* Fernández Lancho, *Escritura;* and Salomon, *Khipus.*
137. Villar, *Lingüística,* 15.
138. Covey, *How,* 186.
139. Villar, *Lingüística,* 3.
140. Europeans referred to the Caribbean basin as the "West Indies" to differentiate that region from the East Indies, what is today India, China, Vietnam, and other Asiatic countries.
141. Also published in 1492 was his *Diccionario latino-español.* His *Diccionario espanol-latino* appeared two years later. Other works followed.
142. Durand, "La biblioteca," 249.
143. Aldrete, *Del origen,* 1:356 (two pages are numbered 356, and the reference is to the second one).
144. Durand, *El Inca,* 145.
145. It is curious that recent DNA testing reveals the DNA in Spaniards from the Bell-Beaker culture that seems to have moved in both northerly and southerly directions in Europe around 2000 BC, but shows no trace of Visigoths, Vandals, or Suevi, peoples we know emigrated to the Iberian Peninsula during the fifth and sixth centuries. See Patterson et al., "Ancient," 1080–81.
146. Aldrete, *Del origen,* 1:360.
147. Aldrete, *Del origen,* 1:139; synthesized in Mignolo, *The Darker,* 30.
148. Aldrete, *Del origen,* 1:362.
149. Mignolo, *The Darker,* 30–32.
150. Aldrete, *Del origen,* 1:144.
151. Fornee, *Descripción,* 17; Referring to other towns, San Antón de Chinchaypuquio, La Visitación de Nuestra Señora de Zamoro, La Encarnación Pantipata, and Santiago Pivil, Fornee writes simply, "la lengua que en estos pueblos se habla es la general." *Descripción,* 21. In each of the remaining quadripartite town clusters, he states, they speak the General Language, either from laziness, or because those ayllukuna had been completely Qheswaized.
152. Aldrete, *Del origen,* 1:144.
153. Mignolo, *The Darker,* 32.
154. Mignolo, *The Darker,* 31.
155. On Garcilaso's relationship to Aldrete, see Durand, *El Inca,* 138, 139, and 138, 1n.
156. Durand, *El Inca,* 145.
157. Aldrete, *Del origen,* 1:356, n* (the first p. 356 of two).
158. As argued by Fernández, "Traducción," 93–104. In our time, there are editions of Valera's work, such as Carrillo's short anthology. For a discussion of Garcilaso's citing of Valera's works, see Hyland, *The Jesuit,* 72–81.
159. Markham, *The Incas,* 12.
160. Markham, *The Incas,* 13.
161. Hyland, *The Jesuit,* 1–2.

162. Markham, *The Incas,* 13.
163. Mannheim, "Una nación," 293.
164. Torero, *Idiomas*, 384.
165. Torero, *Idiomas*, 389; also Pérez Fernández, *Bartolomé de las Casas,* 466.
166. Mannheim, "Una nación," 293; see also Durston, *Pastoral Quechua.*
167. Belarminio, *Declaración*, n.p.
168. Hyland mentions another, Bartolomé de Santiago, *The Jesuit*, 64; On December 14, 1582, the Jesuits voted to prohibit additional mestizos from ordination. Hyland, *The Jesuit*, 179.
169. Walker, *The Tupac*, 259, 269.
170. On the 1981 census, see Klee, "The Acquisition," 402; on the 1993 census, see Comisión de la Verdad, *Informe final*, Conclusiones generales, 1.6.
171. See the *Informe final* of the Comisión de la Verdad y Reconciliación, 160; Anexo 2, 17.
172. Stanish, *Ancient*, 65. There were other substantial cultures, such as the Moche and Chimú, which succeeded it on the north coast of present-day Peru.
173. Villamarín and Villamarín, "Chiefdoms," 583; see also *UN,* 134.
174. For more on Pizarro's daughter, see Rostworowski, *Doña Francisca.*
175. For more on the proper name of Peru, see Porras Barrenechea, *El nombre del Perú.*
176. de Ballester, *Tomo primero*, 127.
177. de Ballester, *Tomo primero*, 126a.
178. de Ballester, *Tomo primero*, 126(dorso)a.
179. Murra, "Andean," 68, 65–66.
180. Arguedas, *Formación*, 90.
181. Andrien, *Andean*, 57, 50.
182. "Jacaru," *Ethnologue: Languages of the World,* www.ethnologue.com/language/jqr (accessed July 20, 2017).
183. Fuenzalida Vollmar, *La matriz*; see also Keith, *Conquest,* 45.
184. Ramírez, *The World*, 25, 26, 12.
185. Cahill, "The Inca," 94, 95, 106.
186. Andrien, *Andean*, 45.
187. Andrien, *Andean*, 50. Italics removed.
188. Riva-Agüero, *Obras,* 4:174.
189. Wallerstein, *The Modern*, 350.
190. Undeniably, the violence could be military, and it could be unleashed with the quill. This is one of the theses of José Rabasa's *Writing Violence* (2000) and of Anibal González's *Killer Books* (2001).
191. Castro Arenas, *La rebelión*; López Baralt, *Guaman Poma,* 34.
192. Arguedas, *Formación,* 71.
193. Arguedas, *Formación*, 40, 173–79.
194. Brotherston, "Indigenous," 291.
195. López-Baralt, *Guaman Poma,* 34.
196. López Baralt, *Guaman Poma,* 40.

197. Arguedas, *Formación*, 173–82.
198. For Cornejo Polar's take on the flag's incorporation, which he calls *azaroso*, perilous, see *Escribir*, 52.
199. Flores Galindo, *Obras*, 3.1:238.
200. As Fernández Cozman shows, Porras Barrenechea introduced the concept of transculturation for the first time in Peruvian historical and literary studies with his 1969 *El sentido tradicional en la literatura peruana* (*Raúl Porras*). For a comparison between "transculturación" and "heterogeneity," see Sobrevilla, "Transculturación y heterogeneidad."
201. Fernández Cozman, *Raúl Porras*, 81, first observed this pre-Ángel Rama use of the term in Peru (also, 85). Rama's book *La transculturación narrativa en Latinoamérica* came out in 1982.

Chapter 4

1. Alarcón, Kaplan, and Moallem, "Introduction," 2.
2. Fernández, "*No hay nación*," 27.
3. Kaplen and Grewal, "Transnational," 349.
4. Yuval-Davis, *Gender*, 2.
5. Yuval-Davis, *Gender*, 3.
6. Yuval-Davis, *Gender*, 2.
7. Yuval-Davis, *Gender*, 27.
8. Franco, *Critical*, 71.
9. Domingo, *Naissance*, 285–86.
10. Butler, *Gender Trouble*, 43–44.
11. Silverblatt, *Moon*, xxvi.
12. Silverblatt, *Moon*, xxvii.
13. Bruhns and Stothert, *Women*, 134.
14. Nuttall, *The Codex*, 44; For a discussion on this woman leader, Lady Nine Grass Death, see Bruhns and Stothert, *Women*, 186–89.
15. Bruhns and Stothert, *Women*, 234.
16. Nash, "The Aztecs," 349.
17. Castro-Klarén, "Huamán Poma," 46.
18. Bruhns and Stothert, *Women*, 133.
19. Blanco, "The Production," 113a-113b.
20. For recent research on Spanish women during that period, see Pumar Martínez, *Españolas en Indias*; Maura, *Women*.
21. León-Portilla, *La filosofía*, 179–88.
22. Caso, *El pueblo*, 18, 19. For Caso, Chalchiuhtlicue was not Tlaloc's wife, but his sister, *El pueblo*, 59. See also Clendinnen, *Aztecs*, 168.
23. Klor de Alva, "Sahagún," 39.
24. Bruhns and Stothert, *Women*, 147, 263, 134, 147.
25. Calnek, "Patterns," 58.
26. Durán, *Historia*, 2:55.

27. Rounds, "Dynastic," 66.
28. Durán, *Historia*, 2:52.
29. Calnek, "Patterns," 48–49; Davies, *The Aztec*, 24.
30. Smith, *National*, 29, explains this notion of feeling.
31. Cline, *Colonial*, 115.
32. Nash, "The Aztecs," 352.
33. Nash, "The Aztecs," 355.
34. Bruhns and Stothert, *Women*, 235. This Atotoztli should not be confused with the earlier Atotoztli, the mother of Acamapichtli. It is also possible she shared power with another male authority, Cihuacoatl (Tlacaelel).
35. Davies, *The Aztecs*, 125.
36. Rounds, "Dynastic," 75.
37. Rounds, "Dynastic," 66.
38. Clendinnen, *Aztecs*, 207.
39. Calnek, "Patterns," 58.
40. Maravall, *Utopía*, 130.
41. Maravall, *Utopía*, 131; Cieza de León, *CP-1*^{era}, fol. 4, p. 8.
42. An entire series of captivity narratives documents this fear. A good place to begin would be Voigt, *Writing Captivity*.
43. Franco, *Critical*, 71.
44. Franco, *Critical*, 71–72.
45. See Fernández Herrero, *La utopía*, 97.
46. For a discussion of purity of blood in a European and Global context, see Mignolo, *Local*, 27–33, and beyond.
47. Paz, *Sor Juana*, 48.
48. Bacigalupo, *A Changing*, 28.
49. Morison, *Admiral of the Ocean Sea*, 291. Adorno reports Guinea was "a general term for the west coast of Africa that later became known as the Slave Coast," *The Polemics*, 67.
50. For Rocío Cortés, the association of Hernán Cortés with Quetzalcoatl became codified in Book 12 of the Florentine Codex, "Motecuzoma/Huémac," 30. Given that Sahagún had to hide this manuscript, Muñoz may not have had access to it. But the story must have certainly also been in the air.
51. Franco discerns that Díaz del Castillo viewed Doña Marina more favorably than did Cortés and López de Gómara in their writings. *Critical*, 69.
52. Adorno, *The Polemics*, 166.
53. Adorno, "Discourses" 257.
54. See Gibson, "The Identity," 195.
55. Mörner and Gibson, "Diego Muñoz Camargo." The historian Muñoz Camargo married a woman of nobility, but as Gibson reports, his mother was not. Gibson, "The Identity," 200, 205.
56. Bruhns and Stothert, *Women*, 235.
57. Davies, *The Aztecs*, 295.

58. Lavrin, "Sexuality," 61–77.
59. Mörner and Gibson, "Diego Muñoz Camargo," 562.
60. Adorno, "Literary," 7.
61. Lavrin "Sexuality," 79.
62. Paz, *Sor Juana*, 26.
63. Benassy-Berling, *Humanismo*, 22–24.
64. Gruzinski, "Individualization," 109.
65. Cline, "The Spiritual," 472–73.
66. Cline, "The Spiritual," 475.
67. Leonard, *Baroque*, 45.
68. Esteva-Fabregat, *Mestizaje*, 35.
69. See Cline, "The Spiritual," 479–80.
70. Blanco, "The Production," 112b.
71. For a discussion of endogamy and exogamy later in the colonial period, see Jackson, *Race*, 43–45.
72. Wachtel, "The Indian," 212.
73. Haskett, "Our Suffering," 451, 453, 452.
74. Lavrin, "Sexuality," 56.
75. Despite the strange rejection of Paz by some scholars, he has advanced the discussion. Franco addresses this issue: "To refer to La Malinche as La Chingada restores the violence of the conquest, which seems to fade into the background for Todorov and Greenblatt whilst at the same time reaffirming the identification of women with territory, or with passive victimization. By transforming her into La Chingada, Paz hides the fact she collaborated." Franco, *Critical*, 77.
76. Smith, *National*, 9–11.
77. Smith, *National*, 11.
78. Haskett, "Our Suffering," 467.
79. Jackson, *Race*, 5, 6.
80. Jackson, *Race*, 12.
81. Yannis Hamilakis, qtd. in Papadopoulos and Urton, "Introduction," 26.
82. Coe, *Breaking*, 48.
83. Bruhns and Stothert, *Women*, 228.
84. Papadopoulos and Urton, "Introduction," 27.
85. Annis, "Story from a Peaceful Town," 155–56.
86. Patterson et al., "Ancient," 1081–82.
87. Garofalo "The Shape," 27–49.
88. Gerhard, "A Black Conquistador," 451–59; Restall, "Black Conquistadors," 171–205.
89. The results are as follows: "the Nahua from Mexico and the Aymara/Quechua from Bolivia have very low European contributions (2.3% and 1.4%, respectively), whereas the Quechua from Peru and the Mayans from Mexico show higher European contributions (8.5% and 9.2%, respectively)." Mao et al., "A Genomewide," 1174. Like the Maya, the Inka has elevated contact with Europeans. See our study in this

chapter that shows that the formerly pure Inka panaka is today the most mixed.

90. Explained more fully with bibliographical references in Ward, *Decolonial Indigeneity*, 43–48.
91. Lovell, "The Highland," 412.
92. Lovell, "The Highland," 412–13.
93. Strasser and Tinsman, "It's a Man's World?" 77.
94. On the genres open to women's cultivation during the colonial era, two very useful studies are Meyers, *Neither Saints* and Merrim, *Early Modern*.
95. Gordon explains their location: "Kindred Zenú peoples lived from the Gulf of Urabá east to the lower Cauca Valley." Gordon, *Human*, 33.
96. Bruhns and Stothert, *Women*, 223.
97. Milanich, "Un nuevo mundo," 76.
98. Gordon, *Human*, 33.
99. Gordon, *Human*, 33.
100. Villamarín and Villamarín, "Chiefdoms," 601.
101. Bruhns and Stothert have been helpful in formulating my views here. See, for example, Bruhns and Stothert, *Women*, 103–4.
102. Helms, "The Indians," 40.
103. Bubano Arias, "Las santafereñas del XVII," 131.
104. Rappaport, *The Politics*, 37. Italics removed.
105. Bruhns and Stothert, *Women*, 262.
106. Humboldt and Bonpland, *Personal Narrative*, 213. He writes, referring to Cieza de León's *Chronicle*, "The Indians of Darien, Uraba, Zenu (Sinu), Tatabé, the valleys of Nore and of Guaca, the mountains of Abibe and Antioquia, are accused, by the same author, of ferocious cannibalism; and perhaps that circumstance alone gives rise to the idea that they were of the same race of the Caribs of the West Indies."
107. Rodríguez Jiménez, "Sangre," 284.
108. Bruhns and Stothert, *Women*, 264.
109. Scopophilia, described by Mulvey, denotes deriving "pleasure in using another person as an object of sexual stimulation through sight." The staring the scopophilic male must undertake has been described by Mulvey as the "gaze." "Visual Pleasure," 10, 12.
110. Bedoya et al., "Admixture," 7234.
111. *MedicineNet.com*, s.v. "Definition of Chromosome," accessed January 14, 2006, www.medterms.com/script/main/art.asp?articlekey=14018.
112. *MedicineNet.com*, s.v. "Mitochondrial DNA," accessed January 14, 2006, www.medterms.com/script/main/art.asp?articlekey=8921.
113. Towns the biologists call "six founder municipalities," Bedoya et al., "Admixture," 7234.
114. Bedoya et al., "Admixture," 7234.
115. Burkholder and Johnson, *Colonial*, 115.
116. Wade, "Patterns," 13.

117. Bedoya et al., "Admixture," 7237.
118. Bedoya et al., "Admixture," 7237–38.
119. Verano, "War," 111.
120. Cordy-Collins, "Labretted," 255.
121. Castillo, "The Last," 309–16. Another discovery was made in 2006; this *cacica* or *sacerdotisa* from around the same period has been dubbed the "Dama de Cao." Much remains to be learned about her. See Redacción, "Quién era la poderosa Dama de Cao, la mujer que gobernó en Perú hace 1.700 años y cuyo rostro acaban de reconstruir," *BBC Mundo*, July 5, 2017, www.bbc.com/mundo/noticias-40502526 (accessed July 27, 2017).
122. Castillo, "The Last," 309–16.
123. Cordy-Collins, "Labretted," 254, 247, 256.
124. Cordy-Collins, "Labretted," 253.
125. Again, *Webster's New World Collegiate Dictionary* defines cacique simply as "an Indian chief" (203b).
126. For more on the *cacica* (*kuraka*) with bibliographical references, see Ward, *Decolonizing Indigeneity*, 192–93.
127. Silverblatt, *Moon*, xxii.
128. Bruhns and Stothert, *Women*, 205–6.
129. Villamarín and Villamarín, "Chiefdoms," 582.
130. Covey, *How*, 14.
131. Flores Galindo, *Obras*, 3.1:40.
132. See Sarmiento de Gamboa, *Historia*, en Garcilaso de la Vega, *Obras*, t. IV, ch. 13, p. 218b; and Rostworowski de Diez Canseco, *Historia*, 25.
133. Porras Barrenechea, *Mito*, 22.
134. For the myth part, see Zuidema, *Inca*, 7–14.
135. Silverblatt, *Moon*, 53.
136. Bruhns and Stothert, *Women*, 240.
137. Andrien, *Andean*, 30.
138. Hernández Astete, *La mujer*, 110.
139. Hernández Astete, *La mujer*, 115–26.
140. Bruhns and Stothert, *Women*, 168.
141. Silverblatt, *Moon*, 14.
142. Zuidema, *The Ceque*, 40.
143. Adorno, *The Polemics*, 50.
144. Mignolo, *The Darker*, 227, 230, 249, 253, etc.
145. Zuidema, *The Ceque*, 40–41.
146. Silverblatt, *Moon*, 68.
147. Silverblatt, *Moon*, 72 (see also 73–75), 74, xxix.
148. Zuidema, *The Ceque*, 44.
149. Zuidema, *The Ceque*, 80, 19n.
150. Cahill, "The Inca," 134.
151. The active-voice construction is appropriate because, as Arguedas explains, "la

transformación [es] conscientemente impulsada por los indios y no según el proceso tradicional inverso de empobrecimiento de mistis o como consecuencia de la bastardía." *Formación*, 37; The notion of illegitimacy is revealing, because that is how the Spanish viewed the non-Qollana secondary wives. Zuidema, *The Ceque*, 40–41.

152. Arguedas, *Formación*, 34.
153. Arguedas, *Formación*, 35.
154. Rowe, *Los Incas*, 45.
155. Zuidema, *The Ceque*, 16, states, "The panaca of the eleventh ruler, Huayna Capac, had no place in the organization of Cuzco, unlike those of the first ten rulers, and the name of this panaca was also different in nature. The panaca of the initial five rulers were said to belong to one-half of the population of Cuzco, which was called Hurin-Cuzco, or Lower Cuzco, and the panaca of the next five to Hanan-Cuzco, or Upper Cuzco"; Zuidema, *The Ceque*, 15.
156. Zuidema, *The Ceque*, 123.
157. Zuidema, *The Ceque*, 128.
158. Chang-Rodríguez describes how what would have been the panaka of Waskar was destroyed, *Cartografía*, 231–33.
159. See Murra, "Andean"; Rostworowski de Diez Canseco, *Historia*, 61–71.
160. Rostworowski de Diez Canseco, *Historia*, 63.
161. Herrero Astete, *La mujer*, 87.
162. Herrero Astete, *La mujer*, 87, 91.
163. Covey, *How*, 110, 146.
164. Murúa, *Historia*, bk. 1, ch. 19, p. 64.
165. Betanzos, *Suma*, 36.
166. Covey, *How*, 116.
167. Covey recognizes this reciprocal element, *How*, 116.
168. Ramírez, *The World*, 22.
169. Riva-Agüero, *Obras*, 4:148.
170. Riva-Agüero, *Obras*, 2:10.
171. Commented on in Kapsoli, *Francisco de Carbajal*, 97; see Calvete de Estrella, *Rebelión*, 156.
172. Adorno shows that the last decades of Guaman Poma's life were completely defined by litigation. See Adorno, *Guaman Poma*, 29–44.
173. Regarding the books Guaman Poma appears to have read, see Pease, G. Y., *Las crónicas*, 270–77.
174. Chang-Rodríguez, *La palabra*, 43.
175. For a discussion on the Christian implications of this passage, see Chang-Rodríguez, *La palabra*, 133.
176. As observed by Chang-Rodríguez and Vicuña Guengerich, Guaman Poma's view of mestizaje is the opposite of Inca Garcilaso's. See Chang-Rodríguez, "Coloniaje," 42 and Vicuña Guengerich, "Virtuosas," 680.
177. For a discussion of Guaman Poma's concept of *Criollo*, see Chang-Rodríguez,

"Cruel Criollos."

178. Adorno, *Cronista*, 73–74.
179. Vega, "La prostitución," 49.
180. Chang-Rodríguez, *La apropiación*, 10.
181. Molina, *Relación de la conquista y población del Perú*, qtd. in *NU*, 123–24.
182. Adorno, *Cronista*, 73.
183. Adorno notes that "the flesh-and-blood priests who populate Guaman Poma's chronicle are overwhelmingly those who served in local Andean parishes in the provinces of Lucanas Andamarca, Soras, and Aymaraes in the southern Peruvian Andes." *Guaman Poma*, 36.
184. Rivarola, *Español*, 46.

Chapter 5

1. Kirk, "Mapping," 997.
2. Hellenthal et al., "A Genetic," 747.
3. Patterson et al., "Ancient," 1065.
4. As mentioned in a note for Chapter 2, Patterson et al., "Ancient," 1081–82, surprisingly could not find the genes of the Suevi, Vandal, and Visigoth peoples, even though they underscore that this indeed happened. What they do find is immigration from North Europe by the so-called "Bell-Beaker culture" around 2000 BC. Patterson et al., "Ancient," 1081.
5. Sicoli and Holton "Linguistic Phylogenies," 1.
6. Scheinsohn, "Hunter-Gatherer."
7. Sandoval et al., "Tracing," 627.
8. See, for example, Yacobaccio et al., who write, "Chemical characterization of lithic sources has contributed to archaeological research as a means of demonstrating contact between two geographical locales: the original source of a lithic object and the archaeological site from which it was ultimately recovered." "Long Distance," 167.
9. Lee, "Fernand Braudel," 1.
10. Doyle, "Inter-Imperiality," 336.
11. Braswell and Glascock, "The Emergence," 34.
12. Papadopoulos and Urton, "Introduction," 21.
13. Papadopoulos and Urton, "Introduction," 26.
14. Ospina, *América*, 55.
15. Papadopoulos and Urton, "Introduction," 1.
16. Bauer, "Toward," 41.
17. Fernández, "Noticias."
18. Shimada, "Evolution," 430–36; Villamarín and Villamarín, "Chiefdoms," 599.
19. On the colonial and ambiguous usage of this term that refers to a people, a concept, and a phenomenon, see Curet, "The Taino." He explains: "We cannot, therefore, say with any degree of certainty that the native people of the Greater Antilles used taíno (term) to refer to their communal identity or ethos. This is all to say that the term

taíno is an Arawak word (adjective) that refers to a concept of goodness or nobility but that has been used with other meanings by scholars." Curet, "The Taino," 470.

20. Ortiz, *Contrapunteo,* 323, for example.
21. Ortiz, *Contrapunteo,* 256–57. Views such as Ortiz's in this regard are disputed. Reid, for example, explains, "The term Ciboney, as applied to the natives in western Cuba and elsewhere in the Caribbean, is a misnomer as the term applies to a local Taíno group in central Cuba and not to Archaic groups found throughout the Caribbean and circum-Caribbean, despite its continued use in this regard." *Myths,* 84; Keegan suggests the distinction between Siboneyes and Guanajabibes is derived from the chronicles, "Creating."
22. *Diccionario de la lengua española,* Real Academia Española, 6: 840.
23. These dates come from Sam Colop, "Introducción," and D. Tedlock, *2000 Years*; Christenson, *The Burdon,* 77, 81, 144, notes Pedro de Alvarado conquered Q'umarkaj with the help of Tlaxcalan allies.
24. Carmack, *The Quiché,* 86.
25. See, for example, Florescano, "Chichén Itza."
26. Van Akkeren, *La visión,* 22; Christenson suggests the Nahuatl name for Q'umarkaj came as late as 1524, when Alvarado's Tlaxcalan allies used it, *The Burdon,* 114.
27. Lesure, "Figurine," 381.
28. Braswell and Glascock, "The Emergence," 38.
29. Lynch, "The Earliest," 252.
30. Verano, "War," 112.
31. Porras Barrenechea, *Pizarro,* 38.
32. McCafferty, "Domestic," 77.
33. Woodward, "Lenca," 4:166.
34. Richardson et al., "The Northern," 437.
35. Kolb, *Marine,* 20–23.
36. Kolb, *Marine,* 19.
37. Kolb, *Marine,* 111–21; Kolb does not theorize an Ecuador to Mexico route, as other scholars have done after him. He recognizes Pacific Coast routes "are more difficult to identify because of 'gaps' in the archaeological surveys." *Marine,* 116. Here, we add recent studies (such as Hosler) regarding the balsa rafts to the archaeological information.
38. Trubitt, "The Production," 244.
39. Hosler, "West," 189.
40. [Xérez], "Relación," 196–97; Porras Barrenechea rejects the notion that the King's secretary, Juan de Sámano, could have been the author of this short chronicle. He merely stamped it as secretary. The author was likely Francisco de Xérez, *Los cronistas,* 53.
41. [Xérez], "Relación," 197.
42. Hosler, "West," 187–88.
43. Hosler, "West," 189.
44. Murra, "Did Tribute," 62; Currie, "Archaeology," n.p.

45. See Trubitt, "The Production," 256.
46. Haskett, "Pochteca," 276; see also Kolb, *Marine,* 107–9.
47. Van Akkeren, *La visión,* 20.
48. Carmack, *The Quiché,* 153
49. Torero, *Idiomas,* 93.
50. For a gender-related analysis on the tomb's contents, see Bruhns and Stothert, *Women,* 184; also Verano, "War," esp. 114–16; and Gálvez Mora and Briceño Rosario, "The Moche," 155.
51. Castillo, "The Last," 314, 317, 318, 321.
52. Trubitt, "The Production," 245–48.
53. Stanish, *Ancient,* 9, 31, 16, 34.
54. Castillo, "The Last," 324.
55. Shimada, *Pampa,* 259.
56. Richardson et al., "The Northern," 437.
57. Jones, "Innovation," 217–18.
58. Bruhns and Stothert, *Women,* 201.
59. Shimada, "Evolution," 430–34.
60. Covey, *How,* 58. Covey considers the possibility the Wari capital was sacked around AD 1100.
61. Hamilakis, qtd. in Papadopoulos and Urton, "Introduction," 26.
62. Bruhns and Stothert, *Women,* 134, 147, 165–67, 156, 79–81, 263. See also p. 140.
63. Helms, "The Indians," 41.
64. Villamarín and Villamarín, "Chiefdoms," 599.
65. Trimborn, *Señorío,* 189.
66. Villamarín and Villamarín, "Chiefdoms," 599, 600.
67. Weaver, *Latin America,* 5.
68. Weaver, *Latin America,* 5.
69. Stanish, *Ancient,* 14.
70. Torero, *Idiomas,* 94.
71. Kosiba, "Emplacing," 101.
72. Stanish, *Ancient,* 12, 24.
73. Murra, "Andean," 66, 70.
74. Betanzos, *Suma,* 36.
75. Andrien, *Andean,* 32.
76. Covey, *How,* 203.
77. Yacobaccio et al., "Long-Distance," 172–73.
78. Yacobaccio et al., "Long-Distance," 187.
79. McNeill, *The Rise,* 584.
80. Sacks, "Introduction," 35.
81. José Ortega, "Las Casas," 83.
82. Morison, *The Admiral,* 43, 49.
83. Klein, *African Slavery,* 17.
84. Manning, "The Slave," 118–19.

85. José Ortega, "Las Casas," 83.
86. Lockhart and Otte, *Letters*, 3; Restall, *Seven*, 28–35.
87. Restall, Souza, and Terraciano, *Mesoamerican*, 6.
88. Lockhart and Otte, *Letters*, 3.
89. Restall, *Seven*, 43, 42.
90. I take the idea of the logic of capitalism from Heilbroner, *The Nature and Logic of Capitalism*.
91. On the Spanish and French bankruptcies, see Wallerstein, *The Modern*, 183–84. Phase two of the World-System would come when England and the northern Low Countries became the new linchpin of the world economic system. On Holland and England, see Wallerstein, *The Modern*, 213 & 230–31, respectively.
92. Guevara, *Relox*, 643. This quotation does not appear in the *Libro áureo* version of the story. The word "steel" did not mean the amalgamated metal we think of today. The *Diccionario de la lengua castellana* from 1726, tomo 1, offers this definition: "metal que se cria en las venas de la tierra de la especie del hierro; pero mas puro, mas fino y mas fuerte que el artificial que se hace del hierro purificado."
93. Hoerder, *Cultures*, 43.
94. Wallerstein, *The Modern*, 17.
95. Yun, "Economic," 115.
96. Robisheaux, "The World," 79.
97. Weaver, *Latin America*, 6.
98. Robisheaux, "The World," 94, 80.
99. Wallerstein, *The Modern*, 20–21.
100. Weaver, *Latin America*, 7.
101. McNeill, *The Rise*, 583–84.
102. Mignolo, *Local*, xi.
103. Casey, *Early*, 1.
104. The links between religion and commerce can be seen in Borges, *The Economics of the Goa Jesuits, 1542–1759*; For the enduring presence of Catholicism and its relationship to money in the Philippines, see Wiegele, *Investing in Miracles*.
105. Mignolo, *Local*, 146.
106. Casey, *Early*, 43.
107. Casey, *Early*, 1.
108. Millones, "Prólogo," xxiii.
109. Andrien, *Andean*, 49.
110. Wallerstein, *The Modern*, 335.
111. Wallerstein, *The Modern*, 337.
112. Keith, *Conquest*, 39–40.
113. DeLeonardis, "Itinerant," 476.
114. Keith, *Conquest*, 40.
115. Wallerstein, *The Modern*, 350.
116. Wallerstein, *The Modern*, 67.
117. Pastor Bodmer, *The Armature*, 41.

118. Mignolo, *The Darker*, 286.
119. Wallerstein, *The Modern*, 170.
120. Fuenzalida Vollmar, *La matriz*, 11.
121. DeLeonardis, "Itinerant," 446; DeLeonardis observes that the Cachimayos in the Ica and Pisco regions eventually took up wine making, inserting them at least into Peruvian markets. "Itinerant," 476.
122. Wallerstein, *The Modern*, 188, 189.
123. Larson, *Trials*, 40.
124. Fuenzalida Vollmar, *La matriz*, 12.
125. Fuenzalida Vollmar, *La matriz*, 13.
126. Keith, *Conquest*, 45.
127. Saint Martin de Porres was beatified in 1837, and canonized by Pope John in 1962. He is the patron saint of, among other things, mixed-race people and all those seeking racial harmony.
128. Torero, *Idiomas*, 161.
129. Wallerstein, *The Modern*, 45.
130. Wallerstein, *The Modern*, 41–45.
131. Munro, "Patterns," 171.
132. Yun, "Economic," 113; on the silver-silk Asian connection, see Weaver, *Latin America*, 10, 20.
133. Smith, *The Glasgow*, 1:185.
134. Restall, Souza, and Terraciano, *Mesoamerican*, 10.
135. Ramírez, *The World*, 8.
136. Larson, *Trials*, 27
137. Vitoria, *Relectio*, 101.
138. Stern, *Peru's Indian*, 36.
139. Arguedas, *Formación*, 37–38.
140. Gutiérrez Arbulú, "Introducción," 15.
141. Quiroz Chueca, "Gremios," 494.
142. Aragón Noriega, "El pan," 257–85.
143. Mexicano Ramos, "'Negocios' menudistas," 311–12.
144. Aragón Noriega, "El pan," 257–85; see also Mexicano Ramos, "'Negocios' menudistas," 311–64.
145. Gutiérrez Arbulú, "Introducción," 13.
146. Adorno hints at this in "Discourses," 250–55.
147. Silva Santisteban, *Los obrajes*, 13.
148. Rivarola, *Español*, 37.
149. Rivarola, *Español*, 45.
150. Silva Santisteban, *Los obrajes*, 15, 22–27.
151. Fuenzalida Vollmar, *La matriz*, 15.
152. Andrien, *Andean*, 80, 81.
153. Andrien, *Andean*, 82.
154. Bonilla's work on the early postcolonial period got me to think along these lines.

He writes, "La inexistencia de mercados nacionales y el aislamiento recíproco entre regiones por la ausencia de rutas de transporte garantizaron el mantenimiento de esta situación." "Etnia," 94. He refers to what he calls "stagnation." After communities were liberated from the mita and the tributo that linked them to places outside their immediate area, they would take refuge in their own intimacy, which is to say, they would become self-absorbed.

155. Wallerstein, *The Modern*, 193.
156. Wallerstein, *The Modern*, 194.
157. Again, see Silverblatt, *Modern*.
158. Jara, "Una investigación," 240, 241; Discussed in Wallerstein, *The Modern*, 94.
159. Wallerstein, *The Modern*, 188.
160. García Bryce, *Crafting*, 26.
161. García Bryce, *Crafting*, 27, 28.

BIBLIOGRAPHY

Archival Sources

Peruvian Manuscript Collection, 1583–1892. Manuel de Odriozola, creator. David M. Rubenstein Rare Book & Manuscript Library. Duke University, Durham, NC.

Published Primary Sources

Acosta, Joseph de. *Historia natural y moral de las Indias.* Edited by Edmundo O'Gorman. México: FCE, 1940.

Aldrete, Bernardo. *Del origen y principio de la lengua castellana ò romance que oi se usa en España.* Edited by Lidio Nieto Jiménez. 2 vols. Madrid: Consejo Superior de Investigaciones Científicas, 1972.

———. *Varias antigvedades de España, África y otras provincias.* Amberes: Hasrey, 1614.

Alva Ixtlilxóchitl, Fernando de. *Obras históricas: incluyen el texto completo de las llamadas Relaciones e Historia de la nación chichimeca en una nueva versión establecida con el cotejo de los manuscritos más antiguos que se conocen.* 1975. Edición Facsimilar, edited by Edmundo O'Gorman. 2 vols. Mexico: Universidad Nacional Autónoma de México/Instituto Mexiquense de Cultura, 1997.

Anonymous. *La mort D'Ataw Wallpa ou La fin de l'Empire des Incas. Tragédie anonyme en langue quechua du milieu du XVIe siècle.* Edited and translated by Jean-Philippe Husson. Geneva: Patiño, 2001.

Anonymous. *El título de Totonicapán. Texto, traducción y comentario.* Edited by Robert M. Carmack and James L. Mondloch. Mexico: FCE, 1983.

Belarminio, Cardinal Roberto, S.J. *Declaración copiosa de las cuatro partes mas essenciales y necesarias de la doctrina christiana compusto por orden del Beautísimo P. Clemente Octavo de felice memoria.* Traducida de Lengua Castellana en la General del Inga por el Bachiller Bartolomé Iurado Palomino, natural de la ciudad de Cuzco. Lima: Jorge López de Herrera, 1641.

Betanzos, Juan de. *Suma y narración de los Incas.* Madrid: Ediciones Atlas (Biblioteca de Autores Españoles), 1968.

Burga, Manuel. *Nacimiento de una utopía: muerte y resurrección de los incas.* 2nd ed. Lima: Universidad Nacional Mayor de San Marcos, 2005.

Cabeza de Vaca, Alvar Núñez. *The Narrative of Cabeza de Vaca.* Edited and translated by Rolena Adorno and Patrick Charles Pautz. Lincoln: University of Nebraska Press, 2003.

Calvete de Estrella, Juan Cristóbal. *Rebelión de Gonzalo Pizarro en el Perú y vida de d. Pedro Gasca.* Ed. E. Paz y Mélia. Tomo 1. Madrid: Imprenta y Fundición de M. Tello, 1889.

Castellanos, Juan de. *Elegías de varones ilustres de Indias. Antología crítica de Juan de Castellanos.* Edited by Luis Fernando Restrepo. Bogotá: Editorial Pontificia Universidad Javeriana, 2004.

Chimalpahin Quauhtlehuanitzin, Domingo de San Antonio Muñón. *Codex Chimalpahin.* Edited and translated by Arthur J. O. Anderson and Susan Schroeder. Vol. 1. Norman: University of Oklahoma Press, 1997.

Cieza de León, Pedro de. *Crónica del Perú: primera parte.* Edited by Franklin Pease G. Y. and Miguel Maticorena E. 3rd ed. Lima: Pontificia Universidad Católica/Academia Nacional de la Historia, 1995. First published in Sevilla, 1553.

Cieza de León, Pedro de. *Crónica del Perú: tercera parte.* Edited by Francesca Cantù and Kart Baldinger. 3rd ed. Lima: Pontificia Universidad Católica/Academia Nacional de la Historia, 1996.

Cobo, Father Bernabé. *History of the Inca Empire.* Translated by Roland Hamilton. Austin: University of Texas Press, 1993.

Coe, Michael D., and Gordon Whittaker, eds. *Aztec Sorcerers in Seventeenth Century Mexico: The Treatise on Superstitions by Hernando de Ruiz de Alarcón.* Albany: State University of New York/Institute for Mesoamerican Studies, 1982.

Colón, Cristóbal. *Textos y documentos completos.* Edited by Consuelo Varela. Madrid: Alianza Universidad, 1982.

Cortés, Hernán. *Cartas de relación.* Edited by Manuel Alcalá. Mexico: Editorial Porrúa, 1983.

Cruz, Sor Juana Inés de la. *Obras completas.* Edited by Francisco Monterde. Mexico: Editorial Porrúa, 1981.

de Ballester, Thomas, ed. *Tomo primero de las ordenanzas del Perú, dirigidas al rey nuestro señor.* Lima: Joseph de Contreras, 1685.

Díaz del Castillo, Bernal. *Historia verdadera de la conquista de la Nueva España.* Edited by Carmelo Sáenz de Santa María. Madrid: Instituto "Gonzalo Fernández de Oviedo," de C.S.I.C, 1982.

Durán, Diego. *Historia de las Indias de Nueva España e islas de la Tierra Firme.* Edited by Ángel María Garibay K. 2 vols. Mexico: Editorial Porrúa, 1967.

Erasmus. *The Education of a Christian Prince.* Translated by Neil M. Sheshire and Michael J. Heath. Edited by Lisa Jardine. Cambridge: Cambridge University Press, 1997.

Fornee, Niculoso de. *Descripción de la tierra del Corregimiento de Abancay de que es corregidor Niculoso de Fornee.* In vol. 2 of *Relaciones geográficas de Indias-Perú,* edited by Don Marcos Jiménez de la Espada, 16–30. Madrid: Biblioteca de Autores Españoles, Atlas, 1965.

Garcilaso de la Vega, El Inca. *Royal Commentaries of the Incas* and *General History of Peru.* 2 vols. Translated and edited by Harold V. Livermore. Austin: University of Texas Press, 1966.

———. *Obras completas del Inca Garcilaso de la Vega.* 4 tomos. Madrid: Biblioteca de Autores Españoles/Ediciones Atlas, 1960–65.

———. *Comentarios reales de los incas.* 2 tomos. Edited by Ángel Rosenblat. Buenos Aires: Emecé Editores, 1943.

———. *La Florida del Inca, historia del adelantado Hernando de Soto.* Lisbon: Pedro de Crasbeeck, 1605.

Guamán Poma de Ayala, Felipe. *Nueva Crónica y buen gobierno.* 3 vols. Edited by John V. Murra, Rolena Adorno, and Jorge L. Urioste. Madrid: Historia 16, 1987.

Guevara, Antonio de. *Libro áureo de Marco Aurelio.* In vol. 1 of *Obras Completas,* edited by Emilio Blanco, 1–333. Madrid: Turner (Biblioteca Castro), 1994.

———. *Relox de príncipes.* In vol. 2 of *Obras Completas,* edited by Emilio Blanco, 1–943. Madrid: Turner (Biblioteca Castro), 1994.

Las Casas, Bartolomé de. *Historia de las Indias.* Edited by André Saint Lu. 3 vols. Caracas: Biblioteca Ayacucho, 1986.

———. *Tratados.* 2 vols. Mexico: FCE, 1965.

León Portilla, Miguel, ed. *Broken Spears: The Aztec Account of the Conquest of Mexico.* Translated by Lysander Kemp. London: Constable; Boston: Beacon Press, 1962.

———. *Visión de los vencidos: Relaciones indígenas de la conquista.* Mexico: UNAM, 1959.

Lockhart, James, Frances Berdan, and Arthur O. Anderson. *The Tlaxcalan Actas: A Compendium of the Records of the Cabildo of Tlaxcala (1545–1627).* Salt Lake City: University of Utah Press, 1986.

Londoño Vélez, Santiago, and Benjamín Villegas. *Colombian Art: 3,500 Years of History.* Bogotá: Villegas Editores, 2001.

Mariana, Juan de. *Obras del Padre Juan de Mariana.* Edited by F[ancisco]. P[i]. M[argall]. 2 tomes. Vols. 30 & 31, Biblioteca de Autores Españoles. Madrid: Atlas, 1950.

More, Thomas. *The Yale Edition of the Complete Works of St. Thomas More.* Vol. 4, *Utopia.* Edited by Edward Surtz, S.J. and J. H. Hexter. New Haven: Yale University Press, 1965.

Motolinía [o Benavente], Fray Toribio. *Historia de los indios de la Nueva España.* Edited by Edmundo O'Gorman. 6th ed. Mexico: Porrúa, 1995.

Murúa, Martín de. *Historia general del Perú.* Edited by Manuel Ballesteros Gaibrois. 2nd reprint, Madrid: Dastin, 2001.

Muñoz Camargo, Diego. *Historia de Tlaxcala.* Edited by Germán Vázquez. Madrid: Historia 16, 1986.

Nuttall, Zelia, ed. *The Codex Nuttall: A Picture Manuscript from Ancient Mexico.* New York: Dover Publications, 1975.

Popol Vuh: The Definitive Edition of the Mayan Book of the Dawn of Life and the Glories of Gods and Kings. Edited by Dennis Tedlock. New York: Touchstone, 1996.

Popol Vuh, Las antiguas historias del Quiché. Translated by Adrián Recinos. 4th ed. Mexico: FCE, 1960.

Popol Vuh: The Sacred Book of the Ancient Quiché Maya. Translated by Delia Goetz and Sylvanus Morley from Recinos's Spanish Translation. Norman: University of Oklahoma Press, 1950.

Popol Wuj Online. Transcription of Father Jiménez's Quiché and Spanish texts. Columbus: The Ohio State University, 2011. http://library.osu.edu/projects/popolwuj/index.php.

Popol Wuj: versión poética kiche. (K'iche'). Edited by Luis Enrique Sam Colop. Guatemala City: Cholsamaj/Quetzaltenango: PEMBI-GTZ, 1999.

Restall, Matthew, Lisa Sousa, and Keven Terraciano. *Mesoamerican Voices: Native-Language Writings from Colonial México, Oaxaca, Yucatán, and Guatemala.* Cambridge: Cambridge University Press, 2005.

Rivers, Elias L., ed. *Poesía lírica del Siglo de Oro.* Madrid: Cátedra, 1983.

Rivola, José Luis. *Español andino: textos de bilingües de los siglos XVI y XVII.* Madrid/Frankfurt: Iberoamericana/Vervuert, 2000.

Royes, Ralph, ed. *The Book of Chilam Balam of Chumayel.* London: Forgotten Books, 2008. First published in Washington, DC by the Carnegie Institution, 1933.

Sahagún, Fray Bernardino de. *Historia general de las cosas de la* Nueva *España.* Edited by Ángel María Garibay K. México: Editorial Porrúa, 1985.

———. *General History of the Things of New Spain* [Florentine Codex]. Edited and translated by Arthur J. O. Anderson and Charles Dibble. Introductory Volume and Books 1–12. Santa Fe: School of American Research/University of Utah, 1978.

Sarmiento de Gamboa, Pedro. *Historia Indica.* En vol. 4 of el Inca Garcilaso de la Vega, *Obras completas del Inca Garcilaso de la Vega,* 189–279. Madrid: Biblioteca de Autores Españoles/Ediciones Atlas, 1960–65.

Valera, Blas. "Selecciones." In *Cronistas indios y mestizos,* edited by Francisco Carillo, 197–212. *Enciclopedia histórica de la literatura peruana,* vol. 6. Lima: Horizonte, 1991.

Vallejo, César. *Trilce.* Versión Quechua. Edited and translated by Porfirio Meneses Lazón. Lima: Universidad Ricardo Palma, 2008.

Velasco, Juan. *Historia del reino de Quito.* Caracas: Biblioteca Ayacucho, 1981.

Vespucio, Américo. *Cartas.* Madrid: Anjana, 1983.

Vitoria, Francisco de. *Relectio de indis. Carta magna de los indios.* Madrid: Consejo Superior de Investigaciones Científicas, 1989.

[Xérez, Francisco de]. "Relación de los primeros descubrimientos de Francisco Pizarro y Diego de Almagro, sacada del códice número CXX de la Biblioteca Imperial de Viena." In tomo 5, *Colección de documentos inéditos para la historia de España,* edited by Martín Fernández Navarrette, Miguel Salvá, and Pedro Sainz de Baranda, 193–201. Madrid: Imprenta de la Viuda de Calero, 1844.

Zárate, Agustín de. *Historia del descubrimiento y conqvista de las provincias del Peru, y de los sucesos que en ella ha auido, desde que se conquistó, hasta que el Licenciado de la Gasca Obispo de Siguença boluio a estos reynos: y de las cosas naturales que en la dicha provincia se hallan dignas de memoria, La qual escreuia Augustin de Çarate, Contador de mercedes de su majestad, siendo Contador general de cuentas en aquella provincia, y en la de Tierrafirme.* Sevilla: Casa de Alonso Escriuano, 1577.

———. *Historia del descvbrimiento y conqvista del Perv, con las cosas naturales que señaladamente allí se hallan, y los sucesos que ha auido. La qual escriuia Augustin de Çarate, ejerciendo el cargo de Contador general de cuentas por su Majestad en aquella provincia, y en la de Tierra firme.* Antwerp: Casa de Martín Nucio, 1555.

Dictionaries

Academia Mayor de la Lengua Quechua. *Diccionario quechua-español-quechua/Qheswa-español-qheswa Simi Taque.* Qosqo (Cuzco): Municipalidad del Qosqo, 1995.

Bierhorst, John. *A Nahuatl-English Dictionary and Concordance to the Cantares Mexicanos with an Analytical Transcription and Grammatical Notes.* Stanford: Stanford University Press, 1985.

Corominas, Joan. *Breve diccionario etimológico de la lengua castellana.* 2nd ed. Madrid: Editorial Gredos, 1967.

Diccionario de la lengua castellana en que se explica el verdadero sentido de las voces, su naturaleza y calidad, con las phrases o modos de hablar, los proverbios o refranes, y otras cosas convenientes al uso de la lengua. 6 tomes. Madrid: Francisco del Hierro (Real Academia Española), 1726–37.

Diccionario de la lengua española. 22nd ed. 10 vols. Madrid: Real Academia Española, 2001.

González Holguín, Diego. *Vocabulario de la lengua general de todo el Perv llamada Lengua QQuicha o del Inca.* Lima: Universidad Nacional Mayor de San Marcos, 1989. First published 1608.

Oxford English Dictionary. 2nd ed. Oxford: Oxford University Press, 1989. Online version accessed through the Loyola/Notre Dame Library, Baltimore, Maryland.

Siméon, Rémi. *Diccionario de la lengua náhuatl.* 8th ed. Mexico: Siglo XXI, 1991. First published 1885.

Stephens, Thomas M. *Dictionary of Latin American Racial and Ethnic Terminology.* Gainesville: University of Florida Press, 1989.

Webster's New World College Dictionary. 4th ed. Foster City, CA: IDG Books Worldwide, 2000.

Eighteenth- and Nineteenth-Century Documents

Alberdi, J. B. "Gobernar es poblar." In vol. 8 of *Escritos póstumos de J. B. Alberdi,* 266–70. Buenos Aires: Imp. Cruz Hermanos, 1899.

Clavijero, Francisco J. *The History of Mexico: Collected from Spanish and Mexican Historians, from Manuscripts, and Ancient Paintings of the Indians.* Translated by Charles Cullen. 2 vols. London: G. G. J. and J. Robinson, 1787.

Humboldt, Alexander von, and Aimé Bonpland. *Personal Narrative of Travels to the Equinoctial Regions of America during the Years 1799–1804.* Edited and translated by Thomasina Ross. Vol. 3. London: George Bell and Sons, 1885.

Matto de Turner, Clorinda. *Leyendas y recortes.* Lima: "La Equitativa," 1893.

———. "Estudios históricos: A la Sociedad Arqueológico-Lingüística." Leído en el "Círculo Literario." *El Perú Ilustrado* 69 (1 de septiembre de 1888). Quoted from *Leyendas,* 91–100.

———. "Estudios históricos: Al Dóctor Luis Cordero." *El Perú Ilustrado* 71 (15 de septiembre de 1888). Quoted from *Leyendas,* 101–11.

Palma, Ricardo. *Tradiciones peruanas completas.* Edited by Edith Palma. Madrid: Aguilar, 1961.

Pardo Bazán, Emilia. *La España de Ayer y la de Hoy. Conferencia de París.* Madrid: Administración, [1899?].

Prescott, William H. *History of the Conquest of Mexico: With a Preliminary View of the Ancient Mexican Civilization, and the Life of the Conqueror, Hernando Cortés.* 3 vols. New York/London: Harper/R. Bentley, 1843.

———. *History of the Conquest of Peru: With a Preliminary View of the Civilization of the Incas.* New York/London/Paris: Harper and Brothers/R. Bentley/Baudry's European Library, 1847.

Renan, Ernest. "Qu'est-ce qu'une nation?" 1882. Reprinted in *Qu'est-ce qu'une nation? Et autres essais politiques*, edited by Joël Roman, 37–58. Paris: Pocket, 1992.

Robertson, William. *The History of America.* London: Printed for W. Strahan, 1777.

Villar, Leonardo. *Lexicología keshua: Uirakocha.* Lima: Imprenta del "Comercio," 1887.

———. *Lingüística nacional estudio sobre la keshua.* Lima: Impr. "El Comercio," 1890.

Secondary Sources

Adelaar, Willem F. H., with Pieter C. Muysken. *The Languages of the Andes.* Cambridge: Cambridge University Press, 2004.

Adorno, Rolena. *The Polemics of Possession in Spanish American Narrative.* New Haven: Yale University Press, 2007.

———. Introduction to *The Narrative of Cabeza de Vaca*, by Alvar Núñez Cabeza de Vaca, 1–37. Edited and translated by Rolena Adorno and Patrick Charles Pautz. Lincoln: University of Nebraska Press, 2003.

———. *Guaman Poma and His Illustrated Chronicle from Colonial Peru: From a Century of Scholarship to a New Era of Reading/Guaman Poma de Ayala y su crónica ilustrada del Perú colonial: un siglo de investigaciones hacia una nueva era de lectura.* Copenhagen: Museum Tusculanum Press/University of Copenhagen and Royal Library, 2001.

———. "Cultures in Contact: Mesoamerica, the Andes, and the European Written Tradition." In *Discovery to Modernism*, vol. 1 of *The Cambridge History of Latin American Literature*, edited by Roberto González Echevarría and Enrique Pupo-Walker, 33–57. Cambridge: Cambridge University Press, 1996.

———. *Cronista y príncipe. La obra de don Felipe Guaman Poma de Ayala.* Lima: Pontificia Universidad Católica del Perú, 1992.

———. "Images of *Indios Ladinos* in Early Colonial Peru." In *Transatlantic Encounters: Europeans and Andeans in the Sixteenth Century*, edited by Kenneth J. Andrien and Rolena Adorno, 232–70. Berkeley: University of California Press, 1991.

———. "Arms, Letters and the Native Historian in Early Colonial Mexico." In *1492–1992: Re/Discovering Colonial Writing*, edited by René Jara and Nicholas Spadaccini, 201–24. Minneapolis: University of Minnesota Press, 1989.

———. "Discourses on Colonialism: Bernal Díaz, Las Casas, and the Twentieth-Century Reader." *MLN* 103, no. 2 (March 1988): 239–58.

———. "Literary Production and Suppression: Reading and Writing about Amerindians in Colonial Spanish America." *Dispositio* 11, nos. 28–29 (1985): 1–25.

Alarcón, Norma, Caren Kaplan, and Minoo Moallem. "Introduction: Between Woman and Nation." In *Between Woman and Nation: Nationalisms, Transnational Feminisms, and the State*, edited by Caren Kaplan, Norma Alarcón, and Minoo Moallem, 1–16. Durham, NC: Duke University Press, 1999.

Almeida, Joselyn L. *Reimagining the Transatlantic 1780–1890*. Surry: Ashgate, 2011.

Anderson, Benedict. *Imagined Communities: Reflections on the Origin and Spread of Nationalism*. New York: Verso, 1983.

Andrien, Kenneth J. *Andean Worlds: Indigenous History, Culture, and Consciousness under Spanish Rule, 1533–1825*. Albuquerque: University of New Mexico Press, 2001.

Annis, Sheldon. "Story from a Peaceful Town: San Antonio Aguas Calientes." In *Harvest of Violence: The Mayan Indians and the Guatemalan Crisis*, edited by Robert M. Carmack, 155–73. Norman: University of Oklahoma Press, 1992.

Anthias, Floya, and Nira Yuval-Davis. Introduction to *Women-Nation-State*, edited by Floya Anthias and Nira Yuval-Davis, 1–15. Houndmills: Macmillan Press, 1989.

Anzaldúa, Gloria. *Borderlands/La Frontera: The New Mestiza*. San Francisco: Spinsters/Aunt Lute, 1987.

Aragón Noriega, Ilana. "El pan, el vino, y otros negocios: aspectos laborales de la mujer." In *Lima en el Siglo XVI*, edited by Laura Gutiérrez Arbulú, 257–85. Lima: Pontificia Universidad Católica del Perú, 2006.

Arguedas, José María. *Formación de una cultura nacional indoamericana*. Edited by Ángel Rama. 5th ed. Mexico: Siglo XXI, 1989.

Arias, Arturo. "Kotz'ib': The Emergence of a New Maya Literature." *Latin American Indigenous Literatures Journal* 24, no. 1 (Spring 2008): 7–28.

Arroyo Reyes, Carlos. "Entre el incaísmo modernista y Rumi Maqui: El joven Mariátegui y el descubrimiento del indio." Accessed January 9, 2018. https://www.scribd.com/document/65917773/Entre-el-incaismo-modernista-y-Rumi-Maqui.

Bacigalupo, Marvyn Helen. *A Changing Perspective: Attitudes toward Creole Society in New Spain (1521–1610)*. London: Tamesis Books Limited, 1981.

Bailyn, Bernard. *The Peopling of British North America: An Introduction*. New York: Knopf, 1986.

Bauer, Ralph. "Toward a Cultural Geography of Colonial American Literatures: Empire, Location, Creolization." In *A Companion to the Literatures of Colonial America*, edited by Susan Castillo and Ivy Schweitzer, 38–59. Malden, MA: Blackwell, 2005.

Beckjord, Sara H. *Territories of History: Humanism, Rhetoric, and the Historical Imagination in the Early Chronicles of Spanish America*. University Park: The Pennsylvania State University Press, 2007.

———. "'Con sal y ají y tomates': las redes textuales de Bernal Díaz en el caso de Cholula." *Revista Iberoamericana* 61, nos. 170–71 (1995): 147–60.

Bedoya, Gabriel, Patricia Montoya, Jenny García, Ivan Soto, Stephane Bouregeois, Luis Carvajal, Damian Labuda, Victor Alvarez, Jorge Ospina, Philip W. Hedrick, and Andrés Ruíz-Linares. "Admixture Dynamics in Hispanics: A Shift in the Nuclear Genetic Ancestry of a South American Population Isolate." *Proceedings of the National Academy of Sciences of the United States of America* 103, no. 19 (May 9, 2006): 7234–39.

Benassy-Berling, Marie-Cecile. *Humanismo y religión en Sor Juana Inés de la Cruz.* Mexico: UNAM, 1983.

Bhabha, Homi. *The Location of Culture.* London: Routledge, 1994.

Blanco, José Joaquín. "The Production of Literary Culture in New Spain." In *Configurations of Literary Culture*, vol. 1 of *Literary Cultures of Latin America: A Comparative History*, edited by Mario J. Valdés and Djelal Kadir, 109–19. Oxford: Oxford University Press, 2004.

Bonilla, Heraclio. "Etnia, religión y la cuestión nacional en el área andina." En *Indianidad, etnocidio, indigenismo en América Latina*, translated by Ana Freyre de Zavala, 87–110. México: Instituto Indigenista Interamericano, 1988.

Borges, Charles J. *The Economics of the Goa Jesuits, 1542–1759: An Explanation of their Rise and Fall.* New Delhi: Concept Pub. Co., 1994.

Brading, D. A. *The First America: The Spanish Monarchy, Creole Patriots, and the Liberal State 1492–1867.* Cambridge: Cambridge University Press, 1991.

Braswell, Geoffrey E., and Michael D. Glascock. "The Emergence of Market Economies in the Ancient Maya World: Obsidian Exchange in Terminal Classic Yucatán, Mexico." In *Geochemical Evidence for Long-Distance Exchange*, edited by Michael D. Glascock, 33–52. Westport: Bergin & Garvey (Greenwood Publishing), 2002.

Brian, Amber. "The Alva Ixtlilxochitl Brothers and the Nahua Intellectual Community." In *Texcoco: Prehispanic and Colonial Perspectives*, edited by Jongsoo Lee and Galen Brokaw, 201–18. Boulder: University Press of Colorado, 2014.

———. "The Original Alva Ixtlilxochitl Manuscripts at Cambridge University." *Colonial Latin American Review* 23, no. 1 (April 2014): 84–101.

Brotherston, Gordon. "Indigenous Literatures and Cultures in Twentieth-Century Latin America." In vol. 10 of *Cambridge History of Latin America: Latin America since 1930, Ideas, Culture and Society*, edited by Leslie Bethell, 287–305. Cambridge: Cambridge University Press, 1995.

Bruhns, Karen Olsen. *Ancient South America.* Cambridge: Cambridge University Press, 1994.

———, and Karen E. Stothert. *Women in Ancient America.* Norman: University of Oklahoma Press, 1999.

Bubano Arias, Grace. "Las santafereñas del XVII: Entre holandas y lágrimas." *Logos: Revista de la Facultad de Filosofía y Humanidades* 9 (2005): 119–38. https://revistas.lasalle.edu.co.

Burga, Manuel. "The Triumph of Colonial Christianity in the Central Andes: Guilt, Good Conscience and Indian Piety." In *The Middle Period in Latin America, Values and Attitudes in the 17th–19th Centuries*, edited by Mark D. Szuchman, 33–52. Boulder: Lynne Rienner Publishers, 1989.

Burgos, Elizabeth [and Rigoberta Menchú]. *Me llamo Rigoberta Menchú y así me nació la conciencia.* Octava edición. México: Siglo XXI, 1992.

Burkholder, Mark A., and Lyman L. Johnson. *Colonial Latin America.* 5th ed. Oxford: Oxford University Press, 2004.

Butler, Judith. *Gender Trouble: Feminism and the Subversion of Identity.* New York: Routledge, 1999.

Cahill, David. "The Inca and Inca Symbolism in Popular Festive Culture: The Religious Processions of Seventeenth-Century Cuzco." In *Habsburg Peru: Images, Imagination and Memory,* edited by Peter T. Bradley and David Cahill, 87–162. Liverpool: Liverpool University Press, 2000.

Calero, Luis F. *Chiefdoms under Siege: Spain's rule and Native Adaptation in the Southern Colombian Andes, 1535–1700.* Albuquerque: University of New Mexico Press, 1997.

Calnek, Eduard E. "Patterns of Empire Formation in the Valley of Mexico, Late Postclassic Period, 1200–1521." In *The Inca and Aztec States, 1400–1800,* edited by George A. Collier, Renato I. Rosaldo, and John D. Wirth, 43–62. New York: Academic Press, 1982.

Camayd-Freixas, Eric. "Enunciating Space, Locating Identity: Garcilaso de la Vega's *Comentarios reales de los Incas.*" In *Mapping Colonial Spanish America: Places and Commonplaces of Identity, Culture and Experience,* edited by Santa Arias and Mariselle Meléndez, 102–20. Lewisburg, PA: Bucknell University Press/London: Associated University Presses, 2002.

Cameron, Euan. *Early Modern Europe: An Oxford History.* Edited by Euan Cameron. Oxford: Oxford University Press, 1999. See esp. "Editor's Introduction."

Carbia, Rómulo D. *Historia de la leyenda negra hispanoamericana.* Madrid: Publicaciones del Consejo de Hispanidad, 1944.

Carmack, Robert M. *The Quiché Mayas of Utatlán. The Evolution of a Highland Guatemala Kingdom.* Norman: University of Oklahoma, 1981.

Casey, James. *Early Modern Spain: A Social History.* London: Routledge, 2002.

Caso, Alfonso. *El pueblo del sol.* Mexico: FCE, 1953. Castillo, Alejandra et al., eds. *Nación, estado y cultura en América Latina.* Santiago: Ediciones Facultad de Filosofía y Humanidades, Universidad de Chile, 2003.

Castillo, Luis Jaime. "The Last of the Mochicas: A View from the Jequetepeque Valley." In *Moche Art and Archaeology in Ancient Peru,* edited by Joanne Pillsbury, 307–32. Washington/New Haven: National Gallery of Art/Yale University Press, 2001.

Castro Arenas, Mario. *La rebelión de Juan Santos.* Lima: Milla Batres, 1973.

Castro-Klarén, Sara. *The Narrow Pass of Our Nerves: Writing, Coloniality and Postcolonial Theory.* Madrid/Frankfurt: Iberoamericana/Vervuert, 2011.

———. "The Nation in Ruins: Archeology and the Rise of the Nation." In *Beyond Imagined Communities: Reading and Writing the Nation in Nineteenth-Century Latin America,* edited by Sara Castro-Klarén and John Chasteen, 161–95. Washington/Baltimore: Woodrow Wilson Center Press/Johns Hopkins University Press, 2003.

———. "Huamán Poma y el espacio de la pureza." *Revista Iberoamericana* 47, nos. 114–15 (Enero–Junio 1981): 45–67.

Cerrón-Palomino, Rodolfo. *Las lenguas de los incas: el puquina, el aimara y el quechua.* Frankfurt: Peter Lang AG, 2013.

———. "El aimara como lengua oficial de los incas." *Boletín de arqueología PUCP,* no. 8 (2004): 9–21.

———. "Examen de la teoría aimarista de Uhle." In *Max Uhle y el Perú antiguo*, edited by Peter Kaulicke, 85–120. Lima: Pontificia Universidad Católica del Perú, 1998.

———. "Estudio introductorio." In *Grammatica o arte de la lengua general de los indios de los reynos del Perú*, by Fray Domingo de Santo Tomás, vii–liv. Cuzco: Centro de Estudios Regionales Andinos "Bartolomé de Las Casas," 1995.

———. "El Nebrija Indiano." In *Grammatica o arte de la lengua general de los indios de los reynos del Perú*, by Fray Domingo de S. Thomas, i–lxiii. Transliteración y Estudio por Rudolfo Cerrón-Palomino. Madrid: Agencia Española de Cooperación Internacional, 1994.

———. "Sobre el nombre quechua." *Lexis* 9, no. 1 (1985): 87–99.

Chabod, Federico. *La idea de la nación*. Translated by Stella Mastrangelo. Mexico: FCE, 1987.

Chang-Rodríguez, Raquel. *Cartografía garcilasista*. Alicante: Universidad de Alicante, "Cuadernos sin nombre," 2013.

———. *La palabra y la pluma en* Primer nueva corónica y buen gobierno. Lima: Pontificia Universidad Católica del Perú, 2005.

———. *La apropiación del signo: Tres cronistas indígenas del Perú*. Tempe: Arizona State University, 1988.

———. "Coloniaje y conciencia nacional: Garcilaso de la Vega Inca y Felipe Guamán Poma de Ayala." *Cahiers du monde hispanique et luso-brésilien* 38, numéro consacré aux consciences nationales dans le monde ibérique et ibérico-américain (1982): 29–43.

Christenson, Allen J. *The Burden of the Ancients. Maya Ceremonies of World Renewal from the Precolombian Period to the Present*. Austin: University of Texas Press, 2016.

———. *K'iche'-English Dictionary and Guide to Pronunciation of the K'iche'-Maya Alphabet*. Cristal River: Foundation for the Advancement of Mesoamerican Studies, 2003. Accessed July 1, 2016. www.famsi.org/mayawriting/dictionary/christenson/quidic_complete.pdf.

Clendinnen, Inga. *Aztecs*. Cambridge: Cambridge University Press, 1991.

Cline, S. L. "The Spiritual Conquest Reexamined: Baptism and Christian Marriage in Early Sixteenth-Century Mexico." *Hispanic American Historical Review* 73, no. 3 (1993): 453–80.

———. *Colonial Culhuacan, 1580–1600: A Social History of an Aztec Town*. Albuquerque: University of New Mexico Press, 1986.

Coe, Michael. *Breaking the Maya Code*. New York: Thames and Hudson, 1992.

———. *America's First Civilization*. New York/Princeton: American Heritage/Van Nostrand, 1968.

———, and Rex Koontz. *Mexico from the Olmecs to the Aztecs*. 6th ed. New York: Thames and Hudson, 2008.

Colom González, Francisco. *Relatos de nación: la construcción de las identidades nacionales en el mundo hispánico*. Madrid: Consejo Superior de Investigaciones Científicas, Instituto de Filosofía: Organización de Estados Iberoamericanos/Iberoamericana/Frankfurt: Vervuert, 2005.

Comisión de la Verdad y Reconciliación. *Informe final*. Lima: CVR, 2003.

Cordy-Collins, Alana. "Labretted Ladies: Foreign Women in Northern Moche Art." In *Moche Art and Archaeology in Ancient Peru*, edited by Joanne Pillsbury, 247–57. Washington, DC/New Haven: National Gallery of Art/Yale University Press, 2001.

Cornejo Polar, Antonio. *Escribir en el aire. Ensayo sobre la heterogeneidad socio-cultural en las literaturas andinas*. Lima: Horizonte, 1994.

Cortés, Rocío. "The Colegio Imperial de Santa Cruz de Tlatelolco and its aftermath: Nahua intellectuals and the spiritual conquest of Mexico." In *A Companion to Latin American Literature*, edited by Sara Castro-Klarén, 86–105. Malden, MA: Blackwell, 2008.

———. "Motecuzoma/Huémac y Quetzalcóatl/Cortés: Referencia mítica sobre el fin del imperio mexica en la *Crónica mexicana* de don Hernando de Alvarado Tezozomoc." *Hofstra Hispanic Review* 3, no. 1 (2006): 26–40.

———. "¿Dónde está Tlaloc? Edificación real y simbólica del imperio en fuentes escritas y materia." *MLN* 118 (2003): 341–62.

Courcelles, Dominique de. "Managing the World: The Development of Jus Gentium by the Theologians of Salamanca in the Sixteenth Century." *Philosophy and Rhetoric* 38, no. 1 (2005): 1–15.

Covey, R. Alan. *How the Incas Built Their Heartland: State Formation and the Innovation of Imperial Strategies in the Sacred Valley, Peru*. Ann Arbor: The University of Michigan, 2006.

Crowley, Frances G. *Garcilaso de la Vega, el Inca and His Sources in 'Comentarios reales de los Incas.'* The Hague: Mouton, 1971.

Curet, L. Antonio. "The Taíno: Phenomena, Concepts, and Terms." *Ethnohistory* 61, no. 3 (Summer 2014): 467–95.

Currie, Elizabeth J. "Archaeology, Ethnohistory and Exchange along the Coast of Ecuador." *Antiquity* 69, no. 264 (1995). Accessed June 13, 2015. doi:10.1017/ S0003598X00081904.

Daneri, Juan José. "¿Tloque Nahuaque o dios desconocido? El problema de la traducción en *La historia chichimeca* de Fernando de Alva Ixtlilxóchitl." In vol. 1 of *Morada de la palabra: homenaje a Luce y Mercedes López Baralt*, edited by William Mejías López, 515–21. San Juan: Editorial de la Universidad de Puerto Rico, 2002.

Davies, Nigel. *The Incas*. Boulder: University Press of Colorado, 1995.

———. *The Aztec Empire: The Toltec Resurgence*. Norman: University of Oklahoma Press, 1987.

———. *The Ancient Kingdoms of Mexico*. New York: Penguin Books, 1982.

———. *The Toltec Heritage: From the Fall of Tula to the Rise of Tenochtitlan*. Norman: University of Oklahoma Press, 1980.

———. *The Toltecs until the Fall of Tula*. Norman: University of Oklahoma Press, 1977.

———. *The Aztecs*. Norman: University of Oklahoma Press, 1973.

Deas, Malcolm. "The Man on Foot: Conscription and the Nation-State in Nineteenth-Century Latin America." In *Studies in the Formation of the Nation State in Latin America*, edited by James Dunkerley, 77–93. London: Institute for Latin American Studies, 2002.

DeLeonardis, Lisa. "Itinerant Experts, Alternative Harvests: *Kamayuq* in the Service of *Qhapaq* and Crown." *Ethnohistory* 58, no. 3 (Summer 2011): 445–89.

Derrida, Jacques. "Structure, Sign, and Play in the Discourse of the Human Sciences." In *The Structuralist Controversy*, edited by Richard Macksey and Eugenio Donato, 247–72. Baltimore, Johns Hopkins University Press, 1972.

Díaz Caballero, Jesús. "El incaísmo como primera ficción orientadora en la formación de la nación criolla en las provincias unidas del Río de la Plata." *A Contracorriente* 3, no. 1 (Fall 2005): 67–113.

Dibble, Charles E. "Sahagún's Historia." In introductory vol., books 1–12 of *General History of the Things of New Spain* [Florentine Codex], by Bernardino de Sahagún, 9–23. Edited and translated by Arthur J. O. Anderson and Charles Dibble. Santa Fe/ Salt Lake City: School of American Research/University of Utah Press, 1978.

Diehl, Richard A. *Tula: The Toltec Capital of Ancient Mexico.* London: Thames and Hudson, 1983.

Dillehay, Tom. "Town and Country in Late Moche Times." In *Moche Art and Archaeology in Ancient Peru*, edited by Joanne Pillsbury, 259–83. Washington, DC/New Haven: National Gallery of Art/Yale University Press, 2001.

Domingo, Paola. *Naissance d'une société métisse. Aspects socio-économiques du Paraguay de la Conquête à travers les dossiers testamentaires.* Montpellier: Université Paul-Valéry-Montpellier III, 2006.

Dore, Elizabeth. "One Step Forward, Two Steps Back: Gender and the State in the Long Nineteenth Century." In *Hidden Histories of Gender and the State in Latin America*, edited by Elizabeth Dore and Maxine Molyneux, 3–32. Durham, NC: Duke University Press, 2000.

Doyle, Laura. "Inter-Imperiality and Literary Studies in the Longer *Durée*." *PMLA* 130, no. 2 (2015): 336–47.

Duncan, David Ewing. *Hernando de Soto: A Savage Quest in the Americas.* New York: Crown Books, 1995.

Durand, José. "La biblioteca del Inca." *Nueva Revista de Filología Hispánica* 2, no. 3 (1948): 239–64.

———. *El Inca Garcilaso, clásico de América.* México: Secretaria de Educación Pública, 1976.

Durston, Alan. *Pastoral Quechua. The History of Christian Translation in Colonial Peru, 1550–1650.* Notre Dame: University of Notre Dame Press, 2007.

Earle, Duncan. "Menchú Tales and Maya Social Landscape: The Silencing of Words and Worlds." In *The Rigoberta Menchú Controversy*, edited by Arturo Arias, 288–308. Minneapolis: University of Minnesota Press, 2001.

Earle, Rebecca. "The Role of Print in the Spanish American Wars of Independence." In *The Political Power of the Word: Press and Oratory in Nineteenth-Century Latin America*, edited by Iván Jaksić, 9–33. London: Institute for Latin American Studies/ University of London, 2002.

Espinoza Soriano, Waldemar. *Los incas: economía, sociedad y estado en la era del Tahuantinsuyo.* 3rd ed. Lima: Amaru Editores, 1997.

Esteva-Fabregat, Claudio. *Mestizaje in Ibero-America.* Translated by John Wheat. Tucson: University of Arizona Press, 1995.

Fabian, Johannes. *Time and the Other: How Anthropology Makes its Mark.* New York, Columbia University Press, 2002.

Fernández, Christian. *Inca Garcilaso: Imaginación, memoria e identidad.* Lima: Universidad Nacional Mayor de San Marcos, 2004.

———. "Noticias del imperio: la crisis financiera de España en la segunda parte de los *Comentarios reales* del Inca Garcilaso de la Vega." In *Entre la pluma y la espada: El Inca Garcilaso y sus* Comentarios reales, edited by Raquel Chang-Rodríguez, 109–18. Lima: Fondo Editorial de la Pontificia Universidad Católica del Perú, 2010.

———. "Traducción y apropiación: Los 'papeles rotos' y la creación de Blas Valera como 'autor' en los Comentarios reales del Inca Garcilaso." In *El Inca Garcilaso de la Vega: entre varios mundos*, edited by José Morales Saravia and Gerhard Penzkofer, 93–104. Lima: Ediciones del Vicerrectorado Académico de la Universidad Nacional Mayor de San Marcos, 2011.

Fernández, Pura. "*No hay nación para este sexo.* Redes culturales de mujeres de letras españolas y latinoamericanas (1824–1936)." In *No hay nación para este sexo. La Re(d) pública transatlántica de las Letras: escritoras españolas y latinoamericanas (1824–1936)*, 9–57. Frankfurt/Madrid: Vervuert/Iberoamericana, 2015.

Fernández Cozman, Camilo. *Raúl Porras Barrenechea y la literatura peruana.* Lima: Universidad Nacional Mayor de San Marcos, 2000.

Fernández Herrero, Beatriz. *La utopía de América. Teoría. Leyes. Experimentos.* Barcelona: Anthropos, 1992.

Fernández Lancho, Manassés. *Escritura incaica: Kellka inkaika.* Lima: Universidad Nacional Federico Villarreal, Editorial Universitaria, 2001.

Florescano, Enrique. "Chichén Itzá, Teotihuacán and the Origins of the *Popol Vuh.*" *Colonial Latin American Review* 15, no. 2 (December 2006): 129–42.

Flores Galindo, Alberto. *Obras completas.* 6 vols. Lima: Sur, Casa de Estudios del Socialismo, 1993–2008.

Franco, Jean. *Critical Passions: Selected Essays.* Edited by Mary Louise Pratt and Kathleen Newman. Durham, NC: Duke University Press, 1999.

Fuenzalida Vollmar, Fernando. *La matriz colonial de la comunidad de indígenas peruanas: una hipótesis de trabajo.* Lima: Instituto de Estudios Peruanos, 1969.

Gadamer, Hans-Georg. *Truth and Method.* Translated by Joel Weinsheimer and Donald G. Marshall. 3rd ed. London: Bloomsbury Academic, 2013.

Galaviz, Juan M. *Juana Inés de la Cruz.* Madrid: Historia 16, 1987.

Gálvez Mora, César, and Jesús Briceño Rosario. "The Moche in the Chicaza Valley." In *Moche Art and Archaeology in Ancient Peru*, edited by Joanne Pillsbury, 141–57. Washington, DC/New Haven: National Gallery of Art/Yale University Press, 2001.

Garofalo, Leo J. "The Shape of a Diaspora: The Movement of Afro-Iberians to Colonial Spanish America." In *Africans to Spanish America: Expanding the Diaspora*, edited by Sherwin Bryant, Rachael Sarah, and Ben Vinson, 27–49. Urbana: University of Illinois Press, 2002.

García Bryce, Iñigo. *Crafting the Republic: Lima's Artisans and Nation Building in Peru, 1821–1879.* Albuquerque: University of New Mexico Press, 2004.

García Canclini, Néstor. *Culturas híbridas: estrategias para entrar y salir de la modernidad.* Mexico: Grijalbo, 1990.

García Loaeza, Pablo. "Fernando de Alva Ixtlilxochitl's Texcocan Dynasty. Nobility, Genealogy, and Historiography." In *Texcoco: Prehispanic and Colonial Perspectives,* edited by Jongsoo Lee and Galen Brokaw, 219–42. Boulder: University Press of Colorado, 2014.

Geertz, Clifford. "The Integrative Revolution: Primordial Sentiments and Civil Politics in the New States." In *Old Societies and New States,* edited by Clifford Geertz, 103–57. New York: The Free Press, 1963.

Gerhard, Peter. "A Black Conquistador in Mexico." *Hispanic American Historical Review* 58, no. 3 (1968): 451–59.

Gibson, Charles. *The Aztecs under Spanish Rule.* Stanford: Stanford University Press, 1964.

———. *Tlaxcala in the Sixteenth Century.* New Haven: Yale University Press, 1952.

———. "The Identity of Diego Muñoz Camargo." *Hispanic American Historical Review* 30 (1950): 195–208.

Gillespie, Susan D. "The Triple Alliance: A Postconquest Tradition." In *Native Traditions in the Postconquest World,* edited by Elizabeth Hill Boone and Tom Cummins, 233–64. Washington, DC: Dumbarton Oaks Research Library, 1998.

Glade, William. "The State in Retreat in the Economy." In *The Changing Role of the State in Latin America,* edited by Menno Vellinga, 93–113. Boulder: Westview Press, 1988.

Gordon, B. Le Roy. *Human Geography and Ecology in the Sinú Country of Colombia.* 1957. Reprint, Westport, CT: Greenwood Press, 1977.

Gott, Richard. "Latin America as a White Settler Society." *Bulletin of Latin American Research* 26, no. 2 (2007): 269–89.

Gover, Keven. Forward to *Nation to Nation: Treaties between the United States & American Indian Nations,* edited by Suzan Shown Harjo, xi–xiii. Washington, DC: National Museum of the American Indian/Smithsonian Books, 2014.

Greer, Margaret R., Walter D. Mignolo, and Maureen Quilligan. Introduction to *Rereading the Black Legend: the Discourses of Religious and Racial Difference in the Renaissance Empires,* 1–24. Chicago: University of Chicago Press, 2007. Ebsco e-book.

Gruzinski, Serge. "Individualization and Acculturation: Confession among the Nahuas of Mexico from the Sixteenth to the Eighteenth Century." In *Sexuality and Marriage in Colonial Latin America,* edited by Asunción Lavrin, 96–117. Lincoln: University of Nebraska Press, 1989.

Gutiérrez Arbulú, Laura. "Introducción." *Lima en el Siglo XVI,* edited by Laura Gutiérrez Arbulú, 13–16. Lima: Pontificia Universidad Católica del Perú, 2006.

Haas, Jonathan, Winfred Creamer, and Alvaro Ruíz. "Dating the Late Archaic Occupation of the North Chaco Region in Peru." *Nature* 432 (December 23–30, 2004): 1020–23.

Hampe Martínez, Teodoro. "La misión financiera de Agustín de Zárate, Contador General del Perú y Tierra Firme (1543–1546)." *Historia y cultura; revista del Museo Nacional de Arqueología, Antropología e Historia del Perú* 17 (1984): 91–124.

Hannaford, Ivan. *Race: The History of an Idea in the West.* Washington, DC/Baltimore: The Woodrow Wilson Center Press/The Johns Hopkins University Press, 1996.

Hardman, M. J. "Aymara and Quechua: Languages in Contact." In *South American Indian languages: Retrospect and Prospect*, edited by Harriet E. Manelis Klein and Louisa R. Stark, 617–43. Austin: University of Texas Press, 1985.

Haskett, Robert S. "'Our Suffering with the Taxco Tribute': Involuntary Mine Labor and Indigenous Society in Central New Spain." *Hispanic American Historical Review* 71, no. 3 (1991): 447–75.

———. *Indigenous Rulers: An Ethnohistory of Town Government in Colonial Cuernavaca*. Albuquerque: University of New Mexico Press, 1991.

———. "Pochteca." In vol. 5 of *Encyclopedia of Latin American History and Culture*, edited by Erick Langer and Jay Kinsbrunner, 276. 2nd ed. Detroit: Gale/Cengage, 2008.

Hastings, Adrian. *The Construction of Nationhood: Ethnicity, Religion, and Nationalism*. Cambridge: Cambridge University Press, 1997.

Heilbroner, Robert L. *The Nature and Logic of Capitalism*. New York: W. W. Norton and Company, 1985.

Hellenthal, Garrett, George B. J. Busby, Gavin Band, James F. Wilson, Cristian Capelli, Daniel Falush, and Simon Myers. "A Genetic Atlas of Human Admixture History." *Science* 343 (February 14, 2014): 747–50.

Helms, Mary W. "The Indians of the Caribbean and Circum-Caribbean at the End of the Fifteenth Century." In vol. 1 of *The Cambridge History of Latin America*, edited by Leslie Bethell, 37–57. Cambridge: Cambridge University Press, 1985.

Hernández Arana Xajilá, Francisco, and Francisco Díaz Gebuto Quej. *The Annals of the Cakchiquels*. Translated by Adrián Recinos and Delia Goetz. Norman: University of Oklahoma Press, 1953.

Hernández Astete, Francisco. *La mujer en el Tahuantinsuyo*. Lima: Pontificia Universidad Católica del Perú, 2005.

Herzog, Tamar. *Defining Nations: Immigrants and Citizens in Early Modern Spain and Spanish America*. New Haven: Yale University Press, 2003.

Hewett, Edgar L. *Ancient Life in Mexico and Central America*. Indianapolis, New York: Bobbs-Merrill Co., 1936.

Hinkelammert, Franz J. "The Hidden Logic of Modernity: Locke and the Inversion of Human Rights." *Worlds and Knowledges Otherwise* (Fall 2004): 1–27.

Hobsbawm, E. J. *Nations and Nationalism since 1780*. 2nd ed. Cambridge: Cambridge University Press, 1992.

Hoerder, Dirk. *Cultures in Contact: World Migrations in the Second Millennium*. Durham, NC: Duke University Press, 2002.

Holt, Thomas C. "Forward: The First New Nations." In *Race and Nation in Modern Latin America*, edited by Nancy P. Appelbaum, Anne S. Macpherson, and Karin Alejandra Rosemblatt. Chapel Hill: The University of North Carolina Press, 2003.

Horn, Rebecca. "The Sociopolitical Organization of the Colonial Jurisdiction of Coyoacan." In vol. 2 of *Ciudad y campo en la historia de México*, edited by Ricardo Sánchez, Eric Van Young, and Gisela von Wobeser, 102–13. Mexico: Instituto de Investigaciones Históricas, UNAM, 1991.

Hosler, Dorothy. "West Mexican Metallurgy: Revisited and Revised." *Journal of World Prehistory* 22, no. 3 (January 2009): 185–212.

Husson, Jean-Philippe. Introduction to *La mort D'Ataw Wallpa ou La fin de l'Empire des Incas. Tragédie anonyme en langue quechua du milieu du XVIe siècle*, edited and translated by Jean-Philippe Husson, 15–36. Geneva: Patiño, 2001.

Hyland, Sabine. *The Jesuit and the Incas: The Extraordinary Life of Padre Blas Valera, S.J.* Ann Arbor: University of Michigan Press, 2003.

Ilgen, William D. *The Bernard J. Flatow Collection of Latin American Cronistas.* Chapel Hill: University of North Carolina at Chapel Hill Library, 2005.

Isbell, William H. "La arqueología wari y la dispersión del quechua." *Boletín de Arqueología PUCP* 14 (2010): 199–220.

Jackson, Robert H. *Race, Caste, and Status: Indians in Colonial Spanish America.* Albuquerque: University of New Mexico Press, 1999.

Jara, Alvaro. "Una investigación sobre los problemas del trabajo en Chile durante el período colonial." *Hispanic American Historical Review* 32 (May 1959): 239–44.

Jones, Julie. "Innovation and Resplendence: Metalwork for Moche Lords." In *Moche Art and Archaeology in Ancient Peru*, edited by Joanne Pillsbury, 207–21. Washington, DC/New Haven: National Gallery of Art/Yale University Press, 2001.

Kaplen, Caren, and Inderpal Grewal. "Transnational Feminist Cultural Studies: Beyond the Marxism/Poststructuralism/Feminism Divides." In *Between Woman and Nation: Nationalisms, Transnational Feminisms, and the State*, edited by Caren Kaplan, Norma Alarcón, and Minoo Moallem, 349–63. Durham, NC: Duke University Press, 1999.

Kapsoli Escudero, Wilfredo. *El retorno del Inca.* 2nd ed. Lima: Universidad Ricardo Palma, 2001.

———. *Francisco de Carbajal o el Genio del Mal.* Lima: Gráfica Horizonte, 2000.

Kauffmann Doig, Federico. "Los liberteños ancestrales." In *Gran Encyclopedia del Perú*, 562–80. Lima: Lexis, 1998.

Kauffmann, Leisa. "Figures of Time and Tribute: The Trace of the Colonial Subaltern in Fernando de Alva Ixtlilxochitl's *Historia de la nación chichimeca.*" *The Global South* 4, no. 1 (Spring 2010): 31–47.

Keegan, William F. "Creating the Guanahatabey /Ciboney~: the Modern Genesis of an Extinct Culture." *Antiquity* 63, no. 239 (1989): 373.

Keith, Robert G. *Conquest and Agrarian Change: The Emergence of the Hacienda System on the Peruvian Coast.* Cambridge: Harvard University Press, 1976.

———. "Encomienda, Hacienda and Corregimiento in Spanish America: A Structural Analysis." *Hispanic American Historical Review* 51 (1971): 431–46.

Kinsbrunner, Jay, and Erick Langer, eds. *Encyclopedia of Latin American History and Culture.* 2nd ed. 6 vols. New York: Charles Scribner's Sons, 2008.

Kirk, Stephanie. "Mapping the Hemispheric Divide: The Colonial Americas in a Collaborative Context." *PMLA* 128, no. 4 (2013): 976–82.

Klarén, Peter Findell. *Peru: Society and Nationhood in the Andes.* Oxford: Oxford University Press, 2000.

Klee, Carol A. "The Acquisition of Clitic Pronouns in the Spanish Interlanguage of Peruvian Quechua Speakers." *Hispania* 72, no. 2 (1989): 402–8.

Klein, Herbert S. *African Slavery in Latin America and the Caribbean.* Oxford: Oxford University Press, 1896.

Klor de Alva, J. Jorge. "Sahagún and the Birth of Modern Ethnography: Representing, Confessing, and Inscribing the Native Other." In *The Work of Bernardino de Sahagún, Pioneer Ethnographer of Sixteenth-Century Aztec Mexico*, edited by J. Jorge Klor de Alva, H. B. Nicholson, and Eloise Quiñones Keber, 31–52. Albany: Institute for Mesoamerican Studies, 1988.

Kolb, Charles C. *Marine Shell Trade and Classic Teotihuacan, Mexico.* Oxford: BAR International Series 364, 1987.

Kosiba, Steve. "Emplacing Value, Cultivating Order: Places of Conversion and Practices of Subordination throughout Early Inka State Formation." In *The Construction of Value in the Ancient World*, edited by John K. Papadopoulos and Gary Urton, 97–127. Los Angeles: Cotsen Institute of Archaeology Press, 2012.

Kubler, George. *The Art and Architecture of Ancient America: The Mexican, Maya, and Andean Peoples.* Baltimore: Penguin Books, 1962.

Larson, Brooke. *Trials of Nation Making: Liberalism, Race, and Ethnicity in the Andes, 1810–1910.* Cambridge: Cambridge University Press, 2004.

Lavrin, Asunción. "Sexuality in Colonial Mexico: *A Church Dilemma*." In *Sexuality and Marriage in Colonial Latin America*, edited by Asunción Lavrin, 47–95. Lincoln: University of Nebraska Press, 1989.

Lee, Jongsoo. *The Allure of Nezahualcoyotl: Pre-Hispanic History, Religion, and Nahua Poetics.* Albuquerque: University of New Mexico Press, 2008.

Lee, Richard E. "Fernand Braudel, the Longue Durée, and World-Systems Analysis." In *The Longue Durée and World-Systems Analysis*, edited by Richard E. Lee, 1–7. New York: State University of New York Press, 2012.

Lehmann, Henri. "The Moguex-Coconuco." In *The Andean Civilizations*, vol. 2 of *Handbook of South American Indians*, 969–74. New York: Copper Square Publishers, 1963.

Leibsohn, Dana. "Primers for Memory: Cartographic Histories and Nahua Identities." In *Writing without Words: Alternative Literacies in Mesoamerica and the Andes*, edited by Elizabeth Hill Boone and Walter D. Mignolo, 161–83. Durham, NC: Duke University Press, 1994.

Leonard, Irving. *Los libros del conquistador.* Translated by Mario Monteforte Toledo. México: FCE, 1979.

———. *Baroque Times in Old México.* 2nd ed. Ann Arbor: University of Michigan, 1966.

León-Portilla, Miguel. *La filosofía náhuatl.* Mexico: Universidad Nacional Autónoma de México, 1983.

———. *Toltecáyotl: Estudios de Cultura Náhuatl.* Mexico: FCE, 1982.

Lesure, Richard G. "Figurine Fashions in Formative Mesoamerica." In *The Construction of Value in the Ancient World*, edited by John K. Papadopoulos and Gary Urton, 370–91. Los Angeles: Cotsen Institute of Archaeology Press, 2012.

Lienhard, Martín. *La voz y su huella: Escritura y conflicto étnico-social en América Latina 1492–1988.* Hanover: Ediciones del Norte, 1991.

Livi-Bacci, Massimo. "The Depopulation of Hispanic America after the Conquest." *Population and Development Review* 32, no. 2 (June 2006): 199–232.

Lockhart, James. *Nahuatl as Written: Lessons in Older Written Nahuatl, with Copious Examples and Texts.* Los Angeles: UCLA Latin American Studies/Stanford University Press, 2001.

———. *The Nahuas after the Conquest.* Stanford: Stanford University Press, 1992.

———. *Nahuas and Spaniards: Postconquest Central Mexican History and Philology.* Stanford: Stanford University Press, 1991.

———. *Of Things of the Indies: Essays Old and New in Early Latin American History.* Stanford: Stanford University Press, 1999.

———, and Enrique Otte, eds. *Letters and People of the Spanish Indies: The Sixteenth Century.* Cambridge: Cambridge University Press, 1976.

López, Carlos M. "The *Popol Wuj:* The Repositioning and Survival of Mayan Culture." In *A Companion to Latin American Literature*, edited by Sara Castro-Klarén, 68–85. Malden, MA: Blackwell, 2008.

———. *Los* Popol Wuj *y sus epistemologías: Las diferencias, el conocimiento y los ciclos del infinito.* Quito: Ediciones Abya-Yala, 1999.

López-Baralt, Mercedes. *Guaman Poma: autor y artista.* Lima: Pontificia Universidad Católica del Perú, 1993.

Lovell, W. George. "The Highland Maya." In part 2 of *Mesoamerica*, vol. 2 of The *Cambridge History of the Native Peoples of the Americas*, edited by Richard E. W. Adams and Murdo J. MacLeod, 392–442. Cambridge: Cambridge University Press, 2000.

Lumbreras, Luis Guillermo. *The Peoples and Cultures of Ancient Peru.* Translated by Betty J. Meggers. Washington, DC: Smithsonian Institution Press, 1974.

Lynch, Thomas F. "The Earliest South American Lifeways." In vol. 3, part 1 of *The Cambridge History of the Native People of the Americas*, edited by Frank Salomon and Stuart B. Schwartz, 188–263. Cambridge: Cambridge University Press, 1999.

MacCormack, Sabine. *Religion in the Andes: Vision and Imagination in Early Colonial Peru.* Princeton: Princeton University Press, 1991.

Maddox, Lucy. *Removals: Nineteenth-Century American Literature and the Politics of Indian Affairs.* Oxford: Oxford University Press, 1991.

Mallon, Florencia E. *The Defense of Community in Peru's Central Highlands: Peasant Struggle and Capitalist Transition 1860-1940.* Princeton: Princeton University Press, 1983.

Mann, Charles C. "Unraveling Khipu's Secrets." *Science* 39 (August 12, 2005): 1005–6.

Mannheim, Bruce. *The Language of the Inka since the European Invasion.* Austin: University of Texas Press, 1991. .

———. "Una nación acorralada: Southern Peruvian Quechua Language Planning and Politics in Historical Perspective." *Language in Society* 13, no. 3 (1984): 291–309

Manning, Patrick. "The Slave Trade: The Formal Demography of a Global System." In *The Atlantic Slave Trade. Effects of Economics, Societies, and Peoples in Africa, the Americas, and Europe*, edited by Joseph E. Inikori and Stanley L. Engerman, 117–41. Durham, NC: Duke University Press, 1992.

Mao, Xianyun, Abigail W. Bigham, Rui Mei, Gerardo Gutierrez, Ken M. Weiss, Tom D. Brutsaert, Fabiola Leon-Velarde, Lorna G. Moore, Enrique Vargas, Paul M. McKeigue, Mark D. Shriver, and Esteban J. Parra. "A Genomewide Admixture Mapping Panel for Hispanic/Latino Populations." *The American Journal of Human Genetics* 80 (June 2007): 1071–81.

Maravall, José Antonio. "La aportación de Ortega al desarrollo del concepto de nación." *Cuadernos Hispanoamericanos* 403–5 (1984): 511–28.

———. *Utopía y reformismo en la España de los Austrias.* Madrid: Siglo XXI, 1982.

Markham, Sir Clements. *The Incas of Peru.* New York: E. P. Dutton and Company, 1912.

Marriot, McKim. "Cultural Policy in the New States." In *Old Societies and New States,* edited by Clifford Geertz, 27–56. New York: The Free Press, 1963.

Maura, Juan Francisco. *Women in the Conquest of the Americas.* Translated by John F. Deredita. New York: Peter Lang, 1997.

Mazzotti, José Antonio. *Coros mestizos del Inca Garcilaso: resonancias andinas.* Lima: FCE/Bolsa de Valores de Lima, 1996.

McCafferty, Geoffrey G. "Domestic Practice in Postclassic Santa Isabel, Nicaragua." *Latin American Antiquity* 19, no. 1 (2008): 64–82.

McEvoy, Carmen. "Indio y nación: una lectura política de la rebelión de Huancané (1866–1868). In *Forjando la nación: ensayos de historia republicana,* 61–118. Lima/Sewanee: Pontificia Universidad Católica del Perú/University of the South, 1999.

McNeill, William H. *The Rise of the West: A History of the Human Community.* Chicago: University of Chicago Press, 1963.

Melo, Jorge Orlando. *Historia de Colombia: el establecimiento de la dominación española.* 1977. Reprint, Biblioteca Digital Andino/Biblioteca Luis Ángel Arango, 2006.

Menchú, Rigoberta, and Elizabeth Burgos. *I, Rigoberta Menchú: An Indian Woman in Guatemala.* Translated by Ann Wright. 2nd ed. London: Verso, 2009.

Menéndez y Pelayo, Marcelino. *Orígenes de la novela.* 4 vols. Santander: S.A. de Artes Gráfica, 1943.

Merrim, Stephanie. *Early Modern Women's Writing and Sor Juana Inés de la Cruz.* Nashville: Vanderbilt University Press, 1999.

———. "The First Fifty Years of Hispanic New World Historiography: The Caribbean, Mexico, and Central America." In *Discovery to Modernism,* vol. 1 of *The Cambridge History of Latin American literature,* edited by Roberto González Echevarría and Enrique Pupo-Walker, 58–100. Cambridge: Cambridge University Press, 1996.

Mexicano Ramos, César. "'Negocios' menudistas y la vida cotidiana en Lima." In *Lima en el Siglo XVI,* edited by Laura Gutiérrez Arbulú, 311–64. Lima: Pontificia Universidad Católica del Perú, 2006.

Meyer, Karl E. *Teotihuacán.* New York: Newsweek, 1973.

Meyers, Kathleen Ann. *Neither Saints nor Sinners: Writing the Lives of Women in Spanish America.* Oxford: Oxford University Press, 2003.

Mignolo, Walter D. *The Darker Side of the Renaissance.* 2nd ed. Ann Arbor: University of Michigan, 2003.

———. *The Idea of Latin America.* London: Blackwell, 2005.

———. *Local Histories/Global Designs: Coloniality, Subaltern Knowledges, and Border Thinking.* Princeton: Princeton University Press, 2000.

———. "El mandato y la ofrenda: la Descripción de la ciudad y provincia de Tlaxcala, de Diego Muñoz Camargo, y las relaciones de Indias." *Nueva Revista de Filología Hispánica* 35, no. 2 (1987): 451–84.

Milanich, Jerald T. "Un nuevo mundo: indígenas y europeos en La Florida del siglo XVI." In *Franqueando Fronteras: Garcilaso de la Vega y "La Florida del Inca,"* edited by Raquel Chang-Rodríguez, 60–86. Lima: Pontificia Universidad Católica del Perú, 2006.

Miller, Marilyn. "Covert Mestizaje and the Strategy of 'Passing' in Diego Muñoz Camargo's Historia de Tlaxcala." *Colonial Latin American Review* 6, no. 1 (June 1997): 41–58.

Millones, Luis. "Prólogo." In *Anales de la Inquisición de Lima*, by Ricardo Palma, vii–xliii. Lima: Fondo Editorial del Congreso de Lima, 1997.

Miola, Robert, ed. *Early Modern Catholicism: An Anthology of Primary Sources*. Oxford: Oxford University Press, 2007.

Miró Quesada, Aurelio. "Cronología." In vol. 2 of *Comentarios reales*, edited by Aurelio Miró Quesada, 285–311. Caracas: Biblioteca Ayacucho, [1985].

Montiel, Edgar, coord. *Hacia una mundialización humanista*. Paris: UNESCO, 2003.

Moraña, Mabel. *Viaje al silencio: Exploraciones del discurso barroco*. Mexico: UNAM, 1998.

———, ed. "Indigenismo y globalización: Debates Actuales." In *Indigenismo hacia el fin del milenio*. Homenaje a Antonio Cornejo Polar, 243–52. Pittsburgh: Biblioteca de América, 1998.

Moreiras, Alberto. *The Exhaustion of Difference: The Politics of Latin American Cultural Studies*. Durham, NC: Duke University Press, 2001.

Morison, Samuel Eliot. *Admiral of the Ocean Sea: A Life of Christopher Columbus*. Boston: Little, Brown and Company, 1970.

Mörner, Magnus, and Charles Gibson. "Diego Muñoz Camargo and the Segregation Policy of the Spanish Crown." *The Hispanic American Historical Review* 42, no. 4. (November 1962): 558–68.

Moseley, Michael E. "Structure and History in the Dynastic Lore of Chimor." In *The Northern Dynasties: Kingship and Statecraft in Chimor*, edited by Michael E. Moseley and Alana Cordy-Collins, 1–41. Washington, DC: Dumbarton Oaks Research Library and Collection, 1990.

Mulvey, Laura. "Visual Pleasure and Narrative Cinema." *The Screen* 16, no. 3 (1975): 6–18.

Munro, John H. "Patterns of Trade, Money, and Credit." In *Handbook of European History 1400–1600: Late Middle Ages, Renaissance and Reformation*, edited by Thomas A. Brady Jr., Heiko A. Oberman, and James D. Tracy. Leiden: E. J. Brill, 1994. 147–71.

Murra, John V. "Andean Societies before 1532." In *Colonial Latin America*, vol. 1 of *The Cambridge History of Latin America*, edited by Leslie Bethell, 59–90. Cambridge: Cambridge University Press, 1984.

———. "Did Tribute and Markets Prevail in the Andes before the European Invasion?" In *Ethnicity, Markets, and Migration in the Andes: At the Crossroads of History and Anthropology*, edited by Brook Larson, Olivia Harris, and Enrique Tandeter, 57–72. Durham, NC: Duke University Press, 1995.

Nash, June. "The Aztecs and the Ideology of Male Dominance." *Signs* 4, no. 2 (Winter 1978): 349–62.

Nicholson, H. B. *Topiltzin Quetzalcoatl: The Once and Future Lord of the Toltecs*. Norman: University of Oklahoma Press, 2001.

Oblitas Poblete, Enrique. *La lengua secreta de los Incas*. La Paz: Talleres de la Editorial del Estado, 1968.

Ohmae, Kenichi. "The Nation State's Response." In *The End of the Nation State: The Rise of Regional Economies*, 117–40. New York: Free Press, 1995.

Ong, Walter J. *Orality and Literacy: The Technologizing of the World*. London: Methuen, 1982.

Ortega, José. "Las Casas, reformador social y precursor de la 'teología de la liberación.'" *Cuadernos Hispanoamericanos* 466 (1989): 67–87.

Ortega, Julio. *La cultura peruana: Experiencia y conciencia*. México: FCE, 1978.

———. *Transatlantic Translations: Dialogues in Latin American Literature*. London: Reaktion Books, 2006.

Ortiz, Fernando. *Contrapunteo cubano del tabaco y el azúcar*. Edited by Enrico Mario Santí. Madrid: Cátedra, 2002.

Ospina, William. *América mestiza*. 2004. Reprint, Bogotá: Mondarori, 2013.

———. *Ursúa*. Bogotá: Alfaguara, 2005.

Papadopoulos, John K., and Gary Urton. "Introduction: The Construction of Value in the Ancient World." In *The Construction of Value in the Ancient World*, edited by John K. Papadopoulos and Gary Urton, 1–47. Los Angeles: Cotsen Institute of Archaeology Press, 2012.

Parsons, James J. *Antioquia's Corridor to the Sea: An Historical Geography of the Settlement of Urabá*. Berkeley: University of California Press, 1967.

Pastor Bodmer, Beatriz. *The Armature of Conquest: Spanish Accounts of the Discovery of America, 1492–1589*. Stanford: Stanford University Press, 1992.

Patterson, Nick, Priya Moorjani, Yontao Luo, Swapan Mallick, Nadin Rohland, Yiping Zhan, Teri Genschoreck, Teresa Webster, and David Reich. "Ancient Admixture in Human History." *Genetics* (November 2012): 1065–93.

Paz, Octavio. *El laberinto de la soledad*. 2nd ed. Mexico: FCE, 1959.

———. *Sor Juana Inés de la Cruz o Las trampas de la fe*. Barcelona: Seix Barral, 1982.

Pease G. Y., Franklin. *Las crónicas y los Andes*. Lima: FCE, 2010.

———. "Estudio preliminar." In *Crónica del Perú-Señorío de los incas*, by Pedro Cieza de León, ix–xxxiv. Caracas: Biblioteca Ayacucho, 2005.

Pérez Fernández, O. P. Isacio. *Bartolomé de las Casas en el Perú*. Cuzco: Instituto de Estudios Rurales, "Bartolomé de las Casas," 1986.

Phelan, John Leddy. *The Millennial Kingdom of the Franciscans in the New World*. 2nd ed. Berkeley: University of California Press, 1970.

Pohl, Mary E. D., Kevin O. Pope, and Christopher von Nagy. "Olmec Origins of Mesoamerican Writing." *Science*, New Series 298, no. 5600 (December 6, 2002): 1984–87.

Porras Barrenechea, Raúl. *Los cronistas del Perú (1528–1650)*. Lima: Banco de Crédito de Lima, 1986.

———. *Fuentes históricas peruanas*. Lima: Instituto Raúl Porras Barrenechea, 1963.

———. *Mito, tradición e historia del Perú*. 1951. Reprint, Lima: Peisa, 1974.

———. *El nombre del Perú*. Lima: P. L. Villanueva, 1951.

———. *Pizarro, Fundador*. Lima: Universidad Ricardo Palma/Instituto Raúl Porras Barrenechea, 2016.

Portocarrero, Gonzalo. *Rostros criollos del mal: Cultura y transgresión en la sociedad peruana.* Lima: Red Para el Desarrollo de las Ciencias Sociales en el Perú, 2004.

Prak, Maarten, ed. *Early Modern Capitalism: Economic and Social Change in Europe 1400–1800.* Florence, KY: Routledge, 2005.

Pratt, Mary Louise. *Imperial Eyes: Travel Writing and Transculturation.* London: Routledge, 1992.

Proulx, Paul. "Quechua and Aymara." *Language Sciences* 9, no. 1 (1987): 91–102.

Pumar Martínez, Carmen. *Españolas en Indias: mujeres-soldado, adelantadas y gobernadoras.* Madrid: Ediciones Anaya, 1988.

Quijano, Aníbal. "Coloniality and Modernity/Rationality." *Cultural Studies* 21, nos. 2–3 (March/May 2007): 168–78.

———. "Colonialidad del poder y clasificación social." *Journal of World Systems Research* 6, no. 2 (Summer-Fall 2000): 342–86.

Quilligan, Maureen, Walter Mignolo, and Margaret Rich. *Rereading the Black Legend: The Discourses of Religious and Racial Difference in the Renaissance Empires.* Chicago: University of Chicago Press, 2007.

Quiroa, Néstor. "The *Popol Vuh* and the Dominican Religious Extirpation in Highland Guatemala: Prologues and Annotations of Fr. Francisco Ximénez." *Americas* 67, no. 4 (April 2011): 467–94.

Quiroz Chueca, Francisco. "Gremios en Lima." In *Lima en el Siglo XVI*, edited by Laura Gutiérrez Arbulú, 493–524. Lima: Pontificia Universidad Católica del Perú, 2006.

Rabasa, José. "Historiografía colonial y la episteme occidental moderna: una aproximación a la etnografía franciscana, Oviedo y Las Casas." In *El impacto del humanismo en el Nuevo Mundo*, edited by Ruscalleda, Rodríguez, Nieves, Gamallo, López, and Damiani, 67–105. Potomac: Scripta Humanistica, 1994.

Radicati di Primeglio, Carlos. *Estudios sobre los quipus.* Lima: Fondo Editorial Universidad Nacional Mayor de San Marcos, 2006.

Rama, Ángel. *Transculturación narrativa en América Latina.* Mexico: Siglo XXI, 1982.

Ramírez, Susan Elizabeth. *The World Upside Down: Cross-Cultural Contact and Conflict in Sixteenth-Century Peru.* Stanford: Stanford University Press, 1996.

Rappaport, Joanne. *The Politics of Memory: Native Historical Interpretations in the Colombian Andes.* 1990. Reprint, Durham, NC: Duke University Press, 1998.

———, and Tom Cummins. *Beyond the Lettered City.* Durham, NC: Duke University Press, 2012.

Reid, Basil A. *Myths and Realities of Caribbean History.* Tuscaloosa: University Alabama Press, 2009.

Restall, Matthew. "A History of the New Philology and the New Philology in History." *Latin American Research Review* 38, no. 1 (February 2003): 111–34.

———. *Seven Myths of the Spanish Conquest.* Oxford: Oxford University Press, 2003.

———. "Black Conquistadors: Armed Africans in Early Spanish America." *The Americas* 57, no. 2 (2000): 171–205.

———. *Maya Conquistador.* Boston: Beacon Press, 1998.

———. "Heirs to the Hieroglyphs: Indigenous Writing in Colonial Mesoamerica." *The Americas* 54, no. 2 (October 1997): 239–67.

Richardson, James B., Mark A McConaughy, Allison Heaps de Peña, and Elena B. Décima Zamecnik. "The Northern Frontier of the Kingdom of Chimor: The Piura, Chira, and Tumbez Valleys." In *The Northern Dynasties: Kingship and Statecraft in Chimor*, edited by Michael E. Moseley and Alana Cordy-Collins, 419–45. Washington, DC: Dumbarton Oaks Research Library and Collection, 1990.

Riva-Agüero, José de la. *Obras completas.* 14 vols. Lima: Pontificia Universidad Católica del Perú, 1962–97.

Rivarola, José Luis. *Español andino: textos de bilingües de los siglos XVI y XVII.* Madrid/Frankfurt: Iberoamericana/Vervuert, 2000.

Rivera Domínguez, Benemérita. "Conflicto entre divinidades por el espacio sagrado." In *Mito, palabra e historia en la tradición literaria latinoamericana*, edited by José Carlos Rovira, José Carlos, and Eva Valero Juan, 81–90. Madrid/Frankfurt: Iberoamericana/Vervuert, 2013.

Robertson, William. *The History of America.* Dublin: Printed for Messrs. Price, 1777.

Robinson, William. *A Theory of Global Capitalism: Production, Class, and State in a Transnational World.* Baltimore: Johns Hopkins University Press, 2004.

Robisheaux, Thomas W. "The World of the Village." In *Handbook of European History 1400–1600: Late Middle Ages, Renaissance and Reformation*, edited by Thomas A. Brady Jr., Heiko A. Oberman, and James D. Tracy, 79–112. Leiden: E. J. Brill, 1994.

Romero Galván, José Rubén. "Los cronistas indígenas." In *La cultura letrada en la Nueva España del siglo XVII*, vol. 2 of *Historia de la literatura mexicana desde sus orígenes hasta nuestros días*, edited by Raquel Chang-Rodríguez, 270–87. Mexico: Siglo XXI, 2002.

Ross, Kathleen. "Historians of the Conquest and Colonization of the New World: 1550–1620." In vol. 1 of *The Cambridge History of Latin American Literature*, edited by Roberto González Echevarría and Enrique Pupo-Walker, 101–42. Cambridge: Cambridge University Press, 1996.

Rostworowski de Diez Canseco, María. *La historia de Tahuantinsuyo.* 4th ed. Lima: IAP Ediciones, 1992.

Rostworowski, María. *Doña Francisca Pizarro, una ilustre mestiza 1534–1598.* 3rd ed. Lima: Instituto de Estudios Peruanos, 2003.

———, and Craig Morris. "The Fourfold Domain: Inka Power and its Social Foundations." In part 1 of *South America*, vol. 3 of *The Cambridge History of the Native Peoples of Latin America*, edited by Frank Salomon and Stuart B. Schwartz, 769–863. Cambridge: Cambridge University Press, 1999:

Rounds, J. "Dynastic Succession and the Centralization of Power in Tenochtitlan." In *The Inca and Aztec States, 1400–1800*, edited by George A. Collier, Renato I. Rosaldo, and John D. Wirth, 63–89. New York: Academic Press, 1982.

Rowe, John Howland. *Los Incas del Cuzco: Siglos XVI-XVII-XVIII.* Cuzco: Instituto Nacional del Cultura, Región Cusco, 2003.

Sacks, David Harris. "Introduction: More's Utopia in Historical Perspective." In *Utopia*, translated by Ralph Robynson (1556 version) and edited by David Harris Sacks, 1–79. Boston: Bedford/St. Martin's, 1999.

Salomon, Frank. *Khipus and Cultural Life in a Peruvian Town.* Durham, NC: Duke University Press, 2000.

Salvatore, Ricardo D. "Conclusion." In *Murder and Violence in Modern Latin America*, edited by Eric A. Johnston, Ricardo D. Salvatore, and Pieter Spierenburg, 235–69. Malden/Oxford: Wiley-Blackwell/Society for Latin American Studies, 2013.

Sam Colop, Luis Enrique. "Introducción." In *Popol Wuj*, 13–20. Guatemala City: Chosamaj, 2008.

Sánchez-Albornoz, Nicolás. "The Population of Colonial Spanish America." In *Colonial Latin America*, vol. 2 of *The Cambridge History of Latin America*, edited by Leslie Bethell, 3–35. Cambridge: Cambridge University Press, 1984.

Sandoval, José R., Alberto Salazar-Granara, Oscar Acosta, Wilder Castillo-Herrera, Ricardo Fujita, Sergio DJ Pena, and Fabricio R Santos. "Tracing the genomic ancestry of Peruvians reveals a major legacy of pre-Columbian ancestors." *Journal of Human Genetics* 58 (2013): 627–34.

Scheinsohn, Vivian. "Hunter-Gatherer Archaeology in South America." *Annual Review of Anthropology* 32 (2003): 339–61. doi:10.1146/annurev.anthro.32.061002.093228.

Schneider, Paul. *Brutal Journey: Cabeza de Vaca and the Epic First Crossing of North America.* New York: Henry Holt and Company, 2007.

Schroeder, Susan. *Chimalpahin and the Kingdoms of Chalco.* Tucson: University of Arizona Press, 1991.

———, Stephanie Gail Wood, and Robert Stephen Haskett, eds. *Indian Woman of Early Mexico.* Norman: University of Oklahoma Press, 1997.

Seed, Patricia. *American Pentimento: The Invention of Indians and the Pursuit of Riches.* Minneapolis: University of Minnesota Press, 2001.

Sharer, Robert J. "The Maya Highlands and the Adjacent Pacific Coast." In part 1 of *Mesoamerica*, vol. 2 of *The Cambridge History of the Native Peoples of the Americas*, edited by Richard E. W. Adams and Murdo J. MacLeod, 449–99. Cambridge: Cambridge University Press, 2000.

Shimada, Izumi. "Evolution of Andean Diversity: Regional Formations (500 BCE–CE 600)." In vol. 3, part 1 of *The Cambridge History of the Native People of the Americas*, edited by Frank Salomon and Stuart B. Schwartz, 350–517. Cambridge: Cambridge University Press, 1999.

———. *Pampa Grande and the Mochica Culture.* Austin: University of Texas Press, 1994.

Sicoli, Mark A., and Gary Holton. "Linguistic Phylogenies Support Back-Migration from Beringia to Asia." *PLoS ONE* 9, no. 3 (March 2014): 1–8.

Silva Santisteban, Fernando. *Los obrajes en el virreinato del Perú.* Lima: Publicaciones del Museo Nacional de Historia, 1964.

Silverblatt, Irene. *Modern Inquisitions: Peru and the Colonial Origins of the Civilized World.* Durham, NC: Duke University Press, 2004.

———. *Moon, Sun, and Witches: Gender Ideologies and Class in Inca and Colonial Peru.* Princeton: Princeton University Press, 1987.

Smith, Adam. *The Glasgow Edition of the Works and Correspondence of Adam Smith.* 6 vols. Indianapolis: Liberty Fund, 1981–85.

Smith, Anthony D. *The Antiquity of Nations*. Cambridge: Polity Press, 2004.

———. *The Ethnic Origins of Nations*. Malden, MA: Blackwell, 1988.

———. *National Identity*. Reno: University of Nevada Press, 1991.

Smith, T. Lynn. "The Racial Composition of the Population of Colombia." *Journal of Inter-American Studies* 8, no. 2 (April 1966): 212–35.

Sobrevilla, David. "Transculturación y heterogeneidad: avatares de dos categorías literarias en América Latina." *Revista de crítica literaria latinoamericana* 27, no. 54. (2ndo semestre del 2001): 21–33.

Spellman, W. M. *European Political Thought 1600–1700*. New York: St. Martins Press, 1998.

Stanish, Charles. *Ancient Andean Political Economy*. Austin: University of Texas Press, 1992.

———. "The Revaluation of Landscapes in the Incan Empire as Peircean Replication." In *The Construction of Value in the Ancient World*, edited by John K. Papadopoulos and Gary Urton, 128–36. Los Angles: Cotsen Institute of Archaeology, University of California, 2012.

Stern, Steve J. *Peru's Indian Peoples and the Challenge of Spanish Conquest: Huamanga to 1640*. Madison: University of Wisconsin Press, 1982.

Strasser, Ulrike, and Heidi Tinsman. "It's a Man's World? World History Meets the History of Masculinity, in Latin American Studies, for Instance." *Journal of World History* 21, no. 1 (March 2010): 75–96.

Szemiński, Jan. "Un texto en el idioma olvidado de los Inkas." *Histórica* 14, no. 2 (1990): 379–89.

Taylor, Diana. "Remapping Genre through Performance: From 'American' to 'Hemispheric' Studies." *PMLA* 122, no. 5 (October 2007): 1416–30.

Tedlock, Barbara. *Time and the Highland Maya*. Albuquerque: University of New Mexico Press, 1982.

Tedlock, Dennis. *2000 Years of Mayan Literature*. Berkeley: University of California Press, 2010.

Thomas, Hugh. *Conquest: Montezuma, Cortés and the Fall of Old Mexico*. New York: Simon and Schuster/Touchtone, 1995.

Thomson, Sinclair. *We Alone Will Rule: Native Andean Politics in the Age of Insurgency*. Madison: University of Wisconsin Press, 2002.

Topic, John R. "Craft Production in the Kingdom of Chimor." In *The Northern Dynasties: Kingship and Statecraft in Chimor*, edited by Michael E. Moseley and Alana Cordy-Collins, 145–76. Washington, DC: Dumbarton Oaks Research Library and Collection, 1990.

Torero, Alfredo. *Idiomas de los Andes: lingüística e historia*. Lima: Editorial Horizonte, 2005.

Townsend, Camilla. "Polygyny and the Divided Altepetl: The Tetzcocan Key to Preconquest Nahua Politics." In *Texcoco: Prehispanic and Colonial Perspectives*, edited by Jongsoo Lee and Galen Brokaw, 93–116. Boulder: University Press of Colorado, 2014.

Trimborn, Hermann. *Señorío y barbarie en el Valle del Cauca. Estudio sobre la antigua civilización Quimbaya y grupos afines del oeste de Colombia*. Calí: Universidad del Valle, 2005.

Troyan, Brett. *Cauca's Indigenous Movement in Southwestern Colombia: Land, Violence, and Ethnic Community.* Lanham, MD: Lexington Books, 2015.

Trubitt, Mary Beth D. "The Production and Exchange of Marine Shell Prestige Goods." *Journal of Archaeological Research* 11, no. 3 (September 2003): 243–77.

Twain, Mark. *Following the Equator: A Journey around the World.* 2 vols. New York: Harper and Brothers, Publishers, 1899.

Uhle, Max. "La posición histórica de los aymaras en el antiguo Perú." *Boletín de la Oficina nacional de Estadística* (Bolivia) 6, nos. 58–60 (1910): 350–56.

Urton, Gary. *Signs of the Inka Khipu: Binary Coding in the Andean Knotted-String Records.* Austin: University of Texas Press, 2003.

Valle Escalante, Emilio del. *Maya Nationalisms and Postcolonial Challenges in Guatemala.* Santa Fe: School for Advanced Research, 2009.

Van Akkeren, Ruud. *La visión indígena de la conquista.* Guatemala: Serviprensa, 2007.

———. "El Chinamit y la plaza del Postclásico: La arqueología y la etnohistoria en busca del papel de la Casa de Consejo." En *XIX Simposio de Investigaciones Arqueológicas en Guatemala, 2005: La arqueología y la etnohistoria en busca del papel de la Casa de Consejo*, edited by J. P. Laporte, B. Arroyo, and H. Mejía, 207–18. Guatemala: Museo Nacional de Arqueología y Etnología, 2006.

Varner, John Grier. *The Life and Times of Garcilaso de la Vega.* Austin: University of Texas Press, 1968.

Vasconcelos, José. *La raza cósmica.* Novena Edición. Mexico: Espasa Calpe, 1995.

Vázquez, Germán. "Introducción." In *Historia de Tlaxcala*, by Diego Muñoz Camargo, 7–65. Madrid: Historia 16, 1986.

———. "Introducción." In *Historia de la nación chichimeca*, by Fernando de Alva Ixtlilxóchitl, 7–46. Madrid: Historia 16, 1985.

Vedia, Enrique de, ed. *Historiadores primitivos de Indias.* 2 tomos. Vols. 22 and 26, Biblioteca de Autores Españoles. Madrid: M. Rivadeneyra, 1853 (vol.1) & 1858 (vol. 2).

Vega, Juan José. *La poligamia española en el Perú.* Lima: Universidad Nacional de Educación, 1968.

———. "La prostitución en el incario." In *Historia de las mujeres en América Latina*, edited by Juan Andreo García and Sara Beatriz Guardia, 45–53. Murcia: Universidad de Murcia, 2002.

Velazco, Salvador. *Visiones de Anáhuac: Reconstrucciones historiográficas y etnicidades emergentes en el México colonial: Fernando de Alva Ixtlilxóchitl, Diego Muñoz Camargo y Hernando Alvarado Tezozómoc.* Guadalajara: Universidad de Guadalajara, 2003.

Villegas Romero, Arturo. *El movimiento de Túpac Amaru II.* Arequipa: Editorial UNSA, 2000.

Verano, John W. "War and Death in the Moche World: Osteological Evidence and Visual Discourse." In *Moche Art and Archaeology in Ancient Peru*, edited by Joanne Pillsbury, 111–25. Washington, DC/New Haven: National Gallery of Art/Yale University Press, 2001.

Verdesio, Gustavo. "Latin America in the Precontact Period." In vol. 5 of *Encyclopedia of Latin American History and Culture*, edited by Erick Langer and Jay Kinsbrunner, 340–42. 2nd ed. Detroit: Charles Scribner's Sons, 2008.

Villamarín, Juan, and Judith Villamarín. "Chiefdoms: The Prevalence and Persistence of 'Señoríos naturales,' 1400 to European Conquest." In *South America*, vol. 3, part 1 of *The Cambridge History of the Native Peoples of Latin America*, edited by Frank Salomon and Stuart B. Schwartz, 577–667. Cambridge: Cambridge University Press, 1999.

Vicuña Guengerich, Sara. "Virtuosas o corruptas: Las mujeres indígenas en las obras de Guamán Poma de Ayala y el Inca Garcilaso de la Vega." *Hispania* 96, no. 4 (2013): 672–83.

Vidal, Gore. *Inventing a Nation: Washington, Adams, and Jefferson*. New Haven: Yale University Press, 2003.

Voigt, Lisa. *Writing Captivity in the Early Modern Atlantic: Circulations of Knowledge and Authority in the Iberian and English Imperial Worlds*. Durham, NC: University of North Carolina Press, for Omohundro Institute of Early American History and Culture, 2009.

———. "Peregrine Peregrinations: Rewriting Travel and Discovery in Mestizo Chronicles of New Spain." *Revista Hispánica Moderna* 40, no. 1 (2006): 3–24.

Wachtel, Nathan. "The Indian and the Spanish Conquest." In *Colonial Latin America*, vol. 1 of *The Cambridge History of Latin America*, edited by Leslie Bethell, 207–48. Cambridge: Cambridge University Press, 1985.

Wade, Peter. "Patterns of Race in Colombia." *Bulletin of Latin American Research* 5, no. 2 (1986): 1–19.

Walker, Charles F. *The Tupac Amaru Rebellion*. Cambridge: The Belknap Press of Harvard University Press, 2014.

Wallerstein, Immanuel. *The Modern World-System: Capitalist Agriculture and the Origins of the European World-Economy in the Sixteenth Century*. New York: Academic Press, 1974.

Ward, Thomas. *Decolonizing Indigeneity: New Approaches to Latin American Literature*. Lanham, MD: Lexington Books, 2017.

———. "Modern Nativist Readings of Garcilaso in Peru." In *Entre la pluma y la espada: El Inca Garcilaso y sus* Comentarios reales, edited by Raquel Chang-Rodríguez, 171–89. Lima: Fondo Editorial de la Pontificia Universidad Católica del Perú, 2010.

———. "From the 'People' to the Nation: An Emerging Notion in Sahagún, Ixtlilxóchitl and Muñoz Camargo." *Estudios de Cultura Náhuatl* 32 (2001): 223–34.

———. "Expanding Ethnicity in Sixteenth-Century Anahuac: Ideologies of Ethnicity and Gender in the Nation-Building Process." *MLN* 116, no. 2 (March 2001): 419–52.

Weber, Katinka. "Chiquitano and the Multiple Meanings of being Indigenous in Bolivia." *Bulletin of Latin American Research* 32, no. 2 (April 2013): 194–209.

Welsh, Frank. *The Four Nations: A History of the United Kingdom*. New Haven: Yale University Press, 2003.

Weaver, Frederick Stirton. *Latin America in the World Economy: Mercantile Colonialism to Global Capitalism*. Boulder: Westview Press, 2000.

Whittaker, Gordon. "Aztec Dialectology and the Nahuatl of the Friars." In *The Work of Bernardino de Sahagún, Pioneer Ethnographer of Sixteenth-Century Aztec Mexico*, edited by J. Jorge Klor de Alva, H. B. Nicholson, and Eloise Quiñones Keber, 321–339. Albany: Institute for Mesoamerican Studies, 1988.

Wiegele, Katherine L. *Investing in Miracles: El Shaddai and the Transformation of Popular Catholicism in the Philippines.* Honolulu: University of Hawai'i Press, 2005.

Wood, Stephanie G. "Pedro Villafranca y Juana Gertrudis Navarrete: falsificador de títulos y su viuda (Nueva España, Siglo XVIII)." In *Lucha por la supervivencia en América colonial*, edited by David G. Sweet and Gary B. Nash, 472–85. Mexico: FCE, 1987.

Woodward, Laura L. "Lenca." In vol. 4 of *Encyclopedia of Latin American History and Culture*, edited by Jay Kinsbrunner, 166–67. 2nd ed. Detroit: Gale/Cengage, 2008.

Yacobaccio, Hugo D., Patricia S. Escola, Marisa Lazzari, and Fernando Pereyra. "Long-Distance Obsidian Traffic in Northwestern Argentina." In *Geochemical Evidence for Long-Distance Exchange*, edited by Michael D. Glascock, 167–203. Westport: Bergin & Garvey (Greenwood Publishing), 2002.

Yun, Bartolomé. "Economic Cycles and Structural Changes." In *Handbook of European History 1400–1600: Late Middle Ages, Renaissance and Reformation*, edited by Thomas A. Brady Jr., Heiko A. Oberman, and James D. Tracy, 113–45. Leiden: E. J. Brill, 1994.

Yuval-Davis, Nira. *Gender and Nation.* Thousand Oaks, CA: Sage, 1997.

Zanelli, Carmela. "La loa de 'El divino Narciso' de Sor Juana Inés de la Cruz y la doble recuperación de la cultura indígena mexicana." In *La literatura novohispana: Revisión crítica y propuestas metodológicas*, edited by José Pascual Buxó and Arnulfo Herrera, 183–200. Mexico: UNAM, 1994.

Zevallos Aguilar, Juan. "Inkarri y J. M. Arguedas. Construcciones y desconstrucciones de un mito mesiánico." *Siete Culebras* 12 (July–October 2006): 20–23.

Zuidema, R. T. *The Ceque System of Cuzco: The Social Organization of the Capital of the Inca.* Leiden, E. J. Brill, 1964.

———. *Inca Civilization in Cuzco.* Translated by Jean-Jacques Decoster. Austin: University of Texas Press, 1990.

———. *Reyes y guerreros: Ensayos de cultura andina.* Edited by Manuel Burga. Lima: FOMCIENCIAS, 1989.

INDEX

References to illustrations appear in italics.